Manly Arts

MANLY ARTS

Masculinity and Nation in Early

American Cinema

David A. Gerstner

Duke University Press   Durham & London   2006

© 2006 Duke University Press

All rights reserved

Printed in the United States of

America on acid-free paper ∞

Designed by C. H. Westmoreland

Typeset in Adobe Garamond

by Tseng Information Systems, Inc.

Library of Congress Cataloging-in-

Publication Data appear on the

last printed page of this book.

For Michelangelo

The function of narrative

is not to "represent,"

it is to constitute a spectacle.

ROLAND BARTHES

Contents

Preface ix

Acknowledgments xv

1 Nineteenth-Century Formulations of Masculinity
and Realism: The Body of Edwin Forrest 1

2 *The Battle Cry of Peace* and the Spectacle
of Realism 51

3 African American Realism: Oscar Micheaux,
Autobiography, and the Ambiguity of Black Male
Desire 83

4 *Manhatta*: A National Self-Portrait 119

5 The Queer Frontier: Vincente Minnelli's
Cabin in the Sky 165

Epilogue 212

Notes 215

Bibliography 281

Index 305

Preface

For many Americans, cinema was, and remains, the national art. During the nineteenth century and the twentieth, the cinema took hold of the public's imagination in the fervent debates about what constituted American democratic aesthetics — debates that were especially couched in concerns over the effeminization of American culture. Not only was the cinema technologically fascinating; it was, more presciently, America's sui generis art form because it arrived on the scene at a crucial moment when the discourses about art and national identity focused on questions regarding what medium best suited the country's aesthetic ideals. Unlike the Old World art forms of painting, literature, and even photography, the cinema represented the New World both in form and content and dramatically shaped that American myth. But what is the American myth that the cinema so successfully captured? And in what way did the cinema express and fundamentally shape it? As I trace in this volume, the American cinema finds its discursive and practiced contours through the cultural dynamics of aesthetics, gender, race, class, and national identity. In what way, then, does aesthetic form serve cultural identity? More specifically, what is the cultural significance of cinema to the ideologies of American masculinity and nationalism?

The American cinema as an American art form had much at stake for those who identified as national artists, patrons of the arts, critics, pundits, and politicians, because it was perceived to mirror the virile attributes that purportedly defined the New World's cultural mythology. Thus, the cinema is situated within the national debate as a key art form that served America's distinct ideological positions about (though not exclusively about) gender. Yet even though the cinema held promise as America's unique, and uniquely, mediated form of representation, it did not simply displace literature and painting. For many, the experimental quality of the new medium provided a way to infuse the European traditions of painting, literature, and photography with new life—that is, with American life. In this way, I take issue with arguments that insist on the Hollywood mode of production as the predominant form through which all cinemas are ideologically and aesthetically conceived. As I see it, the terms for American cinematic form and content wrestled with the long-standing hegemony of the arts in general, even after the so-called classical Hollywood mode of production was in place.

As I researched and wrote this book I was struck by the way in which filmmakers such as J. Stuart Blackton and Theodore Roosevelt, Oscar Micheaux, Paul Strand and Charles Sheeler, and Vincente Minnelli approached the cinema only partially as a new mode of storytelling. This is not to say that the import of national myth making was overlooked or that narrative models were refused in film production. To be sure, narrative was at the heart of Blackton and Roosevelt's anti-pacifist production of *The Battle Cry of Peace* (1915). But, even in the case of this film, Blackton envisaged in direct relationship to the other arts a mode of cinematic production that evoked a multimedia experience as much as a story for propagandistic purposes (as I describe in chapter 2, he experimented with the properties of cinema, painting, and dance with surprising results). Although some viewed film as a logical extension of narrative production found in literature, painting, and theater, others engaged the medium's discrete properties in relationship to the formal dimensions of these and other arts. Indeed, by 1920 Strand and Sheeler (photographer and photographer/painter respectively) explored the cinema as an American modernist response to European cubism. While relying on European tradition for their philosophical foundation, American avant-garde artists persistently turned to the often angst-ridden dialectic of machine and nature to shore up their unique national identity and devise what some consider an American cubism. The cinema machine and its formal possibilities reflected (or so it was thought) the modern American artist within and against the nation's de-natured and urbanized backdrop. In chapter 4 of this volume, I consider Strand and Sheeler's contribution to American avant-garde cinema—*Manhatta* (1921)—in this light.

The aesthetic terms for the cinema, however, were not only navigated through the aesthetic traditions of white Eurocentrism; in the case of Micheaux's filmmaking, for example, slave narratives and other African American arts came to bear so directly that the form often contested more than Anglo-Saxon story content (with *The Birth of a Nation* being the most obvious example). Because Micheaux's films did not entirely turn to white modes of narrative, they challenged the "proper" ordering of things that white narratives purposed as "natural." Because he was torn by pressures to achieve on the one hand a cultural uplift of the Anglo-Saxon (and, certainly, African American) variety, and on the other hand by the desire to declare the aesthetic specificities of African American culture, Micheaux produced a body of work in literature and film that reveals precisely through form and content his troubled ideological position. To be pulled to and fro as a black man by the demands of a white hetero-masculinist world was to experience the modes of cultural production with distinct aesthetic effect and affect. In chapter 3, I study Micheaux's *Within Our Gates* (1920) for the ways that the filmmaker's cinematic aesthetics grapple with the ideological terms for African American manhood.

The creative results, however, were more startling in the cultural context of virile white America when African Americans and white queer modernists collaborated. Like many of his generation, Minnelli came to the cinema via his work in other art forms (he claimed painting as his first love). Once immersed in the 1930s New York theatrical world, Minnelli wrapped himself in the diverse and frenetic milieus of queer American art. Notably, the kinetic arts in which he participated embraced the diversity of race and international culture so often dismissed in heterocentric and Anglo-Saxon pronouncements about art. The commingling of white, queer modernist and African American cultures, enabled by the dynamic context of national and international politics, displayed an aesthetic sophistication of cultural excess that did not sit well with those Americans who wished for the national arts something less pretentious (i.e., more manly and less effeminate). In this volume I conclude with a study of Minnelli's production of *Cabin in the Sky* (1943) because it reveals a somewhat different creative expression of American culture that, not surprisingly, left many critics confused about the state of the national arts in the mid-twentieth century.

Whether the national debate turned on the popular or avant-garde arts, the impulse to position art as "American," white, and *manly* returned again and again to secure a national aesthetic. The terms for "American art" and "manliness" were filtered through an array of cultural producers with surprisingly divergent applications of cinematic form. Perhaps even more trenchant was the way that nationalist and masculinist aesthetics were explained and performed by American artists. The cultural producers discussed here clearly indicate the symbiosis between aesthetics and their corporeal relationship to race, gender, and nation. In this book I seek to disentangle these cultural discourses and practices—the relationships between aesthetics and historical circumstances and between aesthetics and corporeality—to explore how American art and cinema enabled the myth of manly America. The effects of these productions were often ironic, successful as much as they were unsuccessful, and, in an instance or two, beautifully queer.

To wit, my investigation into cinematic America begins in 1849 with the Astor Place Riot where a violent shift occurred in the terms for American masculinity and the arts. Played out against the bodies of the "rugged" American actor Edwin Forrest and the European dilettante actor William Macready, the riot proved to be a significant moment in which the ideals of white American masculine performance were dramatically and spectacularly announced.

The effects of the riot in 1849 remained a formidable force well into the twentieth century, if not through our present time. In fact, the resonance of this historical moment—especially as it takes shape through Forrest's body, gesture, and rhetoric about art—accrues value since it paves the way for the broader issues of race, gender, and nation that in this book I engage as cornerstones of American cinematic production. Forrest's identification with and, as we shall see, feasting on the Other articulated a central trope for the formulation of both the American male artist and the American masculine arts. As I argue, American male artists consistently turned to the Other—or navigated it within themselves—so as to measure their primitive Otherness against their "civilized" selves. In each instance, however, such identification led to a wide range of cultural production and interpretation. Minnelli's identification and experience with the Other, as I explore in chapter 5, carried implications far different from those expressed in the way Forrest and Theodore Roosevelt envisaged their manly truculence. America's assertion of its masculine nationhood through cinematic representation in the twentieth century is thus best understood through a study of the complex nexus of nineteenth-century aesthetics and anxieties of national identity.

Acknowledgments

In the course of my work on this volume, the following institutions were gracious in offering me time and, in some cases, financial assistance: Academy of Motion Picture Arts and Sciences, Margaret Herrick Library; Archives of American Art, New York; Art Resource; Beinecke Rare Book and Manuscript Library, Yale University; City University of New York, College of Staten Island; Duke University Press; Harry Ransom Center, University of Texas, Austin; Hirshhorn Museum and Sculpture Garden, Smithsonian Institution; Interloan Library Office, College of Staten Island; the PSC-CUNY Award; Museum of Modern Art; Shubert Theater Archives; Metropolitan Museum of Art, photography library; New-York Historical Society; New York Public Library, Performing Arts Library at Lincoln Center; Paul Strand Archive, Aperture Foundation, Millerton, New York; Theodore Roosevelt Collection, Houghton Library, Harvard; Schomburg Center for Research in Black Culture; and University of California, Los Angeles Department of Special Collections.

Many voices resonate throughout this text. For support from the emotional to the intellectual to the digital, I'd like to thank Mirella Affron, Kathy Aherne, Sally Banes, John Benicewicz, Janet Bergstrom, John Birdseye, Nick Browne, Catherine Burke, Mary Ann Chach, Jeanine Corbet, Cynthia Chris, Wallace Dailey, Amy Densford, Katherine Dunham, Mika Emori, Justin Faerber, Alistair Fox, Dave and Jean Gerstner, Jeff Harris, Andrew Hewitt, Nicholas Jenkins, Katie Courtland, Karen Lucic, Richard Lummis, Stephen Mamber, Michael Mandiberg, Janet Manfredonia, Paula Massood, Joe McElhaney, Ed Miller, Sally Milner, Sherry Millner, Lee Minnelli, Anthony Montoya, Edmund Morris, Suzanne Gerstner Nixon, Kristine Paulus, Eva Peters,

David Podell, Madeline Preston, Jill Reichenbach, Charles Silver, Jason Simon, Reynolds Smith, Vivian Sobchack, Matthew Solomon, Francisco Soto, Janet Staiger, Janelle Stovall, Valerie Tevere, Sharon Torian, Samuel Weber, Judith Weisenfeld, Cherie Westmoreland, Peter Wollen, Cindy Wong, and Ying Zhu.

Finally, I thank my partner, Michael. As a writer he understands the intensity and time demanded in composing a book; his love and willingness to put up with me for the past ten years guaranteed that this book would be written, and I dedicate it to him.

A portion of chapter 3 was published as " 'Other and Different Scenes': Oscar Micheaux's Bodies and the Cinematic Cut," *Wide Angle* 21.4 (October 1999 [2004]): 6–19.

1

Nineteenth-Century Formulations

of Masculinity and Realism:

The Body of Edwin Forrest

On the evening of May 10, 1849, American art came into its own through an act of masculine bravado and violence. Outside the Astor Place Opera House in New York City, 31 bystanders were left dead and 150 persons were wounded in a clash between an estimated 10,000 to 24,000 civilians and around 200 members of the military and the police force.[1] At center stage of this momentous affair were the bodies of two men, two actors—William Macready of England and Edwin Forrest of the United States. As the story is usually told, the Astor Place Riot was the cumulative effect of the trans-Atlantic rivalry between these two Shakespearean artists. For several years the actors had taunted one another, and a virtual publicity mill was generated from the insults and pejorative remarks that flew not only between the two actors but also between the international presses. What began because of a public "hiss" over what Forrest described as Macready's "fancy dance" in his performance of *Hamlet* in 1846 turned into a contest over the terms for masculine and American democratic art.[2]

Things came to a head when in different venues Macready and Forrest simultaneously (and competitively) performed *Macbeth* in New York on the evening of May 9, 1849. On the following night, the night of the riot (with Macready in the role of *Macbeth* and Forrest in his favored role of *Gladiator*), the stage performances of these actors quite literally collided with and spilled over into the arena of the spectators.[3] With these performances the "friendly rivalry" between the two inter-

Edwin Forrest as Metamora. Engraving after a
photograph by Matthew Brady, ca. 1859. New York
Public Library/Art Resource, New York.

nationally recognized actors escalated into a night of violence in the streets, which was followed by weeks of tension among various political and creative spheres regarding the national interest of the arts. The effect that these two male bodies had on this historical affair, along with the role that their nationally and masculinely defined bodies played in the discourses preceding and subsequently following the riot, cannot be underestimated. These two distinct artistic bodies ushered in the terms for a national sensibility of the American arts. In the end, the situation surrounding Forrest and Macready sharpened the contours and parameters of what would have a resounding impact on the shape of American creative practices and aesthetics.

A tense atmosphere developed throughout Macready's and Forrest's New York theatrical run—especially regarding Macready's performances and his public remarks about Forrest and Americans in general. On the stage, Macready encountered the taunts and jeers (as well as the eggs and vegetables) of America's burgeoning working and immigrant classes. According to most accounts, the groups that caused the most noise at Macready's performance on the night of the riot, as well as in the street prior to it, were led by protonationalist "nativists" who organized under such propagandistic banners as "America for Americans" and the "American Committee." Moreover, these nationalist-led movements were largely composed of groups of recently landed Irish immigrants.[4] Indeed, the Irish American national fervor of the period is key to envisaging much of the anti-British energy leveled against Macready the evening of the riot. Following decades of heinous imperialist rule and domination in their homeland, the Irish placed great stock in the ideological promises of America's economic and political future. The privileged status accorded to the British actor Macready by wealthy and in some cases loyalist Americans did not sit well with the immigrants, who easily recalled memories of the Great Famines and the infamous Penal Colony restrictions of the nineteenth century.[5] This was emphasized all the more by Macready's body and acting style, which were perceived by the Irish as the antithesis to the corporeal form presented by Forrest, whose brash and virile performances were read as thoroughly American.[6] For the young rebellious Irish Americans, Forrest channeled the necessary creative and manly attributes that they identified as American.

The bodies of Macready and Forrest thus became the stage where both ire and nationalist sentiment were rehearsed by those who touted "America for Americans." Forrest represented "democratic" masculinity as the richest and the most ideally "real" form of American representation. And since Macready's body encapsulated a British spectacle —both on stage and on the street—it did not appeal to the Irish and other disenfranchised descendents of the British Empire who sought to carve a national identity outside of Old World sensibilities.[7] For these new Americans, an arrogant display of Britishness was the last thing they wanted to see as they earnestly established themselves in the New World.

Masculine Bodies, Equality, and National Art

Hayden White writes that in times of "sociocultural stress," and particularly in the contested arena of democracy, a "technique of ostensive self-definition by negation" is not unheard of. "If we do not know what we think 'civilization' *is*," he writes, "we can always find an example of what it is not . . . It appears as a kind of reflex action in conflicts between nations, classes, and political parties"[8] In this case, manufacturing a virile America—separate from England—and faith in the dream of a manly and democratic civilization finds an apt point of negation in the body of Macready. For the young "America for Americans," Macready's dilettantish arrogance registered unmanliness and thus, in effect, un-Americanness.[9]

In 1849, at the point of "sociocultural stress," nationhood, class, and masculinity were negotiated through a simple strategy that negated the body of Macready. The British actor certainly did not help matters for himself by wittingly or unwittingly fanning negative flames. His inflated comments about his own self-worth and the intellectual capacity of the American spectator were, to draw out the metaphor, fuel for the quickly burning cultural fire. "Through the years," Lawrence Levine tells us, "Macready's critique of Forrest continued to be coupled to his distaste for Forrest's audience, whom he termed 'vulgar,' 'coarse,' 'underbred,' 'ruffianly,' 'disagreeable,' 'ignorant.'"[10] Macready's effusive commentary, however, was not necessarily received as an affront to the American immigrant's sense of self. In fact, the Americans to whom Macready directed his views were rather proud of their "vulgarity" and "disagreeability" since it measured many of the essential qualities associated with their working-class roots, immigrant status, and rejection of aristocratic British culture.[11] But Macready's attitude must be viewed as something more than a distinction between upper-class and lower-class sensibilities. Indeed, it was his presentation of self, a body that flagrantly distanced itself from the "underbred" corporeality and soul of the American, that provided a symbol and marker for cultural inscription with which Americans could identify as not American. To be precise, the search for an American image of national identity through Macready's body—that is, the artistic European or British man—represented how not to be an American man.

What did Macready present to the American public that triggered such antagonistic patriotic and masculine vitriol? At the outset, Macready labeled himself and his performances as "earnest, majestic, and impassioned."[12] Needless to say, self-aggrandizement of this sort was substantial fodder for anti-British sentiment since Macready's self-image took shape around the visual presence of the "majestic and impassioned" that was immediately associated with British imperialism and its effeminized cultural affect.

As Macready saw it (in his negative dismissal of American culture), Forrest merely yielded to his philistine audiences' lack of knowledge about the theatrical discipline. He performed with "great physical power . . . [but with] no imagination, no original thought, no poetry." In fact, Macready raised the national and aesthetic ante when he stated, "I did not think it the performance of an artist. [Forrest] had all the qualifications, all the material out of which to build up a great artist, an actor for all the world. He is now only an actor for the less intelligent of the Americans."[13] Thus stripped of the accolades and consecration of imperial art, Forrest's artistry and physical presence—applauded by the very vocal and "less intelligent" Americans that Macready belittled— became the visual anchor for the emergence of the ideal, male American artist.

It is easy to see how Macready's heritage, performance style, and relationship to the arts were perceived by Forrest's proponents as extensions of the British actor's masculinity or lack thereof. Around Macready's and Forrest's bodies grew a discourse that threaded a cultural logic where national identity, class, gender, and aesthetics came together and made sense during a particular cultural moment—and thus contingently satisfied the anxieties of American men whose own sense of national manhood was at best uncertain.

Macready's negated body (and Forrest's prescriptive one) both put forth and complicated a key concern: What does (and what should) the body of the American male artist look like? If the traditional idea of the artist in the nineteenth century was a European creation, was it ever desirable to have such a creature grace American shores? Can there be such a figure as an American artist as it was understood in the Continental sense? How might Americans define the American arts through the body of the American artist? Or as the question was more resolutely put, and as Ursula Frohne uncovers in her reading of the nineteenth-century American literary and arts' magazine *The Crayon*: "Has the Artist a right to exist?"[14] Indeed, the figure of the artist was meant to exist and, more important, it would play a decisive role in the development and representation of America as nation. There were, however, some cultural forces with which to be reckoned before such a representation could be placed on the cultural dais. At the moment of the Astor Place Riot, the importance of the arts as a conduit of national identity through the body of the artist became highly apparent. For the American male artist (and certainly for the spectator as well), the artist and the work of art were no longer inseparable. But if such an artist figure were to grace the American stage, a set of guidelines were necessary for his participation in American cultural identity. In fact, the perceived, theorized, and practiced relationship between art and artists spoke directly to the quality of one's manhood.

If by the end of the nineteenth century American male artists found themselves negotiating the angst of homosexuality as an artistic "stereotype" and art itself as a "feminine" activity, the artists and cultural pundits of 1849 were more eager to define the masculine characteristics of American arts and artists in terms of a masculine national sensibility.[15] Certainly, the risks and anxieties about the effeminizing effect of an excessive marketplace were identified in the period just prior to the Astor Place Riot. Hence, homophobia and misogyny were part and parcel of the nationalist sentiment. But the concerns of the artist as effeminized and/or homosexual would be more clearly articulated (or at least categorized) a few years later.[16] In 1849 the concept of the homosexual and his cultural attributes were not yet in place for such distinctions. Specifically, Macready's body, performance, and overconfident public relations bespoke national and class difference rather than gender "perversion." But the uneasy intersections of nation, class, and gender were set in motion over the Macready and Forrest debacle.

Immediately following the events of the Astor Place Riot, the window through which national identity, gender, class, and aesthetics converged was made clear by an anonymous author (identified as "An American Citizen") who published a treatise on America's position in the arts and its necessarily strident relationship to democratic principles. What is noteworthy about this passage is the concept of democratic equality as it is collapsed through nation, class, and gender (particularly in the domain of the arts). "In concluding this work," writes the American Citizen,

the painful reflection is forced upon us, that the causes which led to the deplorable results of the magisterial, inefficiency and wickedness, lie deeper than those presented on the surface of the controversy between Mr. Forrest and Mr. Macready; they are to be found in our social system; in the presumption and arrogance of a class; in the servile and disgusting imitation by the wealthy few of the habits and customs of European, and particularly British, aristocrats. This, of course, will be denied by the persons for whom those remarks are intended; but turn which way we will, on every hand are the evidences of a gradual approach to those odious distinctions which the rich have always been prone to establish between themselves and the poor. The tradesman looks down upon the mechanic; the merchant assumes the superiority over both; the lawyer claims more honor and distinction than his less fortunate, but equally honest fellow citizen; the clergyman, in his own estimation, stands infinitely above them all; and so these lines are drawn until insuperable social barriers have been erected between the rich and the poor. Even the house of God—in which the word of Eternal Truth should sound in the ears of the poor and distressed—has been converted into a temple adorned by the worshippers of Mammon, and its doors are closed to all but the proud and the wealthy of the land. Those stately structures that rise up annually in our midst, and are called ornaments to the city, are but monuments erected to the vanity of men, and in too many instances owe their existence to the avarice and rapacity of their builders. The laborer and producer who looks upon the palace of the *non-producer*, and the gorgeous churches of the aristocracy, *knows* that from his toil has been wrung the wealth thus expended: he knows, too, that the proud dwellers in marble mansions are *not* superior to himself; *that he is, at least, in the eye of the law, their equal, and if he resists*

their encroachments upon the few rights left him, he only asserts his manhood,
and maintains the principle of equality upon which the whole fabric of this
government is based.

The theatre, even, is not exempt from aristocratic rule.[17]

The "American Citizen" tells us, in the same breath, that "manhood"
and the assertion of the "principle of equality" are one and the same.
The confluent variables of masculinity and equality are at the heart
of the artistic matter. As this citizen sees it, manhood is the sine qua
non of the "principle of equality upon which the whole fabric of this
government is based." Moreover, the anxiety of the citizen rests with
the perceived external threat to the principled simultaneity of American manhood and equality, and thus democracy (the "whole fabric").[18]
Most disturbing for him is the "odious distinction" of class perpetu-
ated by the rich (particularly by the *American* rich who, in this reading,
remain ostensibly British), who by their class devalue the true cultural
"producer" of the American economy (the laborer).[19] What the Astor
Place Riot ushered into public consciousness was a central cultural belief that the aristocratic hierarchy of culture (read here British culture
as performed on the body of Macready) was a sham. Furthermore,
the Americans, "prone" to such "disgusting imitation" of European
habits, were leading the young nation's social system of democracy and
equality into ruin.

The "painful acts" of violence on the evening of May 10, 1849, were
a minor revolution of sorts in that they tore away the privilege of "aristocratic rule," particularly in the realm of the arts, and here most specifically in the realm of the theater, which had not been "exempt from
aristocratic rule." The riot, as it is described here, was unequivocally an
American resistance to the "encroachments" of the lie of Old World
social class and hierarchy. To allow this lie to continue — as Macready
purportedly engendered in his very Britishness and disdain for Forrest — was to reject the "assertion" and right of American manhood. To
refuse American masculine assertion is to reject social equality; Edwin
Forrest's masculinity and performance proffered, in the first place, a
break from the deeply embedded aristocratic falsehoods that underlie
the social system espoused by England.

In addition, the American Citizen makes clear that American masculinity is itself threatened by Old World and unmanly aristocratic rule —
and thus the very foundation of the nation's interest is at risk. Indeed,

British pretense was quite literally killing Americans and their way of life. As the American Citizen notes further: "That national antipathies have had much to do in producing the quarrel between Mr. Forrest and Mr. Macready, and the deplorable consequences that followed it, cannot be denied, and it has been clearly proven that Mr. Forrest was not the aggressor; he bore patiently all that man could bear and his assailant must to the latest day of his life be harrowed with the reflection that his insolence and arrogance sent twenty-five [sic] persons to premature graves, and forced him to flee from a land that always welcomed him with open arms" (119). Macready's arrogant presumptions of imperial nationhood (a slap in the face of his host with "open arms") and its path to violence and death sit in direct opposition to Forrest's passive "patience" when confronted with national aggression. This imperial aggression is, however, of a particular sort. England and her American adherents are "jealous" of America's strength and ability to insist on equality for all. "National jealousy is a passion," continues the American Citizen, "that we cannot cherish, but this subserviency to English arrogance, so prevalent in certain circles, deserves the censure of every true-hearted American. England hates because she fears the young giant of the West, and she knows that the easiest way to rob him of his strength, is to accustom him to the luxury and artificial existence that has made her so weak in her old age; therefore, it ought to be the religious duty of every republican to frown upon and oppose every attempt that is made to introduce the habit and customs of an aristocracy among us" (119).

More frightful to consider, and yet another paradoxical rationalization of nation and gender, is the notion that jealousy is an aggressive feminine act (deceptively seductive and propagated by British aristocratic culture) that endangers America's patient and gentle masculine assertion of equality. The ill—if not castrating—effects of England's effeminized culture are not only "her" blindness to her own "artificial existence" in "old age," but also her inability to recognize her own artificiality causes her "fear" of the masculine "young giant," America. It is the job of the young republicans to vigilantly resist these feminizing and dangerous conditions that England imports and that those "non-producing" Americans sanctify as proper culture. For the American Citizen, Forrest symbolized the resistance to the dangerous jealousy that England held against the gentle and patient giant.

Yet Forrest's burly performance style represented more than a break from the old country's notion of art. Forrest's body and his non-British-aristocratic performance (i.e., one that was muscular, ruffian, and working class) was suggestive of, if not alluring for, what the American art and artist should embody.[20] This rough-and-ready manhood so vociferously presented by Forrest on the New York stage was recognized as the very symbol of American equality because his performance asserted manhood in such a way as to sit squarely in relation to the terms of working-class and immigrant manhood that symbolized America's so-called cultural producers of the democratic ideal of equality.

If democracy and equality were the trademarks of American manhood, American pundits and artists emphasized a logic that secured a masculine culture as the ideal of a classless and genderless society. To be clear, the dream of this ideal classless and genderless society was the dream of many American men,[21] and as such this ideal underscored the condition of the American arts. Although American women undoubtedly confronted misogyny in the hierarchies of gender and the larger field of cultural "democracy," a powerful discourse (a rhetoric that served many of the "liberal" men who supported "women's rights") cut across the national campaign set forth by critics, artists, and statesmen. To establish a paradigm of class and gender fortified with the euphemism *equality*, American democracy became synonymous with the cultural models of masculinity. In many ways, and perhaps more perfidious than the tiers of the British class structure, American equality was generated through a broad-based discourse of populist democratic and masculinist sameness at the expense of lived, experiential difference. Equality thus meant a sameness that in turn defined itself as manly, and it coincided with the assertion of virile manhood for both man and woman. A true American man and woman were, in this logic, masculine by nature. The artist and his or her work of art were thus challenged with the project of creating form and content that elicited such democratic Americanness.

For democratic America, Forrest's career came to signify the strong current of American thought held by the "people," the press, and the cultural critics that earnestly sought what David Potter has termed a "national character."[22] According to Potter, what was essential to the successful formations of an American national character were the claims of "democracy" and "equality" that resisted the presumption of external cultural authority (especially from Britain). Potter argues that the "anti-authoritarian aspect of the creed of equality" (16), under the auspices of American democracy, is the impulse behind America's "commitment to progress" that is underscored by a "belief in the perfectibility of man and in the practicability of steps to bring perfection nearer" (17). But the perfectible American man that embodies the national character straddled the tensions and paradoxical maxims that underwrote the idealist and realist principles of democracy and aesthetics: "Americans are committed," Potter argues, "to the view that materialistic means are necessary to idealist ends" (17). If the aporia (the dialectical impasse) that exists between the ideal and the real of the American national character (an unreachable, pure meeting of democratic principles and material goods) cannot be broached, then culture takes its imperfect, yet progressive, form in the practical and ideological processes manufactured in the work of art. As such, Edwin Forrest embodied these perfect imperfections of an ideal national character.

The Body of Edwin Forrest: American Artist

What did this body of masculine creativity and democratic equality look like? How was it "performed" and made to represent what R. W. B. Lewis described as the "American Adam"?[23] What did Edwin Forrest say and do to elicit for the American public such a presence on stage and in the lived world? Although Forrest's hyperbolic manliness may with critical hindsight be perceived as a caricature, his body more concretely and persuasively served as a fecund source for the representation of American democracy. His performance as the popular male artist offered Americans a forceful example of American art and artists as a spectacle of and for the people.

Championed by Walt Whitman's darlings, the predominantly Irish Bowery B'hoys, Forrest was positioned as a vital cultural marker in the American arts. Since Macready solidified British aristocratic and imperialist pretenses, Forrest's virile and gruff demeanor engaged the ethics and demeanor of a strong and hardy (American) working class (the actor's wealth would have suggested something other than working-class wages, however).[24] In 1849, Whitman applauded Forrest's performance style and "manlier aspirations." His reading of Forrest is instructive for understanding the way in which the journalist soon-to-be poet evolved his vision of the American democratic arts and how he carried such central (yet not without contradictory) tenets into his later and extremely influential work—work that will weave its way through the men and art that this book addresses. Richard Moody writes that, at the time of the riot,

> Another perverse complaint came from an inconspicuous reporter on the *Brooklyn Eagle* named Walt Whitman. (This was nine years before the publication of *Leaves of Grass*.) Whitman recognized Forrest's genius in making "the hearts of the masses swell responsively to all those nobler manlier aspirations in behalf of mortal freedom." He [Whitman] deplored the evil influence that he exerted on his vapid imitators, who lacked his [Forrest's] control. "If they have to enact passion, they do so by all kinds of unnatural and violent jerks, swings, screwing of the nerves of the face, rolling of the eyes, and so on . . . It is a common fallacy to think that an exaggerated, noisy, and inflated style of acting—and no other—will produce the desired effect upon a promiscuous audience."[25]

This passage is illuminating in that it tells as much about Forrest as it does about Whitman (and, certainly, Moody). Moreover, in terms of the present study it is important to flag Moody's language that describes Whitman's "complaint" about Forrest's double-edged influence as "perverse," since such rhetoric anticipates contemporary masculinist (if not homophobic) assumptions about the popular arts (assumptions that are particularly rife in some projects in cultural studies and American studies). There is a tendency among some writers toward a simplified, if not romanticized, conflation of the working class with the so-called popular arts. What is posited in this scholarship is the success of the American democratic arts through a working-class sensibility whose leisure activities are rendered as virile and hardy, not effete or decadent. The working class is conceived as down-to-earth, where its members participate in the popular arts or the art of the people. Such an intersection is posited as ipso facto "democratic" while neglecting the hetero-masculinist impulse that underlies such assertions.[26]

Nonetheless, Whitman occupies a complicated station in the context of American art, cultural criticism, and other "manlier aspirations" of the national creative enterprise. He is not easily situated in discussions that bridge the American arts with masculinity because he is at once homophobic, homoerotic, misogynist, liberal progressive, nationalistic, and, later, a proponent of bureaucratic corporations. Whitman's texts, like any others, take on a life of their own in critical debate, with effects that are striking and often paradoxical. That said, it should be noted that Whitman played an instrumental role in equalizing the terms democracy and masculinity.[27]

In terms of this discussion, Whitman's comments about Forrest point to an important shift within the style of American theatrical performance during this period of the nineteenth century. Clearly, as Whitman's remarks suggest, Forrest's influence set a precedent and proscription for an unnatural, or uncontrolled, performance style. In this way, an American sense of naturalism and its attending aesthetic realism were identified through the masculine gestures of Forrest. Forrest's performance, which apparently dispensed with "unnatural and violent jerks, swings, screwing of the nerves of the face, [and] rolling of the eyes," set the terms for what was soon to be recognized as the early style of "realist" representation in the theater and, subsequently, the cinema.[28] Whitman's critical acclaim of Forrest's performance style is indicative of the cultural atmosphere that was seen to be engulfing America's project of creativity and masculinity. If, as Alexis de Tocqueville argued, the United States of the 1830s lagged in the civilized arts and any sort of cultural capital, Forrest's masculine creativity can be seen as a significant point of entry for America's vision of what the arts would look like.[29]

To achieve his sanctioned rank as a "natural" or "realist" performer, Forrest strenuously exercised his body into what he considered to be the real and ideal American artist. Forrest's biographer, Moody, describes in Whitmanesque terms how Forrest conditioned his body to "reflect the sublime sweep of his native land, whose spirit would be imbued with the fresh, free air of the young democracy."[30] In fact, Forrest rigorously developed his well-recognized muscular frame through an exercise program that "went beyond the sheer necessity of developing muscularity for his heroic roles; he was simply fascinated by physical culture" (75–76). "Under the vigorous physical regimen," as Moody describes it,

> Forrest developed a Herculean body. In later years his five-foot-ten frame carried a massive burden of over two hundred pounds. In 1827 he had no excess fat. His legs, arms, shoulders, and even his neck seemed a mass of muscles. When he came on stage, anyone who had not yet glimpsed the new star was immediately struck by his handsome, upright figure and the tremendous display of strength. Most of his roles permitted a free exhibition of his physique—bare legs and bare arms—which made the initial

impact even more provocative. Although not of more than average height, spectators invariably were amazed at his seemingly gigantic proportions. When Fanny Kemble saw him for the first time, she exclaimed: "What a mountain of a man!"(77).

This celebrated "mountain of a man," an ideal body emboldened by the metaphors of "sublime" nature, fascinated and won over scores of followers (both men and women). Through his "provocative" and "free exhibition of his physique," Forrest was the corporeal carrier (in "gigantic proportions") of the new democracy.

In word and deed, Forrest put forth the significant traits that would serve as the model of the American male artist.[31] William Rounseville Alger, Forrest's contemporary biographer who interviewed the actor later in life, recounted in 1877 how his performances were likened to "a whirlwind, a tornado, a cataract."[32] What is clear, then, is that Forrest saw his creative self in symbiotic relationship with nature. Indeed, Forrest believed himself to be "the embodiment of natural power" as well as the artistic conduit through which America's natural essence was revealed. It was more than landscape, however, that signaled the American sensibilities of manliness and creativity. Forrest's bodily regimen and intellectual sense of American creativity tightly wove together the contemporary humanist vernacular of an imaginary transcendent vision (the "sublime"), with practical and virile common sense to evoke America's vast landscape and the native peoples who populated it.

Both Moody and Alger suggest that Forrest amalgamated nativist and "authentic" primitivist cultural tropes so as to incorporate them with his artistic temperament, thereby yielding a "nativist badge . . . as professional trademark."[33] Like other young American artists coming on the scene (e.g., James Fenimore Cooper, Washington Irving, David Thoreau, and Ralph Waldo Emerson), Forrest's melding of body and nature enabled what Richard Slotkin characterizes as "total self-immersion in direct, simple, and unanticipated experience" between man and his environment.[34] But it took shape through very specific avenues. The following account written by Forrest's biographer, Alger, illuminates the way in which Forrest put in place the cult of nativist principles in relation to his body and the aesthetic practices of Western civilization:

One night Push-ma-ta-ha [Forrest's American Indian friend] and Forrest were lying on the ground before a big fire which they had kindled a little way out from the village. They had been conversing for hours, recalling stories and legends for their mutual entertainment. The shadows of the wood lay here and there like so many dark ghosts of trees prostrate and intangible on the earth. The pale smoke from their burning heap of brush floated towards heaven in spectral volumes and slowly faded out afar. In the unapproachable blue over their heads hung the full moon, and in the pauses of their talk nothing but the lonely notes of night-bird broke the silence. Like an artist, or like an antique Greek, Forrest had a keen delight in the naked form of man, feeling that the best image of God we have is nude humanity in its perfection, which our fashionable dresses so travesty and degrade. Push-ma-ta-ha, then twenty-four years old, brought up from birth in the open air and in almost incessant action of sport and command, was from head to foot a faultless model of a human being. Forrest asked him to strip himself and walk to and fro before him between the moonlight and the firelight, that he might feast his eyes and his soul on so complete a physical type of what man should be. The young chief, without a word, cast aside his Choctaw garb and stepped forth with dainty tread, a living statue of Apollo in glowing bronze.[35]

Alger's account presents an important moment in the history of the male gaze and homoerotic manifestations that are persistently raised around the tensions of male-to-male relations in the arts. And since the arts, especially nineteenth-century theater, carried the taint of vulgarity and even of sin, how did the male artist articulate his man-to-man union with the savage Other in the deep recesses of the American frontier without suggesting sodomitic possibilities?[36] In what ways did Forrest and other artists assure America's cultural custodians and gatekeepers that their creative experiences were nothing short of the highest moral quality? The work of art, I suggest, functions as a shield to protect the artist from accusations that his activities are somehow less than manly. The conjuring of an "antique Greek" tradition de-eroticizes Forrest's "delight in the naked form of man." In this way, the encounter that both eroticizes and exoticizes the Indian body is one that romanticizes the mythic placement of the "native" as one who is essential for achieving a true or real moment of pure artistry. Paul Gilmore posits that "by imagining himself as spectator and spectacle, Forrest configures both Indianness and manliness as performative—as, in fact, the same performance. And through his aesthetic (dis)engagement with Push-ma-ta-ha, Forrest not only distances himself from the homoerotic pleasure he gains in looking, but provides himself with a way of at once becoming the Indian by gaining a masculine body while at the same time denying that very embodiment."[37] Gilmore is right that Forrest's disengagement from the "homoerotics" of the scene underlines a more complex dynamic. Hence, Forrest's position as artist in the scene serves as a means for him to protect himself from the homosexual threat through a process of embracing the "primitive" body of the Other as a work of art while simultaneously projecting the ideal self through a transcendent commingling of self and Other.

I would argue, however, that Forrest's positioning of self here is not one of "aesthetic (dis)engagement" or the "denying" of embodiment. Forrest's program to become an American artist insisted that *no* disengagement must exist between the artist and the work of art. To be both spectator and spectacle provocatively calls into play an "imagining" (to use Gilmore's term) where Forrest believes he experiences his masculine embodiment as the complete work of art by "feasting" on the body of the Indian. The spectacle desexualizes the encounter, because spectacle, as Guy Debord would have it, provides a deceived condition of unified consciousness. If Hollywood was later criticized for sublimating sexual desire into romance, it could be said that nineteenth-century male artists sublimated homosexual desire (or homosocial desire, for that matter) through the romanticized relationship of the native body and landscape.[38]

"The acquaintance of Forrest with Push-ma-ta-ha," writes Alger, "was the first of his deep interest in the subject of the American Aborigines, of his subsequent extensive researches into their history, and finally of his offering a prize for a play which should embody a representative idea of their genius and their fate" (128). The later success of Forrest's performance of an American Indian in *Metamora* (the play that came to be because of his "extensive researches") was singled out by audiences and critics for its authentic interpretation of the native. Gilmore argues, however, that Forrest's performances as Metamora, applauded for their thunderous spectacle, were nothing short of racist minstrelsy: "This vision of Forrest emitting natural power—or in fact being the embodiment of natural power—allowed his fans to cast away his white skin in a fantasy of him actually becoming red."[39] As I later note, Forrest is not alone in the "deep interest" of the American Indian.[40]

What was it, however, that Forrest and other American artists believed to have happened to their own physical existence once the presence of the "savage" crossed their paths so that "he might feast his eyes and his soul on so complete a physical type of what man should be"? It is important to bear in mind that the native-as-American discourse ranges greatly and serves varied ideological aims in American history. Nineteenth-century artists engaged the Indian far differently than did, for example, newspaper editorialists, politicians, and the military.[41] For the artists under discussion here, to perform as the "noble savage" took on great weight since the push for an identifiable sense of the American arts was so anxiously demanded: As Philip Deloria notes, "There was, quite simply, no way to conceive an American identity without Indians."[42] The so-called pure corporeality of the Indian was critical for this new identity. In 1825, author John Neal wrote an essay for *Blackwood's Magazine* in which he stated: "We now urge to the writers of America, who are coming out, one after another, in a vile masquerade—putting away their chief properties and aping the style of another people . . . It is American books that are wanted of America; not English books—nor books, made in America, by Englishmen, or by writers, who are a sort of bastard English . . . Come forth naked, absolutely naked, *we* should say, to every real North American—savage, or not; wild or tame; though your muscles be rather too large, and your toes turned the wrong way."[43] The call was now made and the wrappings of virility (celebrated for its imperfections) and creativity were unleashed to supply "naked" savagism. The Indian was successfully catapulted as the carrier of the essential quality of the American arts.

As many scholars have shown, the grand scope of the white man's American arts and his privileged manhood saddled the glories of a "sublime sweep of [the] native land" through, in particular, an elevation of the American Indian and the mythology of a pure native land.[44] Gail Bederman succinctly points out that "white heroes achieve manhood by becoming 'like' Indian Warriors, while nonetheless remaining unmistakably white."[45] Of course, the images chosen to signify the transcendence of America's relationship to the Indian and the land were founded on the gutting of the very thing that represented the "sublime sweep." Indeed, Forrest's beholding, or rather, ingesting of the Other as a pure work of art points to a central concern in the experience of American masculinity and creativity: How did an artist like Forrest ingest the essence of nativeness yet remain pure and white? Moreover, how did the likes of Forrest embrace his symbiotic masculine Americanness with the native?

In his refusal of Western modern decadence (fashionable clothes) and his encounter with the "pure" native, Forrest found the "feast" for "eyes and his soul" in the ideal "physical type of what man should be." And as Gilmore points out, Push-ma-ta-ha's "dainty tread," when understood in its historical context, refers to movement that is "of exquisite taste; delicious . . . and effeminately beautiful."[46] As I pointed out earlier, Alger, Moody, and, to be sure, Forrest, managed (through rhetoric rich in its ability to gloss over its own glaring contradictions) the erotics of man-to-man desire in such a way as to retain a non-homosexualized encounter between Forrest and Push-ma-ta-ha. Thus, Forrest's devouring of the "delicious" primitive male body who moved with a "dainty tread" is cast as an "effeminate" object of desire. The primitive, identified here as "effeminately beautiful," secured the male's object of desire as nothing short of heterosexual (an effeminized Other) while manifesting all the essential (if not savage) qualities of pure American manliness.[47] The native body assumes (simultaneously and paradoxically) the purity of natural origin, a savage "embodiment of virility"[48] yet an "effeminately beautiful" pose, and the privileged identification as a de-eroticized work of art. In a later chapter I will reintroduce the "delicious" Other—with a rather queer and sophisticated inflection.

In the meantime, what is at stake here in Forrest's masculinist gaze on Push-ma-ta-ha (a gaze that is more troubling than placing the native Other on the American pedestal of art) are the conditions that ensured the deeply seated and thoroughly inscribed nationalist "aura" of the American arts. The process—indeed spectacle—of American masculinity and creativity that is found in Forrest's encounter with Push-ma-ta-ha is not an expression of the Othering of pure difference in relation to the white/nonwhite body. Rather, the privileged claims for creativity that the artist as white man exercised were those in which he envisioned both a transcendence beyond his impure modern-civilized self and a deep penetration of his own dark, lost past. But, perhaps more important, the spectacle of art ultimately achieved the perfect balance or commonsense existence between Western culture and noble savagery. Push-ma-ta-ha was the body through which Forrest convened in sublime imbrication with the native Other while his creative essence was concretized and Americanized.

Forrest's body thus might be said to have gentrified the exotic Other's body because he imagined himself as a participant in, and in contact with, the mythological primitivism from which the "noble savage" derived and lived. The civilized white man moves in on, and perceives himself to become one with, the noble savage so as to bestow on him the gifts of Western knowledge and progress that satisfy democratic principles.[49] Under the paradigm of democratic equality—which is, as we have witnessed with the American Citizen, the assertion of manhood—the white American male artist of the nineteenth-century brought himself into a transcendent state where his primitive Being experienced the total oneness of man. There is a creative process here that involves complex acts of consumption and production on the part of the white-settler artist who conjured an experience that neatly bundled his body with subject and object.[50]

Forrest's feasting on the "savage" is also part of a long-standing colonial tradition of captive narratives where cannibalism plays a significant point of anxiety between the white man and the Indian.[51] Forrest's feast, like those of the early Puritans that Slotkin discusses, "culminates in the total absorption of the eater and the eaten in each other, a total sharing of identities."[52] It is precisely the "absorption" and "total sharing of identities" where the white man's fixation on race to regulate the terms for the white man's American arts established an important benchmark for an aesthetic of realism as a projection of American democracy and masculinity.

The Experience of American Masculinity and Creativity

Edwin Forrest turned again and again to the image of the obliging native where he projected and invested a pure ideal of American masculinity into his body. Like the early Puritans, Forrest experienced the "total absorption of eater and eaten in each other," a commingling of identity with the primitive Other. His play, *Metamora* (first performed 1829), ran successfully for years. With *Metamora*, Forrest "might feast his eyes and soul on so complete a physical type of what man should be."[53] As we have seen, at the heart of this experience is the suggestion that Forrest channeled the essence and aura of American Indian nativeness directly into his body, and in so doing wove it in and through his art. As a body unencumbered by civilization's threats of effeminization and other modern excesses (that is, British and American aristocratic cultures), the "naked savage" of America moved elegantly, yet truculently, between the moonlight and the firelight before the white male artist.[54] Thus the artist fulfilled his chosen role as the enlightened translator of the material world and the sublime. The artist who embodied the essence of American creativity and its original spirit of primitiveness eliminated the effeminizing effects of civilization and presented to America its own pure Americanness.

The process of masculinizing the American artist—the work or labor involved in the making of the complete work of art—was based on the premise that art commingled with the (male) artist's body and thus elevated subject and object into a transcendental yet democratic sphere of common sense.[55] This experience of identifying oneself and one's art as American was realized, I would argue, in the following ways: first, in the organization of form and content that framed the image object along traditional academic modes of production where the artist inserted his mark or presence; second, in the use of American Indian/nativist imagery (landscapes and bodies) as a way to ground his presence through the notions of beauty and the sublime in order to sustain the virile essences of masculinity, democracy, creativity, and (industrialized) civilization; and third, in the consecration of the aesthetic of realism (as tied to American theories of the sublime, idealism, and common sense) where art struck a harmonious balance between the popular and its functional use value.

There is one other component of the American arts that is important to note here since it leads to a discussion about masculinity, creativity, and the cinema. In some ways, Forrest had earlier evoked this concept of the cinematic through his experience with Push-ma-ta-ha where the American Indian's movement was framed and observed by the flickering firelight. Lee Clark Mitchell suggests in his study of Forrest's influential contemporary, James Fenimore Cooper—notably in looking at Cooper's major work *The Leatherstocking Tales* (1823–1841)—that in order to grasp fully the rush of the American landscape and its spiritual connection for the white settler on America's frontier it is useful to consider the "brisk cinematic action" at work in the early-nineteenth-century imagination.[56] The notion of the cinematic, as we know, precedes the institution itself.[57] But the later arrival of the mechanical device promised a way to re-present the object in ways not available to the other arts. One of cinema's more specific properties that became central to American artists is its ability to project an ideal self through the terms of realism. To be clear, this projection was not simply that of a mirror reflection of a manly body (though this was important as well). Instead, the key was in the projection of the abstract ideals of masculine democracy through the materialized shadows cast on the movie screen.

Although Mitchell's terms such as "brisk cinematic action" and the sense of rapid movement in nineteenth-century literary fiction offered to the American (and overseas) audience a set of rich, vivid tools with which to imagine the excitement of the frontier, the idea of projecting a vision of self through the arts was significant. Earl Rovit identified "self-definition," or individualism, for artists as a vital part of the American experience. He further suggests that "the American writer characteristically invents or discovers his own peculiar symbolic manner of expressing his projections of, or solution to, his overweening needs for self-definition."[58] The "projections of, or solutions to" individualism solidified a masculine national identity sanctioned by imperialist manifest destiny and the wide-open spaces of the (global) frontier. The land, the native, and the balance of civilization with savagery defined the complete embodiment of individual Americanness. The idea of the cinematic, both abstractly and realistically, projected these nineteenth-century discourses back to America.

Later, when the idea of the cinema became a technological and industrial possibility, the realist aesthetic that the motion-picture camera enabled, as well as its mass appeal in terms of shaping an ideal national identity, clinched what Frederick Jackson Turner recommended some years later in 1903. During this period, when the cinema was rapidly coming into its own, Turner wrote: "The material forces that gave vitality to Western democracy are passing away. It is to the realm of the spirit, to the domain of ideals and legislation, that we must look for Western influence upon democracy in our own days."[59] The popular American arts of the twentieth century, whether experienced or manufactured in the metropolis or the rural countryside, bore the "realm of the spirit" of masculine democracy. The camera's ability to record movement and then project an aped image back to the spectator (including the artist or the artist's idea of himself) was instrumental in capturing America's progressive dreams of the real and the ideal. With the cinema, the artist's projection of his transcendent self, his democratic principles, and his all-encompassing vision of America were fully realized. The ideological success of masculinizing the American arts was thus accomplished through a complex patterning of a spatial and temporal gestalt where realist ideologies took on the force of a *gesamtkunstwerk*—a complete work of art—with the arrival of the cinema.

Framing the American Real: Theories of Absorption

In his book *The Real Thing: Imitation and Authenticity in American Culture, 1880–1940* Miles Orvell tells us that "one dominant mode in the popular culture in the late nineteenth century was . . . the tendency to enclose reality in manageable forms, to contain it within a theatrical space, an enclosed exposition or recreational space, or within the space of the picture frame. If the world outside the frame was beyond control, the world inside of it could at least offer the illusion of mastery and comprehension."[60] The sense of just what this proper frame of reality was, however, was never made clear aesthetically. Yet the myth that realism captured an ideal moment in a frame played a crucial role in setting the terms for American realism.

The artist's ability first to experience and then transpose nature into art—to frame it and manage its uncertainty—was an essential component both of the nineteenth-century romantic movement and of Emersonian transcendentalism. Thus, the landscape within which Forrest posed Push-ma-ta-ha is described by the actor as if it is a painter's canvas or a theatrical stage. Push-ma-ta-ha is framed within a specific field; in both Alger's and Moody's biographies, notably, the body of the Indian remains in an enclosed range and perspective, illuminated by the reach of moonlight and firelight. Here, the worlds of painting and theater are not far apart; the description of the event portrays Forrest directing his gaze (as well as directing Push-ma-ta-ha) on a canvas wherein he orchestrates a living creative force. Furthermore, the position into which Forrest guides his model (the "living statue of Apollo in glowing bronze") is aligned with a historical tradition and a painterly trope that art historian Michael Fried identifies as "absorption."[61] Although part of a long-standing European tradition, the trope was transformed by the likes of Manet during the 1860s and then was defunct in Paris by the 1870s. The import and "primacy" of absorption, however, was still identifiable in American painting as late as 1875. The most salient aspect of the tradition is the paradoxical effect it elicits in the spectator's experience with the work of art: absorption places the viewer at once objectively outside the work while also moving the viewer inside it.

The tradition of absorption, as Fried defines it, "is essentially a realist one, and there is every likelihood that the connection between absorption and realism that it evinces is functional rather than merely accidental."[62] The functionality of absorption, therefore, "serve[s] the ends of pictorial realism by encouraging the viewer to explore the represented scene in an unhurried manner; the same painterly chiaroscuro that lends itself to strong absorptive effects (e.g., shadowing a given personage's gaze, often in contrast to bright illumination on the brow) also yields effects of modeling and atmosphere—of the tangibleness but also the continuity of a perceptual field" (42–43). What can be seen in these works that Fried discusses is a figure in repose or thoughtful contemplation. The model's pose or gesture is thus a performance, a dramatic scene of thinking, gazing, pondering, writing, or reading.[63] The figure performs in the tableau that the artist has directed and to which the beholder is made witness.

We can rightly imagine Forrest assuming the role of artist and spectator who, as was a convention of the day, conceived the American landscape as a painter's canvas only to be filled by the ideal model who in "shadowing a given personage's gaze" by firelight presented the figure of pure American contemplation and repose. What is striking about the pose of absorption, as well as its "functional" realism, is that the figure casts his or her look in such as way as to "neutralize or negate the beholder's presence."[64] Later I will return to the suggestive quality of "neutralization," but here I want to stress the illusion of reality; like Forrest's directing of Push-ma-ta-ha, the framed pose invites a spectatorial position of "unconsciousness or obliviousness" (101). The work of art is, consequently, presented before the spectator as a distinct entity to be observed and contemplated from a distance.

Yet, paradoxically, the beholder is simultaneously inserted into the world of the picture while kept objectively distanced. Indeed, Fried points to the more famous of these contradictory assertions when he describes "Diderot's infrequent but nevertheless far from arbitrary use of the fiction of *physically entering* a painting or group of paintings he is reviewing, a fiction conspicuously at odds with the doctrine of the radical exclusion of the beholder." (118). How might such an incongruous position, one both inside and outside the painting, be explained? For

Diderot, according to Fried, "an essential object of paintings . . . was to induce in the beholder a particular psycho-physical condition, equivalent in kind and intensity to a profound experience of nature." More provocatively, the intense "psycho-physical" experience triggered by the work of art achieved an "existential reverie or *repos délicieux*" (130). In effect, the spectator's experience with the work of art evoked a "fiction of the beholder's physical presence within the painting, by virtue of an almost magical recreation of the effect of nature itself" (132). The tradition of absorption is thus one characterized by the illusion of a "magical" nature—that is, a "functional" realism that is manufactured, on the one hand, by the performative fiction of the figure in the tableau while, on the other hand, by the spectator's transformative and fictional experience of being here yet there. But the spectator is not alone in his or her insertion into the tableau's performance.

In Fried's essay on Thomas Eakins, the American painter who "subscribed to the myth of realism,"[65] he argues, among other things, that Eakin's work bears the signature—literally and figuratively—of the artist. The artist at once projects himself into his fictional tableau, a site of spectacularized Otherness, while remaining in a position of privileged objectivity outside the frame. Eakin's historical and biographical circumstances (psychoanalytically derived for Fried) are traceable in his work and indicate the artist's presence within and without the frame.[66] The insertion of self into the aestheticized frame of realism, the site of Otherness, for both spectator and artist, employs a "repos délicieux," a Burkean sublime measured by the "dialectic of pain and pleasure" (65). To be simultaneously inside and outside the frame is both terrifying and pleasurable because it sets the scene where the masculine self is affirmed through its "psycho-physical" commingling with the Other, the work of art (consider, in this light, Forrest's framing of and feasting on Push-ma-ta-ha). This masculinist scene of threat and narcissistic affirmation, as I show below, is a notion that returns again and again in the experience of American art.

Before I take up the complexity of the American sublime and its troubling dialectic of narcissistic pain and pleasure along with its peculiar relationship to masculinity, it is important first to address the sense of the sublime as a delicious embrace and "re-creation" of primitive nature. These are rich metaphors when we consider Forrest's "feast" of the native body—one that is modeled in the pose of the absorptive tradition and burdened as the marker of a lost savage and pure self.[67]

Indeed, in this manner commingling with the native was a significant step in experiencing the sublimity of nature.

This Shadow of the Soul, or Other Me

Many artists have viewed American Indianness as an aesthetic equivalent for democracy.[68] When shaped as a noble and determined savage, the American Indian served as a recognizable trope for public consumption that held fast the functional realities of everyday frontier life. The "noble savage" ideally represented the hope of the new (white) American for a balance of his own savage and civil sensibilities. How did the figure of the American Indian come to be identified with the frontiersman's savage instinct while maintaining codes of Western civilization? Locating the trace of the "savage" in art is no simple matter given the ties of the American upper class to European notions of taste.[69] In 1845, for example, the author of an essay in the *American Review: A Whig Journal of Politics, Literature, Art, and Science* addressed what he saw as the "condition and prospects of Ideal Art in this country."[70] For the author of this essay, "cultivating a noble taste for the Arts, and nobly encouraging the Artist" on the part of each American was paramount for the "increase in the value of life to himself, [while it added] more to the refinement and glory of the nation" (659). Art was thus undeniably central for social and individual uplift (to be supported by the common citizen) with the added benefit that it created a refined nation (which can explain why Matthew Arnold's treatise on art and uplift were later so well received by a particular class in America).[71] As I discuss in chapter 3, cultural uplift cuts many ways, especially in relationship to race.

An agreement about the route to this progressivist "glory of the nation," however, was not easily reached. Yet certain characteristic themes emerged more powerfully than others in the shaping of American art. As a result of being put through the American filter and dissemination of Rousseauistic philosophies of nature, Kantian and Burkean readings of the sublime, Emersonian transcendentalist poetry, luminist brushstroke techniques, primitivist and romantic theories of the "noble savage," and while, at the same time, resisting and clinging to Old World aesthetic dicta, the condition of art and the artist underwent a process of configuration that forged America's complex national aesthetic.

In this way, the American artist was called on by several cultural forces to establish a virile aesthetic that expunged the decadence of Old World standards of beauty. If we saw in Forrest the idea that the artist could channel through himself the Indian's nativeness, the taking on of this noble savagery additionally lent itself to the idea of an American sublime that was grounded as real, democratic, and virile. Ralph Waldo Emerson's claim that "the high and divine beauty which can be loved without effeminacy, is that which is found in combination with the human will," bespeaks a profound concern about the experience of art, beauty, and the sublime in America where the "human will" is nothing short of manly.[72] At stake are bodies: the body of the artist, the body of the "savage," the body of the nation, all three of which were intertwined, collapsed, and visualized by critics and artists alike in order to achieve a unique aggregate of creative work. A problem, however, existed in the fact that the colonial artist was not very far removed (genetically) from his Anglo cousins,[73] yet the Indian was uniquely American.

Hoxie Fairchild, in his classic book *The Noble Savage*, designates the age of the English romantic period in literature and its popular use of the primitivist noble savage between 1730 and 1830. He stresses, further, that this break does not preclude the romantic ideas of the period from lingering across geographical space and historical time.[74] "Our own Ralph Waldo Emerson's philosophy," Fairchild points out, "has sometimes been hailed as distinctively American." But then he goes on to state that Emerson was wholly imitative in certain writings; as an example he cites the following passage from the 1839 poem "Goodbye":

O, when I am safe in my sylvan home,
I tread on the pride of Greece and Rome;
And when I am stretched beneath the pines,
Where the evening star so holy shines,
I laugh at the lore and the pride of man,
At the sophist schools, and the learned clan;
For what are they all, in their high conceit,
When man in the bush with God may meet?[75]

Not only are these lines "imitative" of English romanticism, but Emerson's text is instructive for the way in which nineteenth-century tensions over the loss of nature and encroaching of civilization are played out within the American terrain. The "pride of Greece and Rome" and the "sophist schools" that surface in civilization are meaningless when one is finally "stretched beneath the pines." When all is said and done, it is to nature we return. For Emerson and the romantics (on both sides of the Atlantic), man must not lose touch with his essence or risk the loss of the sublime experience operating in his creative energies enabled by nature.[76]

But the tension between nature and civilization is not easily resolved through privileging one side or the other. For many American artists the tension itself is where the tapestry of paradoxical cultural equations of the nature/civilization divide supported democratic progress. This was progress in the making. But striking a commonsense balance to contain excesses was where the difficulty lay. Once attained, however, the experience was sublime in its affect. To secure the balanced position of the white man in this place of democratic promise meant identifying a body that was simultaneously civilized yet purely connected to America's rugged landscape. Most important, this body—because of its perceived original connection to the land—signified the true human nature of Americans. Roy Harvey Pearce suggests that the idea, symbol, and image of the body of the Indian (recall Push-ma-ta-ha) was the tabula rasa on which the nature/civilization tension of the white man was battled and masculine-American civilization prospered.[77] At once savage, childlike, authentic, and natural, the American Indian (from no matter what tribe) satisfied Eurocentric notions of what the New World both ought and ought not be.[78]

If man were to conjoin with God and nature or the nature of God where the true byway to democracy awaited, the American artist as a representative of democratic principles conceptually placed his body in this environment free of artificiality shared with the native. Emerson's landscape evoked in "Goodbye," for example, points to where an experience of the sublime was carved through man's encounter with nature that transcends civilization. Nature's landscape, for Emerson (as well as for Thoreau, Irving, and Cooper), is mutually dependent on the idea of the primitive/Indian if not on that group's (metaphysical) presence. Thoreau also merged the idea of Indian with landscape so as to rid man of his harmful existence with cultural institutions, as noted in the following: "If, then, we would indeed restore mankind by truly Indian, botanic, magnetic, or natural means, let us first be simple and well as Nature ourselves, dispel clouds which hang over our own brows, and take up a little life into our pores."[79] Although Thoreau wrote these words at a point after Forrest's and Push-ma-ta-ha's sublime exchange, it remains clearly relevant given Forrest's interest in Emerson and the transcendentalists. Emerson, as Slotkin points out, sees Thoreau's "Indian sensibility in his attitude toward nature, identifying himself with the beasts of prey or with the Indian hunters themselves."[80]

The artist's identification with the "Indian sensibility" was thus the ability to assert oneself (as in manly equality) into the landscape—both physically and metaphysically. Such identification was, therefore, essential to the artist's efforts to Americanize their work. The American artist's creative process communed with nature in such a way that the artist was mystically able to place himself in touch with his purported symbiotic association with the Indian. To become one with the native, the artist must identify himself as and with the savage. This identification was pivotal to the artist's sublime transcendence into the sphere of pure American art. As Washington Irving put it, "There is something in the character and habits of the North American savage taken in connection with the scenery over which he is accustomed to range, its vast lakes, boundless forests, majestic rivers, and trackless plains, that is, to my mind, wonderfully striking and sublime."[81]

Seen this way, Forrest's experience with Push-ma-ta-ha cannot be underestimated for how it served the "wonderfully striking and sublime." Diderot's suggestion of the beholder's insertion into the work of art is constructively recalled here. The belief by critics and artists in America that the encounter with the work (for Forrest, the work of art was Push-ma-ta-ha) established, as Fried argues, a "fiction of the beholder's physical presence within the painting, by virtue of an *almost magical recreation of the effect of nature itself*,"[82] which was solidified by the awe-inspiring ability of the (male) artist to both encapsulate and represent the essence of America. Following the tradition of the artist's romanticized relationship to the Indian (*pace* George Catlin and Frank Hamilton Cushing),[83] Forrest's telling of this meeting with the American Indian in the sublime American landscape tapped into a rich and far-reaching discourse operating in nineteenth-century America.

The spectacle (in its fullest sense) of the experience of Forrest and other American artists is important because it underscores crucial attributes associated with masculinity, creativity, and national identity. Here, Push-ma-ta-ha's pure American body, a body of a mythic past embedded in the original land, conjured what Henry Nash Smith refers to as "ancient mother nature," a notion that defended the line between decadent, effeminate industrialization and original nature. The Indian sublime was thus a romanticized aesthetic during the nineteenth century, where American artists envisioned a return to the "simple life of the savages."[84] Smith argues that "men who felt themselves divorced from nature seemed to hope that by dwelling upon these symbols they might regain a lost imaginative contact with some secret source of virtue and power in the universe" (84). The "imaginative contact" between artist and Other embraced a sense of the true, or real, American experience. Once devoured and absorbed as part of the masculine self, the artist was then able to project himself/Other on stage, in literature, in painting, and ultimately on film as a perfect embodiment of indigenous creativity and masculinity.

Dana Nelson rightly argues that "the abstracting identity of white/ national manhood found one means for stabilizing its internal divisions and individual anxieties via imagined projections into, onto, against Indian territories, Indian bodies, Indian identities."[85] The act of the consuming of and identifying with the Other through an "imagined projection" with the purpose of achieving a sense of one's complete national and natural maleness belies what Lee Edelman theorizes as masculine narcissistic fantasy: "If the fantasy of masculinity . . . is the fantasy of a non-self-conscious selfhood endowed with absolute control of a gaze whose directionality is irreversible, the enacted—or 'self-conscious'—'manhood' . . . is itself a performance *for the gaze of the Other.*" Yet, while manhood is the "display of a masculinity that defines itself through its capacity to put *Others* on display," it resists announcing the very performance that defines the terms for that masculinity.[86]

The history of American white male creativity and art is thus a history of a narcissistic fantasy that defines the wholeness and completeness of a masculine nationalist self. The notion of the Indian is the key for the pure ideal that the white man must achieve if he is to exist in a perfect model of civilization; the Indian serves as the antidote to over-civilization and the metaphoric narcotic used to reach an American sublime. The spectacle of white male masculinity whose "control of a gaze" is measured through his projection of self for the Other (that is, the savage, his audience, and ultimately the primitive Other of himself) is also a history riddled with often ironic yet debilitating effects for the American arts. It is this issue of race, gender, and sexuality that informs my work because these concepts are the long-standing markers of difference that have defined the arts in America as a white masculine enterprise. The homophobia, misogyny, and racism that follow in the wake of the narcissistic fantasy of the white male are well documented. Suffice to say that the masculine display and its naturalness, its "non-self-conscious selfhood," supports itself precisely by these differences. It is through the artist himself, the projection of his self, and his absorptive transcendence of space and time that the true work of art arose and maintained its sublimated position. Through the landscape of nature and the body of the primitive Other, the male artist envisioned his pure American ideal self; that is, he is the spectator of himself. But the ironic manifestations of masculine male narcissism are critical to investigate further since the ironies reveal the masculine performance at work. Hence, imagined projection, where self and Other become one, fails because it can never achieve the totalizing effect for which claims have been made about this experience of cultural androcentricism.[87]

When the cinema arrived in the late nineteenth century it provocatively promised the fulfillment of pure projection so central to the American artist's stakes in masculinity and nationhood. Jane Gaines tells us that "*wanting something back* from the image has the potential to be one of the most radical demands that has ever been made on the cinema . . . [that is,] pure reflection and positive images."[88] Indeed, the cinema—the machine of endless imagined projections—was a useful tool not merely for the reflective representation of ideal masculinity; the cinematic image also projected the determining ideologies—both abstractly and materially—of national masculinity and creativity. Forrest's projection of self through Push-ma-ta-ha was a flashpoint, his "*wanting something back*" in the masculinizing of the American arts. Indeed, the imaginary frame and its projection of a white male-centered sublime were just getting started.

The Nonartist and Gender Neutralization

Before I return to the implications of masculine narcissism and the experience of American creative practice I want to trace the aesthetic of realism that supported the male fantasy of a unified self. What was it that the male artist got back from the work of art that cemented his presence as pure democracy while securing a pure sense of "non-self-conscious selfhood"? Scholars generally accept that American realism is a complex, varied, and ideologically fraught aesthetic.[89] At the same time, it has also proven to be a vital affirmation for the claims by American artists to masculine and narcissistic ideals. Realism holds the promise for "pure reflection," while it also preserves masculinist principles of democracy in the American arts. Elsewhere I have discussed the interlocking relationship between the realist aesthetic in America and masculinity.[90]

Traditionally, American aesthetics are rigorously contained and measured in the work of art by masculinist presumptions. And, as I have noted heretofore, the gender traits of the male artist are also contained insofar as the taint of homosexuality (perceived as "feminized manhood") must necessarily be removed. This does not by any means suggest that the frenetic energies involved in displaying the terms of a masculine artist are not ultimately ironic in their dispatch. Nonetheless, the aesthetic of realism, following American democratic ideals, insists on an equalizing (that is, masculine) effect of gender, especially in relation to the cinematic director's claims to creative control of a work (note that John Ford, Howard Hawks, and Sam Fuller announce similar creative intentions when discussing their work).[91] In America, the male artist works diligently to manufacture an image of himself as the nonartist.

America's break from British and Continental aesthetic traditions, such as the sentimentalism associated with romanticism during the nineteenth century, challenged what was seen as a purely European and "feminine" idealism.[92] However, as Ann Douglas makes clear in *The Feminization of American Culture* the tradition of European romanticism and its attachment to ethical concerns should not be confused with the brand of American romanticism that is more accurately described as an aesthetic of "sentimentalism."[93] Although Emerson and Thoreau did not necessarily simplify the sometimes radical possibilities attending the European romantic movement, it is important to bear in mind that the cultural negation by artists and critics of American "sentimentalist self-absorption [or] a commercialization of the inner life" (255) was warded off by a more aggressive and androcentric campaign of realism. Indeed, Michael Davitt Bell argues that "to claim to be a 'realist,' in late nineteenth-and early twentieth-century America, was among other things to suppress worries about one's sexuality and sexual status and to proclaim oneself a man."[94]

But the worries about manhood as less-than virile and certainly anti-American were on the cultural radar prior to the realism campaigns of late-nineteenth-century literary circles. F. O. Matthiessen, in his elegiac work *American Renaissance*, considered the ascendancy of the mid-nineteenth-century writers as one of virile fortitude.[95] In order for the American arts to survive, it was incumbent on the artists to break from their European dependency on the tradition of the arts. Further, for the American arts to become truly American, a new aesthetic was necessary to distinguish America as American. And, without question, the aesthetic had to be virile if the country was to be identified as such. "But the chief source of power here," writes Matthiessen of, in particular, Thoreau, "seems to lie in the verbs of action: 'front,' barer than the more usual 'confront,' is also more muscular. Behind Thoreau's use of it is his conviction that the only frontier is where a man fronts a fact" (96).

As clear-cut as the guardians of masculine culture hoped the divide between romantic idealism and realist materialism to be, the ideological divide between the two was, at best, tenuous. The interstice became precisely the battleground on which realism and romantic idealism struggled and where the sui generis dynamic of the American arts operates. Herein lies what the art historian Barbara Novak and the literary scholar Eric Sundquist investigate when they refer to the "dilemma" of American realism.[96] At its heart are the economies through which the realness of realism fails to achieve its stated aim: that is, as a pure reflection. Nonetheless, the assertions of reflectivity are powerful currents in the thoughts of American realism and they sustain key ideological positions around relations of class, gender, and race. Novak and Sundquist draw out the interconnectedness between American realism and romanticism by suggesting that it is precisely the overlap of these aesthetics that curtails realism's higher aims of absolute truth. As Novak remarks, if romanticism "never had as extensive or uninterrupted tradition" as did realism, it unquestionably was a "potent secondary strain" (45). So, what cultural forces and strains of romantic sensibilities lent realism its coterminous success and failure? Or, to borrow Novak's characterization of the "dilemma," in what ways were the seemingly opposite positions of the "real" and the "ideal" managed?

The answer to these questions lies, again, in an analysis of America's uneasy situatedness between nature and the quickly developing mechanized and industrialized metropolis (not to mention the country's agricultural garden that sustained these new urban centers).[97] Moreover, the stress of the Civil War hastened and proliferated industrial development while it made manifest the desire for a return to a purer historical moment.[98] The bundling of nature and machine and its attending anxieties was ideologically managed through yet another myth: the frontier.

"That romance remained a persistent force in American Realism," Sundquist writes, "must be ascribed in part to the extraordinary force of the idea of the boundlessness of the country, a wilderness of fancied space that Whitman and [Frank] Norris, for example, could celebrate even as they saw it cut, calculated, sold, and turned into cities" (10). In the era when scientific and statistical "fact" were countenanced as masculine truth, where the mechanization of the body was championed for corporate interests, and where Fredrick Jackson Turner's soon-to-be announced closing of the American frontier struck if not a pragmatic realization then, at least, a deluded utopic one in the hearts of free-land homesteaders, the artist—through his body and work—evoked an aesthetic of realism straddled by a commonsense balance of the real and the ideal. If the physical geography of the frontier had closed (or was near closing, by the end of the Civil War era), its mythic promise of democratic Individualism and yeomen enterprise was not.

Earlier in this chapter I pointed to Potter's argument that the national temperament is grounded in a quest for a democratic ideal through a materialist economy. More specifically, America's ideological parameters were shaped by the myth of the frontier in which, as Slotkin points out, "abstractions like 'American Values' and 'national character' would be related to the concrete matters of land acquisition and agricultural production."[99] The balancing of these two foundational democratic tenets between nature's landscape and the commercial enterprise of agriculture was an essential aim for American artists, because to lose control of these core principles portended a decadent relapse into the excess of European traditions or, worse, the loss of the democratic aura that was the idea of unique America. And there was nothing as unique as the frontier (or, of course, the Indian) for the American mythos.

In this way, America's myth of itself was shaped in the arts through a romanticized realism associated with the frontier where narratological tropes such as the conquering or taming of the "savage" and the evocation of a classless manly society became embedded in the cultural psyche so as to appear natural. Realism and idealism became so inextricably entwined that, as Alan Trachtenberg states, American realism was "nothing less than the extension of democracy."[100] The trick was to identify a balance; that is, to strike the aesthetic balance between realism and romanticism, the savage and the civilized, and the unbridled frontier and the agricultural garden. American realism meant the achievement of American democratic equality, common sense, and, therefore, manliness.

How did the American romantic-real take shape in the arts? The debates on which American realism are founded best demonstrate the contest that framed the latitude given to realist and romanticist practices. Contemporary scholars have provided extensive coverage of the vicissitudes of American realism.[101] Michael Fried argues that Thomas Eakin's realism, in such works as *The Gross Clinic* (1875), is so "overwhelming" that it "goes far beyond the norm of the realist tradition,"[102] while earlier in the twentieth century Lewis Mumford championed the painter's realist "salty directness . . . absence of pretence and sham."[103] The romanticist strain in the American arts has had similar definitional troubles. A heavily romanticized aesthetic might lead either to cultural effeminization (sentimentalism) or a perversion of American aesthetics (as many suggested in their reading of Walt Whitman's notion of manly art). In addition, Sundquist suggests, "romance, as Norris quite correctly saw, remained the visceral, spiritual, essence of the real."[104] In effect, the notions of the "sentimentalizing"/perversion and the primal functioned as the two sides of the romantic coin. Like the savage who was simultaneously considered "effeminate" and primitive and thus reified as the noble savage, the aesthetics of realism and romanticism were put through the filter of gender, class, and nation with the hope that American democracy would find ideal representation.

I See Myself: Common Sense and the American Sublime

Since the variations on American realism and romanticism are many, it is more productive to consider the variation of aesthetic practices that inform the contradictions and artistic interactions as they unfold in their historical setting. By doing so, we can look at how the meaning of aesthetic "isms" are culturally generated. As with Foucault's intense weaving of discursive practices that marshal a discourse (madness, sexuality, surveillance), the aesthetic ideals of American realism and romanticism espoused by painters, photographers, novelists, poets, and filmmakers, although different in means, often overlap and connect (then disconnect, yet reach strikingly similar ends), especially where the gender identity of the artist is concerned.

Here I want to return to the tropes of common sense and the sublime since these terms often appear, as we have seen, in nineteenth-century discourse around the artist's body, the landscape, and the social function of the work of art. "Common sense," on the one hand, ostensibly protected the real from becoming too idealistic or, at the very least, secured idealism with, as Matthiessen pointed out, a "virility" of fact. The "sublime," on the other hand, played to radical or romantic impulses as well as bourgeois sensibilities of nineteenth-century discourse about art and aesthetics. The significance of its use in European circles could not be easily dismissed by American discussions about art, no matter how earnestly some Americans sought a divorce from Continental ideas. The sublime's over-romanticized staging, however, did not, in the purest sense, fit squarely with the American artist's discourse on art.

The idea of common sense is always a bit difficult to define, given (ironically) that its cultural definition is foreclosed at the outset because it is seen as an experience of the obvious, the natural, or the directly perceived. By its very "nature," it precludes definition. Common sense supercedes critical engagement since it just is (as Louis Althusser and Catherine Belsey show).[105] It is possible, however, to trace historically the weight placed on the term from the tracts ranging from polemical to philosophical in American parlance. It made sense, as it were, that the 1776 pamphlet, "Common Sense," brokered the cause for independence since, unlike British policy (as the author, Thomas Paine, assured his readers), it was "nothing more than simple facts, plain arguments, and common sense."[106] Yet, in another register later in the nineteenth century William James rethought the absolutist tendencies behind "common sense." Infused by spiritualism, Kantian aesthetics, and revised Emersonian, Thoreauesque, and Whitmanesque poetic philosophy, as well as by a critique of Hegelian absolutism, James argued that, "common sense is less sweeping in its demands than philosophy or mysticism have been wont to be, and can suffer the notion of this world being partly saved and partly lost."[107] Common sense, for James, is a process of "truth verification" that indeed points toward truth but also takes shape through multiple, yet practical paths.[108] Similar to the artists of whom he was so fond (yet more practically oriented in his theories), James's net was indeed cast far and wide in the search for what encompassed the experience of American common sense: as Smith states, "James is Emerson come down to earth."[109] In this way, such a description of experience underscores the curious brand of American democratic experience that at once has been dynamic and transformative as well as leveled on the cultural playing field.

How, given such vicissitude, do we characterize the aesthetic experiences of the sublime and common sense in the American arts? Steven Blakemore argues that the American "picturesque" was "a word applied to certain kinds of writing by analogy to a type of painting that grew out of the effort to find a middle ground between the sublime and the beautiful."[110] If, as we have seen, the "middle ground" in America is defined through masculinist terms (a position central to America's early avant-garde, as I show in chapter 4), in what way (and why) might the experiences of the sublime and common sense serve the same ends? As W. J. T. Mitchell suggests, "sublimity, with its foundation in pain, terror, vigorous exertion, and power, is the masculine aesthetic mode."[111] Though it is arguable that some nineteenth-century American aesthetics, such as transcendentalism, recommended a sublime in line with Mitchell's definition (one that follows the traditional Kantian and Burkean model), I would argue that this is only partially true (yet certainly relevant) for the experience of the American arts.[112] The American sublime as experienced through realism and framed by democratic principles was a dialectical pull between pleasure and terror to the extent that it was an experience of control and management.

Barbara Claire Freeman notes that the "masculinist sublime . . . seeks to master, appropriate, or colonize the other."[113] As we have seen, Edwin Forrest's consumption of essential savageness through Push-ma-ta-ha confirms Freeman's theory. With Forrest, the American sublime is directly tied to how the hegemony of democratic equality is experienced as, defined by, and translated into art because it achieves a pure representation of balance and common sense through the containment of the (excessive) primitive Other. The sublime exists as the holy trinity configuration of artist, work, and nature (and this includes the primitive Other). It is the recipe through which the masculine artist measures his creative success. To achieve a harmonious unity is to conquer the impasse lodged between the real and the ideal. Thus the technique and gesture of American realism was such that the unified and perfectly balanced presence of the holy trinity was itself pure democracy and the embodiment of American manhood.

Yet, this is the "dilemma" of American realism: If the democratic claims for equality and sameness neutralize difference, how is it possible that the artist remains a figure grounded in common sense yet also sublimely transcendent through the work of art? In what way does the artist move beyond his "real" democratic self into the sublime sphere of pure democracy? If we recall Michael Fried's argument that the trope of "absorption," founded in "functional" realism, "neutralize[s]" the experience of art as art, we have a clue to what ideologically and psychologically constitutes the sublime in the experience of American art.

The Riches and Anxieties of the Democratic Sublime

> "I felt that I saw nobility in people. . . . Not the kind you read in story books, but the kind where people go in to work everyday, they come home every day and dinner's on the table every day. There's people doing this in little ways every day all the time. These are the people that I want to write about. This is what I think is important. That's what moves me. That's what makes me want to sing my song."
> —Interview with Bruce Springsteen[114]

Is art practical? What shapes the terms of American art as democratic? How does American art simultaneously manage the contradictory experiences of the sublime and common sense? If European aesthetics were perceived as aristocratic, sophisticated, and effeminate decadence, then what was democratic and manly American art to look like? Was the notion of a democratic art incommensurate with the very idea of the artist himself? As the above interview segment with Bruce Springsteen highlights, an important and central aspect of what constitutes the long-standing experience of American art is that American art ideally embraces (or as such offers the performative gesture toward embracing) the everyday worker, his or her productive contribution to society, and the sanctity of the heteronormative family. In all, this combination measures at once the ordinary and sublime. What I want to stress here is that the economy of American art is inseparable from the economy of capitalism where the contours of real and ideal masculinity are linked. Moreover, the role of the American artist is one that bridges and collapses materialist and idealist principles so as to make the artist appear as one of the everyday productive members of society. Like Edwin Forrest, Springsteen's platitudes regarding his particular audience neglect the artist's own experiences that are not shared with the workers he praises (e.g., Springsteen's concerns with debt or issues of health insurance are far different from those of many of his fans). This is to say, then, that since the individual — the artist — is obligated to produce (recall the American Citizen's displeasure with the privileged nonproducers, especially those of the theater), he negotiates the perceptions of being an effeminate nonproducer — the artist — by satisfying the virile attributes of being a producer (worker).[115]

Forrest's performance of working-class masculinity that masked his financial wealth was essential to the actor's acceptance by working-class and middle-class audiences, and he worked hard to shield himself from accusations of sophisticated pretense. Thus Forrest (as Springsteen would do 150 years later) walked the walk and talked the talk of the manly immigrant and working-class culture. The performance of hardworking cultural producers served to protect what added up to the (decadent) narcissistic fantasies imputed to male artists. The artist's presentation of self and his ideal principles of masculine democracy not only transcended the impossible breach of realism and idealism but also transcended the fate of class.

Hence, under nineteenth-century capitalism the work of art was for sale alongside the artist himself. The management of the artist/work-of-art cachet straddled the precarious line between realism and idealism so as not to exploit the "purity" of art. In such a system the individual artist is marketed at once as the embodiment of the real and the principle of the ideal. "In this atmosphere [of nineteenth-century capitalism]," Sundquist argues, "the market becomes the measure of man himself . . . inner values of the spirit are drawn outward until they appear at last to merge with the things from which one cannot be distinguished and without which one cannot constitute, build, or fabricate. The self becomes an *image* of the real, and the real becomes an advertisement of and for the self."[116] For the American artist, it is the merger between "inner values of spirit" and "things" — the ideal and the real —

where the appropriate packaging of the American sublime with individuality elicits the aura of democracy. Beyond the material realities of class (since it was held that American democracy did away with such oppressive traditions), the artist uplifted the souls of mankind into the realm of a sublime yet practical America.

Further exploration is needed regarding the issue of the masculine narcissistic experience attending the sale and purchase of the artist's image as well as how the spirit and industriousness of creative masculinity are revealed in the work of art. Bryan Wolf argues that there is undoubtedly something more to the "grandiloquence of an American national sublime." Wolf calls this supplemental experience of the artist (in this case a painter) an "egotistical sublime."[117] As Wolf sees it, the egotistical sublime "plunges the painter (against his will . . .) into a world of suppressed intertextual allusions" where the artist "effaces or rewrites" the work's "textual history" with the purpose of claiming originality or an image of himself.[118] But competitive originality and the experience of the "egotistical sublime" for the American artist suggest both the claim as artist and the refusal (the effacing of history) of that title. The artist's presence in the artwork is necessarily a recording, a stamp, of his masculine and productive experience in the world that is uniquely American and original but not necessarily artistic in the European sense. The American artist is a competitive producer who successfully straddles the status of worker and charmed creator while he shares in, and is representative of, American democratic capitalism.[119] His refusal to identify as an artist because of its effeminized associations thus made perfect sense because it was common sense. His creative mark made visible on the work of art through the knowledge of his lived productive experience proved less egregious than the mere flare of a dilettante's signature.

Hence, when the art critic Henry Tuckerman portrayed the artists of the so-called Hudson River school in his *Artist-Life: or Sketches of Eminent American Painters* (1847), he emphasized that the artist's practical experience in the landscape was as vital, if not as "real," as the artist's landscape painted on the canvas. Thus Tuckerman describes how in nature's landscape Frederic Church "observed, under singularly favorable auspices, the permanent traits of indigenous vegetation, the characteristic phases of atmosphere, and the evanescent phenomena of skies, trees and herbage . . . all the essential features of Nature in her wild primeval haunts, he there faithfully studied, and thus laid the foundation of that breadth and executive skill whereby he subsequently represented, with such marvelous truth, her less familiar traits."[120]

Common sense in art is, as I pointed out earlier, what William James referred to as the "verification" of the "truth process." The artist who experiences first hand "nature in her inanimate forms" experiences a particular production of abstract ideals in collusion with the material world that subsequently renders this truth in creative form and content. Church is at once botanist, primitive man, scientific observer, active producer, and finally artist. He is a "man" first and foremost, and he is one who got closer to the details of nature and thus the truth of masculine democracy. He is the neutral witness and translator of nature in art for Americans. Like Forrest, art and artist are no longer (or so it was argued) a precious production to be viewed by the consecrated few at Parisian salons. His masculine appearance and grounded materialist imprint on his art reflected real manhood and its sublime American spirit.[121]

Neutralizing Aesthetic Terror

Later in the twentieth century the American "photo-realist" painter, Robert Bechte, explained his technique for realism as follows: "I try for a kind of neutrality or transparency of style that minimizes the artfulness that might prevent the viewer from responding directly to the subject matter . . . My subject matter comes from my own background and surroundings. I paint them because they are part of what I know and as such I have affection for them. I see them as particular embodiments of a general American experience."[122] Bechte's comments are instructive because they are not unusual: they underline a discourse of realism that is seen to recur in the American art scene since the point at which the drive to sustain a sense of national art as democratic and down to earth became a matter of some urgency. The idea of "neutrality" or "transparency of style" is a hallmark of the American arts that seeks to put artistic practice and its attending effeminizing-effect under erasure. To erase the taint of the Old World, and its effeminate aristocratic hierarchies, the American artist's gesture equalizes and democratizes the playing field between artist and spectator. The work of art is thus conceived as a tool for maximizing art as a real, democratic process and experience. The "particular embodiments of a general American experience" in a classless and genderless society is thus proven to be egalitarian and all the more authentic when the aesthetic is neutralized through realist tropes because the artist's experience in the world equals that for which he has "affection." The artist is a productive and virile original entity in this quest for the democratic sublime, but because he searches and trudges through the everyday world he is no better or worse than anyone else. In a word, American realism is reported to be the experience of cultural sameness, a transhistorical egalitarian society of artists and spectators. In this way, *e pluribus unum* and the celebration of ideological unity is at the core value on which American realism rests: it is at once sublime and anchored in common sense. American realism is the experience of homeostasis.

How might we describe this experience of masculine authorial privilege, the experience of the sublime where the artist transcends yet remains grounded in the everyday? Authorial insertion (directly or indirectly) in the text is certainly not uncommon. But what is it exactly that is inserted, or indeed projected, from the work of art after all? Certainly, the nonsignatorial mark left behind identifies a "style" that posits the artist's remains of creativity in the work. Is it possible to understand the authorial imprint as the mark of the sublime moment in the American arts? If so, how does such a moment function as an ideological trope with designs on conditioning the national aesthetic? Furthermore, how do the notions of common sense and the sublime function as one and the same in the American tradition of the arts? And what is it that is "neutralized" in terms of the aesthetic and the masculine experience of creativity? In response, I will make the case that the neutralization of the sublime intersects with an infusion of common sense that is crucial—yet terrifyingly so—for the status of a virile American aesthetic.

Mark Noll, in his study of how common sense informed American Evangelicalism, argues that early in American history, common sense (an inheritance of Scottish Protestantism) was understood epistemologically. That is, common sense "was the assertion that our perceptions reveal the world pretty much as it is and are not merely 'ideas' impressed upon our minds by a something-I-know-not what."[123] Direct perception was the experience of the real, and it satisfied the work ethic of Protestantism while it contained the excesses that might occur during evangelical experiences encountering the divine.[124] In fact, the initial contact between common-sense perception and the experience of the sublime can be found in eighteenth-century religious experience. As Roderick Nash points out, the application of the sublime to God and his "awesome power . . . was soon extended to describe objects of the physical world such as mountains, deserts, and waterfalls."[125] And, as I have shown, such rhetoric was extended to Forrest's body. The directly perceived experience in collaboration with a transcendentalist euphoria generated the "sublime" as a "favorite adjective of those who wished to praise wilderness" (532). American nature was simply divine.[126]

The notion in American thought of a materialist nature as sublime was, to be sure, brought together by an array of ideas and lofty assertions. As Thomas Weiskel remarks, "Anyone who reads into the tradition of speculation about the sublime knows in what a variety of ideologies the sublime moment finds a central place. What happens to you standing at the edge of the infinite spaces can be made, theoretically, to 'mean' just about anything."[127] And as Gary Shapiro confirms, "It is not only literary works and landscapes, but also passions, individual and national characters, the division of the sexes, and virtuous dispositions of different sorts which are classified as beautiful or sublime."[128]

For Weiskel, the sublime is more precisely "dynamic" because it is an experience of "movement between the unconscious application of the idea of reason (comprehension) and the self-conscious discovery of its provenance" (41). The movement between the unconscious and "self-conscious"—the id and the ideal ego—further suggests that the sublime functions as a return of the repressed: the sublime "masks the project of an ulterior motive" (37). What is it that the sublime symptomatically and so urgently "masks" in this dynamic moment? As Weiskel sees it, the "sublime is intimately and genetically related to anxiety" and, therefore, is an experience in search of "psycho-physical" neutralization. The sublime, in other words, makes "tranquil" the terror and confusion of the modern world (83).

Weiskel's analysis of the sublime yields two distinct registers from the traditional sublime held most prominently by Immanuel Kant and Edmund Burke. Weiskel's argument is relevant here because it pointedly suggests how and why the sublime is essential to the masculinist terms that frame the experience of art and the fear of effeminization that threatens it. In what Weiskel calls the "negative sublime" the experiential moment occurs at the level of the conscious ego because it is a "response to superego anxiety" (83). The negative sublime is aggressive and dangerous where the conscious ego turns toward the voice of the father forcing the subject into an abject position where the subject becomes the very thing he fears—a totalizing voice of authority. Its opposite is what Weiskel alternately terms the "positive sublime" or the "egotistical sublime," which "seems akin to narcissism" and is "strangely vacant" of superego and patriarchal authority. The positive sublime turns toward the experience of what Freud called "primary narcissism" that "in the end would subsume all otherness" (49). Thus, the version of the egotistical sublime suggests an imaginary encounter of pure self. What Weiskel demonstrates, however, is that these two polarized descriptions of the sublime consolidate and operate simultaneously.

Significantly, the dynamic double movement of the sublime cloaks the anxiety in the realm of the unconscious where "fear of injury" occurs (Burke's terror) or what Weiskel more presciently identifies as "castration anxiety." Since the fantasy of castration is "played out in the imagination," the sublime moment redirects aggression objectively while the onslaught of panic triggers "defense of flight" (93). At the center of Weiskel's theory of the sublime is the process of devouring and being devoured during the experience of narcissistic identification:

> As a defense mechanism, identification is simply a more sophisticated form of introjection or incorporation (the three terms are often used interchangeably). The boy must have introjected or internalized an image of the superior power in order to picture himself the consequences of aggression, and in the reactive defense this introjected image is reinforced as the affects line up on its side. The identification which thus establishes the superego retains an essential ambiguity. The boy neutralizes the possibility of danger by incorporating or swallowing it; it is now within and can't hurt him from without. But he must also renounce the aggression and turn himself into—be swallowed by—the image, now an ideal, with which he is identifying (93).[129]

What Weiskel first makes clear is that the male experience of the sublime is at once a defense mechanism against the threat of castration and the conjuring of an aggressive force to defuse the terror of the threat. Essential to Weiskel's account is that the sublime actually "neutralizes" the danger of "sensory overload" (26); the sublime is "homeostatic." "On the principle of homeostasis," Weiskel asserts, "any excess of stimuli will be felt as pain, even if the stimuli themselves are pleasurable" (104). Homeostasis does not cancel opposing forces as much as it "neutralizes" them, thereby allowing both to function in the service of "tranquility" (92).

How is the anxiety of masculine terror defused in such a way that the very experience of neutralization enables the concurrent experience of pain and pleasure? Weiskel provocatively argues that the experience of anxiety is neutralized by both "swallowing" or internalizing male identification with the superego while, conterminously, the same identification is "swallowed by" and turned into the image of the patriarchal ideal. This psychical experience recalls the descriptions of Edwin Forrest engorging (*repos délicieux*) Push-ma-ta-ha where he not only "seeks to master, appropriate, or colonize the other," as Barbara Freeman posits. Moreover, Forrest imagines an internalizing of a pure original past (marshaled by the superego) through the body of the primitive Other while he is simultaneously "swallowed by" the beautiful but horrific presence that stands before him and, in turn again, "turns himself into" the ideal image escorted by the superego.[130]

The anxiety hence never dissipates. Indeed, it is necessary: it is rechanneled, transferred to and fro, and translated into an experience of the sublime. Where is this anxiety transferred? Weiskel argues that anxiety is projected insofar as "what the ego feels to be threatening and therefore inadmissible is expelled and lodged safely in the outer world without being changed" (141). The projection of the inside outward, or the projection of a pure imaginary past (hosted through the body of the primitive landscape or Other), secures the ideal and original image of American manhood. The American sublime is thus a neutralization of primitive aggression and hetero-masculine narcissism projected and disseminated across mediated spheres and cultural experience.

There is, of course, a good deal of irony in the urgent containment of an excessively sublime experience. In the face of an awe-inspiring threat, practical reasoning associated with realism is conjured. In this way, American aesthetics are continually adjusted in the hope of realizing the tranquil and neutralized experience of American common sense that exists, paradoxically, as an ideal. Thus, the tranquility of the sublime contains excess—that is, it does not reject it—while it neutralizes pain and pleasure via the dynamic of swallowing and being swallowed where an imaginary lost moment is riddled by terror and delight. What is ironic is that if the American sublime evokes imagery that harmoniously unites the real and the ideal, the threat of castration anxiety that defines the experience is deferred only for a moment. The threat of effeminization lurks at every turn.

For the American artist the sublime moment takes place on ever-changing landscapes. But the myth of the ideal (the primitive past, the "frontier," the imagined lost past) persistently emerges through the experience of the sublime eliciting at once fear and the thrill of conquering the repressed that purportedly manifests itself as the "real." Whether the sublime is described and portrayed as the moment when Forrest stands in awe of Push-ma-ta-ha or, later in the cinema, when John Wayne sheds a tear at the sight of naval battle in John Ford's *The Wings of Eagles* (1957), ideal masculinity is vividly displayed in all its terror and awe because it is ubiquitously projected and disseminated onto the pages of the novel, canvas, stage, and screen as the experience of something natural and real.

Coda: Walt Whitman, Degeneracy, and the Democratic Real

In 1915, art lecturer F. W. Ruckstuhl delivered an address, entitled "Social Art," to the by-then conservative Men's Open Table of the National Arts Club in New York, whose founding and honorary members included Theodore Roosevelt, Frederic Remington, and Robert Henri. Besides defining the moral cleanliness of art, Ruckstuhl set out to sweepingly dismiss the decadent and excessive strains of European modernism (cubism, impressionism, fauvism) that he felt were contaminating American sensibilities and aesthetics. Ruckstuhl declared Nietzsche and Baudelaire the progenitors of modernist-aesthetic rubbish, and he offered an alternative definition of American social art: "Every work of art is a social work of art which, in some way, aims, by easily understandable forms of beauty, to unite men in a common emotion, and a common pursuit of social perfection; and a social work of art is great in ratio of its technical perfection and of its lifting, spiritual beauty." He goes on to ask, "will our artists produce great works of art which, radiant with every degree of beauty, from the graceful to the sublime, and animated by a binding *national spirit*, will stir, not the low, but the highest, emotions of our own people, until, like in the Periclean and Renaissance epochs, our artists shall transfigure the art of America, by making it supremely sane and supremely Social?" Art in the service of a strong nation was the heart of Anglo-

Portrait of Walt Whitman. 1855. Collection of the New-York
Historical Society.

Saxon bourgeois virile culture. The rush of modernity threatened these values most especially from within America. Middle-class literature from decadents, such as Henry James, that affirmed Europe's claims on civilization wreaked havoc on ideal (American) social art. Modern decadence such as James's aesthetic tripe thus needed to be stopped.

Ruckstuhl's work followed in the wake of Max Nordau's venomous work *Degeneration*, which was published in English in 1895 and read widely in America. His book was endorsed by the cultural authorities because his social position as a medical doctor and bourgeois art critic lent authority to his biodeterminist model that identified degenerate fin-de-siècle art and artists through a measurement of an artist's corporeal and psychological dimensions. His Darwinian and eugenic theories struck a chord with those American men who guarded the gates of middle-class Anglo-Saxon "nativist" propriety and tradition while believing, as Nordau did, that modern man was in the process of de-evolution.[131] In this way, Ruckstuhl's treatise on moral and aesthetic decay via the decadence of Baudelaire and Nietzsche can be directly linked to Nordau's work that "scientifically" proved that these thinkers and their adherents (Huysman, Wagner, Ibsen) were "insane" and "imbeciles." Although Nordau's emphasis on artistic degeneracy was predominantly reserved for European artists (since he wrote initially for a German audience), one American was assigned to his list of artistic perverts: Walt Whitman. Nordau's bio-critical assessment of the poet was, quite simply, that he was crazy. Since Nordau's thesis was not merely about psychical degeneracy but was tightly woven with what he labeled the "physical stigmata" of the artist, his reading of Whitman echoed those American critics who sought a revirilization of the arts in the early twentieth century but found Whitman an inadequate voice for such a project.

Although many American critics concurred, Whitman was also applauded for the democratic foundations supporting his poetry. In *Democratic Vistas* Whitman makes clear the terms for true American art. The split from European urban decadence marks the moment when America not only discovers its unique voice.[132] More important, America's arts and artists discover their masculine identity when purged of Old World decadence and class society.[133] Whitman further insists, as the American Citizen had earlier proclaimed in his defense of Edwin Forrest's role as an American artist, that the masculinization of the arts is equal to democracy. For Whitman, such democratic equalization cuts across gender because American men and women are to be virile.[134] Whitman's genderless and classless democratization of the arts cemented their functionality and purpose for America's masculine representation of itself.

Whitman's success and influence thus bore considerable weight and placed a provocative tension on the state of the American arts—across gender and across race. On the one hand (if we follow the accounts given by critics such as Nordau and Ruckstuhl), the artist (such as Whitman) was to be analyzed through a study of his physical attributes, his biological race traits, his mental stability, and, finally, his dress. Through a study of these biocultural determinants the marks of creative normalcy or degeneracy could be ascertained. Nordau's phrenological observations that large ears, contorted facial features, or other "physical stigmata" marked degeneracy and made easy the task of identifying the aesthetically ill.[135] Whitman's "loafing" body was indeed suspect. Yet, on the other hand, as David Shi argues, "Whitman became the most potent catalyst for change in nineteenth-century American culture."[136] In what way does Whitman act as such a catalyst? How is it that an artist who was received as a degenerate "androgynous persona"[137] also symbolized a major force in defining American democratic art as masculine and vigorous? Why were African American and queer artists attracted to the poet's treatises? Certainly the interpretations of Whitman's aesthetic are many, as are the varied arguments over the significance of the artist's sexuality.[138] As I point out later in this volume, the interpretive possibilities of Whitman's body and his body of work appear in widely disparate contexts. Whitman's concerns of the material real and the democratic ideal, however, cannot be separated from issues of gender.

Whitman's fit within the discourse of American realism is unique. The canon of American realism is essentially a given: in literature, William Dean Howells, Henry James, and Mark Twain sit high on the list, with Theodore Dreiser and Frank Norris's "naturalism" immediately following in the early twentieth-century. Herman Melville and Nathanial Hawthorne rest alongside the realist school, while figures such as Edgar Allan Poe are significant but marginalized; in Poe's case because of his European sensibility that is at once gothic and decadent. In painting, Tom Cole, Frederic Church, Albert Bierstadt, and the Hudson River school are championed for their sublime, yet realist, tendencies, while the later Ash-Can school took up Norris's urban aesthetic tropes and pushed the naturalist's tendency to explore social issues. Walt Whitman, however, is the odd duck. It is worth remembering that Whitman began his career as a journalist and a champion of the common, democratic man who then later became the raison d'être of the artist's poetic songs: as Shi notes, "By rooting romantic idealism in an affection for the everyday realities . . . Whitman successfully fused romantic and realistic values."[139] An early champion of Edwin Forrest's naturalist gestures of masculinity and creativity, Whitman remained a proponent of the commingling of a virile realism and idealism.

What is further striking about Whitman's work and his ideas on American art is the powerful influence they had on twentieth-century artists, if not on those of the twenty-first century. No other artist symbolized, albeit in contradictory ways, the sutured rift between realist and idealist principles in American art as well as the creative and pragmatic duty of the American artist. The list of artists who paid heed to Whitman's call is staggering.[140]

As I hope to demonstrate in the chapters following, Whitman's call for democratic principles in art and its direct relationship to masculinist and national ideology waxed eloquent for many of America's cultural producers. Getting past the more dodgy aspects of Whitman's biographical legend was the rub that was often sidestepped through dexterous theoretical posturing by the likes of Theodore Roosevelt (as I will point out in the next chapter). Nonetheless, while Forrest's performance of virility informed nineteenth-century aesthetics, Whitman's democratic poetics solidified (although never in quite the same way) what American masculinity and creativity stood for at the opening of the twentieth century.

For filmmakers specifically, Whitman's voice played across the medium's popular and avant-garde aesthetics as well as the issues of race and gender it raised. His voice opened diverse passageways for the American arts while others proposed more monolithic models. Whitman bridged realism and romanticism, the experiences of the sublime and common sense, and, perhaps most important, the corporeal sensuality and intellectual investigation of the lived world. With the tradition of realism and democratic idealism guiding nineteenth-century American arts toward a unique brand of national aesthetics, especially through the national bodies of Edwin Forrest and Whitman, the cinema during the twentieth century proved to be the ideal medium through which male artists embodied and projected—through their feasting on the Other—their narcissistic imaginary of masculinity and creativity. The cinema was thus, indeed, America's art.

2

The Battle Cry of Peace
and the Spectacle of Realism

How did the cinema provide American artists and cinema critics with the means to claim for themselves an art form free of European tradition and provenance? In what way did film preserve the tropes of frontier realism and idealism, particularly after the literal borders of the frontier were declared closed? What cinematic aesthetic anchored American ideas in the industrialized and corporatized twentieth century? In this chapter I explore these questions as they unfold around the American Vitagraph production of *The Battle Cry of Peace* (1915). I argue that the popular film served several functions related to Theodore Roosevelt's philosophy of American art and its moral obligation in a postfrontier culture. Ultimately, the cinema fulfilled Roosevelt's requirement for a moral national art, as well as the aesthetic principles of democratic common sense. Given Roosevelt's stature as an icon (if not the icon) of American masculinity in the early twentieth century, the cinema's vast appeal and wide reception were instrumental in his vision of the virile constitution of a national aesthetic. Hence, the making of *Battle Cry* (if not the broader idea of cinema itself) was an exercise in the realization of American art as a masculine and moral gesture of national creativity that broke from European tradition.

The production of *Battle Cry* for propaganda purposes marks an important moment in the history of film production because it emerged when what is now called the classical Hollywood style took hold, for the most part, as an industrial practice.[1] Tied to this event is the significant critical dialogue that took place during this period over the status of cinema as art or as popular entertainment. In this chapter

Portrait of Theodore Roosevelt. 1885. "Hunting
Trips of a Ranchman." Collection of the New-York
Historical Society.

I sketch the collaboration between Roosevelt and J. Stuart Blackton (director of *Battle Cry*) on the making of the film, as well as the ideologically charged correspondences between Roosevelt and the German philosopher Hugo Münsterberg. The aesthetic and political dialogue in which they engaged intimately converges and richly demonstrates the terms that identified American art as popular entertainment, and the cinema took center stage in these discussions. For all three cultural producers, the stakes over nationalism and aesthetics were pivotal to the view of their own masculinity. For these men, to lose this particular aesthetic battle—particularly as the United States was on the verge of entering the Great War in Europe—meant nothing less than national emasculation.

Spectacular Realism

Prior to September 11, 2001, lower Manhattan had on several occasions experienced, and was the fictional backdrop for, the spectacle of disaster. In 1835, an "ocean of burning waves" ripped through the financial district and cut a swath of disaster thirteen acres wide.[2] Max Page, in his book *The Creative Destruction of Manhattan, 1900–1940*, points out that events such as the fire of 1835 were stimulating fodder for late-nineteenth-century works of literary fiction like that of Joaquin Miller's best-seller *Destruction of Gotham* (1886).[3] Such spectacular realism of the fictional sort satiated bourgeois distrust and disgust with what they saw as urban riffraff and, hence, the decline of civilization.[4] In 1915, the film, *The Battle Cry of Peace*, again delivered to New York its moral comeuppance. The film, now lost except for approximately four hundred feet, was directed and produced by American Vitagraph cofounder, J. Stuart Blackton.[5] In the images of the film that remain there are sequences where thick white smoke and building debris choke and blind city pedestrians as they deliriously make their way through the tattered streets of lower Broadway after a fictional enemy invasion. Unlike its earlier predecessors, *Battle Cry* makes the case that it is precisely bourgeois interests and morality that are at risk because of their pacifist politics and their lax, urbane, and decadent attitudes toward American military preparedness.[6] Spectacular realism thus served as a moral tale and an antidote to a society on the brink of cultural effeminization.[7]

Battle Cry is loosely based on Hudson Maxim's book *Defenseless*

America. Maxim, inventor of "Maximite" explosives (his estranged brother gave the world the Maxim machine gun), wrote *Defenseless America* as both a factual guide to world military apparatuses (and the United States's lagging position therein) as well as a moral treatise on the de-evolutionary state of American civilization. Before Maxim scripted *Defenseless America* he had a history of failures and successes in military arsenal development. And in a different cultural realm, he was recognized for the more creative and poetic sensibilities he intermixed with his scientific proclivities.[8] "Poetry and gunpowder," Maxim dramatically asserted, "were both invented about the same time . . . one of the first uses of poetry was the writing of the Bible, and since then gunpowder has been used mainly to back up that poetry."[9] Maxim's tying together of "poetry and gunpowder" led many to assume, correctly, that his poetic interests were merely in the interest of promoting his military products.[10]

In *Defenseless America* (a book published at the behest of Hearst International), Maxim argues that war is the natural state of a manly society (40), and that the middle-class American culture of 1915 had in particular been led astray by the Women's Peace Party (241). He further notes that such "fanatic" effeminization of culture (and the intellectual dross of pacifist philosophers like William James) is "working evil" because it prevents American military buildup to protect the United States's borders from invasion. "Self-styled peace men," however, are the most insidious (4). These so-called men are "usually brimmed and primed with sacrificial sentimentality" and are the "disciples of soft stuff" (24). "Peace men" are nothing less than sure examples of the "degenerates" described by Max Nordau in his book *Degeneration*. For Maxim, civilization is on the cusp of ruin since "privilege" and "luxury" have become synonymous with "degeneracy and disorganization" (35). To remake American virility, then, Maxim turns to Ralph Waldo Emerson, Theodore Roosevelt, and Herbert Spencer to make his case for a culture of "equilibrium" (245). The excesses of fanaticism will, according to Maxim, destroy the very thing the fanatics are fighting for: peace. Peace must be defended and maintained by the "equilibrium" that military muscle is perceived to offer (along with a strong dose of Maximite explosives).

Written in less than a month and advantageously timed with the sinking of the *Lusitania*, Maxim's book offers detailed maps to demonstrate how an invasion from "external" forces might occur. Among these maps are some that outline how the "Heart of America" (here the northeastern seaboard) is left defenseless under a weak naval presence and how enemies with superior naval power (Germany and Japan) can successfully infiltrate. For such a volume full of maps and theories to serve as the inspiration for a film seems odd, especially given that there is no narrative thread to hold the text together. What the book does provide, however, is the background against which Blackton could dress degenerate and defenseless America with both romance and a moral reminder of the tenuous cultural privilege under which it operates. For Blackton, *Defenseless America*—with its lack of narrative structure notwithstanding—was a book that translated necessarily into cinematic presentation. In Blackton's view his film served a double function: to rally patriotic sentiment and to fulfill the cinema's role as a social art.

Emotional Fervor

The Battle Cry of Peace opens, according to *Variety*, with Maxim addressing an audience at Carnegie Hall about issues of peace through military preparedness.[11] The "development of the story proper, which carries a tremendous dramatic punch," follows the life in New York City of two bourgeois families, the Harrisons and the Vandergriffs. The Vandergriff patriarchy holds pacifist positions about the war in Europe, and at one point the father befriends a nondescript, pacifist foreigner. Although the foreigner's name, Emanon ("No Name" spelled backward), represents no particular country, under the circumstances of the war it was no secret that the filmmakers implied the blank-slate enemy to be German (indeed, the costumes of the invaders were suspiciously German in appearance). Needless to say, Emanon turns out to be a spy who prepares, with his comrades, to invade New York. The Vandergriff family, because of their pacifist leanings, is blind to Emanon's covert activities and are thus complicit in their own demise. Blackton uses the second family, the Harrisons—who are antipacifists—so as to intertwine the two families by creating a romance between the Harrison son and the Vandergriff daughter that emphasizes the pacifist/antipacifist debate. Subsequently, the Harrison father attends a Maxim lecture, is convinced of the necessity of military preparedness, and urgently tries to persuade Mr. Vandergriff that Maxim's claims are accurate and

The "Emanon" enemy invades the peaceful, but naive, American middle classes in J. Stuart Blackton and Theodore Roosevelt's *The Battle Cry of Peace* (1915). Courtesy of Photofest.

that his family's safety is at stake unless he begins to rethink his political ideals. Vandergriff, however, refuses to listen to this reasoning, and thus Emanon and his covert companions successfully invade the city because pacifists are naive and are suckered by the European pretense of intellectual ideas over practical action. When Harrison returns to his home after the bombardment of the city and finds his mother and sister dead, his resolve to support military preparedness is confirmed.

The Battle Cry of Peace opened to mixed reviews. The reviewer at *Variety* called the Vitagraph production "a shining mark" for the film industry. The writer continues by stating that *Battle Cry* is undoubtedly a film that "means something to the world at large," and that it is a film with a "mission." However, because *Battle Cry* was released several months after the megahit *The Birth of a Nation*, newspapers such as the *New York Times* invariably made comparisons to it, such as the following: "For pictorial beauty or for evidence of such cinematographic skills as went into the making of 'The Birth of a Nation,'

'The Battle Cry of Peace' is in no way notable."[12] The film, according to this *New York Times* reviewer, was nothing more than an "elaborate and graphic photo-spectacle" designed for propagandist antipacifist purposes. An earlier account in the *New York Times* that was written after the film's previews in late July 1915 clearly articulated the film's ideological motives: "Mr. Blackton deals roughly with the pacifists and generally advances his argument by bludgeon strokes."[13] The *Independent* commented as well on the film's "demagoguery" while the *New Republic* found the film's propagandistic function "forcible, to say the least."[14] Indeed, the film was seen by many as a clumsy, all-out attack on Wilsonian policy on the war in Europe and on pacifist American sentiment.[15]

The film's spectacle of realism was not merely manufactured through its image. Julian Johnson of *Photoplay* found that *Battle Cry*'s multimedia efforts to enhance the film's realism were too much. Johnson wrote that the film's "mistaken idea of producing realism by hammering the bass drum for every canon shot and bomb explosion, accompanied by a weird assortment of other noises, even to the cries of the scurrying populace and groans of the wounded by a mob behind the screen, made the general effect so confusing that it was impossible to concentrate the mind upon the serious matter presented."[16] The *Independent* called the spectacle "overdone," while the *New Republic* was more forthright and declared the film "nauseating" and "an overdose of poison." Although the press differed on the ideological appropriateness of the film, it was generally agreed that the spectacle of realism was, in the words of the *New York Times* preview notice, "designed to make many a person in each audience resolve to join the National Guard, the American Legion, the National Security League, and the Navy League, forthwith, and to write his Congressman by the next mail."

As a whole, however, the press was enthusiastic about the panorama shots of New York. *Variety* claimed that "from a pictorial standpoint the film is a revelation. There are a score of panorama scenes, some of which have been taken from hydroplanes flying over New York, which are little short of wonderful." The preview notice by the *New York Times* also commented on the "notable novelties" of the film, including the "panorama of Manhattan and its waters taken from a hydro-aeroplane." The *Independent* admitted that "as a feat in photography it is amazingly good . . . and worth an evening off to see the battleships battling, the submarines subbing, the aeroplanes landing." The beauty shots, the spectacular realism of the New York skyline and its subsequent demise were instrumental in what Blackton saw as the cinema's ability to raise an "emotional fervor" around political, cultural, and moral issues (I will return to Blackton's terms below). In effect, by presenting the sheer scale of twentieth-century American modernist capitalism—that is, Manhattan's skyline—and then destroying it at the hands of external barbarians, the spectator's patriotism was raised to fever pitch. Peace at any cost meant, according to the film, the loss of the future of modern civilization symbolized by the great metropolis and, of course, America's new twentieth-century frontier.

Nineteenth-century American realism, as I show in the previous chapter, was equated with the natural or what one late-twentieth-century artist, Robert Bechte, called the "transparency of style." In all its variations, it was conceived as a particular national aesthetic that bolstered the young country's claims for a virile identity through its appeal to its symbiotic and ideal relationship to nature. With the arrival of the cinema in 1895, the ideologies of realism were fait accompli. As cited in the press in July 1916, " 'Realism,' said J. A. Berst, vice-president and general manager of Pathé, 'is the essential quality in a picture—that goes without saying.' "[17] In the article Berst further adds that "extra labor and expense is worth while, and it is evident that along with increased realism of colored pictures comes a greatly added beauty as well." In Berst's logic (and certainly the logic of those steering America's film industry), realism was the standard measurement of beauty—a contested aesthetic at once sublime, spectacular, and picturesque—because it rested within the long-standing tradition of the aesthetic associated with the democratic principles of common sense.[18] Needless to say, *Battle Cry* affirmed these principles. The irony was that the film's excess, as contemporary reviewers noted, overshot the common sense that purportedly determined its moral and masculine aesthetic.

Blackton's aim to make Maxim's book into a film came about even though his long-term Vitagraph partner, Albert E. Smith, refused to participate in the film's production. Indeed, Blackton invested $100,000 into the production (*Intolerance*, as Blackton recalled, cost $1,900,000),[19] and he envisioned a return of over $1,000,000 on the film's domestic release while paying Maxim $5,000 for the book rights.[20] As Blackton tells it, however, the film was not made for profit;

instead, *Battle Cry* was his moral obligation to set Americans' sight on the disaster that awaited them should they not be better prepared militarily.

To maximize the film's urgent political agenda as well as its veracity, Blackton called on his neighbor, the former president Theodore Roosevelt, to consult on and participate in the film's preproduction. "The most influential person," writes Anthony Slide, "with whom Blackton discussed his idea for *The Battle Cry of Peace* was Theodore Roosevelt."[21] Kevin Brownlow notes that although "his part in the production was never publicly admitted . . . Theodore Roosevelt used his powerful influence to ensure the success of one important American film—one that espoused his own passionate cause of unpreparedness —*The Battle Cry of Peace*."[22] An additional part of Blackton's strategy to assure that the film's message was not overlooked was to secure the participation of key military figures whose public position authenticated Maxim's and Blackton's accuracy in depicting a great city's collapse because of a nation's "unpreparedness" and spiral into degeneracy. Thus there were several consultants on the film, including Franklin Delano Roosevelt (assistant secretary of the navy), Admiral Dewey, and Elihu Root, who were key political figures involved politically and personally with Theodore Roosevelt. But none carried the cultural authoritative force held by the former president. In addition, Roosevelt's very vocal diatribe at the time against the Woodrow Wilson administration and other peace-seeking advocates had placed him at the forefront of the preparedness debate and won him considerable press.[23] Roosevelt's high-pitched calls for better preparedness, however, had fallen on deaf ears in the government ever since Germany attacked Belgium. By 1915, he was hardly able to contain his frustration and anger with the administration's lack of military response, and thus Blackton's invitation to consult on *Battle Cry* must have seemed like a godsend.

Although the direct input of Blackton's and Roosevelt's contributions to the film is historically transparent, it is worth asking how these two cultural producers converged in 1915 and simultaneously agreed on an aesthetic of popular film that met their moral standards of patriotism and militaristic interests. What ideas about art and the cinema intersected at the point at which Blackton and Roosevelt produced one of the year's more financially successful films? Several key figures, Hugo Münsterberg and John Burroughs among them, levied important theoretical and moral standards of culture and aesthetics of which Roosevelt, in particular, paid notice. It is instructive, therefore, to weave together the aesthetic discourses that emerged where Blackton, Roosevelt, and Münsterberg biographically intersected because, as will become clear, the assertions of masculinity and nationalism they espoused found no fuller treatment than in the art that represented their ideological vision.

In 1915, *The Birth of a Nation* ushered in a dramatic shift in American film production. And though *Battle Cry* was considered aesthetically inferior by some, it solidified a particularly potent version of American democratic art over which its makers and critics vociferously asserted their manly aesthetic prerogative.

J. Stuart Blackton

The year 1915 was a significant one for J. Stuart Blackton; not only did he produce and direct *The Battle Cry of Peace* that year, but he also received U.S. citizenship. According to his daughter's memoir, Blackton was born in England in 1875; the family subsequently moved to the Bronx in 1885.[24] His daughter emphasizes that her "father yearned to be an artist" (7) and that he embodied an American artist's story of "rags to riches and then back to rags" (3). Blackton, however, had his many irons in the entrepreneurial fire. His energetic skills and talents in magic, quick sketching, and journalism caught the eye of his idol, Thomas Edison, about whom Blackton always spoke highly. As Charles Musser makes clear, however, Blackton's account of the events of his life must be taken with a grain of salt given that Blackton and Edison spent many a year in the courts wrangling over various legal issues of licensing.[25]

In the period after his interactions with Edison, Blackton's career took off in the motion picture industry. With his friend Alfred E. Smith, Blackton formed the Vitagraph Co. (later the American Vitagraph Co.) as a licensee of Edison's Vitascope Company. This event took place in 1898, the year of the Spanish-American War and Theodore Roosevelt's "Rough Riders" campaign on San Juan Hill in Cuba. The combination of Blackton's American patriotism and his sense of artistry resulted in such films as the maritime battle reenactments *Battle of*

Manila Bay (1898) and *The Spanish Flag Torn Down* (1899).[26] As Blackton recalls:

> Whenever "The Spanish Flag Torn Down" was shown it created excitement among war-time audiences. It was suddenly apparent that these little squares of film possessed the power to arouse public feeling to a tremendous pitch of patriotic and emotional fervor. The motion picture was no longer a pleasing novelty. Intelligently directed, it possessed hitherto undiscovered, potential forces. Its latent drama could stir human emotions to their depths. It was capable of moulding and influencing the minds of people to a degree and to an extent impossible to predict, but even then dimly discernible. To thinking minds, it began to loom large as an overwhelming power for good and evil.[27]

Undoubtedly, Blackton saw himself as a "thinking mind" who dedicated his career to directing the higher moral standards that the film industry demanded during the Progressivist era.

Blackton's remarks indicate the ways in which Vitagraph committed itself to producing (what his daughter recounts as) filmmaking to "uplift the masses."[28] For Blackton, the "moulding and influencing" of minds was not a problem in and of itself as much as it was part of the moral obligation presented to artists to achieve good. Because film aroused an audience to an "emotional fervor" it was, as Blackton saw it, "primordial art, freed and empowered."[29] This is true especially about film because "when man was at last enabled to hold the mirror up to nature and capture its reflection and repeat it so that all might see, and see again, there came that phase of human endeavor and achievement" (3). Like his contemporaries in the industry, realism was a commonsense aesthetic for film because its reflective attributes of nature (when "intelligently directed") raised the proper emotional responses in the cause for cultural uplift. Clearly, during times of war, cinematic American realism was the morally consecrated aesthetic for such ends.

There remains something more to consider about Blackton's lifelong desire to be perceived as an artist of proper moral standing; as one who saw the potential for the "little squares of film" as truly radical in the art world. With the cinema, the American artist was at the forefront of a new, historically unencumbered art medium. For the most part, historians portray Blackton as something of an entertainment wizard with the energetic and creative business acumen of an Edison and the creative sense of a Griffith. As Katz's *Film Encyclopedia* puts it, "Next to Griffith, Blackton was probably the most innovative and creative force in the development of the motion picture art."[30] Blackton, however, also moved in other creative circles that were not industry driven.

Blackton is in many ways representative of what typified the conceptual markers of the nineteenth-century artist, since the line between artist and skilled craftsman was sometimes difficult to define by American standards.[31] In fact, Blackton's involvement with other American artists and institutions suggests a provocative way to consider the exchange of aesthetic theory and creative practices that commingled and were exchanged between the practitioners of the traditional arts and those who worked in the rapidly developing industrial arts of the twentieth century. Indeed, the artificial distinctions between what by the end of the nineteenth century was more resolutely divided as high and low, became all the more blurred when considering a figure such as Blackton and his engagement with American painters and literary artists. In the encounter I describe below, modern technological knowhow is filtered through traditional artistic modes of production where artist and techno-wizard convene. For Blackton, the very notion of something called "American modern art" was nothing less than the cinema itself whose aesthetic of realism was trained on (and necessarily drew upon) the cultural forces that shaped the tradition of American art.

The "Living Corot"

In Blackton's second unpublished autobiography, "Silence Was Golden," he dedicates an entire chapter to "Art and the Movies." In this chapter he describes his active participation and membership in New York's Salamagundi Club,[32] which was founded in 1871 as a sketch club by a group of artist-illustrators (Blackton's early and sustained talent). "Members would gather," writes Sarah Burns, "to critique each other's work but also to sing, box, eat, and drink."[33] Like other men's clubs for artists, the Salamagundi Club functioned as the ground where male American artists expressed their creative tendencies as well as their manly social skills. The club housed sketch and illustrator artists such as Blackton, as well as more-standard painters such as George Inness.

In 1910 Blackton discussed with the members of Salamagundi the idea of "motion pictures in color," and he also gave them screenings of Vitagraph films. One screening, according to Blackton, triggered such an enthusiastic response that the art club members visited the American Vitagraph studios in Flatbush the following day in order to witness for themselves the technology that manufactured what one witness called the "living Corot." Blackton's reference to bringing a painting to life is illuminating here for several reasons. First, it suggests the ways in which artists cooperated without traditional lines of artistic hierarchy—a notion that is especially true for American artists. Second, it demonstrates the idea of what constitutes an aesthetic that bridges "high" and "low" standards in the making of American popular cinema, where the goal is to achieve the most "emotional" and ideological effects on the movie-going populace—as *The Battle Cry of Peace* promised.

As Blackton further relates, he "sprang a surprise" during one of his Salamagundi Vitagraph screenings.[34] With the likes of the critically acclaimed American artist Inness in the audience, Blackton superimposed a film of Isadora Duncan dancers on Corot's painting *Spring*. "A group of dancing nymphs," Blackton explains,

> tiny figures in gossamer draperies [flit] like moths in cool shade. The painting was photographed on panchromatic negative. A second negative was taken of a group of Isadora Duncan dancers, softly lighted against a black background, the living dancers in the same relative positions as the figures in the paintings. These two negatives were printed together on one positive film, toned sepia and tinted a delicate green, the two groups of dancers blending one into the other. At first the effect on the screen was a Corot painting, then the living figures began to move in a graceful dance which increased in tempo, then slowed down until the living forms again became stationary.
>
> The result was startlingly beautiful. A classic masterpiece familiar to all came to life and received itself again into a painting (281–82).

The poet Edwin Markham who was present at the screening declared that Blackton's film presented the "living Corot" as "sublimely poetic" (282). Moreover, cinematic technology appeared to have outdone the traditional arts because it brought a work of art to life. In the American context the implications for this technologically superior art was startling, given that the traditional arts were perceived as strictly an overseas phenomenon. When art thus was made by American artists,

Old World traditions contaminated and made impure the search for an American artwork qua American. Thus the cinema took the arts to new heights, as Blackton's experiment demonstrated, since it hubristically completed (the European) Corot's project to transcend the limitations of art itself. More significantly, this new art form and all that it promised to bring to life was seen as a particularly American (via Edison) contribution to art.[35] Cinema thus purportedly leveled the distinction between the divide of high and low by forging an equal partnership between artists and artisans; that is, the nonartist. Hence, the cinema neutralized cultural distinctions by providing the marks of American democracy, pure and simple.

Markham enthusiastically summarized his experience after viewing the "living Corot" (in words that Blackton called the "most perfect definition of Art ever uttered"): "Art is nature idealized." (282). Film offered many creative possibilities, but none more than its ability to record the real, to make it "living," and, through the "little squares of film," to move an audience to moral uplift. The cinematic sublime successfully met American common sense. As Blackton remarked elsewhere on the cinema's triumphant aesthetic possibilities, Vitagraph's "stark realism outdid any great painting or any elaborate stage effect ever attempted."[36] America now had an art form that it could truly call its own—one made through an industrious balance of traditional practice with modern technology.

Meeting Theodore Roosevelt

Sometime around 1911 Blackton purchased an estate adjoining Theodore Roosevelt's home, Sagamore Hill, in the Oyster Bay area of Long Island. Flanked by Roosevelt's brood on one side and by the Tiffany family on the other, the Blacktons were now, according to his daughter, "firmly established in the ranks of the nouveau riche."[37] When Blackton was ready to produce Hudson Maxim's book, *Defenseless America*, into *The Battle Cry of Peace*, his choice of the statesman Roosevelt as neighbor proved fortuitous. Although Blackton consistently praised Roosevelt (as he did Edison) throughout his career, the president's input was assuredly incisive and at times overwhelming.[38]

Roosevelt's interest in the American arts reached as far back as his Harvard days and was key in his mapping of national identity. He was

consistently concerned with what he saw as America's flaccid intellectualism at the expense of a strictly physical culture. Although, as is noted
widely, in Roosevelt's mind the physical was essential to proper civilization, he also insisted that virility was a balance of mental and bodily
exercise.[39] In 1897, in a letter to the British diplomat Cecil Spring
Rice, Roosevelt writes: "[Americans] are barbarians of a certain kind,
and what is most unpleasant [is that] we are barbarians with a certain middle-class, Philistine quality of ugliness and pettiness, raw conceit, and raw sensitiveness."[40] Roosevelt did not reject art as part of
America's future or state that the nation's philistine attributes were
etched in stone (and certainly some American philistinism was essential for American character); indeed, the arts—a commonsense balance
of physical and intellectual stamina—were, in Roosevelt's mind, necessary for America to develop its role as the leader of the civilized world.
He was determined to be a forerunner, if not an active participant, in
the United States's process of civilization. Thus, thoroughly engaged
with the ideas of literary artists and critics of the late-nineteenth century and early twentieth, Roosevelt articulated an aesthetic of "Americanism" that lifted the nation out of barbarianism and into the privileged ranks of Western civilization. What, according to Roosevelt, was
this national aesthetic? Realism. But realism of a certain sort.

As I have described, the debates over realism, while diverse, were directed toward an essentialized version of what constituted American
art. Roosevelt's involvement in these cultural debates was grounded
in his lengthy and earnest correspondences and friendships with such
high-profile figures as Jacob Riis, Henry and Brooks Adams, John Burroughs, Rudyard Kipling, Brander Matthews, Francis Parkman, Owen
Wister, Frederic Remington, Hamlin Garland, and Stephen Crane.
Over many lunches and dinners, as well as in extensive letter-writing
campaigns, Roosevelt diligently and eruditely expressed his positions
on questions of painting, literature, architecture, and the writing of
history. His grasp of at least three languages gave him entrée to cultural
debates occurring on both sides of the Atlantic. Roosevelt published
widely on an array of subjects; his short stories of frontier life, criticism of literary works, book reviews on many topics, and, of course,
his autobiography had an enormous readership.

Roosevelt's sarcastic reviews of exhibitions such as the 1913 Armory
Show, where he labeled the new (especially European) modernists "the
lunatic fringe" and compared their paintings to "the colored puzzle-

pictures of the Sunday papers," won him many friends in both the popular press and in those creative circles in America that urgently sought to protect the arts from European decadence and to secure the populist dimension of American art.[41] Like many conservative critics of the day, Roosevelt was especially angered by such "pathological" painters as Matisse, who painted "misshapen nude woman, repellant from every standpoint" (356). Nonetheless, Roosevelt's views on art (and on science, history, and politics) drew accolades from many of the accredited institutions of the day. In 1910 he was elected vice president of the American Historical Society, and, in the same year, he gave lectures on his "scientific" theories of race at the Sorbonne, the University of Berlin, and Oxford. The National Arts Club in New York lists him as an honorary founding member along with Frederic Remington and Robert Henri.

In one of the more rigorous scholarly works of Roosevelt's involvement with the American arts, Lawrence J. Oliver situates the statesman's aesthetic ideas in relationship to the staunchly traditional literary critic and professor of comparative literature at Columbia University, Brander Matthews, whose theories of American aesthetics were tightly bound by theories of race.[42] As Oliver points out, Matthews and Roosevelt shared readings and ideas that confirmed their anxieties over the "decline of the Teutonic race" (37). In line with late-nineteenth-century social Darwinian dross on race, Matthews and Roosevelt believed in the strength of the "Teutonic heritage" that united the "great nations of Germany, Great Britain, and the United States" (38).[43] Roosevelt was quite pleased that he had encountered an American literary scholar with whom he agreed about "Americanism" in the arts (118). "Americanism" in the arts meant, for both, the rejection of pretentious cosmopolitanism and lofty philosophies of realism (and other aesthetics) while championing evolutionary eugenics in the progress toward a national art.[44]

Roosevelt echoes his conservative contemporaries when he claims, as he does in his essay "An Art Exhibit," that the "modern artists are too self-conscious and make themselves ridiculous by pretentiousness."[45] In a letter to Matthews, Roosevelt applauds Emerson's "American Scholar" and, according to Oliver, "trumpets the cause of literary Americanism." In the same letter, it is worth noting, Roosevelt mentions to Matthews his unease with America "getting some very undesirable [immigrants] now."[46] The rooting out of excess in America (cosmopolitan snobbery and impure race) was, according to Matthews and Roosevelt, the best chance for America to cleanse impurities from any modernist aesthetics that were making their way from decadent Europe (Anglo-Teutonic heritage was another matter). American realism itself was tainted by European snooty arrogance, if not the pathologies that Max Nordau clearly articulated. Roosevelt thus made an aesthetic distinction in his essay "Dante and the Bowery": to aspire to a superior American national aesthetic one must turn to a classical writer such as Dante (a great artist to which all true great American artists have aspired) because he was "quite simply a realist."[47]

As Roosevelt announces in his essay, contemporary artists in their workings with the realist principle had lost its basic thrust: simplicity. And herein lies an important clarification by Roosevelt about Americanism/realism: the literary philosophy of realism was pretentious. To be valued as worthwhile art, the practice of art was to be a realist and functional enterprise. This was, therefore, the aesthetic of "Americanism." Art thus was not the espousal of philosophical tracts but rather the realization of practical truth. For Roosevelt, art was an industrious and virile activity where art and artist were one and the same because art was "quite simply" an extension of the artist's experience.

The Realist Body of Work

In Roosevelt's mind the American experience deserved a specific aesthetic translation in the arts. Under his terms, American art anchored the all-important masculinist and nationalist virtues that he held dear. It is curious that in the same essay that Roosevelt champions Dante's simple and realist aesthetic tendencies, he also allows Walt Whitman a central place in the American cultural vernacular. Like Dante, Whitman's art (not unlike the progressivist Jacob Riis who was, significantly, not American born) used "anything that was striking and vividly typical of the humanity around him" even though when he did create he "was not quite natural in doing so."[48] Nonetheless, "his art was not equal to his power and purpose; and, even as it was, he, the poet, by set intention, of the democracy, is not known to the people as widely as he should be known" (350–51). The few who did know Whitman well were, of course, part of Roosevelt's literary circles. Most central was Whitman's friend since 1863, the naturalist John Burroughs, with whom Roosevelt maintained a long-standing correspondence and friendship.

Roosevelt assuredly read Burroughs's *Whitman: A Study*, where he would have discovered a thorough analysis of Whitman's poetry as well as a rich biographical sketch of the artist.[49] In his book, Burroughs argues that Whitman's importance rested in his *realist realism*: "No such dose of realism and individualism under the guise of poetry has been administered to the reading public in this century."[50] Poetry was merely the "guise" of Whitman's experiential realism. Through Burroughs, Roosevelt learned to admire Whitman's realist tendencies, which were shaped not so much by the literariness of realism (and though Whitman was not "natural" in doing so), but by the poet's conjuring of lived experience with "humanity" that purportedly existed on the Bowery. If, as Roosevelt would have it, the realism of the Russian Tolstoy was not "conducive to morality,"[51] and William Dean Howells took a "jaundiced view of life,"[52] Whitman presented the everyday experience of democratic life. As Miles Orville recently suggested (and Roosevelt might concur), "More than any other artist of his time, Whitman had tried to reproduce in his work the entirety of American civilization — its industrial and urban character as well as its spiritual, aesthetic, and democratic wealth. The life long creation of *Leaves of Grass* was to be a kind of counterpart to the United States, an epic embodiment of the national character and landscape, a poetic equivalent of the new reality of America, and also, of course, the picture of an ideal self."[53] In this way, a realist aesthetic espoused by Whitman equaled and captured the individual vigor and simplicity of experience associated with the American "character and landscape" through which the manly artist was marshaled.[54]

Roosevelt's emphasis on the "realist" artist intersects directly with his treatises on virility and nationalism as well as with his comprehension of the scientific and psychological studies of the era. Roosevelt's notion of the realist artist is formulated through an idea of experiential realness between nature and man which art is morally obliged to address. Furthermore, art must be purposefully directed. Indeed, not unlike Edwin Forrest,[55] Roosevelt posited his realist, "Americanism" aesthetic as an art form where artist and art were intimately bound to the virile and productive principles associated with America's myth of nature and the frontier.[56] For Roosevelt, the art/artist/nature experience is intellectually brought together through, on the one hand, his encounter with Burroughs's "naturalist" real embodied in Whitman and, on the other hand (and perhaps more significantly), through his correspondence and friendship with Hugo Münsterberg, who introduced the former president to a German scientific rigor and to a neo-Kantian aesthetic that detailed an efficient, dutiful, and stalwart account of national, indeed Teutonic, art. Ultimately, Roosevelt held fast to his Americanist aesthetic, which directly informed his concepts for *The Battle Cry of Peace*. His debate with Münsterberg over the *The Battle Cry of Peace* made clear to what extent Roosevelt tolerated Old World philosophies in the name of American art.

Hugo Münsterberg and Theodore Roosevelt

For nearly fifteen years, Hugo Münsterberg and Theodore Roosevelt had an ongoing correspondence wherein both enthusiastically shared their convictions about national uplift and racial purity that, for them, neatly folded into their philosophical discussions about art, scholarship, politics, and manliness. Indeed, the interaction between the two highly recognizable and culturally popular figures is framed by certain striking affinities of their upper-middle-class upbringings. As their biographers indicate, for both men their parental attachments (and the traumatic loss of these relationships, especially with their fathers) played a considerable role in their staunch views of what constituted national pride.[57] Given the intensity of their long-standing friendship, where political, intellectual, and aesthetic views intimately overlapped with their personal lives, it comes as little surprise that a debate about art, cultural uplift, manliness, and its nationalist implications decidedly ended their relationship. Specifically, the aesthetic break that put to rest the friendship took place over the pro-American and anti-German film *The Battle Cry of Peace*.

Münsterberg, who was born 1863 in Danzig, converted from the Jewish faith to Lutheranism as a young adult. Roosevelt, who was born in 1858 in New York City, was raised in a traditional, strongly disciplined Anglo-Saxon family of Dutch Reformed heritage—a family that was noted for its political stature in New York City. Both Münsterberg and Roosevelt had had health problems as young boys that were later overcome through vigorous exercise programs of the body and mind. Athletics and intellectual rigor were thus inseparable in their quest for a healthy and efficient nation (although Münsterberg suffered nervous disorders in his adult life that, in part, led to his death in 1916). As part of their youthful mental and physical gymnastics, the sciences and the arts served as cornerstones to their concerns about securing and advancing Western civilization. As young men, both read and greatly admired the American authors James Fenimore Cooper and Ralph Waldo Emerson, and both also admired the rigor of German scholarship: Immanuel Kant and the *Nibelungenlied*. As adults, they read voraciously and wrote prolifically.

The parental loss experienced by both men came at an early age: Münsterberg lost his mother at the age of twelve and his father at eighteen; Roosevelt lost his father when he was nineteen, then shortly thereafter, at the age of twenty-six, he lost his mother and young wife on the same day. For both, the voice of the father remained an anchor throughout their often-frenetic attempts to set right the moral terms of twentieth-century civilization. Their duty to father was matched only by their duty to country. The overstriving for maximum efficiency and industriousness toward such ends was a hallmark of both Münsterberg's and Roosevelt's personas. It is no surprise, then, that both were intimately connected to America's most prestigious nineteenth-century academic institution, Harvard, for their entire life.

Münsterberg, invited by William James to teach at Harvard in 1892, spent the longest span of his career teaching, completing research, and prolifically writing books in the then newly founded Department of Philosophy, where he initially served as director of the Psychological Laboratory. Harvard and America were challenges to the German scholar because although America represented a formidable, international cultural force, it lacked a rigorous and scientific balance of the mind and body (America, of course, tended toward the latter). According to Matthew Hale, "Münsterberg worked to transfer a 'masculine' German model to Harvard."[58] During his tenure, Münsterberg was awarded a professorship in Experimental Psychology and then the position of chair of the Department of Philosophy. The links between psychology and philosophy were at the heart of Münsterberg's often-controversial interdisciplinary scholarship, which ultimately caused great friction among his colleagues James, Josiah Royce, George Herbert Palmer, and the president of Harvard, Charles Eliot. It was, however, more than his often-rigid approaches to the field (the department was known for radical posturing) that embroiled his colleagues' bitterness.

Roosevelt attended Harvard as an undergraduate and maintained an active and vocal role at the institution during Münsterberg's tenure. As an undergraduate student, Roosevelt attended lectures by James (which he found "extremely interesting"), and it has been noted that his peers considered him to be a New York dandy and, in fact, somewhat "queer."[59] Later, in 1898, Roosevelt rounded up a large group of Harvard men for his Rough Rider expedition during the Spanish-American War, after which he returned to the university to deliver a series of lectures on the expedition and other topics. The institution was an ideal model for Roosevelt's own campaign of intellectual and corporeal rigor; and it was also through Harvard that Münsterberg and Roosevelt began their fifteen-year correspondence.[60]

As Münsterberg's tenure took ground at Harvard, he (like Roosevelt and James) clearly believed that America needed "character building" since the nation was on the verge of "emasculation." For Roosevelt, his relationship with the German-educated scholar who relished "productive scholarship"[61] provided him with yet another collaborator (*pace* Brander Matthews) in the cause for the Teutonic–Anglo-Saxon authority of the Western canon.[62] Münsterberg's commitment to the "Anglo" segment of this heritage, however, wavered during the Great War. In a telling and ongoing debate between the two men, Roosevelt argued aggressively against the use of national hyphens (i.e., German-American). Roosevelt insisted that once an individual emigrated to America, that individual was fully American, and thus hyphens were anti-American. At the same time, Roosevelt did not reject the traces of knowledge and tradition carried by the immigrants to the United States. As Thomas Dyer puts it, Roosevelt's theories of "Americanization" were "primarily . . . the process of absorbing immigrants into the national bloodstream." Americanization thus meant "cultural assimilation," "Anglo-conformity," and "homogenizing the foreign born."[63] But the eugenic beliefs in the Germanic superiority of mind, body, and culture were deeply rooted in the cultural mindsets of both Münsterberg and Roosevelt.

Professionally, Münsterberg identified himself as an idealist, a psychologist, and a philosopher trained in the rigors of German philosophy. His neo-Kantian positions were, as noted by Hale, infused by a belief in a national and efficient duty toward the ideal and pure state.[64] Phyllis Keller points out that Münsterberg dismissed Freud and his concept of the unconscious with "three words: 'there is none.' "[65] However, Hale's rigorous analysis of Münsterberg's work suggests something more precise in the differences between Freud and Münsterberg. If Freud "traced psychoneurosis to a conflict between modern civilization and the nature of man," Münsterberg "identified therapy with resocialization and health with 'self-fulfillment' through recommitment to the social community, as he defined it" (133–34). Moreover, Münsterberg's therapy was good only for those who were "fundamentally moral" (133).

Münsterberg's model of therapy (based on applied psychology and action theory) understood the activity of the mind and body as an exact and measured operation; in his words, "There is no psychological fact which is not at the same time a physiological one."[66] Further, the mechanism of the body/mind relationship was thought to be similar to the mechanism of the efficient state. Corporeal/mental efficiency led directly to social efficiency. The trained muscle of man (of those morally fit) fulfilled the function of the ideal society. Hence, Münsterberg's admiration of Frederick Winslow Taylor and his model of functionality and industrial efficiency are not surprising. Münsterberg, however, believed that Taylor's model was dilettantish and based on "psychological naiveté."[67] Taylorism, in other words, did not go far enough in eliminating those workers who proved incapable of efficient production because of their "mental types."

Münsterberg's psychological studies, moreover, were presented as important contributions to the efficient management of American corporations. In his book *Psychology and Industrial Efficiency*, Münsterberg seeks to outline an "intermediate between the modern laboratory psychology and the problems of economics: the psychological experiment is systematically to be placed at the service of commerce and industry."[68] Since, Münsterberg argues, "the problems of artistic creation, of scientific observation, of social reform . . . must be acknowledged as organic parts of applied psychology," business must not lag behind (16). Thus, like his studies in the "mental states of attention, memory, feeling, and so on" (22), efficient business practices can align themselves with ideal and efficient experiences of artistic creation.[69] To successfully manage the "attention" of the worker (as indeed the spectator of a work of art was to be brought to attention) is to succeed in the management of the ideal state.

Against this theoretical backdrop of efficiency and attention it is worth considering how Münsterberg developed the terms for a moral cinematic aesthetic for the functional and ideal film spectator. What constituted the ideal spectator for film? How was this spectator shaped by the aesthetics of film? In what ways should the production of film engender this ideal spectator? Finally, why did *The Battle Cry of Peace* fail to achieve the aesthetic ideal?

Aesthetic Shortcomings

Frederick Winslow Taylor begins his treatise on efficient labor production, titled *The Principles of Scientific Management*, with the following comment: "President Roosevelt, in his address to the Governors at the White House, prophetically remarked that 'The conservation of our national resources is only preliminary to the larger question of national efficiency.'"[70] Roosevelt's claims for the efficient management of "national resources," like Münsterberg's bundling of the organism of man with the ideal of the civilized State, were directly linked to the moral and virile attributes of the American citizen.[71] For both Münsterberg and Roosevelt, the arts played an instrumental role in raising the individual subject into an industrious and efficient realm of beauty.

Münsterberg, so the story is told, turned to the cinema and deemed it worth studying when, first, he sought respite from the strain of American anti-German sentiment that he experienced during the Great War and, second, when he viewed Herbert Benon's film *Neptune's Daughter* (1914). By 1915 (and especially following the sinking of the *Lusitania*), Münsterberg's hyper-energetic micromanagement aimed at reclaiming Germany's innocence in the war and its cultural superiority had begun to take its physical and psychological toll.[72] Yet he persisted in his defense of Germany. On many (scandalous) occasions, Münsterberg took his research to corporate institutions (or, in fact, they often sought him) so as to disseminate his culturally authoritative theories to the largest possible audience. In 1915 he served as a contributing editor to the *Paramount Pictograph* and wrote articles on film for *Cosmopolitan*.[73] In addition, Münsterberg spent a good deal of time visiting

Paramount Studios, as well as (not insignificantly) the studios of Vitagraph—where in 1915 Blackton was producing *The Battle Cry of Peace*.

Roosevelt's energetic and melodramatic persona made for extremely popular film before and after his death. The American film industry often parodied Roosevelt (for example, *Terrible Teddy: The Grizzly King* [Porter, 1901]) or called on him to authorize or comment on a film's cultural value. Veronica Gilliespie writes about "T. R.'s love affair with the camera" and that he was "one of the most frequently photographed subjects among public men."[74] Further, as an article in *Moving Picture World* suggests, "[Roosevelt is] something more than a picture personality: he is a PICTURE MAN."[75] After his death, the film industry honored Roosevelt by dedicating films to him (*The Covered Wagon*, 1926) or, as Paramount Pictures did in 1927, by making the film *The Rough Riders* so as to remind America that the spirit of Roosevelt would not die.[76] There is, however, very little written about Roosevelt and the idea of film. Although Roosevelt had much to say about painting and the literary arts, he wrote very little about the cinema. When he did mention it, however, it was clear that he did not underestimate its impact on popular opinion.[77] Overall, Roosevelt's direct and indirect involvement with the cinema and other popular arts was considerable.[78] Roosevelt greeted Münsterberg's philosophies on film and art with enthusiasm, which made sense in light of Roosevelt's clearly articulated theories of what constituted American realist art informed by lived-world experience and high moral Anglo-Teutonic values. Roosevelt and Münsterberg both saw the role of art as one that shaped and inculcated proper moral values for an efficient society. And, for both, art worked at the levels of body and mind in coterminous fashion toward an ideal Western civilization. Their aesthetic ideals about the cinema dovetailed and were held steadfast: that is, until the war.

On January 26, 1916, Münsterberg wrote to tell Roosevelt that he had "had the pleasure of a private performance [at the Paramount Picture Corporation] showing your fervid preparedness speech on the piazza of your house. As psychological experiments of mine will appear in the same reel, I shall be with you before many thousands of audiences, but let me assure you once more I am with you in a better sense than a mere pictorial companionship on the screen."[79] This last bit of camaraderie follows several pages of critique by Münsterberg on Roosevelt's position on the war and his theories of American immigrant assimilation. Münsterberg's words of camaraderie were most likely irritating to

Roosevelt by this point, given that Münsterberg had been recently (and falsely) accused of being a German spy and of being a toady to Roosevelt's nemesis, Woodrow Wilson. As Roosevelt and Münsterberg's correspondence indicates, the war put a strain on their long-standing cordial relations. Roosevelt grew weary (if not incensed) by Münsterberg's posturing and over-determined insistence on Germany's stance in the war as purely defensive; and Münsterberg in turn surely found offensive Roosevelt's brash American demeanor.[80] *The Battle Cry of Peace*, however, brought to the fore the clear differences in the one area on which they seemingly agreed: moral and national aesthetics.

Given the paucity of film scholarship written during this period, our view from a twenty-first-century perspective of Münsterberg's 1916 theory of film has been rewarding and exciting. But it is valuable to keep in mind that Münsterberg's theories, as described above, are commensurate with the psychological studies of the period that center on industrial efficiency and social morality. Here I want to emphasize Münsterberg's understanding of "attention" and the "purpose of art" since these analytical tools for the cinema can be traced to both Roosevelt and Blackton's belief ("emotional fervor") in the ideological strength of the cinematic apparatus. Aligned with his earlier studies in applied psychology, Münsterberg's analysis of both film as art and film as psycho-physiological experience confirms the new industrial art (in its corporate and technological senses) as an ideal art form that, when properly produced, engenders a moral and ideal society.

Allan Langdale points out in his introduction to the recent reissue of Münsterberg's *The Photoplay: A Psychological Study* that the book's topical subjects are arranged "in a hierarchical fashion from lower to higher perceptual and mental processes."[81] Münsterberg's perceptual and mental categories are divided into chapters, as follows: "Depth and Movement," "Attention," "Memory and Imagination," and "Emotions." Langdale is right when he states that Münsterberg, as all his studies insist, resists a psychological study that separates bodily response from mental function, while he sees a hierarchy of corporeal and intellectual functions at work with the experience of art. Indeed, in *The Photoplay* Münsterberg provocatively assesses a complex and concurrent psycho-physiological dynamic and response during the moviegoing experience. That is, the intellect double-tasks while watching a film: "we are never deceived," Münsterberg writes, "we are fully conscious of [cinematic] depth, and yet we do not take it for real depth"

(69). On the other hand, he adds, "we feel that our body adjusts itself to the perception" when we view the film. Münsterberg's theory of attention reiterates the simultaneity of experience at the levels of body and mind. Attention is successful when our body and mind focus on a specific place and/or moment through the proper engineering of the artist producer. It is thus, for example, the duty of the filmmaker to create works that maintain spectator attention (Münsterberg's famous claims for the importance of the close-up are a case in point). Cinema's unique properties are sui generis the ideal art for an ideal and moral nation.

In many ways, Münsterberg's theory of attention is similar to Roosevelt's (and Blackton's) belief in a "realist" tendency in art because, for both, art necessarily keeps the spectator grounded, focused, and not distracted by aesthetics that are disrupting or challenging. Furthermore, and again similar to Münsterberg, Roosevelt argued that the work of art achieves its vitality and purpose only when the artist manufactures and elicits such values through his or her designs of form and content. In both cases, Münsterberg and Roosevelt agree that the work of art, the artist, and the spectator are intimately involved—intellectually and physically—in an experience and process that fastens a vigorous national culture. Their theories, however, diverge after this point.

Münsterberg's scientific theories were grounded in his neo-Kantian perspectives on art and on cultural duty. Such claims consecrated what had been perceived until this time as the vulgar aesthetics and moral vacuity of motion pictures. Münsterberg's work delighted Paramount Pictures (as did his earlier work with other corporations) since the studios vied for better-heeled audiences to fill their picture palaces.[82] Münsterberg's aesthetic blessings granted cinema a new function where middle-class audiences might transcend reality and be lifted toward their dutiful ideal. Münsterberg's writings gloriously fused entertainment and aesthetics to the thrill of the industry, and he saw fit in his book to discuss film "as a source of entertainment and aesthetic enjoyment" (45) while applauding the "most fertile idea when the *Paramount Pictograph* was founded to carry intellectual messages and ambitious discussions into the film houses" (57). For Münsterberg, film was a new art form with discrete properties that, when produced properly, promised to achieve the true "purpose of art": to overcome a mimetic relationship to nature and to be "*freed from all connections* [i.e., social] *which lead beyond their own limits, that is, in perfect isolation*"

(117). Film's unique properties situate it in the realm of the other pure arts that fulfill Kantian idealist aesthetics and principles. Münsterberg's aesthetic theory, on the one hand, is not surprising given his philosophical foundations in German scholarship and his stringent ties to Teutonic civilization. On the other hand, his insistence that the work of art—especially film—should break from the mimetic codes of realism indicates an unease and a clear distinction from Roosevelt over precisely what a national aesthetic portends.

Münsterberg's initial praise for the *Paramount Pictograph*, for example, is flagged with a warning to its editors who "will have to take care that the discussions [in the *Pictograph*] do not degenerate into one-sided propaganda" (57). Indeed, this issue is of great concern to him, as described above in terms of the anti-German sentiment during this period in the United States. At stake for Münsterberg was not only his fervent commitment to Germanic cultural ideals relative to vulgar American anti-intellectualism, but also the fact that Germany, the bearer of that civilization, was at risk of being crushed by the (American and other European) barbarians. In significant ways, Münsterberg's writing on film in America was part and parcel of his campaign to enlighten the philistine masses about the pleasures and cultural authority of Germany's intellectual and aesthetic traditions.[83] Indeed, Münsterberg's greatest fights came when he championed Germany's culture and its claims to cultural privilege. His defense of Teutonism saturated every aspect of his work, and *The Photoplay* was no different in its purpose to produce a Teutonic work of art and, more important, a Teutonic spectator.

Although Münsterberg—in line with Blackton's and Roosevelt's ideological positions—considered film an art that should strive for "wholesome influence" and "upbuilding of the national soul" (155), an intellectual debate over aesthetics during a time of war was the furthest thing from Blackton's and Roosevelt's minds.[84] The effeminized pacifists may engage in such lofty banter, but all means, including art, were to be pressed into practical service as the threat of war loomed. Aesthetic principles were nothing less than threats to national security since they were often the trivial fodder for salon and dilettanti parlor discussion. For Münsterberg, war mongering of this sort was dangerous and typical of the vulgar associations that placed social reality on the same dais with art.

In *The Photoplay*, Münsterberg directly snipes at Roosevelt and

Blackton over *The Battle Cry of Peace*. The unified experience of art, writes Münsterberg "is ruined by mixing it with declamation and propaganda which is not organically interwoven with the action itself. It may be still fresh in the memory what an aesthetically intolerable helter-skelter performance was offered to the public in *The Battle Cry of Peace*. Nothing can be more injurious to the aesthetic cultivation of the people than such performances, which hold the attention of the spectators by ambitious detail and yet destroy their aesthetic sensibility by a complete disregard of the fundamental principle of art, the demand for unity" (137).

Roosevelt may well have agreed with Münsterberg over theories of "attention" and art, but the ultimate goal of the psychological function of cinematic aesthetics had a far different meaning for national interests. The noisy multimedia event of *Battle Cry* infuriated Münsterberg's critical sensibilities at the levels of aesthetics and national pride. The loudness and the attempt at spectacular realness superceded his threshold for American vulgarity. The following passage from a letter from Münsterberg to Roosevelt demonstrates with great passion the invective with which Münsterberg felt toward *Battle Cry*:

> Yesterday for the first time I did blame you, and that is the reason why I am writing to you. The Boston newspapers yesterday brought out large advertisements of the Vitagraph Company which contained nothing but your enthusiastic recommendation of "The Battle Cry of Peace." You are made to say that it is "the most educational drama I have ever witnessed." Did such words really come from your lips? I stand aghast. When I saw it some weeks ago and Mr. Blackton asked me for my opinion and criticism, I wrote to him frankly a letter of which I enclose a copy. You see that I close directly with the most sincere exclamation: "I cannot convince myself that men like Roosevelt and Woods will agree with you that it is worthy of the American nation to draw the composite picture of the English, French, German, Austrian and Russian armies as a horde of brutes who deceive, murder and rape." I beg you to read the whole letter. What does your endorsement mean when you say that this is the "primary, the public school and the college of preparedness?" What is to be learned in this college? Is it a schooling for preparedness that the American people is made to believe that when it enters a war its foes are moral degenerates? Or if they are not to think worse of their foes than of themselves, are they then to learn that they ought to prepare for war because war is a splendid opportunity for

robbing private property and for raping all the women in a hostile land? I still feel convinced that preparedness can be reached only by educating the right spirit and that right spirit must begin by taking war as something pathetic and great and solemn. No youth can be prepared for the hour of war, if he is taught to consider the enemy as criminals and degenerates. I have always been convinced that you, at least, would be the man who would take the historic point of view and teach your nation the God in the battle and that you would not descend to those who picture the enemy as beasts because they hope that in the hysteria of the hour everyone in the audience will understand that the anonymous enemy is meant to be the Germans. That may be a good whip for the hour, but it is a wretched schooling for the preparedness which looks forward to the future. I myself believe sincerely in America's duty of preparedness, and believe in it today more than yesterday, because as the ending of the present war becomes from day to day clearer, the psychologist cannot help foreseeing that the time may not be far distant when England will be obliged to try to gain in the battle with America tomorrow what it has lost in the battle with Germany today. I know you have hated England your life long, as you once told me in the White House. But if you really want to prepare for this war, the only one which sober judgment can anticipate for America, then surely you must not send the people of the land into that shameless "Battle Cry of Peace." I cling to the hope that Mr. Blackton's strong suggestive power was this time stronger than your own deliberate idea of the meaning of war.[85]

As mentioned earlier, Münsterberg's hope that Roosevelt's involvement with the film was minimal did not hold true. There is much in this letter that indicates Münsterberg's frustration with having to curry favor with Roosevelt while simultaneously critiquing what he must have found, on occasion, to be oversimplified and reactionary thinking on the part of the statesman. This letter, as with others, is framed by friendly and cordial correspondence suggesting that Münsterberg felt a need to move gingerly with the recalcitrant former president. These eggshell negotiations on which Münsterberg's letters tread form a striking pattern that illustrate the cultural and authoritative uncertainty he experienced while living in America.

Needless to say, Roosevelt found Münsterberg's letter both inaccurate and unrealistic in its timing for such an argument. On November 6, 1915, Roosevelt sent Münsterberg a curt reply (Münsterberg's letter is nine pages in length; Roosevelt's is only one page), a passage of which is as follows: "First, my dear sir, I wish to correct you in an error of fact. You say that I told you in the White House that I had 'hated England my life long.' I never made any such statement about England or about any other nation: and I am quite incapable of making it about any nation."[86] Roosevelt concludes his brief rejoinder with a final note about Münsterberg's "objection to *The Battle Cry of Peace.*" "While I very strongly disbelieve in much of Germany's international attitude," Roosevelt asserts, "I emphatically believe in her efficiency. This efficiency has been shown by the appeal to German patriotism. Surely the play [*Battle Cry*] in question, whatever its aesthetic short-comings, does appeal to American patriotism and it does show just the kind of thing that would be brought on America by pacifist teachings, if they were successful."

In a fashion typical of Roosevelt, the comment "the play in question, whatever its aesthetic shortcomings" is seen to sit squarely with national pride because "it does show just the kind of thing" that serves realist principles of a social art. The film's "appeal" meets the requirement of Roosevelt's aesthetics since the moral quandary over America's role in the Great War surpasses philosophical aesthetic concerns in art. As I describe in chapter 1 regarding Ruckstuhl's talk at the National Art Club where Roosevelt was a founding member, art was mandated to have the social function of galvanizing American spirit, efficiency, and above all, patriotism. Blackton's thrill at generating "emotional fervor" through the movies is the realist art principle that is based on and affirms common sense. The distinction in the purpose of aesthetics was clear between Roosevelt and Münsterberg: For Roosevelt, American art functioned at a practical, material level where idealism hovered in its shadows, while, for Münsterberg, the idealist principles of Germanic philosophies of *kultur* and civilization took precedence in determining one's practical duty in the name of the pure state.

Roosevelt, Art, and the Postfrontier

In 1893 Frederick Jackson Turner presented to the American Historical Association his famous speech "The Significance of the Frontier in American History."[87] In this presentation Turner touted "frontier individualism" as the great promoter of democracy while raising the specter of dramatic change of frontier experience (30). "Thus civilization in America," Turner asserts, "has followed the arteries made by geology, pouring an ever richer tide through them, until at last the slender paths of aboriginal intercourse have been broadened and interwoven into the complex mazes of modern commercial lines; the wilderness has been interpenetrated by lines of civilization growing ever more numerous" (15). As Richard Slotkin points out, this version of America's frontier indicated a "sense of crisis, that the closure of the Frontier, and the bonanza economy its existence had fostered, was no longer a prospect but an accomplished fact."[88]

But Turner's thesis on the frontier, although recognized in scholarly circles, did not have the impact held by Roosevelt's thesis on the frontier—the series titled *The Winning of the West*. And though Turner admired Roosevelt's *The Winning of the West*, Turner's more academic scholarship, to borrow Edmund Morris's phrase, "refined away much of the crudity of Roosevelt's thinking" especially around issues of race.[89] Roosevelt's gallant and highly appealing narrative account of America's frontier cannot be underestimated for its cultural impact on popular culture and the dissemination of its ideologies. Through popular history, storytelling, art criticism, and, as we have seen, filmmaking, Roosevelt's powerful voice informed and saturated the everyday world. As Slotkin succinctly states: "Roosevelt's influence is paramount in the cultural realm . . . the realm of mass culture mythology" (61). Indeed, Roosevelt's influential writings and activities shaped the myth of the American frontier as a "metaphoric extension" of American imperialism (53).

Significantly, film proved to be key in extending the real as well as the idealist boundaries of the frontier for the twentieth-century imperialist enterprise that Roosevelt held dear. As an art form and as a means of mass communication in the postfrontier era, no other medium had the reach and unimagined persuasive capabilities of those held by art. At the turn of the twentieth century, American had claimed its national aesthetic, and the medium through which it would be exported to the world: cinematic realism. *The Battle Cry of Peace*—presented to elicit the spectacle of realism for "emotional fervor"—is an example of America's sublime national art in the name of common sense. On the precipice of ideal beauty (Manhattan's towering glory to capitalism

and the new frontier) and horrific terror (the new frontier's demise),
Roosevelt and Blackton produced a film that charged and uplifted the
audience through the American sublime experience; that is, a sublime experience toward American patriotic and masculine common
sense. And for Roosevelt, of course, this meant white Anglo-Saxon
Americanism.

3

African American Realism:

Oscar Micheaux, Autobiography, and

the Ambiguity of Black Male Desire

When J. Stuart Blackton and Theodore Roosevelt rallied the American arts, including the cinema, around strong nationalist impulses predicated on "emotional fervor" and cultural "uplift," their urgency to do so took form around Anglo-Saxon traditions of aesthetics, gender, and race. Films such as *The Birth of a Nation* and *The Battle Cry of Peace* presented narratives that presumed the righteousness of Anglo-Saxon values filtered through, specifically, American race relations in the former case and imperialist military preparedness in the latter. The American arts, as conceived as part of the myth of the twentieth-century frontier, were determined by and for white men. Indeed, film industry technology, as scholars have recently shown, developed a mode of production in relationship to the hegemony of ideological whiteness. Of course, the idealist principles of a white aesthetic had little to do with the lived experiences of African Americans. Yet the powerful rhetoric of white uplift by the likes of Roosevelt appealed to, and was disseminated through, nonwhite art and culture. Race "uplift" and aesthetics, as I address in this chapter, are a set of complex terms with which African American artists and spokespersons wrestled, especially as these terms drifted into the form and content of their art. For blacks, assimilating into white culture appeared, on the one hand, as a means of access to America's financial (and otherwise) economy. On the other hand, to assimilate put at risk African American identity itself. The arts (literature, theater, poetry, and film) — in both content

Portrait of Oscar Micheaux.
Courtesy of Photofest.

and form—were thus a pivotal battleground on which African Americans struggled over these highly contentious concerns.

Many individuals in a variety of fields have written about Oscar Micheaux, and in so doing they have underscored the tensions of race uplift in his work. Few, however, have studied his negotiation of race uplift in relationship to the tradition of African American aesthetics. While in this chapter I investigate the significance of the African American form to Micheaux's work, I also consider the politically complicated, and particularly American, dynamic of black and white cultural "uplift" as negotiated by Micheaux.

Homage to Theodore Roosevelt

In Oscar Micheaux's film *Within Our Gates* (1920) the male protagonist, Dr. V. Vivian (Charles D. Lucas), is introduced in an image of him sitting at his desk reading a copy of the *Literary Digest*. In this scene Micheaux foregrounds the journal's cover, on which is a full-page portrait of Theodore Roosevelt. Later, in the film's conclusion, Micheaux reiterates through Vivian once again Roosevelt's significance to African Americans. In this final scene (an awkwardly assertive deus ex machina) Vivian embraces the film's heroine, Sylvia (Evelyn Preer), and proudly reminds her (and us): "Be proud of our country, Sylvia. We should never forget what our people did in Cuba under Roosevelt's command." Micheaux's honorific positioning of the statesman, however, raises some curious issues and concerns given Roosevelt's troubled race relations record just prior to his death in 1919. Why would the portrait of a man who espoused the rightness of white Anglo-Saxon culture and who firmly believed in evolutionary race eugenics be notably displayed in the hands of Micheaux's protagonist?[1] On the other hand, why wouldn't Roosevelt receive recognition by an African American filmmaker, since many blacks thought of him as the presidential (and patriarchal) guardian of their human rights?

Roosevelt certainly shined in the eyes of African Americans when in 1901, for example, he ignored the harsh criticisms by whites after he dined at the White House with Booker T. Washington, the first invitation of a black man to such an occasion. The event was both a pivotal and scandalous moment in national race relations, and it caused much friction in both northern and southern quarters.[2] Roosevelt's relationship with Washington carried significant weight among African Americans, especially since Roosevelt affirmed Washington's project of Anglo-Saxon–inflected cultural uplift. Speaking at Tuskegee Institute in 1905, Roosevelt unabashedly applauded Washington's goals of industrial, cultural uplift for African Americans. Roosevelt also turned to Washington for advice on "Negro" national affairs and offered the popular black leader an olive branch dipped in white paternal benevolence, which Washington was always quick and willing to embrace. As a sign of his willingness to better the condition of African Americans, Roosevelt granted federal positions to blacks and, earlier, during the Spanish-American War (1898) included African American soldiers, as Micheaux points out, in the Rough Riders's operation, where he declared that, after a bit of resistance, the "colored cavalrymen" soon "accepted [him] as one of their own officers."[3] Roosevelt's public outcry against lynching and the inhumane treatment of blacks in the South won the hearts of many African Americans. His defense of black rights, however, was tempered by his insistence (an insistence that ultimately belied his moral beliefs about African Americans) that blacks harbored a criminal class. Black leaders, according to Roosevelt, must publicly denounce this furtive class as instigators who antagonize white prejudice. Roosevelt, in subscribing to a well-worn myth, pointedly directed his criticism toward black men who purportedly raped white women. To be a better class of people, according to Roosevelt (and Booker T. Washington), African Americans must become more like Anglo-Saxons.[4]

African American sentiment, however, largely turned against Roosevelt when in 1906 the president dismissed three companies of black infantrymen (167 men in total) without due process following a riot in Brownsville, Texas. When Roosevelt brought Washington into his advisory circles on the Brownsville affair, African Americans disparaged both men for what they viewed as their complicity with southern racism.[5] As Louis Harlan states, "[Brownsville] not only destroyed the benevolent image of Roosevelt and his party among blacks, but brought sharp criticism of Washington's ambiguous role in the dismissal."[6] Roosevelt made shallow attempts in 1912 to rekindle favor with African Americans when he ran for president under the wing of the Progressivist Party. Roosevelt's essay, "The Progressives and the Colored Man," embraced African Americans as full participants of democracy while he simultaneously reiterated his demand that the guaranteed right to life and liberty for "the humblest among us" can only be granted when the "humblest . . . [behave] in straight and decent fashion."[7] Though Roosevelt courted the African American vote, their impact was nominal and had little effect on the election; and, in any event, Roosevelt did not win a place in office that year.

Undoubtedly, Roosevelt's allegiance to bettering race relations was besotted with paradox and was ultimately framed by his staunch belief in the superiority of white Anglo-Saxon civilization. As Thomas Dyer and Gail Bederman point out, Roosevelt's belief in securing Anglo-Saxon civilization was at the expense of the nonwhite Other. In a charitable light, Roosevelt's theories of race might be viewed as a product of historical circumstance; that is, white benevolent paternalism.[8] On the other hand, Roosevelt's theories were, simply stated, racist.[9] Either way, the taint of the incident at Brownsville and Roosevelt's theories of eugenics effectually left a bloody mark on his legacy.

What was it, then, that some African Americans, including Micheaux, found so attractive about the racial and cultural platform on which Theodore Roosevelt stood?[10] I would argue that several complex reasons exist that take into account Micheaux, Washington, and Roosevelt's commitment to the industriousness of the frontier individual. The model of functional efficiency, as I describe in chapter 2, had a direct correspondence with Roosevelt's understanding of the work of art. Micheaux, in part, followed a similar ideological trajectory. Roosevelt's championing of the frontier as the place where the making of American men and individualism occurred sat squarely with Micheaux's belief in blacks pulling themselves up by their own bootstraps and setting their own individualist agenda. By doing so, African Americans surmounted the history of slavery and race prejudice, and an aesthetic of realism thus followed suit. Although I would not go so far as to describe Micheaux as a "Black Turnerian" (as one scholar has named him), Fredrick Jackson Turner and Roosevelt's American individualism served well Micheaux's concept that black American art and artists should glisten with Rooseveltesque practical realism and spirited romanticism.[11] As I have noted, Roosevelt's ideas about popular culture and art had a significant impact on American culture as a whole, including African American artists and entrepreneurs such as Micheaux. Indeed, aesthetic and philosophical lines can be drawn between black cultural uplift and the romantic-realist writers John Burroughs and Walt Whitman—writers who, as we have seen, received Roosevelt's praise for their role in manufacturing an American national identity.[12]

What I suggest in this chapter is that while Micheaux demonstrated a direct aesthetic link to Roosevelt's "realist" principles and Booker T. Washington's moral codes of industry (realist in its pragmatism) for race uplift, Micheaux's cinematic and literary texts partook of, and disseminated, an American realism that was far more incongruous than his ideological heroes proffered. Micheaux may have turned to the tenets of white (and black accomodationist) culture but he more significantly turned to a broad range of contemporary intellectual and aesthetic ideas, as well as specific traditions at work in African American culture to stretch the terms of creativity and masculinity. It is worth noting that while key early-twentieth-century discussions and debates that took place among African Americans were often framed within a North/South and urban/rural divide (e.g., W. E. B. Du Bois/ Washington), Micheaux expanded the discussion when he took himself (literally and figuratively) to the West. But the West was not the end of Micheaux's story, nor was the South for Washington or the North for Du Bois:[13] Micheaux, like many post-Emancipation African Americans, was migratory.[14] To discuss Micheaux's uneven, mobile, and often ironic relationship to realism and black masculinity I turn to what Hazel Carby refers to as his modernist "ambiguity" and the way he negotiated what Jane Gaines calls "racial realism" in the cinema.[15]

Many scholars have pointed out the conterminous relationship between race "uplift" and white, masculine, bourgeois ideology. In its most reductive terms, race uplift is nothing more than an ideological reshackling of black people to white supremacy. Although Kevin Gaines rigorously traces the uneven promises and shortcomings of racial uplift—particularly as it brackets the oft-cited divide associated with the pragmatics of Washington and the intellectual radicalism of Du Bois—he reconfirms the failure of the movement because it was unable to sidestep the moral cynosure of white masculinist culture.[16] More recently, Hazel Carby has underscored the historical movement's emphasis on black manhood by race leaders. As Carby sees it, black "manhood" was not merely a rhetorical device designed to protect African American enfranchisement during post-Reconstruction and well into the twentieth century.[17] Rather, black male intellectuals and leaders framed their political demands in such a way that they consistently neglected any position for black women to assert themselves as race leaders and intellectuals. "It is," Carby writes, "a conceptual and political failure of imagination that remains a characteristic of the work of contemporary African American male intellectuals" (10).

As Carby is quick to point out, the attention paid to identifying a masculinist black "essence" by "race men" within white Anglo-Saxon discourse forgoes the possibility of a more provocative ambiguity of race and gender. It is, initially, quite easy to situate Micheaux within the black masculinist tradition that Carby addresses. His strong and clearly articulated admiration for Booker T. Washington's functionalism is demonstrated in his films, books, and articles in the popular press.[18] Yet, unlike Washington's anti-intellectualism, Micheaux insists that his audience read and watch as much material as possible. Although he often claimed to know best what his black audience desired from books and films, he also dangled before his readers an assortment of intellectual concepts and practical ideas toward race uplift. For example, Micheaux introduced in his works certain ideas held by Du Bois, James Weldon Johnson, and others less in agreement with Washington's agenda.[19] Though it is true that Micheaux was guided by Washington's entrepreneurial model for bettering the race, there is also evidence that Micheaux saw pure practical training for African Americans as a limited means for uplift. If portraits of Washington are sutured into Micheaux's cinematic and literary world to indicate his protagonists' success in society, Micheaux provocatively peppered his works with the images and words of contemporary intellectual authors less aligned with pure industrial and vocational enterprises.

Micheaux's version of uplift called for African Americans to participate and immerse themselves in their own broadly based culture. Micheaux's fictional surrogate, Sydney Wyeth, in *The Forged Note* (1915 —the year of Washington's death) is stunned, for example, that the bookstores of "Attalia" (Atlanta) do not carry copies of *The Climax* (aka *The Crisis*, the Du Bois-edited organ of the NAACP).[20] Micheaux may have been critical of Du Bois but he was also more urgently driven to intellectually stimulate (with practical ends to be sure) African Americans. Connections can also be drawn between Du Bois's and Micheaux's understanding of what constituted African American art.[21] Micheaux's references to Washington, Du Bois, Johnson, and Charles Chestnutt (to name but a few) suggest the wide textual and intellectual breadth that informed his range of race issues through which he sought discussion in the public arena.[22] More significantly, Micheaux's intertextual interweaving demonstrates the complex matrices of black masculinity, creativity, and politics that were taking shape during the early twentieth century. In this way, the complexity of African American experience became the hallmark of Micheaux's ambiguity, or what perhaps Donald Bogle saw as the "mystery and myths" that surrounded him.[23]

This is why, I believe, Carby singles out Micheaux in her treatment of race men. He is one who troubles the unifying principles consistently supporting a modernist vision of a black masculine essence.[24] Carby argues that in Micheaux's film *Body and Soul* (1925) Paul Robeson's double role in the film is a "doubleness that introduces an interesting and very important sense of ambiguity into the modernist search for wholeness and strategies of inwardness. Micheaux confronted the fragmentation of modern life directly by splitting his protagonist into two men who, while identical in outward appearance, are complete opposites in personality and in moral and ethical intent, in other words in their souls" (69).[25] A close reading of Micheaux's work (both novels and films) confirms Carby's brief but nuanced suggestion of ambiguous "doubleness" in his work, or what Corey Creekmur persuasively refers to as Micheaux's "multimedia and multidirectional circulation of texts."[26] Here I would like to advance Carby's and Creekmur's ar-

African American Realism   **89**

guments by suggesting that Micheaux's doubleness is only part of what makes his work "interesting and very important." His "multidirectional circulation of texts" yields more than doubleness: Micheaux's signature across media bears the mark that mobilizes a wide-reaching history and (con)textual corporeal inscription in which his signature is a remaining presence that, as Derrida puts it, is "no *pure* presence, but only chains of differential marks."[27]

Aesthetic of Personalism

The supplemental marks I want to consider in the Micheaux texts (cinematic, literary, and corporeal) are those inhabiting a relationship to American realist aesthetics and black masculinity. Micheaux's texts are dynamic precisely because the registers through which they emanate bear the "differential marks" associated with vital traditions in African American culture. I would argue that Micheaux's texts appear through several imbricated discourses, including slave narratives and their concern with the aesthetic dimensions that shape memory and "authenticity." Micheaux's texts also reveal a complicated relationship to the figure of the trickster and to minstrelsy and passing. Finally, the modernist ambiguity of Micheaux's texts share, I believe, in the (geopolitical) liberating experience of spatial/temporal migration that paralleled the cinema's own specific formal properties of space/time manipulation. By exploring Micheaux in this way, we can identify the specific terms of black-male experience in the creative arts and how a sentient knowledge of the "real," a lived experience, shaped the political contours of black art in the late nineteenth century and early twentieth. As Charles Johnson elegantly puts it: "The issue at stake is how blacks experience their own bodies within a world of racial restriction."[28]

In what ways, then, did Anglo-Saxon American realism inform black aesthetics and bodies in the late nineteenth century? In post–Civil War America, the everyday disorder of modern life often revealed itself to be too much for any bourgeois aesthetic, including realism, to handle: as Kenneth Warren notes, "Lynching, violence against women, child neglect, adultery, and railroad accidents all become indistinguishable intrusions at the middle-class breakfast table."[29] Warren further argues that it was difficult even for northern writers and artists "to reconcile

African-American political needs with the art of the real" (62). But for the likes of the white American realist William Dean Howells, such a dilemma was not insurmountable. Howells's support of Paul Dunbar's dialect poetry (rather than Dunbar's preferred genteel writing style), as well as Howells's own work in his novel *An Imperative Duty*, articulated realism's underlying foundation of "uplift" that marshaled African American politics through the corridor of white American humanist and paternalistic culture.[30]

The white artists who hoped to realize a humanist aesthetic that addressed the trauma of slave culture created a body of work drenched in sentimental romantic realism. Well before the war, the abolitionist writers Harriet Beecher Stowe and William Lloyd Garrison (albeit different in their emphasis) relied on a romantic sentimentalism to draw out the moral infraction that slavery had wrought. Stowe and Garrison's white voices carried long-standing imprimatur and were read in lieu of, and as an authoritative guardian to, the black writer's voice. For example, Garrison's support of Frederick Douglass's writing served well (initially) the white northerner's Christian progressivism grounded in, as many viewed it, moral and intellectual superiority. What Garrison did not count on, however, was Douglass's refusal to abide the preacher's white Christian abolitionist paternalism.[31] Indeed, Douglass soon made known his own authoritative and strident voice. If Garrison highlighted Douglass's "gentleness and meekness" as representing the authentic voice of the freed slave, Douglass insisted that no white man's paternal authority could consecrate the real experience of slavery.[32] What Douglass realized was that his written word, scripted in the style and voice in which he chose to write, was authority enough.[33] If the real experience of the slave was to be known, the slave narrative—including those tales that might offend white middle-class sensibility—can only be told through the authorial voice of the one who lived the actual experience of the event.

Since authenticating and authorizing the slave narrative by whites has long been recognized as a key trope of the genre, what radical move on the part of African Americans was necessary to express their work as "real" and as intimately involved with their lived experience?[34] In what way did form, content, and authorial signature necessarily announce the artist's experience as indeed "black"? Douglass's three autobiographical accounts underscore the existential import of what Gilroy calls the "aesthetic of personalism."[35] That is, that the writing or the "autobiographics" (to borrow Leigh Gilmore's term) of the slave narrative—the organization of its form and content—were directly tied to the slave's "project of self-liberation" and self-constitution.[36] For Micheaux, who wrote consistently in the autobiographical vein, the repetitive model offered by the slave narrative (the multiple retelling of a life story framed by a particular generic format) set a template through which the complex interrelationships between the embodiment of his historical life and the work of art convened.[37] An "aesthetic of personalism" does not, however, achieve pure essence of self and manhood. In Micheaux's case, Carby's view on his modernist ambiguity recommends his "project of self-liberation" as something more intricate. Micheaux's reflection of self in his texts, while often hubristic, suggests more questions about race and gender than it does absolute resolutions of the black male experience. Following the political gesture attending the autobiographies of Douglass and Washington, Micheaux's creates what Maurice Wallace terms "African American identity formation . . . characterized in black male autobiography by a behavioral ambivalence towards the cultural prescriptions of nineteenth- and twentieth-century racial and sexual identity."[38] Indeed, Micheaux's identity formation moves across texts that weave sexual and racial identities and explore the conundrum of black masculinity in white America. African American autobiography and the "aesthetic of personalism" reach across the larger struggle for freedom.[39]

Where is Micheaux's complicated "raced" body in his texts? Micheaux's fictional selves appear in his roman à clef novels and films as a projection of an ideal ego. The realist-aesthetic tendency to equate a one-to-one reflection between work and author looms large in Micheaux's work. The significance, however, of Micheaux's presentation of multiple versions of himself through the filter of romantic, or melodramatic, realism cannot be ignored given the dearth of popular (and, dare I say, "positive") and complex black images in novels and films of the period (or any other medium for that matter).[40] I suggest that Micheaux writes his body into these texts as a projection of a body torn asunder by the trauma of history and the inability to identify an absolute mirror image of pure blackness. In this way, Oscar Devereaux, Sydney Wyeth, Martin Eden, and Jean Baptiste are Micheaux pseudonyms that stress the author's intertextual position within the vicissitudes of the black historical experience.[41] I want to consider Micheaux's sense of the burden of black history as it inscribes his texts (in the broadest definition) and, more important, as the authorial signature transcribes and revises this history.

If the likes of Edwin Forrest gave witness to the reflective impulse of the work of art and projected it as a kind of masculinist and Anglo-Saxon sublime that purportedly unified racial difference as white, Micheaux's realist principles and "aesthetic of personalism" found less success in transcending or happily commingling with the white racist Other. Here Du Bois's oft-quoted remark that black self-consciousness is a "peculiar sensation" when born into white America rings clear: black self-consciousness is "double-consciousness, this sense of always looking through the eyes of others, of measuring one's soul by the tape of a world that looks on in amused contempt and pity." [42] For blacks, the intractable violence associated with whiteness is emblazoned on their souls and leaves little space to declare an essential blackness. A more resilient response to the "peculiar sensation" was thus necessary.

"8000 Feet of Sensational Realism"
and the Signifyin(g) Monkey

In their work both Jane Gaines and Richard Dyer show how the early cinematic apparatus biased what Dyer calls "aesthetic technology" toward an ideal reproduction of whiteness.[43] Such reproduction, of course, depended on constructing whiteness against something it apparently was not. Similar to Forrest's oppositional position to William Macready and his subsequent mesmerizing experience where he manufactured his mountainness of white American manhood by ingesting the savage Other, the cinema's technology calculated, tinkered with, and assimilated shades of difference toward a formulation of ideal whiteness. Through the mechanics of lighting, makeup, and film stock a racial ideal was reflected and represented through the cinematic machine. "Racial realism," as Gaines terms it, was thus aligned with the American idealism of Anglo-Saxon whiteness where the benchmark for realism was established with "Lillian Gish in mind." [44]

How then was it possible for Micheaux to use the cinematic apparatus for the projection of a black self, if not black culture? Gaines suggests that the mechanical and ideological whitening of the cinema carried its own built-in irony. Black-and-white (orthochromatic) film had the unexpected effect of producing shadings or variant gray tones that more accurately represented a range of dark and light skin tones, thereby resisting the simplified racial demarcations of "pure" black and white. In effect, the goal to equalize color variation along clearly differentiated racial lines to achieve "racial realism" failed. To reproduce exact skin tone in the cinema is, as Gaines tells us, both a "functioning misconception" and "approximation of an assumption" (205).[45]

The failure to achieve "authentic" racial realism in film is precisely where Micheaux's engagement with "aesthetic technology" reveals its rich radical ambiguity. Like Garrison's patriarchal interests in marshalling the terms through which Frederick Douglass wrote the slave narrative, the white cinema afforded Micheaux, to paraphrase Audre Lorde, the tools to mark his signature but not the authority to mark it as black (white Hollywood would "authorize" black images only later with the likes of King Vidor's *Hallelujah*).[46] Like Douglass, Micheaux found it necessary to mark his own voice and authority—his "aesthetic of personalism"—in his "race" films (and novels). How do we identify Micheaux's "aesthetic of personalism" in relation to race and masculinity, and how is it embodied in the text? For Micheaux, the black man's "authentic" experience is distressed, but not incapacitated. On the one hand, the figure of Micheaux/Devereaux/Baptiste/Eden/Wyeth moves toward an ideal freedom, yet on the other hand it moves toward freedom where black desire is curtailed in the white man's world. Disenfranchisement, segregation, miscegenation (rape), lynching, and other forms of violence toward African Americans made the very concepts of desire, freedom, and movement practically incongruous. Against the violence to censor, maim, and ultimately annihilate, desire is not something simply stopped.

Micheaux writes his texts through the aesthetic of the "real" insofar as the films reveal the differential and ambiguous marks of black experience. The voice of freedom and black masculinity in Micheaux's world is nothing less than an "approximation of an assumption" but is "sensational realism" nonetheless. Micheaux's aesthetic of realism is at once the same, yet different. Through pseudonymous characters and tropes such as character doubling (as Carby points out in the film *Body and Soul*) Micheaux traces the troubled authorship of black male desire through the very white technology that sought to simultaneously differentiate and erase blackness. Micheaux's projected narcissism reveals the anxieties of desire attending African American men of the late nineteenth century and the early twentieth because the ideological pull *to be* (black, accomodationist, radical, man) is always already contained as white. It is precisely the "pull," the cultural ambiguities, where Micheaux's work resonates the strongest and ironically insists on the uncertainties of authenticity. Micheaux is, in other words, the "Signifyin(g) Monkey" or trickster extraordinaire. He negotiates the white cinematic spectacle of realism by simultaneous turns upon what Gates posits as the "black linguistic sign, 'Signification' " with its attendant gesture of "Signifyin(g)" as well as the white "standard English signifier." [47] The similarity between "signification" and "Signifyin(g)" are nearly "identical" but not quite. That is, the ambiguity of Micheaux's texts rests in repetition and revision where signification/Signifyin(g)/signifier, and thus white cinema/black cinema, "have everything to do with each other and, then again, absolutely nothing" (45).

How do we see this ambiguous black-self struggle within a technology determined as white and thus real? In what way does Micheaux foil the "standard English signifier[s]" of race and gender? Here I would like to turn to the film *Symbol of the Unconquered* where the trickster's work of revision is on display (though this film is not the only text where we see the trickster at work). Micheaux's films negotiate the technology in both form and content. *Symbol of the Unconquered*, in this example, raises concerns of content but the direction of form is inseparable from narrative and representation.

In the film, Eve (Iris Hall), the mulatto female protagonist, wakes afresh in her new cabin in the West after being rescued by the black homesteader Van Allen (Walker Thompson). Van Allen had found an exhausted Eve one morning after she had received hideous treatment by a hotel manager (a hotel for whites) who refused her lodging. Although Eve passes for white, the manager—a mulatto, Jefferson Driscoll (Lawrence Chenault)—detects her blackness by looking into her eyes, a device Micheaux often uses for blacks' recognition of one another. The manager makes Eve sleep in the hotel barn on a horrible stormy night with another African American man (E. G. Tatum) who was also ejected. The following morning she departs and subsequently meets Van Allen. She, like other African American women who settled the frontier, had set out to begin her new life on an inherited piece of land (an ideal woman in Micheaux's view to be sure). When Eve meets Van Allen, she is taken by his charm (read Oscar Micheaux). Van Allen then thoughtfully and tenderly escorts her to her new home.

African American Realism   **95**

Once home, Van Allen helps her to tidy her new dwelling and assures her that she is safe since he lives conveniently nearby (he provides her with a gun in case she needs to call his attention). Finally, Eve crawls into bed and falls asleep.

As she sleeps, images of Van Allen appear in her dreams (Micheaux achieves this through superimposition of Van Allen's close-up above the sleeping Eve). At one point, however, Eve is suddenly awakened by an intruder and, rather than shoot Van Allen's gun, she cries out in horror. Van Allen quickly runs to her side, comforts her, and reassures her that she is safe since he will sit outside to protect her. After Van Allen leaves the house Eve returns to bed, whereupon she sits up and immediately thinks of Van Allen and declaims, "Oh, What a man, he is!" Indeed, Van Allen is Micheaux's ideal projection of black manhood. Neatly dressed in a tie and plaid coat (he works the land in this suit), Van Allen is a visual rendering of the homesteading-man figure of Jean Baptiste, Oscar Devereaux, and Micheaux himself. From the photographic image of Booker T. Washington on Eve's wall to the organization of the manly frontier mise-en-scène where Van Allen successfully resides, Micheaux divines a space for African American manhood within, yet also against, the "aesthetic technology" of whiteness.[48]

Micheaux's emphasis, however, on his projection of manhood in the film further emphasizes the ambiguities of race yet also the determination of race by strictly enforced parameters of color. To be sure, what is striking about Van Allen is his dark black skin. In comparison Charles D. Lucas, who plays Oscar Devereaux in *The Homesteader*, is much lighter in complexion. If the black actors in Micheaux's early films signified the filmmaker's ideal projection, the men he chooses to present his narcissistic ideal are of many different skin tones. *Symbol of the Unconquered*, however, raises not only the frail correspondence between race and skin tone but also, more significantly, the film highlights Micheaux's query of black manhood as one inextricably intertwined with the complexities of race and gender. I suggest that Micheaux's racial embodiment (one that moves through many worlds and crosses many bodies) intersects with his multimediated identification with gender.

The narcissistic projection that elicits the response, "Oh, What a man, he is!" is perhaps an obvious and self-satisfying invention on Micheaux's part (it certainly recalls Fanny Kemble's remarks about Edwin Forrest's mountainous manhood). More obvious is Micheaux's projection of self (especially in his novels) as often witnessed and made visible through the eyes of a female character. Micheaux, through female admiration, describes his male protagonists/Micheaux in his novels as "free of any ostentation and pretence,"[49] having "the strength and courage of a pioneer,"[50] and loved for his "frank and kind disposition."[51] Conversely, when a woman is selfish and self-absorbed, Micheaux (or Wyeth in *The Case of Mrs. Wingate*) chastises her by telling her she is a poor judge of "real men." Real men are principled and "cannot be appeased by a woman throwing herself at them" (238). In these instances, Micheaux's benevolent paternalism guides these women away from disgrace and toward a moral and sound life (but nowhere near him, of course). If his advice is ignored, Micheaux's women receive their comeuppance. Women, however, are also strong and assertive in Micheaux's world.[52] They work the land with men, assist in daring rescues, take charge in events of important decisionmaking, and are mostly portrayed as intelligent if not equal to Micheaux's male protagonists. In what way, then, does Micheaux's "feminism" form the terms for black masculinity?

Women, I would argue, play a pivotal, if not pivoting, role in Micheaux's work on the aesthetic of realism, the aesthetic of personalism, and the identity of his black maleness. The ambiguity that Carby marks on Micheaux's texts and that Maurice Wallace locates in the black male autobiography is the production of sexual/racial desire where Micheaux's "8000 Feet of Sensational Realism" both generates and pulls to and fro myriad aesthetic expressions and incalculable differences of "black" race and gender.

Mother! Mixed Race, Mixed Gender, Mixed Form

Often described, as we have seen, through the eyes of women, Micheaux's hubris secures a reading for itself through his constructed imaginary of women who longingly desire him (Oh, what a man!). I want to argue, however, that black male desire as projected through Micheaux's women is only in part (although not insignificantly) a narcissistic, masculine heterosexuality. Moreover, and again situating the director within a specific African American tradition, Micheaux identifies black male desire with and through black women's struggle for freedom. To be sure, there is an important relationship between feminism and African American race-man politics. Specifically, at the center of nineteenth-century and twentieth-century African American concepts of politicized feminism is the figure of the mother.[53] As I argue below, the trope of the mother in slave narratives and autobiographies brokers the uncertain relationship between father and son in postslave culture.

In her essay "Micheaux: Celebrating Blackness," bell hooks argues that Micheaux's work reveals the "complexity of experience and feeling" in black culture.[54] For hooks, Micheaux goes "beyond the realm of the ordinary" (351) and tantalizingly suggests that when Micheaux "acknowledges female desire" (354) and sensual pleasure he challenges the "dominant" model of cinema where woman are objectified for the cinematic gaze. To consider Micheaux's quality of being "beyond the realm of the ordinary" hooks makes a stunning comparison between Micheaux and Josephine Baker where she argues that Micheaux, like Baker, conjures an "atavism" central to the black imagination affirming "an unbroken diasporic bond with Africa that has not been severed by assimilation" (359). If this is true, how might we account for Micheaux's narcissistic desire for ideal black manhood projected on the screen when women uncontrollably announce, "Oh, what a man, he is"? Furthermore, is Micheaux's "complexity of experience and feeling" diasporic (with the full weight of this term's global implications) or is there something particularly American about the way he navigates black culture? Micheaux's aesthetic of personalism had much to do with the racially charged America in which he found himself.

In her reading of Micheaux's film *Ten Minutes to Live*, hooks states that, "like Baker, Micheaux saw the black body as a site where nakedness, eroticism was not considered a shameful reality to be hidden" (358). This is true to an extent. The novel *The Case of Mrs. Wingate* for example, is packed with erotic pleasures and bodily display between an African American man and the white Mrs. Wingate. The comparison that hooks makes between Baker and Micheaux is provocative, but Micheaux was more conservative than Baker especially where social propriety, heterosexual marriage, and romantic love were concerned (Micheaux's consistent heterosexual coupling in his works cannot be easily overlooked). What hooks opens to discussion, however, is precisely Micheaux's ability to move between the contemporaneous cultural assessments of race and gender associated with white Anglo-Saxon culture and African American culture. As I point out below, the dynamics of gender and race in African American texts are far different than those held in idealist Anglo-Saxon texts.[55]

Moreover, Micheaux's "feminist implications," as hooks refers to it (359), offer important ways to think about the filmmaker/author's concept of form, particularly because if there is something "atavistic" about Micheaux's work it is "primarily connected to a counter-hegemonic sense of history" (359). Is there a direct line that can be drawn between African history and the production of African American literature and filmmaking? Obviously, such an oversimplification would be reductive, but to disregard the production of resistance as it is displayed in form and content in cultural history would be as remiss an effort. The organization of ideas, thoughts, anxieties, and desires cannot be divorced from the ideologies that usher and produce images on the screen. When Micheaux stated that he understood the "philosophy" of his race and made films and wrote novels around which his audience could galvanize their everyday lives, he made clear that his work emerged through the shared cultural histories that took shape and form in ways that white realism could never realize.[56] Thus, hooks's bold leap to compare Micheaux to Baker may be more productively engaged if we first consider Micheaux's "feminist implications" in relationship to the African American idea of feminism and race as he understood them through Douglass, Washington, and Du Bois. Significantly, feminism for these black male authors is recuperated through the mother's voice as a guiding force for the writing of their manhood into history.

As I note above, Hazel Carby suggests that the histories of black uplift, intellectualism, and political movements have been couched in masculinist discourse excluding women as active participants. This is certainly true, yet there are signs that suggest that women's voices powerfully interceded against the "peculiar sensation" that whiteness inscribes on the black body and within the black psyche. This is not to suggest that African American women's stake in political freedom overrode the masculine assertiveness and aggression of black men or that women were allowed strategic placement in the masculine political and cultural arenas.[57] Moreover, I do not mean to argue that black female voices are alternative markers of liberation for African American manhood.[58] Rather, what I posit is that African American women, especially the figure of the African American mother, shaped, generated, and infused a particular sort of black-male resistance to white paternal authority. Seen this way, African American men indeed asserted masculine privilege but not in the same ways that white Anglo-Saxon men claimed their stake in cultural authority.

To understand the contours of African American manhood, it is necessary to signal the role of the mother because she finds a critical historical place in the manufacturing of black manhood; she is a trope with which to be reckoned. The symbolic weight of the African American mother is rooted in what Waldo Martin terms the "nonrelationship" of the (white) fathers with their mulatto sons. Exslave mulattoes (such as Douglass and Washington) who were fathered by an absent white man, however, were not the only black men to illuminate their mother's central role in their masculine maturation. The freeman, Du Bois, also praised his mother and held her dear in light of his father's desertion when he was a young boy. Most often these men's autobiographies paid reverence to the mother figure by emphasizing her double burden of picking up the additional duties usually reserved for the father.[59]

The "race . . . mother," Laura Doyle argues, "is the point of access to a group history and bodily-grounded identity, but she is also the cultural vehicle for fixing, ranking, and subduing groups and bodies. Twentieth-century narrative tells its way around, through, and past her in its determination to reconfigure the phenomenal self."[60] Nowhere is this truer than the narrativizing of the mother by African American men who scripted the terms for black manhood. With the tearing apart of the slave family structure (spatially and temporally), the black body was physically and psychically torn asunder ("Slavery," wrote Douglass, "does away with fathers, as it does away with families").[61] To repair the shattered groundwork for African American manhood, as these writers saw it, the slave mother was thus conceived as the principle reorganizer of space and time for what remained of her family, especially her sons. More specifically, she became the autobiographical site where black boyhood-into-manhood memory was reserved, reassembled, and authenticated, albeit imperfectly and inconsistently. In this way, the African American mother serves as a fictional text through which black men carved their authentic manhood as "not white."

In African American slave narratives and autobiographies by men, the mother resuscitates the structuring absence of the father and gives her black son the organizational semblance of home. The autobiographies starkly remind the reader that the mother struggled to maintain a home in the face of unendurable obstacles and white (paternal) supremacy. Mothers encouraged their sons to read and study, recognized their everyday achievements, and provided hope and promise for the future. African American mothers, in these writings, spare no expense and, as far as possible, sacrifice their own interests (if not well-being) for the betterment and advancement of their sons. "My mother," writes Washington, "sympathized with me in my disappointment, and sought to comfort me in all the ways she could, and to help me find a way to learn."[62] In these autobiographical accounts, the "black masculinist fondness for the home" (to borrow Wallace's terms)[63] is intimately bound to the significance of the mother.

But inconsistencies remain. The formation of an ideal Oedipal structure—framed by Anglo-Saxon uplift—pulled Douglass, Washington, Johnson, and Du Bois in multiple directions and into an ideological quandary. Certainly, African American men who espoused, in part, white genteel cultural sensibilities, took their cues precisely from the Anglo-Saxon stipulations of ideal family organization.[64] Yet, the paternal benevolence of white uplift only served as a reminder of the duplicity of the white father and his purported containment of desire.[65] Should black men entirely reject the white family tradition or reclaim their manhood by asserting a black patriarchy with its own authoritative voice? Needless to say, assuming ideal patriarchal roles was no easy task for Douglass, Washington, or Du Bois.[66] At the point of anxiety, the point at which an ideological position of black manhood was impossible to author, the mother's body and voice usefully registered her son's torn desire between inculcated traditions of white familial models and the radical resistance to it. Indeed, African American men's claims for manhood were negotiated through the historical struggles that the mother figure battled. The symbiotic relationship of the violently traumatized mother/son relationship is precisely where the supplemental mark unfolds and where the uneasy, yet nonetheless essential, alliances of race and gender necessary in the production of black manhood materialize.

Indeed, the African American mother's role is larger than the domain of the singular home and son. She assumes a metaphysical quality for African American men; what she gives to her sons she gives to all black people. For Douglass, as Martin tells us, "the inheritance of intelligence from his Negro mother, by extension an argument for black equality, had to exclude his lost patrimony."[67] Moreover, the struggle for the black man's civil rights was inextricably bound to those of woman, all women: "Every argument for Negro suffrage," writes

Du Bois, "is an argument for women's suffrage; every argument for woman's suffrage is an argument for Negro suffrage; both are great moments in democracy."[68] In this way, Du Bois was oddly similar to Roosevelt who vigorously supported women's right to vote. Lest we forget, Du Bois's aristocratic outlook on African American manhood as well as Washington's regulating of women's bodies into the domestic sphere were, in Carby's words, "irrevocably and conservatively masculine."[69] The key difference, however, between Roosevelt's championing of women's suffrage and Du Bois's call for women's rights was that black men directly linked the rights of African American men to the rights of all women because the suffrage movement was linked to abolition. The intersection and intermixing of race and gender in the production of black male authenticity in the work of art and everyday politics allowed for a far different approach to identifying the "authentic," or the "real," than Roosevelt had suggested.

Where is Oscar Micheaux in this discussion of the mother and her significance to his black manhood? Betti Carol VanEpps-Taylor gives no reason to suspect that Micheaux's all-black family experienced the dramatic fluctuations experienced by Douglass and the others. Yet when Micheaux does refer to his family he excoriates his father when he recalls his adolescence: "My father complained of my poor service in the field and in disgust I was sent off to do the marketing."[70] The father's effeminizing of his son is certainly noteworthy. The most important acknowledgment of Micheaux's own mother, however, comes in his dedication in *The Homesteader*: "Beloved Mother, This is to You." Micheaux's father is nowhere to be seen in his body of work. His roman-à-clefs novels tend to deemphasize his family background but, at the same time, black fathers in his work (such as his first wife's minister father) are harshly criticized for their policing of their daughters.[71] Mothers, alternatively, are often portrayed with dignity and shown to be the victims at the hand of abusive and deceptive men (such is the case with his wife's mother or with the self-hating mulatto Driscoll, who rejects his black mother's love in *Symbol of the Unconquered*).

Micheaux's maligned mother figures return again and again through the two main narratives he retold many times over (the reworking of Chestnutt's *The House Behind the Cedars* and his own autobiographical tomes). There Micheaux draws together the bodily presence of the mother with the tragic historical effects of slavery on herself and on African American manhood. Micheaux's mothers, in other words, are figures of pathos, stained and scarred by the atrocity of slavery, whose very presence marks the burden of the race's history. As carriers of the past, their significance is heightened particularly when neglected by those who can pass (such as their light-skinned sons) and live in the white man's world without the effects of racism.

But Micheaux's mothers are also imperfect carriers of this history. Their desire to see their children liberated is often at the expense of history inscribed by the author on her body. In *The Masquerade: An Historical Novel* (made earlier as the films *House Behind the Cedars*, 1924; and *Veiled Aristocrats*, 1932), which was Micheaux's final literary revision of Chestnutt's *House Behind the Cedars*, the figure of Rena, the daughter who reluctantly passes at the behest of her light-skinned brother and lives with him in a white-southern world, ultimately realizes her place is with her dark-skinned mother and, therefore, the black race. Rena follows her heart and returns to her mother after she (spiritually? psychically?) intuits her mother's illness. Her mother, however, desperate to make her children happy in the white man's world (even Rena desires to be with her race and leaves the embrace of an unknowing white gentleman to whom her brother has introduced her), strategizes a relationship for Rena with a mulatto who is looking for a schoolteacher and a wife. Rena, however, is in love with her dark-skinned neighbor, Frank. Once all of the crossed wires are played out in Micheaux's historical-melodramatic novel and Rena marries Frank, she explains to her husband the "vain and impossible" life that her brother and mother had hoped for her.[72] While her brother is cast as the misled mulatto, Rena apologizes to Frank for her mother's confused way of dealing with the world and assures him that his dark skin is acceptable to her mother: "My poor mother, then, who really loves you . . . is so influenced by the customs around her, and which she grew up under . . ." (399). The return to the mother, although central to the mythic formation of black manhood, is tainted, suspect, and uncertain. The contamination of outside (white) influence and inside (black) "custom" leaves the sympathetic and once nurturing motherly body disjointed and displaced. Likewise, race memory, since it is carried through the mother's body, has been fragmented and rendered imperfect.

Although white authorization of African American's accounts of the slave experience diligently sought the "proper" order of history, black writers necessarily developed storytelling techniques and literary tropes to mark their own voice, a voice that identified the disjuncture between memory and text. The abolitionist Lydia Maria Child, for example, did her best to make changes to Linda Brent's narrative "for purposes of condensation and orderly arrangement,"[73] yet female slave narratives, as Joanne Braxton points out in her reading of several such texts, are "marked by shifts in the patterns of movement that contribute to the overall impression that the story lacks order" (51).[74] Braxton suggests that women's slave narratives have a "disconnected" structure because the writings follow the way that memory is clouded by distance from the actual slave experience. The narratives were also written versions of oral tales that, over time, were endlessly transformed.

To Braxton's analysis I would further add that the disjuncture of memory and time and, thus, narrative organization is not only reserved for the women's slave narratives. Frederick Douglass's three autobiographies are distinct from one another precisely because the individual volumes are characterized by uncertainties of time and space. Douglass's passage to freedom from Baltimore is recounted with different inflection in each of the three volumes.[75] It is when Douglass no longer feared retribution that the details of his escape were subsequently revealed. Perhaps more significantly, the failure of memory is made all the more prescient because, as Douglass himself, we never discover the actual day of his birth. Like Douglass, Micheaux's persistent revision of dislocated space and time sits squarely and necessarily within a tradition underscored by historical trauma.

How then is the complex interaction of race and gender, memory and desire, harnessed and given shape in "black" works? In what African American traditions and cultural productions are race and gender politics traceable in Micheaux's work? In what way do race and gender intersect with the "aesthetic technology" of the cinema and, for that matter, the novel? Micheaux's organization of narrative form in his films and novels reveals the complex patterns of aesthetic production in twentieth-century African American art that negotiated particular, uncertain histories of gender and race.

Black and White Fathers of Cinema

Jane Gaines characterizes D. W. Griffith and Micheaux as the white and black "fathers" of American cinema.[76] As Gaines points out, Micheaux, like Griffith, laid new creative groundwork provided by cinematic properties. Moreover, the directors used melodramatic devices to heighten both spectator response and the spectacle unfolding on the screen (169). The aesthetic choices of the filmmakers, needless to say, were channeled toward different cultural ends. Gaines rightly argues, for example, that the rape scene between Sylvia and Girdlestone in *Within Our Gates* can be read as "a reaction to that other controversial scene—the 'Gus chase scene' from *The Birth of a Nation*" (177). What is striking, however, about the dialogue between these films is their uncannily similar treatment of narrative through formal cinematic devices. Yet, as Henry Louis Gates reminds us, repetition is not equal to sameness: the films have, in other words, "everything to do with each other and, then again, absolutely nothing." I want to argue here that through the use of the cinematic edit Micheaux reveals the African American body—specifically the male body—as one torn asunder by the violent irony of white culture that on the one hand demands his assimilation, while on the other hand rejects his very presence.

If Micheaux and Griffith are the "fathers" of black and white cinema, to what extent can their patriarchal contributions be considered a reaffirmation of, or resistance to, white Anglo-Saxon ideology? What I argue below is that Micheaux's films can indeed be read as a "reaction" to Griffith, but not so much as a negation of the "white father's" formal designs of cinematic aesthetic technology. Rather, the "white father" and the "black father" both turned to a technique of editing (parallel editing to be precise) that Gaines refers to in Micheaux's work as a "temporally ambiguous" effect. I argue, however, that Micheaux's and Griffith's use of the cut must be traced along a different set of cultural and aesthetic paths. Micheaux's use of the melodramatic mode and its formal dimensions rehearsed the genre while investing it with a provocative treatment of race issues in which his aesthetic was, as Michelle Wallace puts it, "often inspired and effective."[77] Indeed, the use of the same technique and generic conventions (parallel editing, melodrama) does not necessarily imply ideological sameness.

In recent years, film scholarship on Griffith has turned its energies toward situating the director uneasily within (or against) the history of the "classical Hollywood cinema" mode of production. Thomas Elsaesser and Adam Barker go so far as to argue that it is "more useful to see Griffith as a representative of non-continuity cinema."[78] Whereas the classical model of cinema is generally understood as an industrial mode of production that yielded an illusory and cohesive filmic representation of narrative space and time, Elsaesser and Barker point to Griffith's formal narrative structure as one "always based on an act of splitting the narrative core or cell, and obtaining several narrative threads which could then be woven together again" (295). The editing technique that "splits" the narrative in this way, Elsaesser and Barker contend, is parallel editing that in the hands of Griffith "pentrate[s] not only [his] formal procedures, but structure[s] his very conception of the diegetic material, including his view of the family, or morality, sexual difference and history" (295). The cut, especially the technique of parallel editing here, is thus inseparable from Griffith's ideological concerns.

For Tom Gunning, parallel editing prior to Griffith introduced a "narrator system" that complicated the simple presentation of action in, say, early "chase films" where "pursuers and pursued were shown together, moving through each shot, never separated by the editing pattern."[79] In these early chase sequences a "strict homology" was maintained between spatial action and its temporal linearity (77). Parallel editing, however, "asserts itself" as a narrator system because the edit seizes "control over the ordering of the film's signifiers, creating new relations to the spectator in the categories of tense and voice" (77). Parallel editing thus introduced significant interpretive possibilities for the spectator at the hands of those "ordering the film's signifiers."

Griffith's use of this mode of editing is seen in such works as *The Lonely Villa* (1909) and *The Lonedale Operator* (1911) and is used to great dramatic effect in the final rescue sequences of these films. But even here, according to Gunning, Griffith's parallel editing was never quite so simple and, significantly, different from what finally became recognized as the classical Hollywood use of parallel editing.[80] In the case of *The Lonely Villa*, for example, Griffith engages a "three-pronged editing pattern" complicating the simultaneity of space/time proximity usually associated with the two concurrent spatio-temporal relations that parallel editing established (197). More significantly, according to Gunning, Griffith's parallel editing achieved something more radical in such films as *A Corner of Wheat* (1909) where the theoretical juxtaposition of three distinctly separate sequences representing class difference—spatially and (possibly) temporally divided—organized "an economic nexus" weaving together Griffith's ideological concerns about class division in America (245).

Griffith's historical relationship to the dominant mode of American film production is viewed by Gunning, Elsaesser, and others as an opportunity not only to stress the aesthetic traditions through which Griffith worked but, more important, the discontinuities he practiced during the emergence of the purportedly monolithic model of "classical" cinema. Yet, the same scholars do not refute Griffith's ties to and hence "conception of the diegetic material" of white bourgeois culture that ultimately informed most Hollywood cinema.[81] Is a discussion of form and ideology moot? Is it theoretically valuable to draw together autobiographic concerns with the formal organization of the text if white bourgeois ideology permeates all cinema at its very seams? If Griffith's organization of ideological principles is privileged by scholars and understood as a theoretical gesture to express the director's cultural position (artistically, politically, morally), I would like to extend such a possibility to Micheaux's own theoretical gesture of form, specifically parallel editing, as it serves different conceptual ends. If Griffith's "view of the family, or morality, sexual difference and history" position themselves precisely through his formal technique, what might an analysis of Micheaux's cinematic address tell about his ideological concerns? What might the black father's revision of the white father's aesthetic look like?

The risk attending a formal analysis of this sort is that it potentially leads down the path of essentialist reasoning. Gaines grapples with this issue when she discusses Micheaux's "temporal ambiguities" and "freewheeling cinematic grammar" (181). To avoid the pitfall that places Micheaux within the confines of an "indigenous African American culture," Gaines treats Micheaux's style "as an ingenious solution to the impossible demands of the conventions of the classical Hollywood style, shortcuts produced by the exigencies of economics, certainly, but also modifications produced by an independent who had nothing at stake in strictly adhering to Hollywood grammar" (181). If this is true, is it not just as feasible to situate Micheaux's "modifications" through the window of African American signification in the manner through which Gates has suggested where repetition and revision display the gesture of *différance*? Is it not possible to view Micheaux's texts as at once transformations of white industrial film practices and traditions of narrative form in African American culture?

Throughout Micheaux's body of work, time and space are reorganized and revealed for the powerful affect they have on the human agents performing within the text. Most famous of these temporal/spatial designs is Micheaux's use of flashback in his films *Within Our Gates, The Symbol of the Unconquered,* and *Body and Soul.* The flashback saturates or "penetrates" the filmic present with the weight of a traumatic past (e.g., Sylvia's extended flashback of her family's lynching in *Within Our Gates* or Driscoll's tortured relationship with his mother in *Symbol of the Unconquered*). Every subsequent move made by Sylvia and Driscoll bears the heavy past that, in turn, affects the present and the subjects who struggle for its historical outcome.

I suggest that Micheaux's flashback is structured as a parallel edit similar to Griffith's parallel editing in *A Corner of Wheat* where "an economic nexus" is organized (though uncertain in its temporality). As Gunning and Gaines point out, temporal ambiguity is significant in these directors' works since the spectator realizes the affect of history but is never given a precise correlation of time between cinematic spaces.[82] For both Micheaux and Griffith, space-time affect is not simply linear. Parallel editing, here, suggests an imbrication of space and time, not the illusion of distinct continuity; the burden of the past (consider *Intolerance* in the case of Griffith) inscribes itself on, and works in parallel with, the present.

To see the way the historically weighted flashback occurs in Micheaux's cinema it is useful to consider the way it takes shape in his novels since his creative career and aesthetic interests began through this medium. It is clear that both media resonate with one another in his work. In *The Case of Mrs. Wingate,* Sydney Wyeth is approached by Kermit Early to produce an anti-Semitic film that proves that Jews have stymied black equality and are thus a racist culture. Wyeth resists Early's political advances and insists that he is a tolerant humanist.[83] In any case, the troubled waters, as Micheaux posits, between African Americans and Jews are introduced through a flashback ("Now let us go back a few years") to the infamous Leo Frank case (1913).[84] The historical past of race relations between blacks and Jews directly effects the moment at which Wyeth must come to terms with anti-Semitism within his own race.

Later, in *The Masquerade: An Historical Novel,* Micheaux alternates chapters of historical documentation (the Emancipation Proclamation, the Dred-Scott Decision, transcripts of the debates between Steven Douglas and Abraham Lincoln, and the full text of Lincoln's inauguration speech) with his final retelling of Chestnutt's *House Beyond the Cedars*. As I discussed earlier, *Masquerade* recounts the story of light-skinned Rena who confronts the challenges of passing and negotiating her place within black culture. In a key scene, after Rena returns to "her people," her mother throws a party for her where she is introduced to Wain (the unscrupulous mulatto) who later escorts her to another county where she will assume a teaching position and, if Wain has his way, the role of his lover. This scene at the party is important for the way Micheaux describes Rena's experience of *other* time and space and its affect on her body:

> Rena did what, conscientiously, she thought politeness required. She went the round of the guests in the early part of the evening and exchanged greetings with them. To several requests for dances she replied that she was not dancing. She did not hold herself aloof because of pride; any instinctive shrinking she might have felt by reason of her recent association with persons of greater refinement was offset by her more newly awakened zeal for humanity; they were her people; she must not despise them. But the occasion suggested painful memories of other and different scenes in which she had lately participated. Once or twice these memories were so vivid as almost to overpower her. She slipped away from the company and kept in the background as much as possible without seeming to slight any one.[85]

Rena's history of passing, the uncertainty of her mother's goals for her, and the ambiguity of her identity and relationship to "her people" remains powerfully "other and different." Micheaux plays a startling hand here because he "cuts" back and forth between earlier scenes—scenes conjured, but unseen—revealing not simply the traces of Rena's biographical narrative; that is, more significantly, Micheaux marks the "other and different" as her experience of passing as well as the Emancipation Proclamation and the Dred-Scott Decision. History inscribes Rena's "painful memories" on her torn body (a mulatta, neither white nor black). In Micheaux's novels (and, certainly, his films), the flashback is sometimes difficult to distinguish from parallel editing because space and time bear on one another between scenes.[86] The affect of the past is both present (parallel) and past (flashback).

Micheaux's modernist "ambiguity" is thus one of disjuncture—yet simultaneity—between past and present. In his novels, space and time are, like the bodies that people his world, torn asunder by the editorial cut so well rehearsed in the tradition of the slave narrative and African American autobiography. His films are similarly dynamic in their space-time relations. If, as Gunning points out, Griffith complicated the parallel editing sequences by introducing a "three-pronged editing pattern" ("split" at the core as Elsaesser and Barker would have it), Micheaux took parallel editing further along a more multipronged editing pattern. This multipronged system, I think, often has much to do with critical readings of his films that consider his work hastily constructed, completed on the financial sly, or as negotiated texts that address the concerns of the censors. I'd like to argue otherwise (without denying the financial difficulties shaping Micheaux's film production and the issues of censorship he faced by both black and white audiences and exhibitors). In *Within Our Gates* (but not this film exclusively) multipronged editing patterns suggest, like his novels, the burden of both historical and concurrent events on a single moment. What follows is an analysis of Micheaux's multipronged parallel editing pattern in a scene from *Within Our Gates*. Micheaux's aesthetic impulse here highlights both his formal interests as well as the terms for black manhood as he understood them.

In the film *Within Our Gates* the character of Sylvia is injured in a car accident while rushing to save a child's life. Soon after the accident she discovers that the philanthropist Mrs. Elena Warwick (Mrs. Evelyn) is the owner of the car that struck her. While Sylvia is in the hospital, Mrs. Warwick visits her and is charmed by her dedication to education for African Americans in the South. Sylvia tells Mrs. Warwick that the school in which she has been teaching is running extremely low on cash and she is unsure whether it will be able to continue operations. In response, Mrs. Warwick invites Sylvia to her home to discuss this situation once she has recuperated.

The following sequence of scenes where the philanthropist convenes with Sylvia and considers the value of her contribution demonstrates Micheaux's complex multipronged parallel editing nexus that, I argue, reveals the weight of events on the African American body, especially that of the African American man. The "Mrs. Warwick" sequence (as I call it) opens with an establishing shot of Mrs. Warwick's large sitting room in her bourgeois home; it is elegantly appointed for the period and managed by a white maid. Sylvia enters the room and is welcomed by Mrs. Warwick; they then proceed to the sofa to chat. Before Micheaux cuts to the two-shot "dialogue" between the two women, Micheaux startlingly cuts away to Dr. Vivian (in his office) who, as we have seen earlier, is both Sylvia's love interest and the epitome of proper African American manhood. The cut away to Vivian immediately associates the doctor with the dialogue, albeit in an ambiguous space and time dimension, because the cut occurs precisely at the moment when Mrs. Warwick and Sylvia are about to be seated. With the cut, it appears as if he (since he is sitting in the direction Sylvia is facing before she sits) assumes the place of Sylvia. After we see Vivian, however, we cut back to the two-shot between Mrs. Warwick and Sylvia. Vivian's presence, indicated several times through a temporally ambiguous series of parallel cuts, will prove, as we will see, indispensable for understanding the affect that Mrs. Warwick's and Sylvia's conference has on African American manhood. The brief encounter between the two women is shot simply as a two-shot. Mrs. Warwick tells Sylvia that she intends to make a considerable effort to help the school. As Sylvia prepares to leave, Micheaux cuts to the establishing shot of Mrs. Warwick's sitting room. Sylvia exits.

At this point, Micheaux cuts back to Dr. Vivian who then has a flashback of himself flirting with Sylvia in his office. Given what has preceded and what is about to follow, this sequence serves as an important bridge and reminds the spectator who and what is at the heart of all the narratological activity going on in the film: that is, heterosexual romance between strong intelligent African American men and women. Once the flashback to Sylvia is complete, Micheaux cuts back to Vivian alone in his office. The connection has thus been made between Vivian and Sylvia, their desire for one another clearly communicated, and Micheaux's desire for the optimal couple also stated.

Following the Vivian bridge, the film cuts back to Mrs. Warwick's sitting room where the philanthropist remains a bit hesitant about her commitment to the school. Therefore she is pleased when her friend, Geraldine, arrives to give her advice. Geraldine is from the South, and Mrs. Warwick thus considers her an expert on the dilemma she faces. In many ways, Micheaux echoes the editing pattern used for Sylvia's reception (establishing shot, two-shot). The sequence plays out a bit longer, however, since Geraldine has much to say about Mrs. Warwick giving money to African American education; in her opinion learning

"Again I've sold my birthright. All for a miserable 'mess of pottage.' Negroes and whites—all are equal. As for me, miserable sinner, Hell is my destiny."

Stills from the "Mrs. Warwick" sequence from *Within Our Gates*.

only "makes their heads hurt." Geraldine recommends that she instead give one hundred dollars to the Reverend Old Ned (rather than the five thousand she planned to give to Sylvia). As in the prior sequence with Sylvia, Micheaux, during the dialogue between Geraldine and Mrs. Warwick, cuts away to another setting. This time, Micheaux cuts to Old Ned where we see him foolishly and exaggeratedly performing a religious service. Subsequently, we see him dealing with some shady business about the church collection, acting subservient to white men, then chastising himself for selling his "birthright . . . for a 'mess of pottage.' "

The contrast is striking in terms of Micheaux's parallel editing sequences since the scene between Sylvia and Mrs. Warwick is intercut with the single shot of Dr. Vivian while the more elaborate Old Ned sequence runs parallel with the Geraldine and Mrs. Warwick scene. In the Geraldine/Mrs. Warwick scene, Micheaux's parallel editing pattern takes on its multipronged complexity. Is this a flashback or a projection of Geraldine's race-fueled fantasy? At what time is Old Ned preaching? When does he visit the white folk? Is any of this simultaneously occurring while Geraldine and Mrs. Warwick are in conversation? The elongated Old Ned sequence is significant on at least two counts. First, the sequence primarily establishes Micheaux's perspective of the tragic place that the black minister holds in both white and black culture (the black minister was a figure that raised the ire of both Micheaux and Du Bois). Old Ned is in direct contrast with the ("other and different") parallel sequence of the successful and self-assured Dr. Vivian. Thus, when Micheaux cuts to Old Ned who toadies to white folk and rebukes himself in shame, Vivian shines because he has his own business and loves a dedicated woman (dedicated to him and the cause). The distinction between proper, uplift manhood is clearly spelled out in this sequence — the "economic nexus" (in its fullest sense) — of the parallel editing pattern.

When the Old Ned sequence is complete, Micheaux cuts back to the two-shot of Geraldine and Mrs. Warwick who, after the Old Ned story told by Geraldine, is more confused and uncertain about what to do for Sylvia's cause (she eventually comes around and gives Sylvia ten times more than she initially promised). Upon Geraldine's exit Micheaux makes the final cut of the "Mrs. Warwick" sequence, where he returns, full circle, to the sitting room of the white philanthropist's bourgeois home. However, Micheaux's parallel editing structure reveals something else. As noted above, parallel editing presents an obvious comparison between two different types of African American men (and it is no secret to which version Micheaux subscribes). This exercise in parallel editing is not, however, simply reserved for men but also assays what is presented as the important "feminist" concerns of African American men as such concerns relate to the securing of their heterosexual black manhood. Thus, the second area of significance for Micheaux's use of parallel editing and of flashbacks is that the cut serves to project Sylvia's and Geraldine's fantasy of African American men. Through the mirroring of the sequences (Mrs. Warwick/Sylvia, Mrs. Warwick/Geraldine) the fate of the black man is cast. The decision made by Mrs. Warwick, the philanthropist, in her choice of how to help the race is directly tied to how she ultimately understands — an understanding inscribed through the camera that writes the feminine body — the African American man.[87] The stakes are high because the projection of the black man (a projection based on the intelligent black woman or the ignorant southern white woman) to the white woman philanthropist will shape the destiny of the race. Micheaux manages the outcome; he makes the white folk see the "truth" at work in the spirit of African American men and women. Micheaux "authenticates," through the black man and woman's perspective, his version of the proper order of things. Yet, the struggle to be a black man in a white man's world — whether the struggle is filtered in Micheaux's world through the bodies of Vivian, Old Ned, Driscoll, Early, or Wyeth — remains one of uncertainty, danger, and ambiguity. Micheaux's multipronged parallel editing pattern, the affect cut, underscores the complexity of space and time while it reveals the work of historical affect on the human agents who struggle in its wake.

The Pleasure and Pain of Passing

In the novel *The Wind from Nowhere*, Micheaux's last revision of *The Conquest* and *The Homesteader*, Martin Eden/Micheaux gives his white lover, Deborah, a copy of James Weldon Johnson's *The Autobiography of an Ex-Colored Man*. When Deborah opens the gift "she murmured to herself, half aloud[,] 'A strange title, must be a strange book. I'll bet it's interesting.' "[88] Eden's gift to the white woman he loves (she, it turns out, is of mixed blood) is indeed "strange" but "interesting" because it reveals the ambiguity so relevant to Micheaux's grappling with the terms of African American manhood in the twentieth century.[89] If Micheaux praised Booker T. Washington in the earlier work *The Conquest* (251–53), he soon after queried in *The Forged Note* (65) why he could not find a copy of *The Climax* (that is, Du Bois's *The Crisis*) in a major black urban center. Likewise, Micheaux's similarity to James Weldon Johnson—the author of the book that Eden uses to reveal himself—cannot easily be dismissed (Johnson, after all, befriended and shared aesthetic interests with Brander Matthews who, we saw earlier, was simpatico with Theodore Roosevelt).[90] To simply fix Micheaux within Washington's ideological (and aesthetic) framework of practicality and segregationist politics is to ignore the complexities of Micheaux's place within the African American male experience. To fully realize Micheaux's understanding of black creativity and its role for black manhood it is necessary, I suggest, to attend to the slippages that inform Micheaux's autobiographics (by which I mean his work and body, as I argue above).

Micheaux's bid to (auto)biography functions within a tradition that at once seeks an authentic "aesthetic of personalism" through white "aesthetic technology" while it refuses to provide consistent evidence to authenticate itself. That is, given the dearth of historical, tangible, and ordered evidence (let alone a large body of missing filmic evidence), to "know" Micheaux is to "know" the remains of the text. As Ann duCille argues in her review of Zora Neale Hurston's work: "Her autobiography is an exercise in omission and misinformation, full of fantastic adventures but ultimately telling us very little about her art, her ideas, her amours or even her age."[91] The same review could be made of Micheaux (or indeed Douglass or Du Bois). The gaps and revisions are endless in these writings. I disagree, however, with duCille's conclusion that such "omissions" tell us "very little about her art." Instead I would argue that the "omissions and misinformation" tell us so very much about the writer's art.

It should be noted, however, that duCille later concedes that Hurston was "a master of double-entendre, [and that she] was 'playing' . . . the way a trickster might play the master" (13). The trickster playing the master is precisely the aesthetic strategy at hand in the black texts of Hurston and Micheaux. The "aesthetic technology" that contained the nonwhite gesture and manufactured an impenetrable divide between black and white always failed because the cultural imperfections that stain the ideality of whiteness (the very marks of difference that produced the claims for the ideal in the first place), necessarily remain present because they sustain the principles of that ideal. In such ideological movement to and fro the African American trickster's resistances are of particular note.

In the following passage from *The Conquest* Micheaux remarks on the experience of minstrelsy: "As the Reverend was then some three hundred and seventy-five miles south of Chicago attending a conference, I couldn't see how we could get together, but we put in the Sunday attending church and Sunday School, and that evening went to a downtown theatre where we saw Lew Dokstader's minstrels with Neil O'Brien as captain of the fire department, which was very funny and I laughed until my head ached" (198). In this passage, Micheaux participates in what W. T. Lhamon refers to as cultural "transactions." That is, "every motif or gesture is embedded in a train of previous such gestures which pull it to the present . . . [Such transactions] do not replace the part of one's identity but, instead, compound who one is."[92] Lhamon's play on "transaction" and "train's action" ("continual, but uneven in their flow and spread") is well suited to his argument about the ambiguity of minstrelsy, its inherent racism yet place as a site of resistance for African Americans. Minstrelsy, as demonstrated by Kevin Gaines (and others), was a form of performance that negotiated the matrices of class and race by allowing for a myriad of cultural response.[93] For many blacks, minstrelsy offered a site of resistance to the rigid ideals of assimilation while it fed transformative modes of black aesthetics and cultural practice. "Other blacks," writes Gaines, "less burdened with the demand to be respectable were also manipulating and reclaiming minstrelsy and were exploring different modes of cultural expression in ragtime, blues, and Negro dialect literature and in the performances of barnstorming Negro vaudeville troupes" (346). The experience of participating within, yet against, the mode of minstrelsy was indeed at the extreme that marshaled simultaneous pleasure and pain: "I laughed until my head ached."

Lhamon's metaphor of the trans/trains thus suits Micheaux, the former Pullman porter with his love of travel between the rural frontier (South Dakota) and urban landscapes (Chicago especially). The Pullman porter, Lynne Kirby suggests in her book *Parallel Tracks*, "did much to link black male identity with the railroads."[94] But for Micheaux, the role of porter was co-active with his role as trickster.[95]

Kirby argues that the "unstable western subject" was "embodied" in the modern experience of both the movie spectator and train passenger. Micheaux serves as no better example of this "unstable western spectator" and passenger of modernity. But he is significantly something more: Micheaux was a cultural producer where the "train's action" and "transaction" generated the disjointedness of modernity through the complexity of his texts. The split narratives, the compulsion to rewrite and revise, the hauntings of fathers both white (Griffith, Roosevelt) and black (Du Bois, Washington, Johnson), and the uneven mixed relations of race and gender are the mobile (con)texts through which the experience of African American masculinity and creativity emerged in Micheaux's texts.

4

Manhatta:

A National Self-Portrait

The terms for a national Anglo-Saxon, hetero-masculinist aesthetic did not stop short with the popular arts. American avant-garde artists took up similar points of cultural reference to announce what they viewed as the necessary aesthetic for America's modernist position in the twentieth century. Though the formal ends were different, the debates that measured the outcome of the popular arts often found common ground with the young American upstart modernists and their concerns over gender and national representation. Moreover, and again similar to the discourse firming up the popular arts, the avant-garde rigorously claimed aesthetic territory as American and as not European. Nonetheless, the young moderns writ large the nation's anxieties over industrialization, urbanization, nature, and modern humanity in general. Significantly, the artists of the period (predominantly white men) established the benchmarks for what it meant to be a creative member of the so-called high arts. As I demonstrate in this chapter, the artist's signature performatives and narcissistic projections (in everything ranging from mode of dress to art philosophy) were bundled with aesthetic form to the extent that form followed identity.

The anxiety over the bureaucratization of American culture and its materialist effects was heightened during the period expressed in the titles of works such as Robert Wiebe's *The Search for Order, 1877–1920* and Richard Hofstadter's *The Age of Reform: From Bryan to FDR* (the post-Reconstruction period of 1877 through the 1930s). Henry May further argues that the twentieth-century cultural tug-of-war—the assertions and debates over progressivist, traditionalist, and radical philosophies—tore at the very fabric of America's finely tuned (or so it was thought) theories of nineteenth-century realism and idealism. By 1912, May argues, concerns over the fractured unity of Anglo-Saxon culture gave way to the more functionalist chants of "practical idealism."[1] As it had for the artists of the previous century, the appropriate balance between realist and idealist aesthetics was the benchmark on which theories of modern aesthetics occurred. But the resulting cultural strain during the rise of the machine age pitted the perceived groundedness of realism not so much against idealism (although principles of democratic idealism remained central to the creative energies American artists engendered), but instead against a more dangerous precedent confronting humanity in the mechanical age: abstraction.

Following the Civil War, America's immersion in the sweeping changes of global economics, new technologies, and industrial communications dominated its cultural psyche. While swimming through the tides of industrialization, the nation simultaneously negotiated torrents of racism, xenophobia, and protonationalism. And though critics and pundits were enthusiastic about America's energetic emergence on the world stage, they wrung their hands with concern over what they saw as the moral conundrum, if not crisis, of excessive materialism that Americans embraced during the industrial age. Walt Whitman, for example, praised the business initiatives of the late nineteenth century and applauded America's entrepreneurial spirit but warned of monopolistic chicanery and "the God damned robbers, fools, stupids, who ride their gay horses over the bodies of the crowd."[2] Theodore Roosevelt later expounded on the debilitating consequences of materialist greed and its consequences for the body and mind. His counteractive prescription to the excesses of culture was to strenuously exercise individual corporeal and intellectual stamina. Social-cultural critics and artists such as Thorstein Veblen, Marsden Hartley, Paul Rosenfeld, Van Wyck Brooks, and Waldo Frank lamented profligate and conspicuous consumption at the expense of higher spiritual, intellectual, and idealist (manly) pursuits. Those who practiced "immoral recreations, private bestialities, and the like"[3] under the gluttonous attributes of capitalism eschewed America's founding principles of thrift and common sense. The philistines "lust[ed] for prosperity" (Hartley) and were nothing less than barbarians (Veblen); they were hypocritical "Puritan-Pioneers" (Frank), and, quite simply, out-and-out "lazy" (Rosenfeld).[4] What was required, according to Brooks, was a "middle tradition," stoked by Whitman's poetics, to contain the excesses of American "high-brow" and "low-brow" cultures.[5]

For many cultural critics, spiritual deprivation—directly linked to materialism—was the most unfortunate, if not most dangerous, calamity of machine culture. The decadence of the modern age thus promoted the slow rotting of America's spiritual innards. To counter the chilling effects of the machine's ubiquity, artists and writers pitched a resurrection (religious entendre intended) of spiritual wealth to achieve a nationalist sense of pure oneness in the face of mass-produced, self-indulgent gratification.[6] Modernist American art—of a very specific kind—revived spirituality but remained beholden to the terms of twentieth-century modern progress. The blame, however, for America's moral and spiritual quandary was not merely reserved for the rabid captains of industry and their inhumane schemes of profit grabbing: European influence remained a bête noir. At the turn of the nineteenth century, Americans maintained their love-hate relationship with the Old World from where the imports of culture, carried by millions of immigrants each year, frustrated America's efforts to purge the standards of Europe and its designs on a racially pure and nativist culture. Old World detritus was as perfidious as new-fangled machinery and the corporate managers who "rode their gay horses over the bodies of the crowd."

Following years of uncertain economic markets and what was viewed as the decay of urban and rural communities in post-Reconstruction America, the country underwent a philosophical and bureaucratic reevaluation, a commonsense recounting of its moral and economic constitution.[7] Through opposing (yet "absolutist" and enthusiastic) movements led by Anglo-Saxon progressivists and nostalgic-utopic populists, it was hoped that Americans would "master an impersonal world" of so-called civilization.[8] The ideological paradoxes, however, of American capitalism and democracy refused to budge. On the one hand, the rapid growth of corporate standardization, increased production of material goods, growing consumerism, and dissemination of excessive wealth marched forward (albeit for a select few); on the other hand, idealist-myth principles remained tied to a concoction of yeomanry agrarianism, frontier truculence, and quasi-nonsectarian spiritualism. To find the ideological and practical balance between America's uncertain moral condition and excesses of materialist production a number of political and cultural agendas fomented. As Leo

Marx indicates, the tensions taking shape around the torn visions of modern industrialism and romanticized pastoralism in the nineteenth century marshaled the quest for a "middle state." [9] Again, with full force in the early twentieth century, the idea of "middle-ground" common sense netted a nineteenth-century perception of ideological balance and the measurement of all things true and American. Ironically, the very drive to contain and control modern culture was managed by an inordinate amount of hyperbolic manly activity. [10]

How did American artists respond to these anxieties of machine culture and the reframing of frontier/pastoral mythology in the first part of the twentieth century? What aesthetic concepts resisted Europe's continued hegemony in the arts and promised to secure America's creativity as American? More precisely, how did the artists position (or, more accurately, project) themselves as American artists in machine culture? In what way did the ideological arguments for an American avant-garde echo those for the popular arts? Finally, how did the cinema prove to be a ripe testing ground where the antithetical suppositions between modernity and spiritualism were bridged? As described in earlier chapters, through the popular cinema in the guise of the urban landscape Theodore Roosevelt imagined (and strenuously defended) America's idealist principles of the frontier. Yet, for many American artists, the popular cinema did not own the formal acumen to address the new age, especially when the European artists' imaginative and provocative aesthetics hit the streets of New York. While the twentieth century bore witness to the psychological-economic standardization of labor and industry (including that of the film industry), American avant-garde artists, or what Edward Abrahams calls the "Lyrical Left," found themselves tackling hegemony of a different sort—an aesthetic hegemony—in the dramatic postimpressionist, European movement of cubism. [11] In 1913, the Armory Show put American artists on notice and cataclysmically restated the question, What is American art? [12]

Here I would like to address these particular twentieth-century anxieties of machine and spirituality, realism and abstraction, and creativity and manhood as they are filtered through the painters-photographers Charles Sheeler and Paul Strand. Their 1921 film *Manhatta* reveals not so much an American aesthetic that romanticized modernity; rather, the film projects an aesthetic narcissism that announced the nationalist and masculinist enterprises of America's avant-garde. [13] *Manhatta* emerges at the moment when American artists perceived a decided break from the tyranny of the Old World. America's machine culture, therefore, was both a blessing and a curse since the machine stood for all things progressive about America while it simultaneously put at risk the essence of the nation's humanity. To begin an analysis about how an ideological "middle state" between machine excess and spiritual expression was met through the cinematic aesthetics of *Manhatta*, it is necessary to work through the cultural milieus and theoretical models in which Sheeler and Strand found themselves. At the forefront of this aesthetic inquiry is Alfred Stieglitz.

America and Alfred Stieglitz

Alfred Stieglitz embodied the quintessential scope of early twentieth-century American modernism: Old World knowledge, philosophical élan, and urban chutzpah. From the way he dressed to the sports he admired to the machine apparatus with which he created modern art as American, Stieglitz—body and soul—was acknowledged as the conduit through which the nation's avant-garde dispersed its creative forces. Paul Strand, as a young photographer, was particularly mesmerized by Stieglitz's claims for a new American modern art grounded in the camera-machine. Strand, however, was far from alone in his devotion to the impresario artist. Stieglitz held an enormous aesthetic sway over many American artists that resonated well into the middle of the century.

To be sure, the encomiums for the American modern master were many. In 1934, Waldo Frank, Lewis Mumford, Dorothy Norman, Paul Rosenfeld and Harold Rugg—all members at one time or another of photographer/art mentor Stieglitz's creative circles—edited an anthology titled *America and Alfred Stieglitz: A Collective Portrait*. This project, done for the occasion of the photographer's seventieth birthday, was to portray to the volume's reader Stieglitz's contributions as a "communal work" in order "to present the body of the subject in concrete social terms."[14] The editors hoped to convey the "world which Stieglitz has embodied and projected through nearly fifty years of intricate creative action" (5). Thus, the editors and artist-writers such as Paul Strand, Charles Demuth, Sherwood Anderson, and Edna Bryner devote a good number of pages to discussing the socio-historical and aesthetic condition of American arts and politics before they ever approach their discussion of the book's central figure, Alfred Stieglitz. Stieglitz is thus presented as a corporeal vessel through which American artists and critics evaluated the place of American art. He "embodies" or is indeed the "body of the subject in concrete social terms" before he is elevated (for the most part) to the status of the great man.[15]

What the collective portrait illustrates (and portraits were important to this group of modernists) is the long-standing and foundational concept of "embodiment" held by the artists in Stieglitz's circle. Although much has been written about Stieglitz's influence in early American twentieth-century arts, and on the diverse group of artists, patrons, and critics who were intimately involved with the photographer, little work has analyzed the group's emphasis on the intersection between machine-culture aesthetics and corporeal-aesthetic embodiment—an aesthetic with broad implications regarding concepts of gender and creativity.[16] Between 1902 and 1917 Stieglitz's photo-journal, *Camera Work*, and his "Little Galleries of the Photo-Secession" (or "291" as it became known for its Fifth Avenue address) introduced a broad spectrum of multimedia works from Europe, Africa, and America. In the rooms of 291 Stieglitz presented the first works seen in America by Auguste Rodin, Henri Matisse, Paul Cézanne, Constantin Brancusi, and Pablo Picasso, as well as photographs and sculpture of African art. The gallery was soon recognized as a hotbed for modern art and cultural debate led by the often-intransigent Stieglitz, but his strongest commitment was to American artists and the idea of American art. Stieglitz supported and fostered the talents of painters such as John Marin, Arthur Dove, Marsden Hartley, Charles Demuth, and many others. Most significantly, he provided the professional forum and launch for Georgia O'Keeffe (who later became his wife). He is also credited with breaking the gender barriers in his treatment of several women artists including Gertrude Käsebier, Dorothy Norman, and, of course, O'Keeffe. It appears that Stieglitz was also tolerant of homosexual artists (Demuth, Hartley, and, although they parted ways, photographer F. Holland Day), many of whom were personal intimates as well as artists consecrated by the master.[17]

One of the last artists introduced to the art world through 291 was photographer Paul Strand. Photography was Stieglitz's first love and Strand was his protégé who carried (for a time anyway) the patriarchal torch. Fellow travelers in the circle (albeit less directly associated but nonetheless significant) included the photographer Eduard Steichen, the art patrons Walter Arensberg and Mabel Dodge Luhan (who held court for artists at her salon), and the writers William Carlos Williams, ("anarchist"-pragmatist) Randolph Bourne, Waldo Frank, and Theodore Dreiser. The painter Charles Sheeler sat at the margins, as we will see, but he drew on Stieglitz and his disciple's theories.

The cross-section of Europeans and non-Americans who moved through this New York arena was indeed impressive: among others were Marcel Duchamp, Francis and Gabrielle-Buffet Picabia, Marius de Zayas, and the expatriates Leo and Gertrude Stein.[18] Through *Camera Work* and 291 Stieglitz introduced (among others) cubism, synchronism, and Dadaism to his young acolytes. Though Stieglitz adamantly marked New York as the seat of new American art, he never rejected in toto the influences of the European art world. "What is certain," Waldo Frank dramatically wrote of Stieglitz, "is that he embodies and projects for the experience of the coming generation a *variant value* within the old world, significant and perhaps crucial to the new world which all minds feel now stirring in the anguish of our epoch."[19] Like W. E. B. Du Bois, Stieglitz's earlier studies in Germany had much to do with his resistance to oversimplifying the Euro-American creative (and, certainly, political) relationship. However, American artists (unlike their European counterparts) were forced to deal with "practical considerations," according to Stieglitz, that made American artists the unique individuals they were meant to be.[20] Indeed, Stieglitz insisted American art existed sui generis. Yet, the prevailing and narrow acceptance of American realism as the national aesthetic by his contemporaries in the visual arts (the "Ashcan group" led by Robert Henri, for example) was, as Stieglitz would have it, shallow, "mediocre," and lacked "a sense of touch."[21] "American" art and its achievement of truth and the real had yet to be fully theorized; Stieglitz, of course, saw himself as the man to propose and practice such a theory.

Throughout the 1920s Stieglitz remained active in the New York art scene but moved into the social background adding his editorial voice to the onslaught of new art/political journals that flooded the market after World War I while continuing his unwavering support for his immediate circle of artists.[22] By 1934, when *America and Alfred Stieglitz: A Collective Portrait* was published, the group of photographers, painters, and writers who were part of the Stieglitz group (many of whom were the publishers of the new art/political journals) were well versed (thanks to Stieglitz) in the theoretical debates deriving from both sides of the Atlantic.[23] Immediately at hand were the aesthetic concerns of the machine as a result of the quickly industrializing and corporatizing face of America. The rush of machine culture had appeared on the American landscape, inscribing it and the bodies that peopled it in unforeseen ways. As we have seen, the tradition in the American arts was loaded with discursive and phenomenological theories that commingled the artist with the landscape. The landscape, however, had now dramatically and, not insignificantly, artificially altered with the machine. If the work of art necessarily enmeshed the artist and the artist's lived world, what sort of modern human relationship could exist between artist and machine? Although the camera-machine presented new hope, of paramount concern were the moral and ethical challenges to the artist's cultural purpose in the new landscape.

Again and again American artists, like their predecessors in the nineteenth century, parsed the specific properties of both their particular medium—especially the camera—and the nationalist aesthetic it licensed. The shock of European cubist painting and its aesthetic analysis of modernity relentlessly resonated for American artists. But cubism arrived, as did the other aesthetic movements and media before it, from across the Atlantic, and American artists again scrambled to identify their own national aesthetic. After nearly plagiarizing the formal designs of Cézanne and Picasso between 1913 and 1918, American artists queried the aesthetic and political world in which they found themselves while they struggled to pinpoint the essential Americanness of the era. Once the astonishment of the European movements was digested and the theoretical debates about machine-made America took shape, American artists claimed an aesthetic victory during the period around which *Camera Work* closed (1917) and World War I ended (1918); indeed, the latter event delivered the first of many severe cultural blows to Europe's artistic preeminence.[24] By 1922 art critic Henry McBride declared that Whitman's "lusty" American artists stood strong against the French "advantage" in the arts.[25] While many new "isms" were bantered about at this time, many critics and artists more generally heralded the new American movement as "precisionism," or as what Milton Brown suggests was the inevitable "outgrowth or domestication of cubism."[26] More precisely, Brown coined the terms for the movement in his title "Cubist-Realism: An American Style."

For the Stieglitz circle, the cultural shift in modern aesthetics and the lived world was best studied and artistically realized through understanding of the machine's relationship to the body and to its modern environment. As these artists viewed it, America's twentieth-century body had little to do with nineteenth-century concerns of oneness between body and traditional nature.[27] For young moderns, to conceive of America's new landscape and its bodies was to necessarily envisage the centrality of the machine. The machine and its corporeal affect thus merged with the new twentieth-century landscape: the camera was the machine in the American garden. Indeed, the machine in the landscape was the point at which the realist aesthetic, in particular, revealed and converged with the truth and the real of American idealism. "We believe we are the true realists," Waldo Frank polemically announced in 1919, "we who insist that in the essence of all reality lies the Ideal. America is for us indeed a promise and a dream. But only because we are sure that in discovering and controlling the complex conditions of our land, we shall find inviolate within them the promise and dreams whereof I speak."[28]

In his conversations with Dorothy Norman, Stieglitz reflected on his creative process and his relationship to the machine-camera. "I found it difficult," Stieglitz stated, "to understand how with society supposed to be 'in the hands of the engineers,' machine-made objects were looked down upon. In a sense, a camera and lens are mere mechanical objects. Nonetheless, without being one with them, what aroused admiration for my pictures could not have existed. I developed a natural respect both for well-made machines and for whatever they produce that is beautifully created."[29] By echoing the concept of oneness with the work of art that informed the trajectory of the American arts, Stieglitz reconfirmed the long-standing tradition that masculinized the American arts. The unity of artist, work of art, and subject allowed for a complex aesthetic experience at once sublime and pragmatic. The act of introducing the machine into the equation, as Stieglitz had, was troublesome, but not illogical. Indeed, it was the ultimate declaration of twentieth-century American modernity where the sublime and common sense were bridged. The new American landscape not only was not forgotten but was fully incorporated into the new epoch's evolutionary advances.

Stieglitz's aesthetic and philosophical studies in Germany, his reading of Whitman and the American transcendentalists, and his "affir-

mation" (a favorite term of the photographer) of the individual artist directly fed his theoretical designs on the American arts in which
the place of the artist must work with the machine while refusing its
potentially decadent excesses.[30] What Stieglitz theorized into cultural
discourse was the provision for twentieth-century material matter (the
machine) as a uniquely American tactile and practical experience (i.e.,
the "sense of touch" he saw lacking in the Ashcan paintings).[31] For
Stieglitz, to reject the place of the machine in the experience of American art was to reject the very concrete matter that identified American
art as American. That is, since French impressionists and German expressionists express their national sensibility precisely through the particular material worlds in which the European artist lived (and thus as
more philosophical and less practical, as Stieglitz saw it), American artists must concentrate and channel their creative efforts through their
very own sensuous ("practical") experience.[32]

Stieglitz's theories opened new spiritual vistas on the modern landscapes for many artists who were eagerly attending their master's discourse.[33] As factories and urban sprawl exponentially increased, nostalgia for Hudson River views did little to generate the new art that
affirmed America's rematerializing of itself.[34] In this way, the spiritual
transcendence of God-inspired compositions from the nineteenth century held little value for twentieth-century American moderns. America's fresh crop of intellectuals and artists anticipated something far
different on the strangely formed horizon, yet sought a convergence
between the tensely paired concepts of spirituality and industrialization. If God no longer served as the imperial master of the higher order
of things, to what transcendent order does one turn? Was God meant
to disappear in the progressive twentieth century? In reponse, a "new
God," as we will see, was anticipated by the likes of Paul Strand.

America's love affair with Darwinism and its bastardized cousin, Social Darwinism (pace Herbert Spencer), had much to do with the
altered cultural logic associated with humanism and spirituality during
the industrial age. Science and the social sciences elevated the human
condition to superior standing in the evolutionary chain of species
production. The advanced biological position of mankind over other
species displaced God's traditional role in the process of creative inspiration. In this way, twentieth-century mankind's creative authority
rested within its very own highly developed organism. In facing the
threat of industrial monopolization (a real concern for the place of

the evolved individual), humans, it was thought, must forge ahead and bypass the developmental chain of other species. By doing so, not only could humans master the machine, they could become its equal if not its superior. By asserting this place of "equivalents" (as Stieglitz termed it, and as I will discuss below) between man and machine, the photographer-cum-philosopher sought a modernist art that reached pure truth and a transcendent, spiritual Americanness.

Stieglitz's palavers on art, modernity, and "equivalents" wended their way through much of the writing and artwork of the young American artists of the period. In what follows I want to discuss several areas in which Stieglitz's theories resonated and disseminated into the American art scene, particularly as they inform the aesthetic contours of Strand and Sheeler's work, especially *Manhatta*. Their work conjoins in 1920 through different arts—Sheeler trained in the tradition of painting and Strand in photography—and hence their vision of American modernism was viewed through dissimilar cultural lenses. Yet, painter and photographer were brought together in the medium of the cinema, where the variations on their theoretical concepts projected and secured, or so it was thought, a unified twentieth-century American idealist realism.

For the Stieglitz group, theory was as central as the actual making of art. Stieglitz once claimed that 291 was "devoted to ideas" and not simply "the ultra modern in painting and sculpture."[35] In many vital ways, practice followed theory in this modernist coterie. In what follows I would like to highlight four theoretical areas in the Stieglitz group's conceptual program of American art that, while distinct in their formulation, often overlap and dialogue with one another: these areas include the individual artist as sportsman/worker (or nonartist); gender and aesthetic "equivalents"; primitivist and spiritual modernism; and the place of New York City.

Art/Artist Sport/Sportsman Work/Worker

Alfred Stieglitz loved sports (baseball and running were his particular favorites). "I always have had," Stieglitz wrote later in life, "a feeling of sport in relationship to everything I have done."[36] For Stieglitz, photography was a healthy competitive sport about to meet a fateful and vulgar demise when Kodak, in 1891, introduced the slogan, "You press the button, and we do the rest"; to this, Stieglitz grieved, "it seemed rotten sportsmanship."[37] The intellectual and creative management of the machine ran afoul, according to Stieglitz, when the unique individual interaction with the camera was set aside for instantaneous production and gratification. Though Stieglitz had little tolerance for and vociferously campaigned against the rote arguments over whether or not photography's artistic integrity could ever rival painting, he did not reject the vitality of the artist's hands-on involvement with the photographic apparatus. Like the painter, the photographer's hand directed the unique aesthetic quality of the work. The act of simply pressing the button meant losing the work that led toward higher achievement in the photographic "moment," or in what Stieglitz referred to as "equivalents" between machine and human. The theory of "equivalents," as we will see, infused the machine/human dynamic with certain genderless qualities.

As Richard Whelan notes, "Truth, running, photography: the common denominators for Alfred were the intensity of striving, the testing of oneself, and the honor of the gentleman-sportsman."[38] Stieglitz encapsulated the odd (and often peculiar) pairing of American twentieth-century competitive enthusiasm with a romantic aesthetic spirit. Given Stieglitz's embrace of the aesthetic-machine, the merging of these two disparate forces grounded key aspects of his aesthetic theories. If the industrial age stripped away the aesthetic spirit of the traditional arts, Stieglitz was not in a position nor was he willing to simply dismiss de facto the industrial moment. Rather, as the good gentleman-sportsman figured, "It's not whether you win or lose, it's how you play the game."[39]

The artist must play fair and work hard. Little room was given (as Stieglitz insisted) to silly attempts at artistry or banal conceptual theories about art.[40] The ideal sportsman was equal to the ideal worker for Stieglitz because both created masterful objects (the body in the case of the sportsman) unparalleled in their dedication to detail, hard work, skill, and craftsmanship. The work ethic behind the object—no matter how sublime its affect—was lodged in the core principles of common sense. Thus, Stieglitz admired the "workingmen's quiet persistence, in the simple satisfactions he felt they derived from craftsmanship, the pride taken in a job well done."[41] As a well-trained craftsman, Stieglitz deciphered, analyzed, and developed the most efficient possible way to complete the best possible job (short of merely pressing the button). By negotiating the time-honored tension between the sublime and common sense, Stieglitz romanticized a functional American artist devoid of European pretense (but not necessarily of European theory). The artist was thus molded into nothing less than the nonartist, a figure at once transcendent, sublime, genderless, and grounded (albeit romantically) in the common sense of artisanship.

Gender Equivalents

As Christine Stansell writes, the "self-conscious attentiveness [of early twentieth-century bohemian culture] to the needs of and sensitivities of the New Woman would become, over the next two decades, a leitmotif of heterosexual relations in bohemia. In its own way, it would end up a liberal version of swagger, reworking feminist ideals of a sexually egalitarian life into a different set of male imperatives."[42] For the feminists of the first decade of the twentieth century, the step out of Victorian standards of womanhood often ushered a subsequent step into modernist performatives contained by masculinist ideology. To declassify oneself from the moral and practical dictates of traditional white womanhood and break into the manly terrains of, say, the arts and politics, meant assuming a masculine "swagger." In this logic, Stieglitz himself was attentive to what he called the changing "Social Order" and "the needs and sensitivities of the New Woman." Yet he had clear "male imperatives" about what sort of artist a woman must be in the era of twentieth-century "liberation."[43]

The ever-practical Stieglitz briskly dismissed excessive "femininity" and the decorative ornamentation associated with it, especially in the arts (or on the body of the artist—male and female). As Dorothy Norman observed, "He detests fuss and shopping, has no interest in fashion, cares about simplicity and quality. It matters little to him that his clothing is shabby, but it must be clean."[44] Edmund Wilson described his attire as one of an "expert 'technician' [rather] than the artist."[45] Likewise, his galleries were "undecorated . . . simple and unfinished."[46] He was attracted to women (such as O'Keeffe) who were practical. O'Keeffe's simplicity in dress (usually black or white or a combination thereof) appealed to Stieglitz's sense of an aesthetic that bespoke a pristine common sense.[47] Like the smooth-running machine and the well-trained athlete, the artist (women included) was to be a hardworking crafts*man*.[48] In living the poetic injunctions of Walt Whitman, a writer he greatly admired, Stieglitz had little patience for dilettantes and effusive cultural expenditure in the American arts.

This view of an efficient life and, especially, a stripped-down version of gender waxed eloquent for Stieglitz and his theory (nestled in the age of "enlightened" feminism) of equivalents. If the enthusiasm for the machine risked a culture of chaos and excess—gender included—Stieglitz sought for art a mechanical reproducibility that unified and made coherent a lived "moment" that was always under the pressure of modern disequilibrium: "My photographs are a picture of the chaos in the world, and of my relationship to that chaos. My prints show the world's constant upsetting of man's equilibrium, and his eternal battle to reestablish it . . . What is of great importance is to hold a moment, to record something so completely that those who see it will relive an equivalent of what has been expressed."[49] Stieglitz's dialectic presents, if only for a moment, an equivalents or synthesis that chaos yields. It comes as no surprise, then, that Stieglitz saw the greatest of his equivalents in his Whitmanesque series titled *Song of the Sky* where the images of clouds display the purest objective moment of nature—that is, of mechanically recorded nature.[50] For Stieglitz, the machine allowed for the ideal tactile moment—both sublime and concrete—between artist and object.

How was the twentieth-century artist to strike this moment of equivalence? Were women artists capable of such transcendence and common sense? For Stieglitz in 1919, the twentieth-century artist must bear in mind that while "man, the male, had thus far been the sole creator of ART . . . there is a new order in the course of development—if it is not already right with us—for those who see."[51] To "see," however, meant to maintain the traditional binaries of male and female essences that framed the equivalence of gender differentiation a priori masculine and heterosexual.

Although Woman, Stieglitz posited, "*feels* the world *differently* than Man feels it," the conjoining of abstract difference (gender-specific feeling) commingles at the point at which the tactile experience (aesthetics, sex) makes gender one. Further, the male artist must experience the changing "Social Order" through modern aesthetics where, by accepting women's place in the arts (a productive muse of sorts), he might, in turn, produce offspring (modern art) that transcends the limitations of gender. "Woman is still Woman," Stieglitz argues, "but not so entirely *His* Woman. The potential child [modern art] brings about its equivalent in other forms. It may be in Color and Line—Form—Painting. A need. Woman finding an outlet—*Herself*. *Her* Vision of the World—intimately related to Man's—nearly identical—yet different." [52] Modern artists—man and woman—produce an equivalent, the "potential child," or the moment of pure modern art. The artist's gender difference, presciently necessary, brings to the world new life through art that transcends, makes equivalent, those differences. Modern art is thus conceived here (and Stieglitz's inflection gives this a certain literalness) as the great equalizer of difference. Difference, however, always yields oneness only through and with Man. Thus, although a Woman rehearses her particular experiential feeling in art (that which is "distinctly feminine"), her rise to equivalence is measured against the terms of difference that are always already masculine: "Her Vision of the World [is] intimately related to Man's." To be a Woman artist was to be indeed the equivalent of Man to the extent that both male and female artists reproduce the masculine discourse of (gender) difference. Put another way, the artist purportedly transcends him/herself—the nonartist—yet preserves the gender-specific qualities of heterosexual (re)production. Ultimately, while Stieglitz welcomed Woman into the modern era of the arts, his equivalents meant something far less than a utopic genderless experience: Woman assumed at once a masculine "swagger" and maintained her reproductive "nature." [53] Moreover, Man's "need" to give birth, to reproduce an ideal genderless Other (modern art), preserved masculinist privilege and status in the American arts.

The Primitive Modern

When, as I describe in chapter 1, Edwin Forrest found his spiritual Otherness in the body of Push-ma-ta-ha, it was the Indian's sublime primitiveness (his national essence) that countered the decorative excesses of civilization (European tradition) that purportedly threatened the purity of the actor's masculine creativity. During the early twentieth century, the appeal to primitiveness for succor from artificial civilization had hardly waned. In fact, the frenzy of machine-age culture only heightened the call, especially for artists, to identify a pure primitiveness that would rein in the dangers that heartless, twentieth-century modernity proffered. For Strand, Sheeler, and the rest of Stieglitz's coterie, the search for spiritual primitivism was instrumental in the definition of American modernism because it revealed, as it had for Forrest, that which was specifically American. Critics and artists of the twentieth century discovered American primitivism (and, by extension, its rejection of European civilization) in an array of unexpected cultural venues.

In *Adventures in the Arts: Informal Chapters on Painters, Vaudeville, and Poets*, Marsden Hartley (Stieglitz's acolyte) tells his readers that he is "preoccupied with the business of transmutation—which is to say, the proper evaluation of life as idea, of experience as delectable diversion."[54] *Adventures in the Arts* thus sets out to explore the "moments" of the particularly American experience as it is served up in the traditional arts and in popular culture. Hartley, in his essay, "Vaudeville," applauds the peculiar uniqueness of these American cultural performances and insists on "severing" the art form from its "frayed traditions worn plush and sequin" and "rid them of the so inadequate back drop such as is given them, the scene of Vesuvius in eruption, or the walk in the park at Versailles" (162). Instead, American vaudeville actors and acrobats, like all American artists, "need first of all large plain spaces upon which to perform" (162). The break from the "frayed" backdrop of Europe (Vesuvius, Versailles) toward the "large plain spaces" of an American mise-en-scène makes way for a "place of laughter of the senses, for the laughter of the body" (173). Hartley, like his contemporaries, evokes the body's sensual experience in a minimalist space as part of the complete American work of art because, given freedom from materialist dross, the unencumbered (artist's) body explores itself while it creates art.

"I think a larger public," Hartley posits, "should be made aware of the beauty and skill of these people [vaudeville performers], who spend their lives in perfecting grace and power of the body, creating the always fascinating pattern and form, orchestration if you will, the orchestration of the muscles into a complete whole" (164). The "power of the body" derives from the total work where the perfection of grace and beauty is performed and unified. The pure, graceful, and beautiful body that performs on the plain and simple stage is thus uniquely American.

The vaudevillian acrobat is, more curiously, a body in the tradition of the American Indian. In this instance, Hartley's vaudevillian body is strikingly similar to Forrest's evocation of Push-ma-ta-ha's pure, pre-modern body. Hartley, for example, writes in his essay "The Red Man" that the American public must come to "cherish" the Indian since "he remains among us as the only esthetic representative of our great country up to the present hour" (13). The "red man" has inscribed, or left his "racial autograph," for Americans to realize the essence of their country. His "autograph" through the "beautiful gesture of his body" makes the name of America "something to be remembered" (13). As a "feast for the eye" (23), American artists (like Forrest's "feast" before them), must necessarily consume and ingest the American Indian and his pure Americaness in order to achieve the natural essence of their own American creativity. In fact, the American artist's turn toward the red man's "spiritual drama" will cleanse away any artificiality and immoral materialism plaguing the often "mediocre" (as Stieglitz would have it) aesthetic of realism.[55] The Indian ideally combines the effects of realism and nature: "It is therefore of a piece with his conception of nature and the struggle for realism is not necessary," Hartley argues, "since he is at all times the natural actor, the natural expresser of the indications and suggestions derived from the great theme of nature which occupies his mind, body, and soul" (18).

Recalling Push-ma-ta-ha's transcendent yet visceral place for Forrest in the arts (the "feast for the eye" where the "real" is determined as natural), Hartley's "red man" is conceived here as the ideal work of modern art. The Indian's authorial signature, especially through his ritual primitive dances, is the "living embodiment" of America's landscape (20), the "poet and artist of the very first order" (26), and he who must be preserved as a "sign of modernism" (28). Yet if, as Hartley states, the "primitives created a complete cosmos for themselves" that supports the terms for American modernism, how might noble-savage primitivism dovetail with machine-culture modernity and civilization? Indeed, the concatenation between primitivism and spiritualism rescued modernity from the materialist risks that machine culture portended.

James Harvey Robinson, founder of the New School for Social Research and a well-known figure among members of the Stieglitz circle, delighted in the knowledge that civilization—following the treatises of Darwin and other post-Enlightenment thinkers—was now understood as a shining example of the thinking human mind. In his book *The Mind in the Making: The Relation of Intelligence to Social Reform*, Robinson demonstrates the progression of "our animal heritage" to our modern intelligence. Although we never entirely lose the primitiveness of "our savage mind" we, as an advanced people of modern civilization, quite simply *see*. Those who see, however, are more rare and more intelligent than the common garden-variety human. "The seer," Robinson tells us (and recall here Stieglitz's emphasis on his ability to "see")

> is simply an example of a *variation* biologically, such as occurs in all species of living things, both animals and vegetable. But the unusually large roses in our gardens, the swifter horses of the herd, and the cleverer wolf in the pack have no means of influencing their fellows as a result of their peculiar superiority. Their offspring has some chance of sharing to some degree this pre-eminence, but otherwise things will go on as before. Whereas, the singular variation represented by a St. Francis, a Dante, a Voltaire, or a Darwin may permanently, and for ages to follow change somewhat, the character and ambitions of innumerable inferior members of the species who could by no possibility have originated anything for themselves, but who can, nevertheless, suffer modification as a result of the teachings of others. This illustrates the magical and unique workings of culture and creative intelligence in mankind.[56]

Thus, the modern (highly evolved) "seer" gives to civilization the gifts of knowledge and foresight. Among those privileged few are those artists such as Stieglitz who, in Lockean fashion, pour both the knowledge of a lost primitive past and transcendent future into the minds and bodies of the select few. But in what way does the trace of the primitive remain in modern civilization? In what way might primitivism preserve the spiritual possibilities of modernity?

Robinson, reiterating a commonplace of the period, states "it is certain, as many anthropologists have pointed out, that customs, savage ideas, and primitive sentiments have continued to form an important part of our own culture down even to the present day. We are met thus with the necessity or reckoning with this inveterate element in our present thought and custom" (87). For Robinson, this is a universal "reckoning." Paris, Berlin, London, and New York must confront the remains of their savageness and engage with it as part of contemporary existence. And though "chemists and physicians have given up talking of spirits" in their discussions of social and economic questions, "we are still victimized by the primitive animistic tendencies of the mind" (89). To refuse spirit, as chemists and physicians have, is to forgo a productive possibility between our (spiritual) savage and modern urban selves.

The primitive, potentially, resuscitates for modern man the spiritual that dissolves away in machine culture.

But if the "chemists and physicians" have shelved God and spirit, was it even possible to evoke a modern spirit in art? Ironically, the further that twentieth-century artists and philosophers moved away from what they saw as romanticized and God-inspired knowledge, the closer they approached the nineteenth-century views they disparaged. Though "victimized by the primitive animistic tendencies of the mind" it was precisely the truculent past that refashioned God as the spiritual guide to modernity. Push-ma-ta-ha and Hartley's "red man" both were to be "cherished" because they saturated the cold logic of modernity with a vigorous and primitive American spirit. The trick, however, was how to identify the primitivist and spiritual attributes of the modern machine.

With modern man's spirit secured through a vision of primitivism, twentieth-century modernists also turned to the "primitive" for all sorts of cultural and political reasons, not the least of which was to confirm the essence of modern whiteness. As Fatimah Tobing Rony suggests in her analysis of ethnographic culture and Robert Flaherty's 1922 film *Nanook of the North*, "Nanook was thus something of a mirror for the white audience: he too was from the North, and . . . like the Nordic, was seen as embodying the Protestant values of patriarchy, industriousness, independence and courage."[57] Moreover, if the primitive Other infused America's avant-garde with a sense of spiritual purpose, he also embodied the limitations of savage culture and affirmed the advancement of white civilization. This is to say, then, that the political modernist Left (I include here the Stieglitz milieu) was "fascinated" with the racial Other to the extent that their patronizing recognition of the "primitive" (not dissimilar to their views on women) confirmed their own evolutionary progress toward higher civilization.[58] American modernists thus turned to primitivism as a way to privilege, if not "mirror," their own cultural authority. The American modern spirit of the avant-garde was, in a word, white.

New York City

Perhaps nowhere was the dialectic impulse between primitiveness and civilization perceived more strongly than in the urban arena of New

York.[59] How was it possible, given the urban commotion and materialist excess that defined the city, for a transcendent spirit to even exist there? The oft-cited "savagery" of city life was easier to locate, especially since its discourse wended its way through editorial pages and the new sciences of anthropology and ethnography. Needless to say, the cultural stratosphere of "primitiveness" was grounded in a wide-ranging ideological framework. But the tension between "old" and "new" was not only reserved for the distinction between a prelapsarian age and twentieth-century American modernity. The long-awaited break from Old World institutions such as the Louvre and Parisian boulevards (not to mention Vesuvius and Versailles) took formidable shape in the place of New York when artists like Paul Rosenfeld remarked, "What had their beauty [of the Louvre, etc.] really to do with us? . . . It was the towers of Manhattan one wanted to see suddenly garlanded with loveliness." As Rosenfeld continued,

> One wanted life for [the towers] and for oneself together. Somewhere in one always there had been the will to take root in New York; to come into relation with the things and the people, not in the insane self-abnegation of current patriotism and nationalism, but in the form of one's utmost self; in the form of realizing all the possibilities for life shut inside one, and simultaneously finding oneself with people. Somewhere within, perhaps in obedience to some outer voice trusted in childhood, there was a voice which promised one day the consummation. One day a miracle should happen over the magnificent harbor, and set life thrilling and rhythming through the place of New York.[60]

If only, according to Rosenfeld, the moderns listened to the primitive "outer voice trusted in childhood," the city would provide a "fundamental oneness" through its "very jostling, abstracted streets" (292).[61] New York is the "embryo" ("faint" but "none the less evident" [292]) out of which American modern art will emerge. The paeans to New York such as Rosenfeld's were many. The city was American modern art itself; in the city machine modernity merged successfully with the spirit of the savage because, "one wanted life for [the towers] and for oneself together."

In New York (or, more aptly, because of New York) painters and photographers collapsed into their work Dada-inspired machine aesthetics, primitivist instincts, and the energetic charge of the American spirit.[62] John Marin, Charles Demuth, Charles Sheeler, Joseph

Stella, and Paul Strand embraced the city's energy as a sign of America's unique place in the international arts. Likewise, Alfred Stieglitz's photographs of the city's street scenes (*Fifth Avenue* [1893] and *The Terminal* [1893], as well as his skyline shots *City of Ambition* [1910] and the newly erected Flatiron Building [*The Flatiron*, 1902–3]) recognized the new America as an assemblage of primitive frontier myth and modern progress flanked by the modern progress of towering architecture, the remains of nature, and bustling street scenes. "The tree in the foreground," Karen Lucic suggests about *The Flatiron*, "seems to embrace the building; both grow out of the same earth."[63] Indeed, New York embodied the ideal fusion of an eternal nature and modern urbanity (and Theodore Roosevelt might very well have agreed with this view).

Yet, the city's spirit was also one of frenetic frisson and thrilling surprise precisely because of its jumbled existence of primitive modernity. The artist's body was intimately entwined with this production of the modern world. In 1929, Stella reflected on his experience painting *The Bridge*, his vision of the Brooklyn Bridge in 1922:

Many nights I stood on the bridge—and in the middle alone—lost—a defenseless prey to the surrounding swarming darkness—crushed by the mountainous black impenetrability of the skyscrapers—here and there lights resembling suspended falls of astral bodies or fantastic splendors of remote rites—shaken by the underground tumult of the trains in perpetual motion, like the blood in the arteries—at times, ringing as alarm in a tempest, the shrill sulphurous voice of the trolley wires—now and then strange moanings of appeal from tug boats, guessed more than seen, through the infernal recesses below—I felt deeply moved, as if on the threshold of a new religion or in the presence of a new DIVINITY.[64]

Thus, the city comprised the ideal (and so, spiritual) commingling of modern primitiveness ("mountainous" skyscrapers, "sulphurous" trolley wires, guttural "moanings" of tug boats), bodiliness ("like the blood in the arteries"), and American spirit ("DIVINITY"). The view of the city as the creative force through which the primitive spirit melded with modern technology helped to mitigate the risks that more-obscure abstractness purportedly held.

As many of these artists quickly realized, however, if twentieth-century America was a place, an idea, like nothing before it, the traditional arts could hardly account for the nation's—especially New York's—kinetic newness. The struggle to identify American modernity through painting and literature had, for many, run its course (which was hinted at by Duchamp when he laid down his paintbrush in 1918 — a suggestion well understood by several American artists).[65] Photography, certainly apposite as a mechanical tool for revealing modernity, was very much a nineteenth-century (and, to be sure, European) medium. Though photography set the stage for the mechanical arts, it was the Americans, according to the Americans, who theoretically and practically transformed it into a twentieth-century modern art form. Yet photography was not entirely satisfactory for registering the energy of America. The cinema was in place — begrudgingly for some, enthusiastically for others — to be not merely the art form of the twentieth century. More significantly, the cinema stood in position as America's art form precisely because it was derived from the machine. Since, as Leo Marx suggests in another context, "Americans have seized upon the machine as their birthright" and the "best of the fine arts — statuary, painting, and architecture [was] still to be found in the Old World,"[66] the cinema was an art form built upon a specifically American industrial enterprise. But, more important, it was perceived as a medium untouched by the hands of European artists and cultural tastemakers. The cinematic machine also embodied, as we will see, the ideal mix of primitivist and modernist instincts.

After twenty-odd years, the American artists Paul Strand and Charles Sheeler rejected the film industry's drive toward popular narrative, and in 1920 they shot and produced what is thought of as the first American avant-garde film, *Manhatta* (or, as it was renamed by the owner of the Rialto during the film's first run in a mainstream theater, *New York the Magnificent*).[67] The spiritual transcendence of the American artist, emboldened by New York's savage modernism, solidified in this cinematic experiment. Clearly thought of as a modernist intervention by its Stieglitz-trained makers, it would take, ironically, an international jury of artists to recognize it as cinematic art; that is, a work of cinema that was both art and American.

Film as American Art

In 1915 (the year that *The Battle Cry of Peace* and *The Birth of a Nation* were released) Vachel Lindsay published *The Art of the Moving Picture*. Lindsay's book caused somewhat of a sensation, not because it was the first critical study of film as art but because it awakened for museum curators and university professors a way to explore this popular phenomenon in terms reserved for those holding a certain academic savoir-faire. The call to position cinema as art, however, did not prevent Lindsay's endorsement of the commercially successful D. W. Griffith (the "king"). Lindsay applauded the cinema in its popular form when, in the hands of directors such as Griffith, it achieved "moods" found in "Whitmanesque scenarios."[68] Though the director worked within the industry, Griffith achieved filmic "splendor" because of his cinematic "simplicity" (85). Unlike the overstated Italian, Gabrielino D'Annunzio, Griffith (more like Whitman from Lindsay's perspective) organized the richness of historical glory and patriotism by making the "sophisticated" democratic (93).[69] Griffith thus fulfilled Lindsay's analytical premise of his book: "*The motion picture art is a great high art, not a process of commercial manufacture*" (45). Griffith's films, according to Lindsay, might emerge from a commercial industry, but his artistry transcended such vulgarity. The experiences of sublime cinematic encounters were rare and identifiable only in a very select group of films. Yet, since so few directors existed who pushed cinema outside the aesthetic impurities of commercialism as Griffith had, Lindsay augured a Whitmanesque model of cinema for other filmmakers that followed Ezra Pound's imagist aesthetic.

Imagism (founded the year of the Armory Show) was an ideal modernist aesthetic—albeit a literary one—through which Lindsay sought to map a new American cinema. In line with his contemporaries, Lindsay envisioned a cinematic art drawn from a principle of primitive hieroglyphics and modernist poetry. The cinema, as Lindsay saw it, was a primitive art whose language had yet to "evolve" as it had for literary masters of prose such as Mark Twain and William Dean Howells (211). Twain and Howells, however, were of the nineteenth century while imagist poetry elevated language to a new stage in the twentieth. Though Lindsay does not draw a direct link between his discussions of hieroglyphics and imagist poetry, his interest in both forms' structure (a series of distinct juxtaposed images that realizes a complex idea) is at the heart of his larger theory. Imagism (an aesthetic form destined to move beyond its literariness) and Egyptian hieroglyphics suited the cinema's primary property of montage. "Imagist photoplays," writes Lindsay, "would be Japanese prints taking on life, animated Japanese paintings, Pompeian mosaics in kaleidoscope but logical succession,

Beardsley drawings made into actors and scenery, Greek vase-paintings in motion" (268). The fusing together of "Pompeian mosaics in kaleidoscope" with "Beardsley drawings," of primitive and modern civilizations (in "logical succession" of course), set the stage for a Whitmanesque form of discrete fragmented images (akin to Whitman's poetic lists) of Americana that recalls the particular aesthetic that Milton Brown termed "cubist-realism."

Lindsay's treatise called on the artist-filmmaker to stimulate the primitive past (the hieroglyphic parlance of Egypt) to successfully bring forth a higher spiritual realm in which crass and materialist America was tempered. A full and rich modern American art would thus emerge. "And this invention, the kinetoscope," writes Lindsay, "which affects or will affect as many people as the guns of Europe, is not yet understood in its powers, particularly those of bringing back the primitive in a big rich way. The primitive is always a new and higher beginning to the man who understands it" (290). The primitive will rescue the spiritual death that Americans confront in the age of the mechanically recorded motion picture: "By studying the matter of being an Egyptian priest, the author-producer may learn in the end how best to express and satisfy the spirit-hungers that are peculiarly American. It is sometimes out of the oldest dream that the youngest vision is born" (288).[70] For Lindsay, the machine, especially the cinematic machine, could bring about a spiritual art because it ultimately and deeply emerged from primitivist beginnings.

As a coda to his discussion of "Imagist cinema," Lindsay argues that motion pictures should "confine" themselves to "a half or quarter reel, just as the Imagist poem is generally a half or quarter page" (268). Lindsay's claims for cinematic brevity are at once primitive and modern. That is, situated within "Imagist textures" the cinema should elicit a complex mood yet be simple in its delivery. There is no need for overextravagant images and unnecessarily long films.[71] Although Lindsay did not discuss *Manhatta* specifically in his later writings, Strand and Sheeler's film clearly met his terms for an "Imagist" cinema because it juxtaposed carefully selected and measured images of "sulphurous" yet modern New York that (indeed directly) evoked the simplicity of Whitmanesque scenarios. The film came in just over seven minutes long.

Charles Sheeler

> MARTIN FRIEDMAN: Do you think that there is—this is a
> very grim question—such a thing as American art today?
> CHARLES SHEELER: Oh, yes, I think so. I think so.
> MARTIN FRIEDMAN: What do you think are its qualities?
> CHARLES SHEELER: Well, that's the sixty-four million dollar
> question.
> —interview with Charles Sheeler, 1959

As we have seen, the identity of the American artist during the early part of the twentieth century was developed through the miasmic whirl of modern *isms*. Charles Sheeler, like his contemporaries, viewed the American artist as one who embodied the conflict between the tradition of commonsense realism and machine-inflected abstraction. Though Sheeler was predominantly a painter (he did, however, work from photographs to execute his paintings), the industrial arts provided for him the provocative means with which to breach the schism between realism and abstraction. Perhaps more important, and central to Sheeler's work, the camera-machine sutured the artist into this aesthetic-cultural gap.[72] Sheeler's recognized achievement to bridge the seemingly indissoluble relationship between realism and abstraction found its success precisely through his inextricable linking and projection of the work of art with the artist's body. That is, his commingling of art and artist, realism and abstraction, the machine and nature, and the primitive with the spiritual portrayed Sheeler himself as the ideal modernist work of art.

For many, Sheeler's industrial-pastoralized abstract realism successfully signaled American art as American. Indeed, Constance Rourke, when writing her book *Charles Sheeler: Artist in the American Tradition*, impelled Sheeler to frame his work within a cultural context, a modernist force, indubitably American.[73] Sheeler's belief in, yet uncertainty about ("the sixty-four million dollar question"), the existence of "American art" did not prevent him from articulating the aesthetic qualities of a national art that punctuated his work. Throughout their extensive correspondence during her book's preparation, Rourke persistently requested that Sheeler describe, clarify, and define his visual concept of America and his aesthetic of realism. "I suppose the theme of [my] whole book," Rourke informed Sheeler, "is that of realism, your approaches to it and your final definitions."[74] Rourke, preempting Sheeler's response to this letter, goes on to articulate how she envisaged his "major progress . . . to have been from an interest in transitory to the permanent in appearances—and what constitutes permanence is in one way or another what you develop later, showing the contributory influences—photography, architecture, the crafts, these on the American side." As Rourke viewed it, and as Sheeler confirmed throughout his career, his view of American realism did not solely draw on the abstract qualities of the modern plastic arts. More important is that Sheeler's art accentuated the "permanence" of Americanness (at least in "appearance") that is found in American craftsmanship and in the crafts themselves. The labor involved in and the materialist "sensuous expression" of American products, according to Rourke, concretized the more "transitory" idealism of America that found its fruition in Sheeler's aesthetic enterprise.[75] Indeed, Sheeler's aesthetic seemingly resolved the all-important balance between modern abstraction and the tradition of realism: "I had come to feel that a picture could have incorporated in it the structural design implied in abstraction and be presented in a wholly realistic manner."[76]

Nonetheless, as Sheeler told art historian Martin Friedman in 1959, "I'm still fussing around being written about as a realist."[77] This was most likely because Sheeler claimed that American realism culled a complicated nexus of multiple and variable realisms that he alternately called "direct realism" (7) and, more often, "selective realism" (11; in Sheeler's mind these terms uneasily referred to Thomas Eakins, Shaker arts and crafts, and industrial factory and barn architecture).[78] As Sheeler recognized, many American realisms existed. Yet, Rourke accurately indicated and identified a strand of realism favored by Sheeler that emerged through the painter's own theories of functionalism artistically rendered through his "precision of vision and hand."[79] To be sure, Sheeler consistently qualified "selective realism" with his emphasis on its aesthetic relationship to craftsmanship, especially the functional and precisionist craftsmanship associated with the Shaker community of Pennsylvania. In this way, Sheeler drew a direct line from the simple efficiency of Shaker architecture, folk-art craftsmanship, and functional design to his own paintings and photographs.[80] But "selective realism" was not exclusively dedicated to theories of functionalism and machine efficiency. The "spirit" of modernity also moved Sheeler, as I will point out, as it had moved his contemporaries.

Born in Doylestown, Pennsylvania, in 1883, Sheeler later studied at the Pennsylvania Academy with the traditionalist dandy William Merritt Chase, who taught his students "to catch the fleeting moment" with quick brushstrokes. At this time, Sheeler befriended student-artists Walter Pach and Morton Schamberg with whom he traveled and studied in Europe in the early 1900s. While in Europe the student-artists studied and were trained in the works of Velásquez, El Greco, and Hals. Friedman and Rourke both argue that Sheeler viewed Cézanne's and the cubists' paintings as early as 1909; works that profoundly influenced him, as they did many other American artists.[81]

While many artist-émigrés returning at the time stationed themselves in New York, Sheeler frequented the city only as a visitor until he moved there more permanently in 1919. On his return from Europe in 1910, Sheeler instead went to Philadelphia where he rented a small weekend barn/studio in Bucks County, not far from Doylestown and near his beloved Shakers and the Barber Collection of Pennsylvania German crafts. Later, Sheeler shared the studio with Schamberg with whom he had become extremely close.[82] Doylestown lent Sheeler an environment more practical both for making a living and for developing his American "selective realism." In Pennsylvania, Sheeler received a steady income when he turned his talents to architectural photography. Subsequently the camera played a central role in Sheeler's approach to painting in America where the photograph often recorded the objects he brought to the canvas. It is possible, as Lucic suggests, that photography "helped Sheeler to overcome his over-dependence on foreign precedents in his painting practice."[83]

Loosely connected to the Arensberg Circle, Sheeler, when visiting New York, met Duchamp and Picabia at the art patron's late-night salons. Sheeler spent time at 291 with the members of the Stieglitz milieu, particularly with the other Pennsylvanian, Charles Demuth, and, later, with Paul Strand. While much of the New York art scene developed under Stieglitz's tutelage, Sheeler only partially immersed himself in the energy of modern urbanity, preferring instead to hone his aesthetic interests around the more "native architecture" (as Rourke termed it) of Bucks County where "the functional intention was very beautifully realized."[84] This does not mean to suggest, however, that

Sheeler entirely unplugged himself from New York events or Stieglitz's aesthetic theories. As early as 1913, Arthur Davies, an artist and the principal organizer of the Armory Show, invited Sheeler and Schamberg to participate in the exhibit where they presented their Cézanne- and Fauve-inflected work. After Schamberg's sudden death in 1918, Sheeler sold his Pennsylvania dwelling and made his move to New York. Sheeler, however, still shied away from the more hypermodern lifestyle in which New York artists imbibed. His "fine workman's sensibility"—a persona he cultivated—was considered to be more precise and acute because it evolved from the more placid surroundings in which he worked. The "artist-craftsman" dualism, as Friedman points out, "never seems to have concerned him."[85] Indeed, in rejecting the dilettantish identification with effete and urbane artistry, Sheeler marched strongly to the American beat of craftsmanship where his worker-creator persona transcended the dilettantish idea of the artist. Sheeler's nonartist presentation of self ideally suited the nonartsiness of his work.

Although removed from the onslaught of urban modernist theories and aesthetics that his more citified contemporaries parlayed, Sheeler's form-follows-function aesthetic fit snugly with the American modernist tendencies couched in "cubist-realist" precisionism, romanticized nature, and the "middle tradition" framed by the spirit of Whitman on which Van Wyck Brooks insisted. Whitman certainly played a decisive role in Sheeler's more spiritual concerns with modernity. But Sheeler's work also evoked its spiritualness through the American amalgam of primitivism and modern individualism. Unlike Stieglitz's aesthetic that carried a residue of the Old World, Sheeler's work, it was thought, let go of that albatross and liberated America's reliance on someone else's past. America's "spiritual hunger" was thus satisfied in the hands of the American craftsmen.

Self-Portraits, Embodying a National Spirit

Sheeler's painting and photography was directed by a functional idealism, and as such it supported the artist's theory that, as cited above, "a picture could have incorporated in it the structural design implied in abstraction and be presented in a wholly realistic manner." Leo Marx's suggestion that Sheeler's painting *American Landscape* (1930)

Charles Sheeler, *American Landscape*. 1930. Oil on Canvas. Museum of Modern Art/Licensed by SCALA/Art Resource, New York.

was "industrialized landscape pastoralized" rightly emphasizes the realist/idealist tensions underlying the production through which Sheeler's American "selective realism" came to terms with modernist abstraction.[86] Yet, in what way did Sheeler's vision of American industrialization encapsulate the spirituality for which most moderns so achingly searched? How did Sheeler "select" the modernist tropes of realism and abstraction, primitivism and modernity, to project the creative energies of the individual and unique American artist? Sheeler's turn to "Greek, Egyptian, Persian, and Negro art" was surely, Rourke tells us, "in part at least an effort to find an answer to the primordial question."[87] From the "Aztec to the Pennsylvanian," Rourke posits, the "structural truth, and a singular unity" of form revealed Sheeler's quest for an artistic essence cradled in a truly American craftsmanship whose materialist roots came from a pure primitivist past. Indeed, American modernity reached a crucial moment when its artists, pace Sheeler, recognized the complex cultural and spiritual intersections formed through the nation's indigenous origins (the "red man"), the agrarian-myth foundation, the machine-based present, and the artist himself. *Side of White Barn* (1917), *Self-Portrait* (1923), and the later works *Upper Deck* (1928) and *View from New York* (1931) are modernist because they convey the spiritual "structural unity" built at the crossroads of the primitive and modern, the "industrialized" and "pastoralized," and realism and abstraction: "Few primitives have been at the same time so simple and complex," Rourke cheers (143).

Shortly after completing, with Strand, the film *Manhatta*, Sheeler presented his drawing *Self-Portrait*. This work is instructive because it draws together the multiple levels at which the twentieth-century American artist cast himself as a modern work of art. In the drawing, a telephone is in the foreground, situated on a table in front of a window. The grayed window serves as the telephone's background and bears the shadowy reflection of, presumably, the artist whose head is out of frame and, in the space of the drawing, is hidden by the window's shade. Lucic argues that *Self-Portrait* and other key works such as this (e.g., *View from New York*) are "playfully perverse" while also pointing to Sheeler's uneasy and ironic relationship with machine culture.[88] Carol Troyen and Erica Hirshler suggest that the work is an "expression of loneliness," while Susan Fillin-Yeh more provocatively declares: "The telephone is the artist."[89] I'd like to follow Fillin-Yeh's assertion that

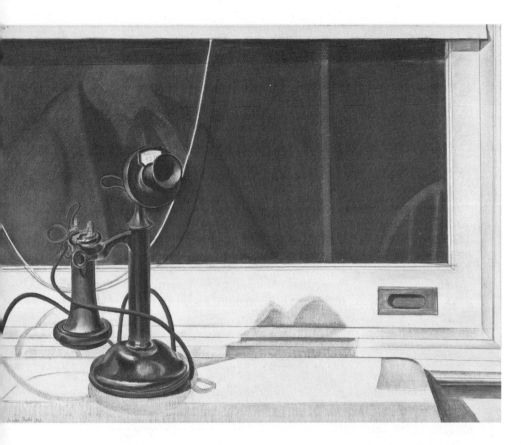

Charles Sheeler, *Self-Portrait*. 1923. Conte crayon, gouache, and pencil on paper. Museum of Modern Art/Licensed by SCALA/Art Resource, New York.

Sheeler's *Self-Portrait* (and this is the obvious example, but his body of work I believe bears this out) projects the artist as machine.

In her assertion Fillin-Yeh redirects the concept of identity in twentieth-century self-portraiture toward an analysis of masculinist narcissism and the embodiment of a modernist sublime. In other words, the twentieth-century artist's body presented in a performative repose as industrialized object (recalling albeit transforming Fried's arguments about "absorption" as a performance) is disclosed as a transcendent yet materialist identification with modern machine culture. The shadowy figure that once stood for the traditional artist's self-portrait merely haunts the image from its margins and foregrounds Rourke's suggestion that Sheeler's work continually shifts between the transitory (shadowed corporeality) and the permanent (the machine), with an accent on the permanent. Where permanence is ultimately achieved, however, is through the artist's projection of self, a self realized concretely in its embodiment with the machine. The artist's body, like the work of art itself, in Sheeler's view, achieves a unified oneness, a modern spirituality, reached at the apex between realism and abstraction, a commingling of body and machine.

But how does Sheeler surmount the spiritual battle with the machine if the machine signals overmaterialist permanence and the loss of human spirit? How does Sheeler's art forge a revival of spirituality within materialist-crazed modernity? Does *Self-Portrait* lay bare the more painful realization of man's lost spirit in the machine age? James Maroney, in his 1999 essay "Charles Sheeler Reveals the Machinery of His Soul," challenges the notion of Sheeler's "playfully perverse" occupation with machine culture. Maroney argues against Lucic's contention, for example, that Sheeler's evocation of formal simultaneity between his paintings *Criss-Cross Conveyors* (1927) and *Chartres Cathedral—Flying Buttresses at the Crossing* (1929) recommends the artist's belief in a transhistoricity between machine culture and architecture.[90] As Maroney sees it, such arguments neglect Sheeler's more complicated theories of modern space that yearn for a spiritual reawakening, and that his "deeply personal philosophical issues" in his approach to art undermine a strictly formalist and functionalist characterization of his work. "Just as a cathedral is a container of spirit, not a representation of stone," Maroney points out with regard to Sheeler's modernist vision, "a ship too [or factory!] is a container of spirit, not a representation of mechanical hardware" (34). This is true, to an extent, but I'd like to cast

Sheeler's mutual theoretical interests in precisionism and spirituality as an intricate component of narcissistic projection operating within the discourses of "simple," yet "complex," American craftsmanship and machine-based industrial labor.

Sheeler's projection of self in his work suggests two things. First, the ideal, unified structural balance between the real and the abstract, machine and human, and artist/craftsman and work of art is inextricably linked to Sheeler's position as a "precisionist" who believed it necessary "to eliminate the means to the end, meaning the technique as far as possible and to present the subject in itself without the distraction of the means achieving it."[91] The artist's technique as well as the artist himself were no longer, according to Sheeler, a "distraction" when the "means to the end" was "eliminated." Since Sheeler conceived modern art as precision based, it was so to the extent that art functions as a sublime experience at once real and ideal. To announce one's disappearance from the creative process as artist thus projects a privileged authorial presence of labor both seen and unseen. That is, the labor of art making and, indeed, craftsmanship of the traditional sort, is posited here as a commonsense activity, a natural and transparent practice. Craftsmanship is simply a performance of unexcessive labor: it just is, one just does it. The Shaker's construction of the unadorned and useful chair thus should be, as Sheeler would have it, no different than the artist's construction of a painting or photograph. Simplicity. Hard work. Labor as common sense. And in such quiet manual labor involved in the work of art, a modern spirit is achieved.

How was the purported simplicity of labor reified yet simultaneously eliminated from a decided materialist presence? Moreover, how was the artist/laborer's authorship spiritually and materially marked if authorial presence was to be eliminated? Sheeler (like Stieglitz and many others) championed the intimate use value associated between the craftsman's experience of work and the object itself. Sheeler, following Stieglitz, invested the concept of the portrait with the necessary theoretical tools to facilitate the work of art as a totalizing experience.[92] In this way, the intimate bonding of artist-worker, machine, and art object was one of spiritual transcendence, not disappearance. The dramatic display of technique may have been "eliminated" but the presence of the artist remained in its simplest form. In other words, the concrete object of labor (the chair, the painting, the photograph) was nothing less than the artist/craftsman's self-portrait.

The second area of significance in what I see as Sheeler's narcissistic projection is the infusion of primitive spirit into the modern machine. In Sheeler's work, it is the machine's spiritual nature—the youngest vision built from the "oldest dream," to paraphrase Linsday—with which the American artist's identification is made. Sheeler secures both his primitive and modern self (from the "Aztec to the Pennsylvanian") by ingesting the modern-primitive Other (machine) and projecting it onto the canvas and the screen. By othering the machine as primitive (that is, by assigning a primitive spirit to it), Sheeler is similar to Edwin Forrest when the actor euphorically ingested the primitive other's essence so as to project his idealized masculine and national identity in the American arts.

All Sheeler's works are thus "American" self-portraits. Paul Strand echoes this concept of the self-portrait in allowing for the suggestion that *Manhatta* is the artists' self-portrait extraordinaire. Sheeler's act of projecting the telephone as his "self-portrait" was not so much meant as irony or as a critical engagement with machine culture; rather, his projection of the modern machine—his projection of self—asserts his artist-craftsman's identification with modern civilization and savagery as one wedded to a "middle tradition" ensconced in American realism and idealism. Because the artist reproduces, embodies, and identifies the self in unison with the work of art—an "equivalents" rendered in line, color, and form—he himself is de facto American modern art.

Paul Strand

The aesthetic and spiritual place of the American modern artist figure signaled an urgent philosophical-creative matter for the young Paul Strand: to what extent should the artist concern himself with abstraction over materialism? The stakes were high for the photographer since his theories of machine-age art were predicated on the expression of "life" itself and between concerns of the permanent and the transitory. "For Strand," Milton Brown tells us, "modernity if not modernism lay in the machine rather than abstraction."[93] Strand's theories and practices of creative abstraction, like those of Sheeler, remained "within the mode of realism; his images are always recognizable traces of a familiar world."[94] But Strand's aesthetic interests deeply coincided with Alfred Stieglitz's belief in American individualism and the unique "moment."

In 1917, Strand declared that "absolute unqualified objectivity" specifc to photography must achieve "living expression" through its ideal fusion of abstraction and realism.[95] Moreover, photography's properties allow for something more than the traditional arts offered. In the photograph, Strand contends, "the objects may be organized to express the causes of which they are the effects, or they may be used as abstract forms, to create an emotion unrelated to the objectivity as such." But the organization of materials for the camera is secondary to the "shallow or profound" spiritual expression brought to the object by the artist who, like all artists, moves "toward the common goal, which is Life" (525).

Americans, according to Strand, were ahead of the game in unleashing the "living expression" latent in the machine arts. In his writings on photography and American art, he remarks: "There is no real consciousness, even among photographers, of what has really happened: namely, that America has really been expressed in terms of America without the outside influence of Paris art-schools or their dilute offspring here."[96] As this statement makes clear, Strand believed in photography because it vitally presented America through the work of Americans. For Strand, the aesthetic truths inherent to the photographic medium were fostered (unlike any other place in the world) because of American journals such as Stieglitz's *Camera Work*. In these pages, artistic expression was privileged as the giver of "Life"; artistic expression found its fullest manifestation through photography because a there does exist there and the machine's social relationship to the world comes to light in this particular art (although the "social" value of art is always present in Strand's thought and work, it was not until the 1930s that it took on its strongest characteristics).[97]

Strand was raised in a middle-class family on New York's Upper West Side; his father was involved in the manufacture of lathes (indeed, Strand's 1923 photograph *Lathe* is perhaps an homage to, or a projection of, his father). At the age of fourteen (in 1904) Strand entered the Ethical Culture School (which was initially conceived as a "Workingman's School") where a science teacher, Lewis Hine (the soon-to-be social-realist photographer), introduced Strand to photography and, significantly, Stieglitz's 291 gallery.[98] The wide socio-aesthetic differences imposed by Hine and Stieglitz apparently left their mark, since Strand's career was one that consistently battled the perceived chasm between the social implications (Hine) and the aesthetic theories (Stieglitz) of

Paul Strand. *Lathe, Akeley Shop, New York. 1923.* © 1971 Aperture Foundation Inc., Paul Strand Archive.

art.[99] Stieglitz, however, heavily guided Strand's early work, as did the European modernism to which Stieglitz introduced the young photographer at 291 and at the Armory Show.

In 1918 Strand was drafted into the military where he served as an X-ray technician and developed an interest in shooting medical films. Prior to entering the military, as Naomi Rosenblum points out, Strand's antiwar position aligned with that of Stieglitz and with the outspoken pacifist Randolph Bourne, with whom he had corresponded about wartime politics. Once drafted, however, Strand formed an allegiance to the military because he found it a "character-building" experience that "enriched" his skills as a photographer and cinematographer.[100] In 1919 Strand returned home and found work in advertising where he photographed Hess-Bright ball bearings while he continued to expand his portfolio and theoretical positions on art.

According to Jan-Christopher Horak, Strand met Sheeler as early as 1917 at Stieglitz's gallery. By the time Sheeler moved to New York in 1919—the year Strand returned home from the military—both had formed strong aesthetic philosophies about the camera and its relationship to the other arts. The painter/photographer Sheeler and the photographer/cinematographer Strand joined forces when, as legend has it,

Sheeler showed Strand his newly purchased French Debrie motion picture camera. Thrilled by their mutual theoretical interests and enthusiasm for the camera-machine, the two artists set out to explore the limits of the cinematic arts. Both strove to situate the industrial visual arts as both a recognized form of art and a representative of distinct American modernism. Furthermore, Strand, like Sheeler, claimed the centrality of the spiritual if not religiosity of the machine—a spirituality made necessary in godless modernity. In Strand's view, a new modern God revived the now-chilled spirituality of modernity and brought "living expression" to mechanical vacuity. Unlike the Dadaist playfulness of, say, Morton Schamberg's plumbing-trap sculpture *God* (1917–18), Strand earnestly reached for God's more spiritual, life-affirming function.

In his essay "Photography and the New God," Strand called on American photographers to embrace the discrete creative possibilities that the camera-machine made available. The camera, as Strand viewed it, elicited a "new religious impulse" and integrated the "intuitive and aesthetic [and] conceptual and scientific."[101] The American artist, according to Strand, stood front and center of a new era in which he might transform the new God (the camera-machine) into creative expression just as scientists before them had transformed God (the labor-machine) into "practical expression" and efficient craftsmanship. Strand warned, however, that the artist would lose his individuality and be "quickly ground to pieces under the heel of the new God" unless he managed the "tremendous task of controlling the heel" (253). If he met such a task, the artist would find "immense possibilities in the creative control" of the machine and "the new God" would be humanized.

To support his case for the new American God, Strand turned to the "American in America," Alfred Stieglitz, to make his case for human expression in the mechanical arts. It was, after all, Stieglitz who led photography out of the European traditions of pictorialism; placed the camera "here in America, the supreme altar of the new God"; and tempered unwieldy acts of mechanical excess in the photographic arts (257). Because of Stieglitz, Strand declares, "we find a highly-evolved crystallization of the photographic principle, the unqualified subjugation of a machine to the single purpose of expression" (255). Stieglitz showed the artist that the "moment" recorded by the photographer was one "significantly related to other moments in his experience" (256). If we recall Stieglitz's theory of "equivalents" we can see, concomitantly, Strand's view of "crystallization" as one that underscores the intimate and historically layered moment, the relationship of "other moments," realized between photographer, subject, and machine. The implications of the direct recording of space and time are even more dramatic since, "so perceived, the whole concept of a portrait takes on a new meaning" (256). Indeed, the complex experiential moment between photographer and subject is revealed in its entire objective truth ("Life") precisely because of the machine. That is, the mechanical work of art displays something more than painting ever could: "The portrait of the individual is really the sum of a hundred or more photographs" (such postulates later informed the theoretical concepts held by the artists who published Stieglitz's *Collective Portrait*).

In Strand's Bergsonian inscription of time and space the individual and the artist's spirit are revealed precisely because the photographer's eye has joined—is embodied with—the "eye of the machine" (256). An intricate converging of artist, subject, and machine reaffirms yet reconfigures the time-honored belief that man is made in the image of God. As Strand would have it, man, in the twentieth century, is both the image and humanizer of God. The modern (self-)portraits of man are conceived, therefore, as a mechanical recording of a lived moment, a unique divine equivalent. In this way, the mechanically recorded image projects the sublime portrait of man as the "new God," revealed as clouds for Stieglitz; the telephone and factory for Sheeler; and the lathe and automobile axel for Strand. But the most sublime American portrait that reflected the American artist was the "divinity" of New York City.

Manhatta: An American Self-Portrait

From its outset, the cinema presented "views" of New York street scenes and its skyline that were enjoyed by popular audiences. At the turn of the century New York City's skyline was both applauded and disparaged by critics,[102] but for many, including Theodore Roosevelt and J. Stuart Blackton, the city's skyline celebrated America's new frontier and its hefty ideological promise of national progress. The very threat of its demise, as *The Battle Cry of Peace* strongly implied, was a threat to American progress itself. In another register (yet not necessarily unlike Roosevelt's partial rooting of America's new frontier in

Walt Whitman's odes to the city), American avant-garde artists posited Manhattan, as I sketched above, as the creative center where the whole of the country's miasmic sensibilities (creative and otherwise) were digested and funneled into art.[103] New York was America's cultural modern center for the future. In reading William James's claims for a truly American philosophy, Ann Douglas points out, "The real greatness of America, in James's view, is its 'energy' and its 'light.' Boston and New England are the past; New York, the present and the future."[104] Stieglitz and his fellow modernists couldn't have agreed more, and they would most certainly have added Paris to the short list of modern cities manqué (it is worth noting that Stieglitz's last trip to Europe was made in 1912). Strand and Sheeler's designs on American modernity—couched in primitivism, machine culture, and "Life" spirit—thus found an ideal medium in the cinema to "register directly the living forms" of the city.[105] Although writers have criticized *Manhatta* for, in the words of Horak, its "lack of interest in human subjects" and for its dwarfing of humanity in the impersonal cityscape,[106] I'd like to argue that, in the minds of the film's makers at least, the film succinctly embodied human subjectivity—especially that of the artist-craftsman and the city. *Manhatta*, put quite simply, is a portrait of America's twentieth-century modernity and the twentieth-century artist.

When *Manhatta*, as *New York the Magnificent*, screened at the Rialto it was no wonder that it was received like any other New York "view." The film's dramatic shots of the thriving metropolis interlaced with Whitman's encomiums presented a towering and efficient Manhattan. Yet, why is it that this film could be successfully received both as a mainstream short film and as an avant-garde work? Ideologically, the film, according to Horak, "position[s] the spectator in a discourse of symbiosis in which nature and technology harmonize" (15). This may be true, in part, but for New York artists the film generated something altogether quite different. And although Horak stresses *Manhatta*'s "romanticism . . . of a particularly American variety, visionary and utopian, yet simultaneously naïve, trapped in the norms of bourgeois idealism" (15), the film is also the embodied projection of masculine narcissism (of a particular "American variety"). Paul Rosenfeld's declaration that "one wanted life for [the towers] and *for oneself together*," finds fecund realization in *Manhatta* in that the American *gesamtkunstwerk* that Rosenfeld sought takes place through the kinetic energy of the film where a living expression of modernity—the commingling of artist and machine art—is corporeally and spiritually embodied though and with Manhattan's towers cinematically recorded.

In their 1921 press release, scripted by Strand, the filmmakers (promoting the film under the title *New York the Magnificent*) state that the artists' collaborative "special knowledge gained from experiments in still photography" has allowed them to turn to the motion-picture medium and "register" the "elusive spirit of a place." In "restricting themselves definitely to the towering geometry of lower Manhattan and its environs" the photographers have "tried to register directly the living forms in front of them and to reduce through the most rigid selection, volumes, lines and masses, to their intensest [*sic*] terms of expression."[107] What this collaborative "registration" of lower Manhattan's "living forms" evokes, Strand concludes, is "spirit manifest itself." The towers are not merely "geometry," they are life expressions; the cinema brings forth something more than photographic stillness. With the cinema, Stieglitz's equivalents took on new life.

To claim the self-portrait as something more than a direct reflection of the artist is not new. Stieglitz's aesthetic theories of "embodied formalism," as discussed earlier, provide for a much wider definition of the traditional "self-portrait." Given the urgency that America's modernists confronted to identify and project their nationalist experiences into a work of art, the jury was still out as to whether or not painting and photography could convey this twentieth-century challenge. Though after *Manhatta* Sheeler would return to painting for the remainder of his career and Strand would dedicate most of his time to photography and work only intermittently as a cinematographer, the cinema in 1920 held significant promise for these artists since it brought to life their aesthetic theories of equivalents and craftsmanship prescient to the machine age. The cinema-machine opportunely supplied the means to render an American self-portrait like none other before it.

Seen as a self-portrait, it is instructive to consider how *Manhatta* draws together a set of cinematic images to project the American artist's embodied experience. The film, I argue, explores four theoretical areas about the artist-filmmakers' relationship to what was perceived as the specific quality of American art: first, the film posits that the artist and city laborers (the artists-craftsmen) work as co-equal builders of the city through the use of primitivist and modernist tools; second, the artists-filmmakers work in the consecrated tradition of Whitman to emphasize the transcendent intermingling of the worker with the artist in the material world; third, the film reiterates the artist-filmmaker as a twentieth-century body who "sees" where an equivalence is made when the artist's eye becomes "one together" with the work and the mechanical apparatus; and, fourth, the film demonstrates the cinema-machine as a tool that fulfills the experience of modern and spiritual expression. Further, although writers such as Alan Trachtenberg, Thomas Bender, and Wanda Corn dismiss the Stieglitz circle's photographs and paintings of New York as devoid of political, social, or cultural value and, therefore, as removed from the everyday practice of urban life, I argue that *Manhatta* suggests otherwise; that is, Strand and Sheeler's city film posits the film, the artists, the city's workers, and the city itself as a unified and embodied entity where the division of labor in creating the city is shared equally among the artists-craftsmen.[108] The consequence of this unified embodiment, however, was that the film's political contours were braced by a narcissistic nationalism.

Here I would like to discuss the film's significance as a "self-portrait," since it emerges as such through the theoretical contexts I have sketched throughout this chapter. *Manhatta*, as I see it, is an American machine-age work that has much to do with a strong current of ideas privileging a nationalist, embodied narcissism ensconced in high art that simultaneously bridged the "practical" (recalling Stieglitz's use of the term) attributes of American culture. The working together of the (high) theoretical and the (low) practical yielded interesting results for *Manhatta* insofar as the film managed to reach a broad spectrum of film viewers. The film's screening in both popular and art-centered venues was yet another striking way that "high-art" theories in America engaged with the "popular culture" toward a middle ground (consider Lindsay's appeal to Griffith's work as Whitmanesque). In other words, to create "art" in America (keeping in mind all the ideological baggage discussed in this book) meant negotiating "high-brow" and "low-brow" sensibilities to reach Van Wyck Brooks's holy grail: the "middle tradition." What could be more Whitman-like? What could be more modern? If the ends of what defined American art were often different, the ideological means by which artists (from Griffith to Stieglitz) envisaged American art were quite similar, since it was filtered through the undulating visions of common sense (folk art) and transcendence (the sublime). *Manhatta* is, therefore, strangely uncanny— indeed, strangely successful—precisely because it meets the crucial criteria of an American middle tradition.

It is also worth bearing in mind here that the theoretical and aesthetic discourses of a middle tradition, on which Strand and Sheeler settled when they made their film portrait, were theories that romanticized the craftsmanship of the working classes. Strand's conflicted ethical relationship to the worker à la Hine and Stieglitz mixed oddly yet in tandem with Sheeler's idealist folk-craftsman. Indeed, the working-class craftsman we see in the film (and read about consistently in their work and in their contemporaries' theories) bolsters the artist/craftsman identification central to America's portrait of the artist. Ironically, the makings of what amounted to the avant-garde's modernist nostalgia for a manly, working-class artist-craftsmanship was no different than the virile, nationalist virtues of hard work and "practical" common sense disseminated in Roosevelt's vision of the popular arts.

To construct the unified work of art at the hands of American artist-craftsmen, Strand and Sheeler followed a Whitmanesque scenario borrowing snippets of the poet's work for the thematic intertitles that matched the film's images.[109] The film's organization hence abides a cubist-realist structure similar to Lindsay's plans for an imagist cinema (a juxtaposition of primitivist and modernist images). The very form of the film — its length and editing style — fulfills the hieroglyphic-imagist requirements that Lindsay outlined. But Strand and Sheeler further insist on — as my analysis below will bear out — an embodied convergence with the artist-craftsman in the film. To critique the film's "lack of interest in human subjects"[110] actually neglects the emphasis that Strand and Sheeler put on human agency — a narcissistic agency to be sure. To sweep their aesthetic concepts under a "denial of history," as Bender does, is, in fact, to deny history.[111] In this film, the imbrication of artist and worker underscores the necessary virtues for the production of American art. This is not an apologia for the Stieglitz circle's reification of the worker (a gesture about which Lewis Hine and the Ashcan group are arguably as guilty). Rather I wish to highlight the way in which Strand and Sheeler viewed their identification with the worker since it informs a key structuring model in the production of American art. Indeed, the film is precisely about an interest in human subjects whose presence is felt materially and spiritually. In the "spirit" of Whitman, the artists insert their cultural-producer presence at the beginning of the film as intimate correspondents with the workers we see in the film. Strand and Sheeler's embodied projection formulates a sort of narcissistic "equivalents" where the artists' work is an active part in the making of the city.

Manhatta's construction around Whitman's poetry draws attention to movement that creates unique city moments. For Strand and Sheeler, the living moments are cinematically "registered." The film's first intertitle, "City of the World (for all races here), City of tall facades of marble and iron, Proud and Passionate City," is juxtaposed with views of downtown Manhattan, taken from a boat moving through the harbor. The subsequent text reads, "When million-footed Manhattan unpent, descends to its pavements," and it is followed by the arrival of a ferry into lower Manhattan. A tightly framed shot shows workers disembarking from the ferry, in the repetition of what is clearly a daily activity. The moving film takes the concept of Stieglitzian equivalents to a new level because the cinema adds living expression and order to chaos in a world that "battled to reestablish" its equilibrium. Thus, while the routine of disembarking each day is always the same, the cinema reveals the endless variations of movement that human subjects create.

The fourth intertitle, which directly inscribes the corelationship between the filmmakers and the workers of the city, reads as follows: "The building of cities—the shovel, the great derrick, the wall scaffold, the work of walls and ceilings." The film cuts to a series of shots of men working with shovels on a construction site, a giant derrick, and a wall scaffold. The merging of the primitive tools (shovels) and the modern (derrick and crane) to build the city conjures the spirit of labor through which Strand and Sheeler identify and insert their embodied vision of urban modernity. The presentation of the construction workers early in the film reveals the direct projection of the artist-craftsman into the building process of the city. Moreover, for the filmmakers the realization of the towers as central to the concept of American modernity depends on the artist's ability to turn the cityscape into art. The construction-site worker's labor is, therefore, incomplete until the artist-craftsmen visualize the towers—the artist brings life to the concrete towers and, more significantly, the worker's labor itself. For the city to exist, therefore, the labor of the artist is as significant as the labor of the construction worker.

But Strand and Sheeler's self-portrait is also one that projects their identification with the towers themselves. As the film progresses after

Workers build the great city towers in the fourth-stanza sequence from
Strand and Sheeler's *Manhatta* (1921).

leaving the construction site, a montage of cubist-realist images are formed by Manhattan's ever-widening skyline and gridlike model. At all moments, the film shows the activities and movements (mechanical and human) that crisscross the avenues, sidewalks, and the buildings themselves. Whitman's poetic chants about the city's aesthetically and culturally interdependent relationship to its harbor galvanize the machines and the humans around a life force that may only be found in the poet's favored urban landscape. By the film's end, the bridges, barges, steamships, and "ceaseless crowds" are "drenched in the splendor" of nature's sunshine. Beyond the obvious modernist fusion of nature and machine, *Manhatta* marks the site, or so the filmmakers hoped, where artists unveiled a self-portrait through a medium thought of as purely American. Hence, Paul Rosenfeld's quest for American beauty and aesthetic independence appears to be found in the frames of *Manhatta* where the towers of Manhattan are "suddenly garlanded with loveliness" and, most important, where life was given to those towers and "for oneself together."

Manhatta is less a narrativization of city life (like those of the later city films) than a film about the materialist and idealist moments that Manhattan generates as modern art.[112] The city is, therefore, a series of discrete moments in which an embodied equivalents, a modern spirituality, occurs. The artist-worker-craftsmen create, with the primitive-modern tools of the cinema, the spirit that is the material oneness of New York City.

Whitman's Bodies and the City

It makes sense that Strand and Sheeler closely adhered to what Michael Moon reads as Whitman's "transformative equations between 'body' and 'text' on which he insists [and through which Whitman's] own body can be successfully projected through, and partially transformed into, his printed text, and his readers *can* engage in contact with the actual physical presence of the author."[113] By drawing on Whitman's bodiliness of the text and Stieglitz's equivalents, Strand and Sheeler undoubtedly viewed *Manhatta* as the most modern of modernist self-portraits. As I mentioned above, I do not, by any means, overvalue Sheeler and Strand's political championing of the working class (although Strand, as time went on, would become more engaged with issues of class). Instead, what I have been interested in showing is a way to conceive of *Manhatta* as inextricably linked to the abundant aesthetic theories that the Stieglitz circle held in their hopes to create a truly national art signaled by its embodiment with the American (male) artist. Therefore, to reject in haste the significance of the filmmakers' aesthetic interests in human subjectivity misses an essential and complex area of American aesthetics where the artist actively viewed his work—a narcissistic projection—as an intricate component of modern subjectivity in American culture. This position may not satisfy the domain of what some call the "political" or the socially engaged, but it was a position that inscribed much of what generated the concept of art in the United States. The political may not be "obvious" in the work of art. Yet—and especially with the cinema—if we have learned anything from Walter Benjamin, it is that aesthetics are densely political with powerful implications. The cinematic self-portrait that I claim *Manhatta* to be speaks forcefully to the naturalized nationalist and masculinist conditions at work in the American arts (with the artists' most liberal assertions of genderlessness notwithstanding).

Received in both popular and art venues, *Manhatta* signaled a vital moment in the American arts because the cinema-machine, the artist, and the work of art were declared victorious in their struggle to break from the influence of Europe and to surmount the apparent gap between spirituality and modernity and, not insignificantly, realism and abstraction. The triumvirate convergence of machine, artist, and work identified a sublime experience for artists that celebrated their visions of a pure nationalist oneness. It was not until twenty-odd years later that such nationalist enthusiasm around machine-based aesthetics revealed its more dangerous potential.

But New York and its creative forces were not known for their singularity of thought. Hence, while the Stieglitz circle's New York powerfully carved the dialectical experiences of nature and machine with abstraction and realism to identify their unique national sensibility, the city also made way for the production of aesthetics and aestheticized bodies that queerly navigated—that is, made archly "*divine*"—the more hetero-masculinist and white determinants of American art.

5

The Queer Frontier:

Vincente Minnelli's *Cabin in the Sky*

In 1937 Vincente Minnelli spoke to the "Fashion Group," where he made the following remarks: "The designers in the theatre today are at last on familiar ground. They are utterly in accord with their audience because their audience is part of the show. The barriers of footlight and stage door have never been so nebulous. The theatre and life have at last decided to meet on common ground, and that common ground—let's face it—is madness. Never, I think, has satire in the theatre been so spirited—color so unrestrained, sophistication so genuine."[1] Minnelli's remarks recall the impresario Lincoln Kirstein and his account of the "Loge Infernale" at the French Opéra. As Kirstein describes it, "Le Jockey Club," an early nineteenth-century group of aestheticized spectator-performers seated in the theater's loge, "detonated" the house "when they released bravos or hisses."[2] Minnelli's theatrical "common ground" on which "theatre and life have decided to meet" also brings to mind Lynn Garafola's telling of the dandified audience spectacle at the Ballets Russes during the early twentieth century where the director, Serge Diaghilev, "flooded . . . the boxes and stalls, illuminating the antics and outfits of their smart occupants."[3] At the Ballets Russes, it was indeed difficult to demarcate the line between a performance by Nijinsky and that of the gay dandies in the illuminated boxes.

But Minnelli's remarks also invite a return to the beginning of this book, where the spectacle of Edwin Forrest and William Macready's performance styles triggered the collapse of the proscenium's bound-

Vincente Minnelli, "Paradise Night." 1936. Set design based on the *Uncle Tom's Cabin* narrative for *The Show Is On*. Courtesy of the Shubert Archive, New York.

aries between spectator and performer and, in doing so, brought to full view the nationalist import elicited by the theatrical experience. There, the "audience [was] part of the show" with significant impact on the culture as a whole. For Oscar Micheaux, likewise (as discussed in chapter 3), the blurring of stage and of real life historically weighed on the impresario/artist's domain, particularly when he attended a minstrelsy program in Chicago and laughed until his "head ached." The history of the blurred relationship between spectator and performance is not only long; it is, to many different degrees, at the heart of the performative spectacle itself. In the cases discussed heretofore in this book, the interactions between the bodies in the audience and those on stage or in film have evoked provocative performatives in the cultural realms of nation, race, and gender. As I will discuss in this chapter, queer culture engaged the arts similarly, but with a different set of corporeal and aesthetic outcomes in mind.

Minnelli's comments also foreground yet another aesthetic gesture discussed earlier that is attributed to the "designer" or cultural producer's lived experience in a multimediated modern world. Minnelli's courting of an array of arts and his use of their various possibilities as mise-en-scène in which he emplaced bodies echoes J. Stuart Blackton's experiment with motion-picture technology that I elaborate in chapter 2. There, Blackton inserted the dancing Isadora Duncan into the world of Corot's painting *Spring*. Blackton's cinematic divertissement, in which the filmmaker forged the three discrete works of art together into film (dance, painting, film), quite literally forced a reconsideration of the dynamic relationship between mise-en-scène and bodies (if not the media themselves), something so instrumental to Minnelli's aestheticized landscapes and, I believe, his view of the "accord" between "designers" and "audience." Minnelli's aesthetic fusion of mise-en-scène and bodies, however, leads us to something more deviant and decadent than the cultural uplift that Blackton recommends because, like Micheaux, Minnelli's view of American culture was registered through complex aesthetic responses to Anglo-Saxon ideologies about hetero-masculinity and race. Minnelli, for example, took issue with the ludicrous arguments about gender and art; he did not, as witnessed in earlier chapters, quibble with the title "artist" as did so many other American male artists. He "was never told that creativity was unmanly," and he was never bashful about his "feminine traits."[4] Moreover, Minnelli rehearsed his "feminine" artistic principles against the grain of racist sentiment so entrenched in American discourses of creativity. As I explore in this chapter, 1930s queer and African American cultures found a unique "common ground" that generated what was perceived to be incongruous aesthetic practices that discomfited and confused white and black American critics alike. In this way, Minnelli recast Blackton's nationalist and Anglo-Saxon "emotional fervor"—an experience enhanced by cinematic spectacle—as aesthetic "madness" and "sophistication." Thus, I argue here, Hollywood's *Cabin in the Sky* (1943) is a significant cultural by-product of New York City's sophisticated and multistranded queer and African American aesthetics in which Minnelli moved. The movement of bodies, the conceptualization of art and/as bodies, and the centrality of an urban-modernist milieu all contributed to Minnelli's queer realization of the cinematic experience.

Dancing Bodies, City Streets

Though Isadora Duncan proved useful for Blackton's ideological interests, her bodily movements bore directly on those American aesthetics through which bodies and mise-en-scène moved and fused; a fusion that introduced a new facet to Minnelli's queer modernist "madness."[5] Kirstein, in his 1935 book *Dance: A Short History of Classic Theatrical Dancing* (a book dedicated in part to Minnelli's soon-to-be colleague, George Balanchine), claims that the American Duncan and the Russian Michel Fokine are the "two perfect champions of the initial contribution" to American dance in the twentieth century (I will return later to the significance of Russian-American creative relations).[6] "Duncan," Kirstein firmly announces, "stands for the new West" that "typified a . . . breathless, expansive, divine new continent" fed by the poetry of Walt Whitman (264–65); and he quotes Duncan as stating: "I have discovered the dance that is worthy of the poems of Walt Whitman. I am indeed the spiritual daughter of Walt Whitman" (265). The San Francisco–born dancer further wrote that, through dance, she sought "divine expression of the human spirit" and her only "dance masters" were Rousseau, Whitman, and Nietzsche.

Duncan's "dance masters" are indicative of a twentieth-century queer rechanneling of Whitman that certainly would have made Whitman purists (if not Whitman himself) uncomfortable, while also infuriating, as noted in chapter 1, the author of *Degeneration*, Max Nordau. Yet, Duncan sits squarely and, as Kirstein elaborates, instrumentally in the currents of American modernism that, against the backdrop of virile, nationalist aesthetics, took hold in the early part of the twentieth century as peculiarly queer. That is, by choreographing Whitman, Rousseau, and Nietzsche together on the same stage and through her body, Duncan announced an American modernism that refused to refuse European (degenerate) aesthetics as part of the American landscape.[7] When Kirstein writes, "Whitman so often means America to Europeans" and, more to the point, that "Whitman's America never realized itself" (265), he is showing his queer cards precisely because he not only unapologetically embraces that which Nordau viciously dismissed in his book but, more significantly, he challenges the very premise of Americanist art as an art marshaled by pure nationalism. For queer modernists, America (like their queer bodies and their lived world) was nothing less than impure. That is, the flows and exchanges of aesthetics and bodies among nations—that is, America (especially New York), Europe, and Russia—stoked an Americanist aesthetic that painter Thomas Hart Benton anxiously snubbed as "homosexual."[8]

How, then, do we take into account Minnelli's "madness," this "sophistication so genuine," indeed, so queer? In an earlier work I discuss Minnelli's favored European aesthetics, their queer inflection, and how they made their way into Hollywood in his musicals and melodramas.[9] I'd like to pick up from where I concluded (in fact, from Minnelli's thoughts given to the Fashion Group in 1937) to draw on the director's urbane mise-en-scène to identify the "nebulous barriers between the footlights and stage door" as they fold into one another. I suspect that it is in the fold that we will discover the imbrication of queer American bodies and queer American aesthetics.

To begin, it is necessary to situate Minnelli within the kinetic energies of New York since the city space played a vital role in his queer corporeal aesthetics. Unlike Alfred Stieglitz, Paul Strand, or Charles Sheeler's "Divine" urban transcendence (to recall, from chapter 4, Joseph Stella's treatise on New York) or Blackton and Theodore Roosevelt's hope for the new progressive urban frontier, Minnelli's urban experience is acutely similar to Micheaux's. In other words, both filmmakers experienced their corporeality as if pushed and pulled by nationalist modernism steeped in white common sense that claimed the city as the site of, again, white masculine progress. Interestingly, both filmmakers spent time in Chicago where, on the one hand, Micheaux raised his financial and cultural capital while, on the other hand, Minnelli acquired many of his early aesthetic interests and skills. For both, however, Chicago left them with a sense of malaise especially in relationship to their views about manhood. Micheaux remained wary of Chicago since it was the place that, because of urban temptation, threatened the goals of proper uplift for African American men.[10] In Minnelli's view, Chicago was a bit too rugged and lacked a certain urbaneness.

Minnelli's move to New York in 1931, however, was experienced somewhat differently from Micheaux's encounter with the city. Micheaux's version of uplift that positioned black manhood more in line with Theodore Roosevelt's masculine frontierism eschewed the urbane aestheticism Minnelli came to adore. Hence, while Minnelli relished the opportunity to move within the elaborate web of creative milieus including many middle-class artists associated with the "last stage" of the Harlem Renaissance, Micheaux saw himself pushed to the outer circles of New York's consecrated African American cultural production.[11] For Micheaux, New York's African American bourgeoisie, and certainly the white, queer middle class that participated within this milieu, rehearsed an aesthetic that had little to do with the filmmaker's romance with American homesteading.[12]

Though David Levering Lewis marks 1935 as a decisive end to the Harlem Renaissance, its effects resonated for quite some time (and continue to do so).[13] Minnelli was fully immersed in the creative flux of ideas from black culture that had its most potent form during the 1920s. He established key collegial relationships across the assorted avenues of New York's sophisticated aesthetics, including African American arts. And yet, though it is easy to celebrate the New York in which Minnelli immersed himself as a bastion of creative freedom among homosexuals and blacks, such an oversimplification ignores the cultural complexities of homophobia and racism that saturated Manhattan at this time.[14] At the same time, I am not suggesting that Minnelli's cultural border-crossings were easy or devoid of an oversimplified "tolerance" of the Other; indeed, as I will demonstrate, his less-than-manly qualities in dress and demeanor unsettled the masculinist sensibilities of many observers.

Nevertheless, Manhattan was the site for a creative commingling of black and white, queer and not-so-queer, cultural production (even Micheaux's misgivings about cities were at times overlooked when the city played a central role in his work—creatively, socially, and financially). Although the city space would lead Micheaux and Minnelli down different aesthetic and cultural paths, it generated a tension that inscribed multiple matrices of ideology (race, sexuality, gender, and nationalism) and left an indelible aesthetic mark on their work and their bodies. Queer and African American artists (and, in many cases, queer African American artists) danced across the everyday urban stage to produce a world divinely perverse.

Uptown and Downtown at the Minnellium

In 1936, the director of collections at the Museum of Modern Art, Alfred Barr, presented two "blockbuster" exhibits, "Cubism and Abstract Art" and "Fantastic Art, Dada and Surrealism." Barr's celebrated exhibits canonized a select group of European artists and movements while minimizing the modernist work of Americans. The museum director, in fact, "was polite but lukewarm" when the place of American twentieth-century modern art was discussed. As Barr saw it, according to Alice Goldfarb Marquis, "American avant-garde artists [and this meant Charles Sheeler, Georgia O'Keeffe, Arthur Dove, and, to a lesser degree, John Marin] seemed to have no ideology except individualism and no coherent development that could be traced in other European terms."[15] Needless to say, Alfred Stieglitz was not pleased with such a summation of contemporary American art. In the same year that Barr sanctified European modernism, Stieglitz was asked to contribute work for a proposed photography show at the museum. Stieglitz refused the request, stating: "I have nothing against the Museum of Modern Art except one thing & that is politics & the social set-up come before all else . . . In short the Museum has really no standard whatever. No integrity of any kind . . . [and] in spite of its good intentions the Museum [is] doing more harm than good."[16]

To be sure, Barr's dismissal in 1936 of American art—especially painting—as something less than "modern" would not have sat well with Stieglitz since he dedicated so much energy to building his milieu of "American" artists. And though around 1937 New York saw the formation of the abstract artists (a group of artists soon to be championed as American art extraordinaire by the art critic Clement Greenberg), it wasn't until 1943 that Barr finally purchased a Jackson Pollock painting (and that feat came about only after six months of trying to convince the museum's trustees that it was worth buying).[17] Concomitant with Barr's assessment of art in the United States, the *Partisan Review* in 1936 published the proceedings from a symposium, the title of which begged the persistent question: "What is Americanism?" Serge Guilbaut posits that this debate "had become central to the problem of defining the role of the artist in a time of cultural crisis."[18] But, as we have seen, the "crisis" of the "role of the artist" in American culture was certainly not something new.

What is important to note, however, is that Barr did not believe that American art as a concept was impossible. In fact, his enthusiasm for *American cinema* (he was a principal proponent of its place at the museum) suggests just where he and others in his cultural milieu saw a glimmer of American modernist hope. Given the widespread cultural interests of his circles, the cinema was perceived as especially modern since it simultaneously broke from the traditional arts while giving them fresh life. These modernists' tastes in the cinema were, indeed, eclectic. The Hollywood systems of production, for example (genre, narrative, stars), were not necessarily rejected by Barr's critical round-table at MOMA or by those with whom he socialized.[19] At times, Hollywood even served up a pleasurable combination of aesthetic style and melodrama that helped stimulate new and creative dimensions in the other arts. Yet, as I demonstrate below, it was not only the Hollywood mode of production to which artists turned for their concept of cinema. If J. Stuart Blackton and the artists of the Salamagundi Club imagined the cinema's promise as one of cultural uplift—one that affirmed masculinist Anglo-Saxon notions of art—then queer modernists played with many different aesthetic and corporeal possibilities through their uses of the cinema. By institutionalizing both European aesthetics and Hollywood at MOMA, Barr and the queer coterie that surrounded him championed an "American art" in the early twentieth century that egregiously challenged the battle cry for an American "middle tradition" destitute of Old World sensibilities in the arts, pure and simple.

MOMA's location in Manhattan (by 1936 it was in its second home) on West Fifty-third Street was instrumental in the shaping of creative sensibilities by queer modernists. According to George Chauncey, "The streets of the East and West Fifties, 'once given over to the homes of New York's wealthiest families,' one observer noted in 1932, were 'now filled with smart little shops, bachelor apartments, residential studios and fashionable speakeasies.' "[20] Several doors down from the museum were the studios and living spaces of several of Barr's immediate artist-friends who drove the cultural capital behind New York's modernist cachet. Vincente Minnelli located his studio right next door to the museum (his home was on Fifty-second Street). Within the range of only a few blocks, figures such as Minnelli, George Platt Lynes (who Minnelli claimed photographed him), George Balanchine (who was not homosexual, but comfortably worked within these circles), Lincoln Kirstein, Monroe Wheeler, Pavel Tchelitchev, and Carl Van Vechten lunched, had sex, and made art.[21] And, after years of introducing his broad range of modern art to the public below Forty-second Street, even Alfred Stieglitz opened a gallery in the area, at 509 Madison Avenue just east of MOMA. Opened in 1929 and called An American Place, it would be Stieglitz's last gallery.[22]

There was, however, another history with lingering cultural affect held by Fifty-third Street. According to Lewis, at the turn of the twentieth century the area around West Fifty-third Street was called "Black Bohemia."[23] There, Bert Williams (friend of James Weldon Johnson) performed what Ann Douglas characterizes as a "double mimicry," a black-on-blackface routine at Jimmie Marshall's Hotel.[24] But West Fifty-third Street was not Harlem. Indeed, while it was possible that queer white artists rubbed shoulders (aesthetically at the very least) with African Americans on the West Side (Platt Lynes, for instance, lived quite far west on Fifty-third), it was ultimately Harlem where the geographical and creative lines became quite porous and (historically) integrated. White and black artists living in their varied quarters of Manhattan (cordoned off by class and race) more presciently shuffled between downtown and uptown during the 1920s and early 1930s. Yet, if George Hutchinson celebrates this urban cultural exchange (some call it "slumming") as the success of Deweyesque pragmatism and a "striking experiment in cultural pluralism" that melted difference into twentieth-century American modernism,[25] queer (white) artists were doing something more perverse than simply reifying "cultural pluralism." American queer circles — including Minnelli's — eagerly searched for and feasted on the cultural "differences" of Harlem as a point of marginalized identification. If Forrest (and, more contemporaneously, Marsden Hartley) had ingested the American Indian toward securing and containing the perceived excesses of his own savage otherness, Minnelli and his queer coterie feasted on the Other precisely to identify and to display their excessive internal otherness. In other words, the queers of midtown who clearly announced themselves as different were resolute that Harlem was different. And through these cultural differences African American and queer white artists intermingled and enabled a mutual feasting of, by, and with the Other.

This is not to dismiss the troubling effects of class, exoticism, and primitivism that queer modernists brought to the table. Unlike Edwin Forrest's "repos délicieux," however, where the feasting by the "non"-Other of the Other's difference was thought to produce the well-balanced, white male artist (the commonsense embodiment of American civilization and savagery), queers and African Americans ingested, through "theft and parody," one another's cultural excess to produce a shared aestheticized and sophisticated world quite distinct from the dominant and more banal commonsense aesthetic environments that surrounded them. The history of *Cabin in the Sky*, I argue, provides a view into this cultural mixing of sophisticated American modernism that resisted hetero-masculinist Anglo-Saxon nationalism.

As Joseph Litvak reminds us, the notion of sophistication must not be forgotten for its earlier meaning of "perversion" and for its important relationship to cannibalistic feasting.[26] Sophisticated taste "rather horrifyingly involves the consumption of the 'edible bodies,' not just of those lesser animals that ordinarily pass for, or end up as, food—symbolically at least—of other consumers. To be sophisticated, that is, is to be more sophisticated than, and to outsophisticate the other is to incorporate the other; to incorporate, at any rate, the other's way of incorporating" (9). In a world where Minnelli, impresario/artist Carl Van Vechten, and actors Ethel Waters and Lena Horne feasted on one another's creativity (they also dined together in the traditional sense), the cultural exchanges in Manhattan suggested something more narcissistically satiating and gratuitously pleasurable than humanist pluralism.[27] Thus, Minnelli's queer milieu explored what Litvak would characterize as "the fantasies of what other people taste like" (12).

In order to see how Minnelli's "sophistication so genuine" permeated queer taste in 1930s New York, I'd like to consider the aesthetic consumption and production of his colleagues George Balanchine and Pavel Tchelitchev who, Minnelli recalls, attended his salon—the venue that composer Kay Swift dubbed the Minnellium. Balanchine and Tchelitchev provided for Minnelli a theoretically rich palette of modernist aesthetics that helped to produce queer American art. Though offering differing perspectives on the relationship between the artist's body and the work of art, Balanchine and Tchelitchev's modernist impulses stirred Minnelli's cinematic imagination in provocative ways.

Minnelli and Balanchine's Bodies: The Corps de Ballet

Born 1903 in Delaware, Ohio, Vincente Minnelli moved to Chicago in 1919 where he was hired to design window displays for the Marshall Fields Department Store. He also attended art classes at the Chicago Art Institute (and painting would remain his first love).[28] In 1931 Minnelli moved from Chicago to New York to work as a production designer (from costuming to set design) for Paramount-Publix's Balaban and Katz. Minnelli was glad to make the move from Chicago since he found the town to have an "impudent style with little class."[29] Its "sleeves rolled-up" sensibility reminded him of the work of the writers Theodore Dreiser and Sherwood Anderson—the sometime members of Stieglitz's more practically oriented American circles. From Chicago, however, Minnelli brought to his New York productions his wide-ranging interests in painting, performance, dance, window-display design, and (to a lesser degree) photography. His aesthetic influences drew on a modernist tradition at once academic (Velásquez, the Flemish masters, Whistler, the French impressionists) and decadent (Aubrey Beardsley, Ronald Firbank, surrealism, Marcel Duchamp, Ballets Russes). His early New York stage productions for *Vanities* and *Du Barry* were "inspired" by the Russian Léon Bakst (who, like Minnelli, was a modernist designer of sets and costumes), Robert Edmond Jones (the well-known white stage and costume designer who in 1917 created sets for the first all-black-cast Broadway drama, *Three Plays for a Negro Theatre*), and the aristocratic aesthetics of Louis XIV.[30] Minnelli's brand of modernism thus fit squarely within queer, urbane, aesthetic parameters.[31]

Minnelli also took aesthetic pleasure in the popular arts such as vaudeville (the theatrical background in which he spent his childhood), the movies (he preferred Jacques Feyder, Max Ophüls, and Sergei Eisenstein but loved the "sophistication" of Rouben Mamoulian's *Love Me Tonight* [1932]), and magazines and newspapers (*Vanity Fair* and the *World*). When he first arrived in New York he returned again and again to Times Square to revel in the "color and fire of all that neon."[32] The converging of mass popular culture with "high" modernist art, for Minnelli, facilitated an aesthetic experience where the body (artist, spectator) sensually meshed with the work of art. Echoing his speech to the Fashion Group, Minnelli told the *New York Journal-American*, "Nowadays, the scenic designer must be part of the idea. The contribution of the designer as expressed in his décor gives personality to his efforts."[33] For Minnelli and other queer artists, the bringing together of lowbrow and highbrow arts did not yield so much a pure middle tradition in the arts as it did for such artists as Strand and Sheeler. Rather, the collision of high and low cultures produced an aesthetic of excess, the "décor" of one's personality.[34]

What (or, more succinctly, who) was exchanged when the so-called high and low culture convened in these urbane theatrical settings? How did these aesthetic mixes give form to the queer bodies of both the artist and spectator on and off stage? The year that Minnelli began his career at Radio City Music Hall in New York was the year Kirstein convinced choreographer Balanchine to move to the United States to build a ballet company. In 1933, four years after Serge Diaghilev's death (with whom Balanchine had worked as choreographer for the Ballets Russes), the ballet master had few prospects left in Europe, and Balanchine thus accepted Kirstein's offer. One year later, they opened the School of American Ballet (SAB). The hurdle to create a successful ballet, let alone an American ballet, was daunting. To lend ballet an aura of American-ness, Kirstein, in particular (but Balanchine did not disagree), hoped to "make the company more 'Buckeye' and less Russian."[35] The stakes were high (financially and creatively) for Kirstein and Balanchine. As Kirstein saw it, the audience in the United States needed to be convinced that ballet was not strictly a continental by-product. Yet the aesthetically astute Kirstein was not one to reject European tradition in toto.[36] Given this cultural predicament, the question remained of how the taint of European decadence associated with ballet might be filtered so that both the prospective American audience (albeit banal in their cultural tastes) could find common ground with the more urbane, sophisticated crowd.

Two years after SAB opened, Kirstein and Balanchine organized the Ballet Caravan that toured during the company's summer recess. It was then that the school's directors crafted a shrewd explanation of American dance. In a promotional brochure for the Caravan, American dance is announced as "at once sophisticated, accomplished, and vitally entertaining. Young, gay, vivacious, these youthful Americans prove it is not necessary to look to Europe for fine ballet. Trained in the best tradition of international classic dance the Caravan is noted for its virtuoso style, versatility, and delightful humor, the good looks of the girls, its manly boys. Gay music and brilliant costumes, commissioned for the Caravan by America's outstanding composers and designers, have shown delighted audiences from Maine to Cuba the glamour and excitement of contemporary atmosphere."[37]

The brochure is revealing for the way that Kirstein negotiated the nationalist and aesthetic conundrum he faced.[38] Although, for example, American ballet does not "look to Europe," as he writes, its students are "trained in the best tradition of international classic dance." Indeed, the national boundaries characterized here extend from "Maine to Cuba." And while "America's outstanding composers and designers" procure a national aesthetic and identity, these artists present "glamour and excitement" which is "sophisticated" and "gay."[39] A bit of gossip, I think, reveals itself here as well. His references to "manly boys," for example, may have calmed concerns of some audience members about the virility of male dancers, but Kirstein's affair with the seaman Carl Carlsen (an affair redolent throughout his life), suggests that the author may have had an alternative type of manliness in mind.[40] In any case, what the brochure indicates is the way in which the pressures for ballet to survive in the United States urged a discursive formation at once manly and national while deliciously queer. Kirstein's and Balanchine's strategies apparently worked—in 1948, they established the New York City Ballet.

Where does Minnelli fit within these enterprises to make American art "American" while also sophisticated and glamorous? Between 1933 and 1943, Minnelli's and Balanchine's careers shared significant, if brief, overlap. Minnelli also worked with the same publicist as Kirstein, fashion expert Eleanor Lambert, who distributed Minnelli's talk to the "Fashion Group" cited at the opening of this chapter.[41] Minnelli's and Balanchine's worlds intersected on creative projects and through mutual, professional acquaintances such as the lyricist Ira Gershwin, the composers George Gershwin and Vladimir Dukelsky (aka Vernon Duke), the costume designers Irene Sharaff and Barbara Karinska, the performers Josephine Baker and Ethel Waters, and the painter Tchelitchev. Minnelli and Balanchine also worked together with Duke's scoring of Ira Gershwin's lyrics in the *Ziegfeld Follies of 1936* where they designed costumes and choreographed for Baker and Bea Lillie in a successful run.[42] Both men later directed Waters in *Cabin in the Sky*—Balanchine on Broadway and Minnelli in Hollywood. In this way, Minnelli and Balanchine directly and indirectly cooperated in the vital formulations of American modernist aesthetics of the 1930s.

Georgi Melitonovich Balanchivadze (meaning "jester's son") was born in 1904 in St. Petersburg (though he always considered himself Georgian). Balanchine (the name given to him by Diaghilev for ease in pronunciation) was raised in a middle-class family who had tremendous interests in the arts but whose fortunes were consistently uneven.[43] As a young boy, Balanchine read Jules Vernes, Sherlock Holmes, Nick Carter, and Pinkerton crime novels. His favoring of adventure and detective stories as a child later translated into equal adoration of the Western film genre as an adult in the United States (he often wore a western-style shirt and string tie). He also loved music (he played piano), acrobats, vaudeville, and the movies in general. Thus, from the start, in Balanchine's mind the popular arts were in many ways inseparable from "high" art and subsequently were imported into his ballets. In fact, in addition to ballet, Balanchine's career as a choreographer crossed into an array of media, including musical revues (the *Cochran's 1930 Revue* in London); Broadway (*Ziegfeld Follies of 1936*, *Cabin in the Sky* [1940], and *On Your Toes* [1936]); and Hollywood (*The Goldwyn Follies* [1938], *On Your Toes* [1939], and *Star-Spangled Rhythm* [1942]).[44] He even choreographed for elephants in Stravinsky's *Circus Polka*: "I am a circus man," he once confirmed.[45] The mixed-media conceptions that Balanchine executed led Ray Bolger to state that working with the choreographer "was like spinning from Julliard to the Louvre to the Royal Academy of Dramatic Arts to Stillman's Gymnasium."[46] Most significantly, Balanchine incorporated African American dance as early as 1921 in his work and continued to draw on its influences throughout his career, especially when he worked on *Cabin in the Sky* with Katherine Dunham, the first recognized African American choreographer.[47]

In 1913, Balanchine was unexpectedly accepted into the Imperial School of Ballet (it was his sister who sought a scholarship for dance; Georgi planned to have a career in the navy). Under Czar Nicholas II, ballet was financed by imperial funds and thus was regularly attended by the czar and czarina. Once the Bolshevik Revolution took place in 1917, however, the fortunes of the czar as well as those of Georgi's family were precipitously undermined. While he continued to study dance, to make ends meet under the new Soviet regime Balanchine used his musical talents with the piano to accompany silent films.[48] Later, when Balanchine went to Hollywood in 1938 (one year after Minnelli made his first trip west), the choreographer enthusiastically hoped, according to Buckle, "to make dance effective on the screen."[49] Minnelli had similar aspirations.

Balanchine's first assignment in Hollywood was to choreograph a ballet for *The Goldwyn Follies* (1938) set to George Gershwin's composition *An American in Paris*. Balanchine envisaged the ballet sequence to be shot from a diverse assortment of angles. Producer Samuel Goldwyn, however, roundly rejected Balanchine's wish to rework the typical Hollywood rendering of dance (i.e., a staged, theatrical style).[50] Nevertheless, the ballet sequence in the film is expectedly impressive for the period.[51]

The significance of music to Balanchine's choreography for the dancer's body is worth exploring here because it helps situate, comparatively, the particular aesthetic direction that Balanchine refused and Minnelli followed. Balanchine viewed ballet as an ephemeral art—"a breath, a mere memory" as Kirstein puts it;[52] an art, therefore, not unlike music and, certainly, not dissimilar to the cinema. Minnelli would have partially agreed with this assessment, but even the most ephemeral arts leave a lingering aesthetic trace, an excess, on the bodies produced through and on those receiving the spectacle. Whereas Minnelli more often used mise-en-scène (spatiality) to generate the corporeal experience (if not corporeality itself) as an aesthetic phenomenon that bridged the stage and the lived world, Balanchine stressed music (temporality) as the "breath" that gave ephemeral form to the body. Both men, however, ventured beyond a simplified and rigid division between the visual and the sonorous.

Minnelli and Balanchine's aesthetic spectacle was inseparable from what Erving Goffman termed the "presentation of self in everyday life."[53] In light of this it is worth noting how both men were recognized in popular discourse. Balanchine was described by Kirstein, for example, as "never wholly discouraged, often depressed, absent as a tangible personality when not in actual labor onstage or in rehearsal"; and Vernon Duke characterized the choreographer as lovely but "disorganized and ill-assembled to the naked eye."[54] On the other hand, there are endless accounts of Minnelli's exquisite dress and persona. "He often looks as if he had wandered out of an art gallery," one paper writes. Minnelli's flamboyancy—a work of art right from the gallery—was often an enigma to those who encountered him.[55]

Sound, Movement, Bodies

"It was music," Buckle informs us, "not painting that filled [Balanchine's] mind, guiding his brain and hands."[56] Indeed, the discussions about Balanchine's so-called plotless ballets are framed by the choreographer's decision to excise decor (a focal point in Diaghilev's productions) from the dancer's staged world. For Balanchine, his 1928 work *Apollon Musagète* (later *Apollo*) "seemed to tell me that I could dare not to use everything, that I, too, could eliminate . . . I began to see how I could clarify, by limiting, by reducing what seemed to be multiple possibilities to the one that is inevitable . . . It was in studying *Apollon* that I came first to understand how gestures, like tones in music and shades in painting, have certain family relations."[57]

Apollo is strikingly different from the Diaghilevian theatrical excess that used mise-en-scène painted by the likes of Henri Matisse, Maurice Utrillo, Max Ernst, Joan Miró, Alain Derain, Georges Rouault, Christian Bérard, and Tchelitchev: painters to whom Minnelli consistently turned for inspiration and incorporated into his work. *Apollo*'s white costuming, bare stage, and minimalist props were in complete opposition to Diaghilev's "passion" for painting. The unadorned stage, therefore, limned the "tones" of pure gesture.[58] The effect was startling, especially because Balanchine's attention to the dancer was not merely reserved for the singular ballerina or the pas de deux. For Balanchine, the corps de ballet—predominantly formed by women—performed a crucial role in evoking the gestural tone; indeed, Balanchine dancers *were* the mise-en-scène.

Balanchine's illumination of the dancer's body as an expressive conduit of musical sound and not as a figure expressed by the decor led some to criticize his work as too abstract. Balanchine rejected these accusations. As McDonagh puts it (supporting Balanchine's position): how is it possible that "ballets with people in them can be considered abstract"?[59] To be sure, Balanchine's denuded mise-en-scène did not abstract the body as much as it projected an ideal female form. It is precisely in this quest for the elimination of decorative excess, the removal of that which "distracts the public," where Minnelli would differ from his colleague. I do not mean to oversimplify Balanchine's pull away from an over-aestheticized set as something that disassociated the spectator from the performance of the dancer's body. In fact, an argument can be easily made otherwise, since Balanchine's choreographed events often electrify the audience. But his display of the dancer's body, hyperrealized on the cleansed set, presents the dance and dancer on a theatrical pedestal. What is most intriguing about such emplacement is how Balanchine conceived this pedestal specifically for the ballerina and the female corps (this is especially worth keeping in mind since his mentor, Diaghilev, emphasized the male dancer). For Balanchine, the ballerina was a projection of the ideal marriage—with all the weight that this term suggests—between art and gender. Ballet was thus a truly hyper hetero-masculine experience, shockingly beautiful, and over-determinedly so.

Balanchine's fixation on the female body, as biographers (including his wives) thoroughly recount, was one of manipulation and control. His (in)famous statement, "Ballet is woman," provocatively suggests how he manufactured this idealization on his minimalist stage.[60] "I consider that woman is queen of the dance," Balanchine stated in 1962, "and that man is but her page, her aid. I am always extremely sorry if some beautiful, talented ballerina expresses through her movements only some literary theme. The human body and particularly the feminine body is truly beautiful itself."[61] In an interview with *Life* magazine, Balanchine further makes clear the position of woman in his work: "Woman is the goddess, the poetess, the muse. That is why I have a company of beautiful girl dancers. I believe that the same is true of life, that everything a man does he does for his ideal woman. You live only one life and you believe in something and I believe in a little thing like that."[62] In identifying his "queen," "goddess," "poetess," and "muse" Balanchine upholds the "ideal woman" in his terpsichorean imaginings. Because he lifts the ballerina beyond the tedium of "some literary theme" and ushers her into "plotless" idealism, Balanchine celebrates the spectacle of female form as man's creation of transcendent beauty.[63] As her "page" and "aid" he does "everything a man does for his ideal woman." The abject man's power rests, therefore, in his manipulation, his choreography of the woman's body so that she delivers beauty to a world in which the heterosexual romance is managed by man's desire.

Once in America, Balanchine's molding of "ballet as woman" into the ideal marriage between art and artist struck a curious nationalist note that is reminiscent of Edwin Forrest's encounter with Push-ma-ta-ha. As mentioned, Balanchine had an abiding love affair with American culture—from dime novels to African American culture to Fred Astaire to, unequivocally, the Western. His choreography for *Western Symphony* (1954), *Square Dance* (1957), *Stars and Stripes* (1958), and *Ragtime* (1966) represents his continued homage to his adopted country.[64] When Balanchine married the American Indian dancer Maria Tallchief, he "felt he had married America."[65] Indeed, when Balanchine was traveling in a train and passed a reservation in Oklahoma, he exclaimed to his traveling companion, Nicholas Nabokov, "Look, those are my relatives!"[66] As Balanchine viewed it, through his marriage to his "ideal" woman (ballerina, American Indian), his blood was injected with pure, primitive beauty. But Balanchine's inserting himself (through blood) into his vision of an American aesthetic cedes ironic consequences since the Russian-born Balanchine's impurities as an American were not something easily erased through his marriage to an American Indian. As I demonstrate below, it is precisely his national outsiderness, his position as a male, non-American artist that allowed him to move comfortably within American queer and, not insignificantly, African American circles. In fact, Balanchine's New York urbane sophistication came to be through his feasting more and more on America's cultural diet (including his "idealized" woman). Needless to say, his manic imbibing of the Other made him something of a freak; and freaks were gladly accepted by queer moderns.

Yet, the "little thing" that Balanchine demurely calls his idealization of woman suggests an important distinction between the way that queer modernists produced the performativity of their body in relationship to the Other/Art and the way that Balanchine staged his own. Queer modernists, such as Minnelli and Tchelitchev, viewed themselves as "blurred" with the spectator at the theatrical event, while Balanchine maintained the deceptive ruse of placing the femininized Other on a spectacularized pedestal. The line is fine here because my argument is not that Balanchine is somehow "wrong" or "bad" in the way that his heterosexual desire reveals itself through formal expression.[67] Indeed, there is no more lovely expression of obsessive heterosexuality on the stage than a Balanchine ballet. But Minnelli and Tchelitchev's aesthetic sophistication and its relationship to Otherness played out differently. Balanchine stripped bare the theatrical stage to announce his union between artist (man) and art (woman). Minnelli and Tchelitchev, however, found a more apt realization of their own feminine Otherness in the excessive decor without which the queer impresario Diaghilev could not do. Their queerness, their perceived interior, excessive, and feminine Otherness necessitated a projection of mise-en-scène that did not project a purportedly ideal realization of heterosexuality. And for this reason Tchelitchev disagreed with his friend Balanchine and saw the elision of the other arts from theater and dance as, ultimately, a failure. Likewise, Minnelli continued to "Diaghilevize" his mise-en-scène on stage and in film.[68] Kirstein, although greatly admiring of Balanchine's work, ultimately sided with the painter Tchelitchev and his theories of bodies and aestheticized place.[69] The projection of Minnelli's and Tchelitchev's own queer Otherness—most precisely, their bodily Otherness—was thus imagined far differently from that of Balanchine.

For Minnelli and Tchelitchev, the work of art was a corporealized experience intimately linking subject and object (artist and work) where they identified the beauty of their queer and creative freakishness. Undoubtedly, Minnelli kept an eye on the New York avant-garde coterie to which Tchelitchev belonged and on the dramatic interventions they made—particularly regarding their views about international aesthetics, the human figure in art, and, significantly, the cinema. Hence, the painter's visits to the Minnellium fully resonated for Vincente because Tchelitchev, like Balanchine, reaffirmed Minnelli's impulse to explore the aesthetic interrelationship between so-called high and low art. The mundane aesthetic that this divide potentially suggested (yet that was insisted on by so many) said little to queer artists whose own lived experiences generated something far more varied, perverse, and sophisticated. In what way, then, do Minnelli's "nebulous" barriers between footlight and stage door, between art and life, dialogue with Tchelitchev's collapsed aesthetic boundaries in his work in theater and painting? The commingling of aesthetics, the expression of the inward outward, and the embrace of dilettantish sophistication provocatively challenged the cultural standards of American commonsense artwork. Along with international artists such as Tchelitchev, Minnelli instrumentally facilitated New York's queer freak show and ultimately took it with him to Hollywood.

Pavel Tchelitchev's Interior Landscapes

If, as Minnelli contends, Pavel Tchelitchev attended the Minnellium it was most likely only on rare occasions since the painter's most intimate circles were aligned with a more painterly crowd of expatriates and homosexual surrealists. This is not to say that Minnelli was not plugged into Tchelitchev's creative milieus, because he most certainly was. His love of painting kept him directly tied to gallery openings and exhibits. Further, this is also not to suggest that Tchelitchev's infrequent visits to Minnelli's salon, where their mutual colleagues Vernon Duke and Balanchine networked, indicated the painter's dislike for popular culture. Tchelitchev greatly admired Todd Browning's film

Freaks (1932) and he thoroughly enjoyed the circus; his aesthetic concepts drew heavily from his pleasures with popular culture, especially with the cinema. In fact, Tchelitchev and his work carried valuable currency among the queer jetset of New York and Hollywood. The playwright and screenwriter Somerset Maugham, for example, once sent to the MGM director George Cukor a Tchelitchev drawing; preceding the arrival of the artwork was a note that read: "You will receive within the next three weeks a drawing by Tchelichieff which Monroe Wheeler (of MOMA), who helped me to choose it, thinks one of the best he has ever done. His only doubt is whether you might think it a trifle indecent, but I said that to the pure all things are pure, and anyway you were too high minded to notice gentleman's private parts. I am sending it to you has a recollection of the happy visit I paid you."[70] The exclusive club to which Cukor, Minnelli, Maugham, Wheeler, and Tchelitchev belonged was one in which the "pure" took great pleasure in the exchange of the "gentleman's private parts" that only the privileged "high minded" could appreciate.

Thus, when Minnelli identified Tchelitchev's presence at his Minnellium he situated himself within a cultural milieu and movement of art known for its resistance (perceived by some to be "demonically" so) to commonsense realism, rural regionalism, and the hetero-masculinist abstract American art charging its way forward.[71] For Minnelli, the heightened virility associated with the abstract expressionist's aesthetic, similar to that which he sensed in Chicago's realist environment, foreclosed the sophisticated high-mindedness he embraced. But to understand here how "sophistication" and "high-mindedness" worked as a refusal of pure transcendent American hetero-masculinist aesthetics, I'd like to consider the way that Tchelitchev felt unable (in a way similar to Minnelli) to articulate a pure maleness as an artist—a necessary trait espoused by Clement Greenberg and his abstract apostles. I use the word "felt" here because Tchelitchev's rejection of abstract virile aesthetics directly reconfigured transcendence—a queer "high mindedness," an arch "Divineness"—directly with his bodily experience, an experience rendered quite distinct from the purported pure nature abstraction divulged.[72] It should be noted that like his compatriot Balanchine, Tchelitchev was a Russian émigré; his relationship to America was thus impure from the outset. And, indeed, it is precisely this outsiderness that spoke presciently to the internal outsider Minnelli.

During the early 1920s Vladimir Dukelsky (Vernon Duke) moved to Constantinople from Russia to immerse himself in Continental modernism.[73] While he continued his piano training he, like Balanchine, worked as a silent-film accompanist. He also became friends with Tchelitchev and his then lover, composer Allen Tanner, and it was Tanner who, after Duke spent time in New York among the urban sophisticates, introduced Duke to Diaghilev in Paris. Through his work with the Ballets Russes, Duke ultimately worked with Balanchine and, once in America, with both Balanchine and Minnelli.[74] After a creatively successful run in Paris where he engaged visual arts with music (and with those who embodied these arts), Duke returned to New York in 1929. Tchelitchev, with his by-then ex-lover Tanner and new boyfriend, Charles Henri Ford, arrived in Manhattan in 1934.[75]

Tchelitchev was born in 1898 in Kaluga outside Moscow. Torn between a career in dance (he loved ballet) or painting, and in deference to his father's fear that these choices were too "effeminate," Tchelitchev dutifully entertained his father's entreaties to study geometry, astrology, and anatomy.[76] Although the first sight of a cadaver made him ill, these disciplines proved indispensable for his later series, "Interior Landscapes" (1943–52). While studying the hard sciences Tchelitchev could not resist his "effeminate" interests, and he immersed himself in the decadent pages of Diaghilev's journal the *World of Art*, which featured avant-garde theatrical designs by the likes of Léon Bakst.[77]

As with the Balanchivadzes' fortunes, the 1917 Revolution devastated Tchelitchev's family and stymied his initial creative impulses. Tchelitchev thus left Russia, and between 1919 and 1934 he lived and worked as a stage designer and aspiring painter in Constantinople, Berlin, and Paris.[78] In so doing, Tchelitchev found a cultural milieu where "art, fashion, nobility and journalism had been at their highest fusing point."[79] Once in New York, Tchelitchev and Ford served as hosts for the soon-to-arrive surrealists (who were forced to emigrate because of World War II), including the poets André Breton and Edouard Roditi as well as the painters Max Ernst and Yves Tanguy.[80] Their creative and social circles reached far and wide and included Duchamp, Van Vechten, Florine Stettheimer, Helena Rubinstein, and Djuna Barnes. Tchelitchev's reputation as an enfant terrible grew with the recognition of his European paintings and elaborate stage designs that incorporated film, virtually nude costuming, and complicated lighting schemes.

When Tchelitchev met the enthusiastic American Charles Henri Ford (in Paris through Gertrude Stein), an important aesthetic and sexual relationship bloomed as a result.[81] As part of his modernist vision, Ford declared his homosexuality to be part of his poetic aesthetics. Tchelitchev soon channeled this sensibility into his own art. His relationship with Ford pushed the phenomenological dynamics between art and body that, although present earlier in Tchelitchev's work, significantly imbued the painter's art during the 1930s. As one commentator saw it, "About 1932, [Tchelitchev] began to see people in landscapes, the idea first suggested to him by the mountainous limbs of a Polynesian model . . . he will focus on a texture, say the human skin, until it has come alive into what he calls a termitère, — an antheap of crawling lice."[82] But texture and human skin had fomented earlier in Tchelitchev's aesthetic concepts, and cinema played a key role in this phenomenological development.

Diaghilev's production of the ballet *Ode* (1928) illustrates Tchelitchev's conceptualization of cinema as part of the modern theatrical experience (though his production of *Errante* for Balanchine's Les Ballets 1933 also used cinema for its mise-en-scène). For Tchelitchev, the cinema's discrete properties took the traditional arts (such as dance and painting) in innovative modernist directions. If, as we have seen, a powerful modernist impulse had been one premised on forging an alliance between the modern world (machine) and nature in the works of Strand and Sheeler, Tchelitchev in his production of *Ode*, according to Kirstein, "announced that he was rivaling Nature herself on the stage."[83] The cinematic machine thus became Tchelitchev's aesthetic tool with which to wrestle nature.

In 1928, Balanchine claimed that *Ode* was "far ahead of its time."[84] As mentioned above, 1928 was also the year that Balanchine choreographed *Apollo*, the ballet in which he realized the ways that the bare stage accentuated the contours of the dancer's body. Though Tchelitchev and Balanchine worked on projects together in the coming years, *Ode* and *Apollo* measured the distinct ways that the two artists viewed the body's dynamic relationship to the stage. Tchelitchev's production was more attuned to Diaghilev's treatment of ballet — at least in part.[85]

Both Kirstein and Tyler in their descriptions of the production refer to *Ode*'s libretto and quote at length from the "majestic document [that] indicates a scenario for cinematic treatment."[86] Indeed, by drawing on his love of Brothers Grimm, Aesop, *The Arabian Nights*, and Mark Twain, as well as the circus (especially the Medrano) and the often-electrified dancer Loie Fuller, Tchelitchev created what Lynn Garafola describes as a "visionary integration of dance and film."[87] Here it is worth taking a look at *Ode* since it presages the Minnellian cinematic spectacle that announced itself as queer.

The ballet *Ode* is based on Mikhail V. Lomonosov's poem *Ode to the Grandeur of Nature and to the Aurora Borealis*. In creating his production, Tchelitchev designed his own sets and costumes and used Nicholas Nabokov to compose the music, Boris Kochno and Nabokov to cowrite the libretto, Léonide Massine to choreograph the ballet, and Serge Lifar to dance the principal role. Most accounts of this "odd ballet" recall the centrality of cinema to its production, where, as Tyler records, Tchelitchev dictated that "five projection machines will be necessary" to produce his desired affect.[88] In the ballet sequence where a pagan fete occurs, for example, cinematic light is used to create a setting in which "the vision and the actual dancers mingle like one scene" (333). Cinematic nature (flowing water, blossoming flowers, "pale blue" cinematic dawn) was projected as a "lightplay" to be poured over and into the dancer's bodies. The "mingling" of bodies and light thus provocatively suggested a fragmentation of the bodies on stage. In one movement described in the libretto, "La Nature leads in from the wings mysterious figures, only parts of whose bodies are made visible by light; some seem to have only a leg, others only an arm, and so forth" (332).[89] Tchelitchev's mingling of the de-natured theatrical body was not so much an effort toward a transcendence of unified corporeality as it was a visceral penetration of its materiality where the body literally is torn to pieces. Finally, the cinematic-theatrical spectacle intensified when "a giant spotlight [was] shot into the eyes of the audience."[90] In so doing, Tchelitchev violently blinded the audience, thereby fragmenting their experience by blurring them within the fullness of the spectacle.[91]

Tchelitchev wrote to Stein that the theater's management was so concerned about the aesthetic excess he envisaged that they "stopped us from using the luminous blue lines because they require 120,000 volts —the theater would have exploded."[92] The theater nonetheless did explode: through projected cinematic light, the simultaneous fusion and dispersal of spectacularized bodies (both on stage and off) "mingled like one scene"—a scene, paradoxically, only made coherent by all that was torn asunder. Tyler describes the aesthetic explosion as part of Tchelitchev's master metaphor: the circus.[93] And, significantly, this balletic circus was, as Tchelitchev recalled it, "my first phenomena of Nature, later to become 'Phenomena' of Mankind in 1938."[94] For Tchelitchev, nature was spectacle. Balanchine, the other "circus man" who considered *Ode* ahead of its time, carried Tchelitchev's mise-en-scène of cinema to New York where he, with Minnelli, incorporated it into the *Ziegfeld Follies*.[95]

But Minnelli did more than simply translate Tchelitchev's unique experiments with cinema to the stage. He positioned himself within what Tchelitchev theoretically conceived as aesthetic "metamorphosis" or "simultaneity."[96] In 1928, when Tchelitchev sought at once to fuse and tear apart the body in *Ode* by means of flickering cinematic light, he also developed, according to Kirstein, his "idiosyncratic perspective systematically; a single composition included multiple vanishing points." Kirstein further notes that multiplicity was the cornerstone of Tchelitchev's "obsession with simultaneity, in his mind a magical state of bi-location, of seeing two things or being in two places at the same moment."[97] Tchelitchev, from an early age, was interested in what he described as "how things are one and not one."[98] To be sure, in 1942 Kirstein wrote, "With Tchelitchev the double image is by no means merely double, it is multiple; it is no trick to be pulled, but rather the employment of the principle of *metamorphosis*."[99] Moreover, Tchelitchev's theories of multiple "simultaneity" were "nourished" in popular culture at the circus and sideshows where "lurid, varicolored street-fair banners hung over booths advertising snake-charmers, strong-men, giants, dwarves, shooting galleries."[100] For Tchelitchev, like Minnelli, "simultaneity" translated as the kinetic experience of bodies between art and the lived world in which the "color and fire of all that neon" (recalling Minnelli's encounter with Times Square) detonated as it did when Browning's MGM *Freaks* merged in Tchelitchev's "high-minded" canvas *Pip & Flip* (1935).[101] Hence, at the Minnellium, painting, dance, cinema, and bodies were the kinesthetic sine qua non for a queer modernist aesthetic. Minnelli's salon, the Minnellium, was, in many ways, the queer Salamagundi Club.

In 1935 (a year after moving to the "diversity, tempo, and strangeness" of New York), Tchelitchev began work on his major canvas of the period, *Phenomena* (completed in 1938).[102] With only a few stage productions on which to work in New York, Tchelitchev turned his energies to painting.[103] But the direct line between his "first phenomena of Nature [*Ode*]" and his circus canvas extraordinaire, " 'Phenomena' of Mankind [*Phenomena*]," had been drawn. It was also at this time that Tchelitchev identified himself as a freak, as a member of the beautiful people.[104] Indeed, in a strange medical twist, a tapeworm inside Tchelitchev's intestines (a parasite he considered female because of its ability to replant its eggs after it was thought purged from his system) was literally ripping apart his internal organs. Tchelitchev recognized the tapeworm as an internal "feminine" Other that he had not only ingested but now ingested him. Thus, while Tchelitchev fed on the feminine Other it simultaneously fed on him. Perversely "nourished," Tchelitchev's "aesthetic vivisection" splayed itself in his art.[105] If Edwin Forrest and Balanchine's ingestion of the feminine Other sought to complete their imaginary manhood (ideally heterosexual), Tchelitchev's feminized Other mirrored his freakish gender imbalance as both man and 'feminized' artist, which he projected in his art.

In *Phenomena* (which features an assortment of artists and other parasites) Tchelitchev introduced his personal sideshow, or what Minnelli's colleague Cecil Beaton called "his interpretation of the universe in terms of freaks" in which the "beautiful people" of the artist's world disseminate the earth.[106] Tchelitchev's tapeworm-cum-skyscraper holds a prominent place in the upper-right corner of the canvas while the caricatured figures of such friends as Stein and Alice B. Toklas hold court and Ford exposes himself to the diverse freak show that is Pavel Tchelitchev. Tchelitchev's ruined body, revealed in his later "Interior Landscapes," was, like *Phenomena*, intimately interwoven with his lived aestheticized world of beautiful freaks. Unlike Balanchine (or Strand and Sheeler for that matter), Tchelitchev was hard pressed to design, or project, a spectacularized minimalist world for his impure body since such a place had little to do with his beautifully queer body. Tchelitchev's American world looked extraordinarily different than did Balanchine's. Tchelitchev's explosive painterly and theatrical mise-en-scène was undoubtedly nourishment for Minnelli's perception of his "feminine" Otherness in masculine America.

Pavel Tchelitchev, "Final Sketch for *Phenomenon*." 1938.
Hirshhorn Museum and Sculpture Garden, Smithsonian Institution,
the Joseph H. Hirshhorn bequest, 1981. Photography by Lee Stalsworth.

How did Tchelitchev's world of beautiful freaks—a world inspired by New York's "diversity"—make its way into Minnelli's hyper-aestheticized mise-en-scène? How did these aesthetic interests that projected a freakish inside outward travel from New York to Hollywood and into Minnelli's first feature film, the adaptation of Broadway's *Cabin in the Sky*, directed by George Balanchine? James Naremore rightly contends that in order to understand the "real story" about the film *Cabin in the Sky* (1943) it is necessary to study "the photography, the art decoration, the costuming, the performances, and the musical numbers."[107] Naremore places *Cabin in the Sky* within competing discourses that, as he describes it, give the film its "historical specificity" to show how "Minnelli and several artists at MGM responded to the racial dialogue of their day" (54). Broadly speaking, Naremore situates *Cabin in the Sky* in the film's historical context of MGM studio production and the predominant discourse of African American folk culture. Only the fourth all-black feature film to be produced in Hollywood, *Cabin in the Sky* is an important study of the way white institutionalized "aesthetic technology" (to recall Richard Dyer's use of these terms) was navigated to develop Hollywood's new market of filmgoers in a racially divided country. I would like here to investigate further the "real story" of *Cabin in the Sky* as it was guided by Minnelli so as to elaborate the interrelationship between white, queer, and (the by then well-placed) "New Negro" modernisms. In what way does the relationship between "New Negro" folk culture and white queer modernism inform Minnelli's *Cabin in the Sky*? What aesthetic concepts converged on the stage and in the subsequent film to forge a "common ground" on which straight and queer African Americans along with white queers expressed a sophisticated aesthetic that disturbed both "liberal" and "conservative" aspirations for ideal American culture, especially for an ideal American "folk culture"? To get to Hollywood, however, we must first return to New York.

When *Cabin in the Sky* opened on Broadway in 1940 the dance critic for the *New York Times*, John Martin, like many others, enthusiastically welcomed the musical to the stage. Martin opens his review by telling his readers that they will be "amply rewarded," especially those audience members who have followed the careers of the choreographer Katherine Dunham (who played the temptress Georgia Brown) and the actor/singer Ethel Waters.[108] But Martin was also confused by what appeared on stage. While Martin celebrates co-choreographer Dunham's contribution to African American dance in the production, he queries the role that George Balanchine played in his directorial debut of the Broadway production ("The combination is a curious one, but it bears fruit," the critic declares). Martin, although not a fan of Balanchine until later in his career, extends a backhanded compliment to the white, non-American director of an all-black musical: "There are numerous directors who have more knowledge of Negro dancing in their background, for the Georgia that is the birthplace of Balanchine happens to be not in the U.S.A. but in the U.S.S.R., but how many are there who would have the intuition to use Miss Dunham and her group instead of the more typical Harlem steppers?" If Martin applauded Balanchine's savvy use of the Dunham troupe, it was Dunham's "intuition" and "innately lyric" talents that should have been put into full service. For Martin, Balanchine's "intuition" (Martin evokes this term to describe both choreographers) "forced . . . his own patterns" onto the African American performance, thereby stripping it (particularly the "sizzle" of Dunham's Georgia Brown) of its racial "flavor." As Martin asks: "[Would] the result have been more pungent if Miss Dunham had been responsible for the choreography, even without so much knowledge of musical comedy routine?"

What is the "flavor" lost, as Martin sees it, in the "Negro dance" because of Balanchine's intervention? Martin's emphasis on Dunham's and Balanchine's "intuition" to parse discrete creative impulses by race suggests, initially, a call for a more direct involvement of African American talent in vehicles designed around African American culture. But Martin, who later argued that African Americans were not meant to dance classical ballet, posits, in effect, a strict aesthetic divide along racial lines.[109] Martin, however, is not alone in his estimation that aesthetics and race are necessarily concomitant variables. In other words, Martin lacked the imagination to recognize the transformative space made available precisely because of Dunham and Balanchine's collaborative, international choreography. For many, like Martin, "folk culture" (black and white) was the nostalgic bastion of an imaginary pure American past — a past to be protected from the onslaught of commercialism by adhering to an essentializing discourse not only of the pure and true "folk," but of art itself.

By the late 1930s, Dunham's training in anthropology also informed an idealist centerpiece for her choreography directed toward the realization of a "utopian folk society."[110] In a 2004 interview about her choreography with Balanchine in *Cabin in the Sky*, however, Dunham does not view a "utopian folk society" as something pure and authentic.[111] Instead, she argues that different cultures share a "universal" quality that takes shape across a broad spectrum of peoples. Individual qualities of these different groups are then developed and expanded through creative working interrelationships (such as dance) across communities. This is not to say that groups of people cannot be identified by sets of different cultural values (Dunham holds fast to this). Yet, even though these cultural qualities exist, they transform as they participate in the larger world. How, then, do these different and distinct cultures overlap and create new and vibrant art? For Dunham, they connect through their experiences of cultural sound. As Dunham explains it, the choreographer's work can be seen as the creative impulse that draws a direct line from the cultural phenomena of music and sound — sonorous experiences grounded in everyday life — to a dancer's performance of different cultural expressions. This is why, Dunham suggests, American dance, especially African American choreography, was "part of a cultural being, a living expression of people in general." African American everyday practices that included such events as church outings and family picnics encouraged and generated a culture of "movement." It is the job of the choreographer(s) to bring this everyday "movement" to the dancer on the stage. Seen this way, Dunham realized that dance was in need of a "new vocabulary" no longer based on European en pointe.

In this way, Dunham fondly recalls working with Balanchine on *Cabin in the Sky* and the success that they had in their "fusion of different cultures." Balanchine, according to Dunham, was a "unique person" whose tacit understanding of black culture derived from his Russian experience that, like African Americans, was one in which people had "to surmount and overcome" obstacles.[112] Kate Baldwin confirms Dunham's suggestion of an international alliance between Russians and African Americas since, historically, "anxieties about cultural imperialism, national assimilation, and suspicions of backwardness along with general enmity that traditionally plagued some Russians also tormented racially oriented African Americans."[113] Significantly, this cultural alliance played out sonorously in Dunham's mind as it assuredly did for Balanchine. For her, the mutually shared experiences of cultural "anxieties" between herself and Balanchine led her to believe that their work succeeded because of their creative responses to "sound" and body. As we have seen, Balanchine's emphasis on the relationship between music and the body, rather than mise-en-scène and the body, sat squarely within Dunham's theories of sound. African American folk rhythms thus took on new life as both Dunham and Balanchine opened alternative, indeed, international directions for just where that "folk" culture might go.[114] The *Cabin in the Sky* that Dunham produced with Balanchine presented at once a key trope of African American culture (the folk) while reshaping (that is, internationalizing) the romanticized nationalist model that had assumed an air of racial essentialism by black and white critics.

Indeed, four years after *Cabin in the Sky* opened on Broadway and one year after the film premiered, James Agee contributed his essay "Pseudo-Folk" to the *Partisan Review*. Agee, the author who reified white southern sharecroppers in *Let Us Now Praise Famous Men*, and who considered the Russian filmmaker Dovzhenko a great "primitive tribal poet," was distraught over what he saw as the commercialization, in fact, vulgarization of black culture.[115] As Agee viewed it, however, a trace of hope lingered in the "back country South . . . [in the] records by Mitchell's Christian Singers." Such music, for example (ironically, a recording), was "sophisticated" in "relation to its source" but not put through the "softening" process of "sophisticating" by the "tricky little midgets like Raymond Scott" (405). The loss of an originary quality of (unsoft?) Negro culture is made all the more "disastrous," according to Agee, because African Americans hegemonically participate with the cultural production of the "pseudo-folk" so "dangerously corrupted" by the white "middle-class audience" (406–7). "The pity of it," he laments, "is that Negroes themselves seem to be as often fooled by this sort of decadence" (405), blinded by white commercialism and the sale of their unique essence.

Given his strong distaste for what he saw as the ruinous state of black folk culture and his populist realist impulses, *Cabin in the Sky* must have disturbed his poetic view of earthbound cultures of "the people."[116] Moreover, in his account of the "pressures" that "produce pseudo-folk art" Agee directly points to the "dreadful pseudo-savage, pseudo 'cultured' dancing of Katherine Dunham and her troupe" (408). Dunham, who drew on lived experience in both her anthropological studies and her choreography, must have been stunned to learn that she contributed to a "pseudo-folk" art.

To be sure, the arguments that Agee espoused in "Pseudo-Folk" were not reserved for white middle-class sensibilities about African American folk culture. Such discussions about the essential spiritual quality and historical specificity of the folk were focal points of twentieth-century African American cultural deliberations. The Harlem Renaissance period was couched in formidable debates over what constituted authenticity with regard to the "New Negro" movement and its relationship to folk culture. Key Harlem Renaissance scholars, such as David Levering Lewis and Houston Baker, reiterate the significance of black folk culture in their work as the political and aesthetic cornerstone of African American nationalist aesthetics. For Lewis, in particular, the "failure" of the Harlem Renaissance was, in part, because of the decadent intervention on black folk culture by white interlopers (in this regard is the "high-minded" Carl Van Vechten who, according to Lewis, is almost "unknown today").[117] Although Baker's deconstruction of the "Harlem Renaissance" elicits a wider reading of twentieth-century African American culture than does Lewis's, Baker also seeks in the movement an "immanent quality" (63) and "foundation for authentic and modern expressivity" in folk culture (91). As J. Martin Favor points out, "Engaging marginalized folk culture and celebrating its forms insufficiently disrupts entrenched notions of identity and hierarchy; the valorization of folk strength still caters to and derives in part from African American marginality in a way that is effective as a voice of protest but not necessarily one of revision or revolution."[118] I do not intend to argue here that *Cabin in the Sky* is a revolutionary intervention. Yet, against the backdrop of unyielding voices (white and black) who clamored for an authentic black folk as the sine qua non of twentieth-century African American (and de facto heterosexual) culture, those involved in the making of the stage play and the film eschewed such doctrine and created something messier and more sophisticated.

Sophisticated Folk

In what way, then, did the forging of American black culture with international aesthetics, ideologies, and sensibilities (such as the relationship between Dunham and Balanchine) evoke the uneasy response that it did from the likes of Martin and Agee? What was it about this internationalizing of Americana that appeared so confusing, so queer? Since we have seen some of the key tropes that informed white, queer middle-class aesthetics, it is necessary to consider—and so to bridge— queer African American aesthetics as they worked concomitantly with queer white culture. At the heart of what we now identify as the Harlem Renaissance was a group of queer men and women who dynamically, yet often contentiously, commingled with white queers to produce a decadent and sophisticated modernist "folk." Through this intermingling of international and queer black and white aesthetics Minnelli's sophisticated folk emerged.

On a Web site dedicated to Alain Locke, the founding leader of the "New Negro" movement, the philosopher is described as a "humanist who was immensely concerned with aesthetics."[119] Like most descriptions of Locke, his interest in aesthetics "metaphorically" suggests his less-than-manly disposition and, of course, his uncertain sexuality. Lewis, for example, describes Locke as the "delicate academic," "exquisite," "habitually ceremonious to the point of prissiness," and prone to a "weakness for his male students" (Lewis later translates these traits as ultimately misogynist).[120] Despite this, Locke's queer sexuality is only intermittently, if at all, evoked when critics discuss his life.[121] Locke himself only once took up the issue of homosexuality in his unpublished and untitled critique of society's antagonistic and unfruitful chastisement of "eccentric individuals" and of those viewed as "insane" (posited here as African Americans, Jews, and homosexuals).[122] In the tradition of the closet as a discursive container of repression, the scholarly positioning of Locke's "immense concern" with European aesthetics betokens a failed hetero-masculinity. Ironically, by pejoratively commenting on Locke's so-described effeminate qualities, Lewis unwittingly subscribes to Malcolm Cowley's impulses (the white writer he challenges) about African American "cultural innocence and regeneration": "One heard it said," Malcolm Cowley remembered, "that the Negroes had retained a direct virility that the whites had lost through being overeducated."[123] If Cowley was wrong (and Lewis, in the end, agrees with Cowley's assumption regarding raced masculinity), Lockean overeducation and overaestheticization mangled not only the "virility" of early-twentieth-century black culture, it threatened the hetero-masculinist legacy of the Harlem Renaissance. In this way, aesthetic decadence (that is, queer sophistication) is, at bottom, the "failure" of the movement. But the milieu of Harlem during the 1920s and well into the 1930s was decidedly queer.[124]

Lewis's punishing estimation of Locke is one that aligns the professor, therefore, within the "salon exotica" of decadent queer whites such as Van Vechten, his wife Fania Marinoff, and the "foreign sojourner," British photographer-aesthete, Cecil Beaton. Lewis's critique of Van Vechten and Beaton's purported gratuitous and momentary pleasures taken with African American culture, however, neglects the artificiality of an arch performative for which both black and white queers were notorious. When Lewis, for example, records Van Vechten's remarks to H. L. Mencken from 1924—"Doubtless I shall discard [African Americans] too in time"—he is blind to the ironic bite that Van Vechten levied in this remark and the pleasure he must have taken in Mencken's earnest response to such an announcement.[125] Lewis's cultural oversights notwithstanding, Van Vechten's relationship to black artists during this period was complicated but not racist. "I never thought of things, that way, you know," Van Vechten emphasized, "I never think of people as Negroes. I think of them as my friends."[126] Ethel Waters, blues singer and prima donna of the Harlem Renaissance era, couldn't have agreed more. "Carl and Fania Marinoff, his wife and a good actress," Waters recalls, "became my dearest friends. Sometimes it seems to me that Carl is the only person in the world who ever has understood the shyness deep down in me."[127] Lillian Faderman, in fact, posits that the experience of white queers in Harlem ranged from those who reveled in the "fruits of colonialism" and "*used* Harlem as a commodity, a stimulant to sexuality" to those who "compared their social discomfort as homosexuals [or queers] in the world at large with the discomfort of black people in the white world."[128] But the "comparison" was not merely observed from a distance; Waters, Countee Cullen (consider his poem "Tableau"), Richard Bruce Nugent, Nancy Cunard, Van Vechten, and Minnelli intermingled creatively and, at times, physically.

Van Vechten's queer society had few boundaries for those who identified themselves in his at once privileged yet liminal world. Though Locke never publicly commented on Van Vechten or his scandalous novel *Nigger Heaven* (1926) their cultural philosophies and lives intimately overlapped.[129] Locke's call for a "free-trade in culture," where "culture-goods, once evolved, are no longer the exclusive property of the race or people that originated them," indicates the "delicate academic's" philosophy of *différance*—albeit a sophisticated one, which queers such as Van Vechten, if not Minnelli, would have endorsed.[130] As Helbling succinctly puts it: "Locke understood that diversity, complexity, and the act and art of imagination constituted the elements of an African American identity."[131]

The place of popular (folk) culture—and it did have its place—was undoubtedly a complex concern for Locke, especially since he enthusiastically participated in Harlem Renaissance cultural milieus and dedicated a great deal of time to academic philosophy. Educated at Harvard (where he studied with William James and Hugo Münsterberg) as well as overseas in England, France, and Germany (like Du Bois), Locke turned to both classicist aesthetics and the populist sentiment of Walt Whitman for his vision of African American folk culture; one that was couched, however, in a "dethroning of absolutes" that simultaneously did not "exile our imperatives, for after all, we live by them."[132] In 1935, though he had been developing these ideas since his 1918 dissertation, Locke repudiated the "ultimates" of "common sense and the practical life" that inform a "chronic and almost universal fundamentalism of values in action" (35). Locke embraced what he viewed as Whitman's sensuous spirituality and individuality (especially as he observed it mixed in Langston Hughes's work) because it meshed perfectly with "African American expressive traditions" that, as he countenanced it, was sentient but not absolute.[133] The senses of the body were, for Locke, where one's individual truth took shape on multiple levels of lived and historical experiences (not simply, as I point out below, through the privileged sense of sight).

Hence, Locke's critique of absolutism provided provocative inroads to the creative contours of American twentieth-century popular culture. Although it is hard to ignore what Lewis points out as Locke's interest in the arts as "highly polished stuff, preferably about polished people, but certainly untainted by racial stereotypes of embarrassing vulgarity,"[134] Locke did not completely dismiss the import of the popular arts, a point of view in keeping with his view of cultural diversity. To be sure, musical revues such as *Shuffle Along*, though including Josephine Baker and Paul Robeson, did not meet Locke's expectations of high African American art. On two separate occasions, however, Locke applauded Hollywood for what he determined to be richly formed representations of African Americans. In his essay "Folk

Values in a New Medium," written with Sterling A. Brown, Locke expressed satisfaction over Hollywood's use of its new technology—sound—in the film *Hearts in Dixie* (the writers, however, were not as taken with King Vidor's *Hallelujah*).[135] Sound technology, as the writers considered it, finally revealed a "more purely Negro voice." Similar to Dunham's theories on sound, Locke and Brown underscore that the folks' aural presence in the film, in fact their "real individuality," is made complex and "achieves an artistic triumph" precisely because one hears the "vital realism" of African American culture in film rather than seeing the representation of "hackneyed caricatures."[136] For Dunham and Locke the failure of visual representation was, in fact, its insistence on sight (the often absurd and insidious determination of "race").

Sound, because of its richness and "vital realism," revealed a more sensual experience of American black culture that Locke suggested was the "more purely Negro thing."[137] Indeed, "A nation's emergence," as Baker contends for the shaping of African American national culture, "is always predicated on the construction of a field of meaningful sounds." Following Locke, Baker tells us that "sounding" renders a "field of possibilities."[138] Though he was the aesthetic priest of bourgeois high black culture, Locke recognized the "possibilities" of popular culture as a key ingredient to his high mindedness, but only to the degree that it enabled an exploration of a wide-ranging sensual experience. As Locke viewed it, to rely on the hierarchy of sight and the canon of art was to miss the wide-ranging experiences of "authentic" folk.

In light of Locke's interest in "free-trade in culture," and the significance of sound as part of the cultural exchange, *Cabin in the Sky* must have intrigued Locke on several fronts. Immediately, he was most likely taken with the fact that the Russian-European crafted ballet master Balanchine (who, as pointed out) reveled in the corporeality of sound, was to direct the all-black-cast Broadway show. But perhaps more presciently for Locke was Dunham's role as both choreographer and performer in the play. It was, after all, Alfred Dunham, Katherine's brother, who "rekindled Locke's interest in publishing philosophical articles."[139] Between 1918 and 1935 Locke wrote few philosophical tracts. From 1928 through the mid-1930s Alfred Dunham and Locke maintained an ongoing correspondence leading to Locke's "reentry into the doing of philosophy directly rather than through the mediation of other literary genres."[140] Through his relationship with Alfred,

Locke would have been aware of Katherine's deep interest in anthropology and Haitian culture; her multivalent approach to a "utopian folk society"; the use of dance and sound to express her academic interests; and her high profile at the University of Chicago.[141] Thus, while John Martin at the *New York Times* was confused about the pure (visual) representation of the black race because of who choreographed *Cabin in the Sky*, Locke would have knowingly tipped his hat to Dunham and Balanchine's successful "interrelationship" in which their choreographic "interpretation" of sound "fused" and "mixed" an international universality of folk cultures.

Given Minnelli's involvement in and awareness of these cultural happenings in African American popular arts, I'd like here to consider his first Hollywood feature film as something more than a display of his mannered mise-en-scène. As a collaborator with and student of the Russians Balanchine, Tchelitchev, and Diaghilev; as a decadent flâneur of European painting whose own paintings were inspired by the Continental tradition; and as an active participant in the swirl of New York's queer and African American creative and social circles (Waters, Lena Horne), Minnelli (turning to a sophisticated fusion and explosion of mise-en-scène and sound) produced *Cabin in the Sky* with a fantastic toolkit of sensual modernism.

Queer as Folk

At first, Minnelli was not necessarily thrilled to be in Los Angeles in 1940. He signed his contract with MGM after leaving a lucrative and rewarding career in New York in which he "had forged an identity as one of the liveliest minds on the musical stage—an aesthete with a strong pragmatic bent who managed to translate his esoteric notions of beauty into punchy Broadway vernacular."[142] Lena Horne recalled running into Minnelli outside Louis B. Mayer's office when she first signed with the studio. "We seemed to be the 'New York group,'" Horne reminisced, "a little bit at bay, making a sort of informal, unspoken contact of friendship among the Hollywood crowd."[143] In fact, Horne and Minnelli had been friends in New York where, sometime in late 1938, Minnelli approached both Horne and Ethel Waters to star in the never-produced *Serena Blandish*, an all-black-cast musical comedy. In many ways *Serena Blandish*, if produced, would have been Minnelli's swan song to the New York modernist impulses he so adored. "I wanted to do a sophisticated black show," writes Minnelli, "because I felt uneasy about the conventional stereotype of the Negro as simple, naïve, and childlike."[144] In Minnellian fashion where detailed mise-en-scène displayed the "personality" of the show's producer and the performers on stage, he demonstrated that he was not only intellectually engaged in African American arts, he was an early participant in the ways that racial stereotypes were reconfigured in popular culture.[145]

Of course, certain important and "sophisticated" all-black-cast productions such as *Four Saints in Three Acts* had received high marks by the cultural literati. Minnelli was aware of these productions and enthusiastic about his own contribution to the New York scene.[146] As Harvey points out, with Waters on board for the Hollywood project and with "a score by Vernon Duke, an old colleague from the *Ziegfeld Follies of 1936*, and the addition of Lena Horne to the cast, this was the very combination of talents that Minnelli had tried to forge when *Serena Blandish* foundered three years before."[147] Assuredly, his "old friend" George Balanchine (who moved in and out of Hollywood at this time) and his work with Katherine Dunham (who was also working in Hollywood) were not far from Minnelli's creative thoughts, especially considering MGM's refusal to include the Dunham dancers as part of the *Cabin in the Sky* film.[148] *Cabin in the Sky* thus appeared as the perfect vehicle with a strong dose of New York cachet to begin Minnelli's film career in Hollywood. What did Minnelli aesthetically pilfer from queer white culture as well as Russian and African American cultures and export into the Hollywood version of *Cabin in the Sky*? What queer sophistication saturated his cinematic spectacle and adapted to an African American context?

The film, adhering closely to the Broadway play, tells the story of Petunia (Ethel Waters) and "Little Joe" Jackson (Eddie "Rochester" Anderson). Petunia, a faithful member of God's church, works diligently to save Little Joe's soul from the demons of gambling and adultery with Georgia Brown (now played by Lena Horne). The story opens with Little Joe agreeing to transform his ways and mend his marriage with Petunia. In one of Minnelli's first prosaic moving-camera shots (among many in the film), we see Petunia's church congregation singing a spiritual while they gossip among themselves about Little Joe's return to the church. As the church members sing, Minnelli follows the gossipers in a zigzag crane shot over the church pews. Little Joe, of course, does not last long in this holy spectacle because temptation (three of his gambling cronies) awaits outside the church doors with the promise of a winning dice game.

Little Joe is lured away again. During the dice game, however, he is shot by the smooth talker Domino Johnson (John William Sublett). Petunia runs to the "Paradise" saloon where the action has occurred to see her husband stumble out the door. Once back at the cabin, the doctor assures Petunia that Little Joe will mend in time. When Petunia asks the doctor if she can see Little Joe, the doctor agrees but warns that he may be "out of his mind." When Petunia enters the bedroom, Little Joe is delirious and mumbling to himself, which sets the stage for the dream visions that constitute the remainder of the film. Similar to *The Wizard of Oz* (1939), the protagonist's dream sequence incorporates their "real world" characters (in fact, the tornado used in *Oz* is the same prop used at the end of *Cabin*). For Little Joe, his visions of heaven and hell are hence personified through his church's reverend who is now the Lord's "general" (Kenneth Spencer) while his gambling buddy, Lucius, now plays "Lucifer Jr." (Rex Ingram). Petunia and Georgia Brown, however, assume the same character roles in Little Joe's dream. During his dream, Little Joe confronts and struggles with choices of good and evil when, at the dream's climax, he finds himself and Petunia facing judgment day. In the end, because the good deeds that Little Joe ultimately performs result in changing the ways of Georgia Brown, he is given entry with Petunia to the Pearly Gates (where an enormous and spectacular staircase leads the way). When, after the dream, Little Joe awakes, Petunia is at his side—glad that he is alive and well and hopeful that he will turn away from the devil's work.

Recent scholars remain unsure (not unlike John Martin writing in the *New York Times* in 1940) about how to situate *Cabin in the Sky* because of the film's complex relationship to African Americans and white Hollywood. Naremore's analysis provides the most generous consideration of these issues given the aesthetic line he draws from the film to Minnelli's New York modernist impulses. Yet, Naremore concludes, "the film is never free of racism" as it sits "uneasily among . . . conflicting discourses about blackness and entertainment in America during World War II."[149] Ed Guerrero finds that all-black-cast films of the period present the "entertaining, folksy" musicals "inaccurately polarized as 'good' or 'bad,' thus articulating an imposed sense of Western, Platonic-Puritan, aesthetic binaries." At the same time, however, he singles out *Cabin in the Sky* for its "clever scene of comic fantasy" in which "Louis Armstrong performs masterfully as a devil, playing jazz in hell, while Duke Ellington's music is depicted as sinful temptation set in a saloon."[150] Harvey finds "the absence of [African American] anger and disaffection" the reason it is "palatable to white audiences."[151] Adam Knee contends that the film only "allows Little Joe and Petunia one route of escape" from their economically marginalized world, and this route is in the "form of a shared dream of ascendance to the heavenly cabin of the film's title, a site presumably of happiness and intimacy." This "transition" toward the "shared dream," unfortunately, is one "predicated on their demise." For Knee, "This space of potential fulfillment is so outside the usual boundaries of the diegesis as to render it largely unrepresentable; it is conjured up only in such special registers of the filmic discourse as an emblematic drawing behind the credits and a sung reference in the titular musical number."[152]

To read the film's cabin as a reductive retelling of the simple folk's grappling over good and evil is to neglect the complexity of cultural circumstances in which the film comes to be. In other words, these readings ignore the queer savoir-faire generated during a particular time and place that the cultural producers involved in the film's making bring to its production. What we see in *Cabin in the Sky* is far from simple. As we saw earlier in Minnelli's concept for *Serena Blandish*, the black "folk" were both the embodiment of mythic qualities (poor and simple folk) and also modern sophisticates who were in no way simple-minded and naive (to suggest this about Waters and Horne now or during the making of the film is at best inadequate).[153] In my effort here to reconsider *Cabin in the Sky* as a modernist fusion of queer and African American international folkism, I'd like to return to the "drawing behind the credits and [the] sung reference in the titular musical number" to suggest that the "shared dream" is not one fulfilled through the characters' demise (indeed, the film does not end with the character's "demise"—they are only dead in Little Joe's dream).[154] The "unrepresentable" may be more present than we think.

Thierry Kuntzel stresses that "the *beginning*—the credits and opening sequence—[is] endowed with a certain structural autonomy (the sequence) and as a privileged link in the chain that constitutes the film: a segment where the entire film may be read, *differently*."[155] Kuntzel's "close reading" of a film's beginnings reveals "the fact that, in the space of a few images—a few seconds—almost the entire film can be condensed" (24). I'd like to extend Kuntzel's close-reading theory because, as he states, "what is fascinating about beginnings is that the film, gathered upon itself, exposes its signifying chain—its successive order —in simultaneity" (24). To add to Kuntzel here, I draw on the historical signifiers of interrelational cultures that simultaneously cut across *Cabin in the Sky* and are launched in the film's credit sequence and detonate throughout the film.

The title sequence for *Cabin in the Sky* opens with a series of twelve title cards on which a small cabin is seen. The title sequence drawings are bordered by a decorative frame that is, in turn, nestled in a bed of petunias (of course). Flowers and mirrors are motifs that persistently recur in Minnelli's oeuvre. In his discussion of *Cabin in the Sky*, Harvey remarks, "In his later work, mirrors become the most emotion-fraught objects in Minnelli's universe, whose gaze exposes his protagonists' worst fears about themselves."[156] I'd argue that ornate frames and mirrors also display what Minnelli saw as beautiful, or, to recall Parker Tyler and Tchelitchev's notion, the beautiful freaks (consider Judy Garland in *Meet Me in St. Louis* and certainly Waters and Horne). By framing at the beginning of the film the cabin as work of art and a place of art, Minnelli indicates the tropic transformation from one of nostalgic fantasy of the naive and simple folk to that of savvy creative engagement.

The cabin we see in the drawings is, in fact, quite similar to Minnelli's internationally inflected modernist sketches for his New York productions that recall the Mexican-born Miguel Corarrabius, Italian-born Paolo Garreto, and the American Ralph Barton's work for *Vanity Fair*. Minnelli's idea of the cabin is far from the image cast by the romanticized writings of Agee and the photographs of Walker Evans that nostalgically evoked a "folksiness" of southern sharecroppers. Instead, Minnelli's cabin is rendered as a hotbed of "soundings." As the cabin in the credit sequence arcs its way in each drawing from left to right then back again through puffy clouds (not unlike Minnelli's sketch for "Paradise Night") it is seen as a lively house where trumpets protrude from its windows while musical notes engulf the place. In the drawings, it appears as if the cabin is bursting with groove and pleasure. Indeed, given the weight of the film's beginnings, it is possible to see the cabin-home not as the framing of the simple black folk's attempts to mimic white middle-class sensibilities. Rather, the cabin is the site of queer and African American "sophisticating."

The film's scene in the Paradise club is likely to be considered most representative of Minnellian urbane modernity, notably because of its glamorous Harlem-style club setting and its knockout numbers performed by Horne, Waters, and Sublett (ironically, Busby Berekely directed Sublett's "Shine" number at the club). However, I'd like to examine a more prescient scene in the film where the "sound" of the folk evokes a traditional spiritualness at the same time that it evokes a knowing, urbane sophistication. In the number "Takin' a Chance on Love" (originally composed by Vernon Duke for the play), Little Joe has just purchased a washing machine for Petunia for her birthday. Overwhelmed, she begins to tear up. To change the mood, Little Joe asks her to sing the song that she first sang, as he reminds her, "when they first . . ." Petunia blushes and quickly stops Little Joe from revealing just what the event was that caused her to break into song in the first place. Petunia—like Waters herself—is not exactly the perfect angel.[157] As she begins the number, one of the deliverymen, Bill (Bill Bailey)—a friend of Little Joe's who helped bring Petunia her gift—enters the cabin.[158]

As Waters begins to sing, the cabin evolves into a Minnellian stage on which she has before performed on Broadway. The "humble shack" where the Jacksons live becomes a sophisticated site for dancing and singing. In a tightly framed three-shot we see Little Joe playing guitar, Petunia singing, and, forming the apex of the shot, Bill adds additional sound and dance. What is striking about Bill is his style. Dressed similarly to the way Minnelli often dressed on the set (slicked hair, sport jacket, opened-collar dress shirt, pleated pants, dual-toned dress shoes), one can't help but notice the uncanny doubling of Bill and Vincente (a projection?). Indeed, Bill and Vincente dance together with camera and body. As the camera pulls into a wide shot, Minnelli gives full view to Bill's ecstatic tap dance in a manner that is far different from Berkeley's more straightforward direction of Sublett at the Paradise. Indeed, Minnelli's moving camera penetrates the musicalized world of the cabin and becomes part of the performance. The cabin explodes with sound and movement as it echoes the vibrant cabin we see in the credit sequence from where a "constellation" of meaning has been dispersed; the initial set of images, the cabin, is thus a "floating figure which the narrative will take up again, vary, displace, transform."[159]

The Broadway Musical Play
'CABIN IN THE SKY'

1

Starring

Ethel Waters
Eddie 'Rochester' Anderson
Lena Horne

Associate Producer
Albert Lewis

3

With

Louis Armstrong   Rex Ingram
Duke Ellington and his Orchestra

The Hall Johnson Choir

Screen Play by
Joseph Schrank
Based Upon the Musical Play
Book by LYNN ROOT
Lyrics by JOHN LATOUCHE
and Music by VERNON DUKE
Produced on the Stage by ALBERT LEWIS
In Association with VINTON FREEDLEY

5

"Happiness Is a Thing Called Joe"
"Life's Full O' Consequence"
"L'il Black Sheep"
Lyrics by . . . . E. Y. HARBURG
Music by HAROLD ARLEN

"Going Up" . . . . DUKE ELLINGTON
Musical Adaptation . . . . . ROGER EDENS
Musical Direction . . . . . GEORGIE STOLL
Orchestration . . . . . GEORGE BASSMAN
Choral Arrangements . . . . . HALL JOHNSON

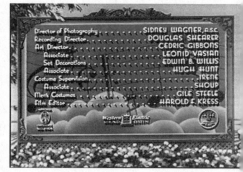

Director of Photography . . . . . SIDNEY WAGNER, A.S.C.
Recording Director . . . . . DOUGLAS SHEARER
Art Director . . . . . CEDRIC GIBBONS
Associate . . . . . LEONID VASIAN
Set Decorations . . . . . EDWIN B. WILLIS
Associate . . . . . HUGH HUNT
Costume Supervision . . . . . IRENE
Associate . . . . . SHOUP
Men's Costumes . . . . . GILE STEELE
Film Editor . . . . . HAROLD F. KRESS

7

9

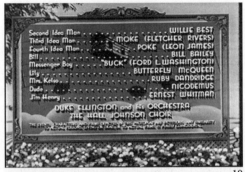

10

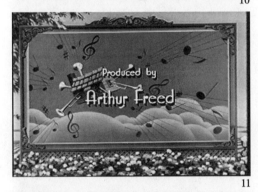

11

12

Title and credit sequence from Minnelli's *Cabin in the Sky* (1943).

Petunia and Little Joe's "humble shack" is now a sphere of floodlights, music, and cinematic decor where the performative barriers between screen and spectator, director and performers, commingle with the delicious and (recalling Litvak) sophisticated taste of one another.

But Minnelli, Waters, Anderson, and Bailey's performances also explode the strict divide of color. To be sure, critics commend Minnelli's "sensitive" direction of the film and its performers and his "handsome sepia-tone surface."[160] Minnelli was, as well, pleased with this aesthetic decision that he and Arthur Freed decided to use. "The film was transformed," Minnelli lauded, "It seemed more magical. Sepia created a soft, velvety patina more flattering to the actor's skin tones."[161] *Cabin in the Sky* thus expanded on the technicalities of sound and the cursory division of "black and white." If Hollywood's "aesthetic technology" historically insisted on a hard separation of blackness and whiteness, Minnelli imbued *Cabin in the Sky* with a "soft, velvety patina" to melt the aggressive edges of the technical color line. Just as Minnelli had sought to dissolve the barriers between "foot-light and stage door" in his work in New York (or as Litvak describes it in another context, the "blurring of the line between eaters and eaten"),[162] he collapsed the ideological and strictly demarcated lines of black and white that Hollywood emphasized in its industrial production. The expanded spectrum of sepia thus provided Minnelli with a richer aesthetic more attuned to his lived world.

In an interview in 1962, Minnelli suggests that "color should be used in a realistic context, the limits of which are dictated by the subject of the film."[163] He then goes on to say, "The filmmaker must have a point of view toward his subject . . . which gives the film unity and the audience must feel this unity" (107). Throughout his career, Minnelli reiterated his sense of color and realism, a queer American realism, as one couched in the imbrication of the artist, the work of art, and the "audience." Minnelli's American realism was a sophisticated taste flavored by the internationalism of George Balanchine, Pavel Tchelitchev, Ethel Waters, and others of the 1930s New York queer roundtable. His was an aestheticized world made glamorous by the "color and fire" that he experienced in 1930s New York. Minnelli was once asked how one develops a sense of color; in response, he stated: "By learning to *see* color. We are all surrounded by color if we will only learn to notice it" (107). To "see" color, however, was not simply accomplished by sight as we have seen. Minnelli's senses of "color" were embraced as multiple

(*Above*) Bill Bailey, Eddie "Rochester" Anderson, and Ethel Waters performing in Minnelli's "sophisticated" cabin during the number *Takin' a Chance on
Love*. *(Below)* Mervin LeRoy, Vincente Minnelli, Eddie "Rochester" Anderson, and Jack Benny on the set of *Cabin in the Sky*. Note the similarities
between Minnelli's and Bailey's suits in these two photos. Photographs and
Prints Division, Schomburg Center for Research in Black Culture, the New
York Public Library, Astor, Lenox and Tilden Foundations.

sensory experiences channeled by the kinetic energies of light, sound, and touch.

Theory of the Pleasure Class

Katherine Dunham recently expressed her pleasure with the "sophistication" of contemporary African American music, such as hip hop. When pressed to explain the difference between the "sophistication" of 1920s and 1930s New York and that of contemporary culture, she concluded that earlier concepts of sophistication were more about the "primitive and baser instincts," the "sexual."[164] Yet, to separate the "primitive" and the sexual from "sophistication" is, in fact, to "de-queer" sophistication. If the "bourgeoisie," as Litvak contends, "has so much at stake in reorienting society around the values of naturalness and unpretentiousness,"[165] then it is incumbent on queer culture to conjure the effete, exotic, and decadent terms of sophistication in order to remain as pretentious and, certainly, as sexual as possible.

As I have argued in this book, the feasting of the Other in order to author and hold fast the tenets of white American masculinity has been a performative gesture that seeks to de-sophisticate by reining in the excesses of culture (i.e., that which is not identified with hetero-masculinist culture). Indeed, the taste of the Other (white queers feasting on African Americans and African Americans feasting on white queers) is precisely the engorgement of Otherness that takes aesthetic pleasure in the commingling of difference. In a manner different from Edwin Forrest's devouring of Push-ma-ta-ha for the sake of defending his nativist, virile masculinity as an artist, the queer feasting of Otherness, as discussed above, reveals a perverse and decadent cannibalism that satiates both the eater and the eaten.

In the productions of *Cabin in the Sky* the queer tastings of cultural difference exposed an aesthetic integration that left many in the audience—including the critics of the period as well as more recent writers—uncertain about just what it is that has been projected on the screen. Unless, as Matthew Tinkcom rightly insists, "we can make some leap between the bits of gossip lore that situate the films in differing accounts of Hollywood history and the potential for remarking on the stylistic anomalies of the films, we foreclose the possibility for acknowledging an articulation between queer producers of popular culture and their idiosyncratic products."[166] To my mind, *Cabin in the Sky* is an "idiosyncratic product" that recommends an opportunity through its "stylistic anomalies" to consider the American frontier at once international, multiracial, and superfluously queer.

Indeed, the uncertainty, the ambiguity, and the queerness of the delicious intermingling of aestheticized Otherness is nothing less than the success of pretentious sophistication.

Epilogue

In 1991 Marlon Riggs, in an interview for his controversial film *Tongues Untied* (1989), stated that in order for the revolutionary act of black men loving black men to occur, it was first necessary to "get at the issue of black gay men loving white gay men."[1] To this end, Riggs, in *Tongues Untied*, provocatively intertwines the poetic rhythms of Walt Whitman and Essex Hemphill—mediated through cinematic form and content—to evoke the complex and inextricable experiences of race, desire, and sexuality. Certainly, Riggs's production reveals a central query of this book: that is, the issue of specifically what cultural (gender, race, sexuality, class, national) and aesthetic (form and content) effects are generated, assumed, and challenged through the intermingling of artist and Other. Riggs's evocation of the taboo relationship of "black gay men loving white gay men" draws to the surface those uneasy aspects of cultural desire and corporeal communion that American artists have either repressed deeply, engaged circuitously, or expressed forthrightly as part and parcel of their creative enterprise. In this way, Riggs's overt articulation of penetration and exchange of bodily fluids between queer bodies in *Tongues Untied* partakes of the long tradition held by American artists and pundits where the national artistic experience takes shape through cannibalization.[2] Moreover, and as Riggs's work makes clear, the relationship between the eater and the eaten is not unidirectional and operates through discrete power relations.

As I have demonstrated in this book, the "feasting" of the Other suggests sharp ideological contrasts over what such aesthetic ingestion yields. Edwin Forrest's claim, for example, that his specifically contoured body mirrored both the nation's "sublime," rugged landscape as well as the noble savagery of Push-ma-ta-ha (the American Indian body he "devoured") provided a far different version of the American male artist than the one encountered in Vincente Minnelli's queer commingling with African American artists associated with the late Harlem Renaissance period. Minnelli's sophisticated designs for theater and film (enabled precisely because of such intercultural ingesting) put forth a queer American aesthetic that celebrated the perverse decadence and internationalized cultural milieus of the urban landscape (and thus quite distinct from Forrest's purported embodiment of pure nature and indigenous culture).

Both Forrest's and Minnelli's feasting of the Other tell of the myriad strategies that American male artists put in motion to establish their sui generis national artistry as well as their national manhood. As I have argued here, many intricate cultural and biohistorical threads weave together, overlap, disperse, and reconnect to generate the conditions of an American work of cinematic art. Thus, this book's aim has been to identify significant cinematic works that dramatically—if not spectacularly—reveal the uneven production of a masculinist and nationalist discourse in the American arts, particularly in the American cinema.

To step into the realm of the American arts is a complicated "field of cultural production" (to borrow Bourdieu's terms). It is my hope that the countless intersections between discursive/aesthetic practices and historical lives traced in this book have made themselves known if only to indicate additional and possible points of entry that might be entertained.

In fact, many possible inquiries stem from the imbricated discourses attended to here about American nationalism and masculinism in relationship to the cinema and other arts. We might, for example, revisit the strains of cultural practices operating in American cinematic art to consider the intricately conjoined issues of corporeality, race, gender, sexuality, and class that inform the images we see on the screen after World War II. In what way, for example, does Stan Brakhage fit into the ideological thinking that took shape under the tutelage of Clement Greenberg and the abstract expressionists, especially in terms of masculinity, race, nationalism, and avant-garde form? How might one map the historical legacy of racism and homophobia attending the creative milieus of New York underground filmmakers and pop or minimalist artists during the 1960s? Though some scholars have provided critical studies of racism in the work of Andy Warhol and Robert Mapplethorpe, historical analyses of works such as Shirley Clarke's *Portrait of Jason* need further investigation so as to unpack the racist and homophobic ideological tropes of the film as they run concurrent with American avant-garde strategies and practices.[3] In this way, it is worth considering the ways that the filmmakers Marlon Riggs and Todd Haynes aesthetically confront these avant-garde tensions between racist and homophobic discourses in their "queer cinema." Finally, it is necessary to continue the investigation into the aesthetic of realism: what are the historical conditions that facilitate the never-ending crusade to secure American realism as the national aesthetic well into the twenty-first century? (The Christian-painter Thomas Kinkade and the Hollywood directors Mel Gibson and James Cameron initially come to mind here.) What ideological forces sustain this privileged aesthetic as American?

Yet, the repetition of discourse and practice that organizes the terms for American masculinism and nationalism by no means augurs a homogenous ideological culture. Instead, it is the ironic failings, the peculiar twists and turns, and the over-determined polemical pronouncements that generate—with powerful affect—the uncanny resiliency of masculinist nationalism in the American cinematic arts.

Notes

1 Nineteenth-Century Masculinity and Realism

1 Riots and rowdiness are long-standing issues in the history of the American theater. As Butsch points out in *The Making of an American Audience* (54–55), the most volatile era for theatrical outbursts began around 1817 and closed with the Astor Place Riot in 1849. For a detailed account of the Astor Place Riot, see Moody, *Astor Place Riot*, 12 (see 172 for casualty statistics). In addition, the following works give descriptions of the event: Ellis, *The Epic of New York City*, 255–65; Reynolds, *Walt Whitman's America*, 163–65; Levine, *Highbrow, Low Brow*, 63–69; and Burrows and Wallace, *Gotham*, 761–68.

2 Moody, *Astor Place Riot*, 56.

3 "The proscenium," writes Wilentz, "proved no barrier to active participation" during Bowery productions (*Chants Democratic*, 259). "Inattention and free trespass," Butsch writes, "of the boundary between performer and audience [during the pre-revolution era] were practices that served to affirm gentry status and the general hierarchy of colonial life. While the upper class predominated, a few commoners appear to have attended as well" (*The Making of an American Audience*, 23). Indeed, by the time of "the Jacksonian era, roughly 1825–1850, theater belonged to the common man" (44). Levine confirms that "the theater in the first half of the nineteenth century played the role that movies played in the first half of the twentieth; it was a kaleidoscope, democratic institution presenting a widely varying bill of fare to all classes and socioeconomic groups" (*Highbrow, Low Brow*, 21). The boundary between stage and audience where an ideal, middle-class, well-behaved spectator silently watched the theatrical spectacle—especially in young America—was not yet earnestly divided by middle-class proprieties. In fact, America's immigrant and working-class audiences had historically, yet certainly uncomfortably, mixed with those of America's landed gentry

in a wide variety of theatrical venues. I would suggest, however, that it was not simply the mixing of classes as such that initiated the chaotic events that took place at the Astor Place Opera House on the evening of May 10. Indeed, the violence occurred around concerns of class, but more important were the issues of nationhood, aesthetics, and masculine identity.

4 Irish American national sentiment and the Irish involvement in the Astor Place Riot are recounted in Wittke, *The Irish in America*, 47; and Shannon, *The American Irish*, 40. Additional material on Irish American immigrants can be found in Greeley's *That Most Distressful Nation* and Wakin's *Enter the Irish American*. For an account of Irish unrest with Britain and parallel rebellious interests with America, see Maier, *From Resistance to Revolution*, 178–79, 255. A useful background to Irish immigration (which was in the thousands as early as 1818) and immigrant living conditions in New York is given in Burrows and Wallace, *Gotham*, 401–2, 478–80, 543–46, 735–60. Foner, in *Free Soil, Free Labor, Free Men* (33–34, 230–32), provides an illuminating account of Irish American opposition to the antislavery movement as well as how the Irish were perceived in the U.S. Northeast.

5 Those Americans who at the time supported Macready and came to his defense included Longfellow, Washington Irving, and Herman Melville. Macready was not the first to disparage American audiences and in turn receive their wrath. George Farren, a British actor, was mobbed by anti-British protestors in 1834 when it was reported that he had "insulted the American flag" and attacked a butcher (reported in Wilentz, *Chants Democratic*, 265).

6 Shannon, *The American Irish*, 40.

7 Burrows and Wallace note that "the combination of nationalist pride and hatred of Great Britain . . . was integral to popular culture in New York" during the late eighteenth century and well into the nineteenth (*Gotham*, 427). For an additional discussion of the historical disdain for Britain during the nineteenth century, see Smith's *The Virgin Land*, 26, 42. See Butsch's valuable work on anti-British sentiment and its relationship to the development of American theater in *The Making of an American Audience*, 26–27, especially 53. See also Burrows and Wallace, *Gotham*, 453, 557.

8 White, *Tropics of Discourse*, 151–52.

9 Pure negation is, of course, no simple matter. What White's account ignores is that the act of negation is haunted by the very historical conditions it seeks to refuse. Ironically, traces of the British Empire continued to linger as part of America's definition of self, no matter how earnest and violent (and no matter the form of) the break from British culture in 1849. Edwin Forrest still performed Shakespeare (as does today the Joseph Papp Public Theater in New York), albeit in what Levine in *Highbrow, Low Brow* (14)

positively describes as a "mutilated" version. Mutilated or not, Old World cultural traditions linger across the American arts. The uses (and abuses) of these traces, however, spoke directly to the variants of masculine creativity in American culture. Indeed, "Declarations of affection for Britain," writes Maier, "continued and hopes that independence be averted were expressed on into late 1775, even by the man who finally wrote the Declaration of Independence" (*From Resistance to Revolution*, 228). Maier covers similar tales of American colonial obsequiousness and resistance to Britain throughout her book (see 23, 100, 106, 134). Nineteenth-century America's competitive, if not angst-ridden, nostalgia for its British heritage was excessively demonstrated with the construction of the ornamental Crystal Palace in New York in 1853 (Burrows and Wallace, *Gotham*, 669).

10 Levine, *Highbrow, Low Brow*, 66. See also Moody, *Astor Place Riot*, 45.

11 The pride of, for example, the Irish and their rebellious and rowdy spirit is documented in Wittke, *The Irish in America*, 40–51; and Greeley, *That Most Distressful Land*, xxvi, 19–27. See Altschuler and Blumin's insightful analysis of America's "disdain for the formalities of polite address" in *Rude Republic*, 8.

12 See J. C. Trewin's introduction to *The Journal of William Charles Macready*, 44.

13 Macready, *The Journal of William Charles Macready*, 205–6.

14 Frohne, "Strategies of Recognition," 211–44, 215.

15 See, for example, Smith's *The Virgin Land* where he discusses Kit Carson's work during the period of 1849 in relation to an aesthetic that "developed entirely apart from the genteel conception" (94).

16 See Foucault, *The History of Sexuality*; and Sinfield, *The Wilde Century*.

17 An American Citizen, *A Rejoinder to "The Replies from England, etc.,"* 115.

18 In this way, "American Citizen" anticipates Griselda Pollock's critique of masculinity, democracy, and equality: "The pre-eminent ideological figure is MAN which immediately reveals the partiality of their democracy and universalism. The rallying cry, liberty, equality and fraternity (again note its gender partiality) imagines a society composed of free, self-possessing male individuals exchanging with equal and like." "Modernity and the Spaces of Femininity," 67.

19 Wilentz writes, "At the turn of the nineteenth century, several writers pointed out that England's wealth was being absorbed by 'non-producing,' parasitical landlords and the military; twenty years later, William Thompson, John Gray, Thomas Hodgskin, and other radical publicists turned these charges against the capitalist credit and wage system" (*Chants Democratic*, 158).

20 Forrest patriotically claimed, "the time would come when American actors would do the American acting" (quoted in Moody, *Astor Place Riot*, 85). See also Alger's *Life of Edwin Forrest*, 28.

21 See Hofstadter's comments in his elegiac *Anti-Intellectualism in American Life* on the masculinist underpinnings of American democracy. According to Hofstadter, "Something was missing in the dialectic of American populistic democracy. Its exponents meant to diminish, if possible to get rid of, status differences in American life" (155). As if to recapture what is conceived of as a phallic lack and thus insure a genderless (that is, masculine) society, American men urgently reframed the terms of equality: "If women invaded politics, they would become masculine, just as men became feminine when they espoused reform. Horace Bushnell suggested that if women got the vote and kept it for hundreds of years, 'the very look and temperament of women will be altered.' The appearance of women would be sharp, their bodies wiry, their voices shrill, their actions angular and abrupt, and full of self-assertion, will, boldness, and eagerness for place and power. It could also be expected that in this nightmare of female assertion, women would actually 'change type physiologically, they will become taller and more brawny, and get bigger hands and feet, and a heavier weight of brain,' and would very likely become 'thinner, sharp-featured, lank and dry, just as all disappointed, over-instigated natures always are' " (190).

22 Potter, "The Quest for the National Character." Forrest fits Slotkin's definition of the "populist" hero: "They are freedom loving individualists who defend worthy folk who are oppressed or dispossessed by powerful men and combinations bent on monopoly" (*Gunfighter Nation*, 216).

23 Lewis, *The American Adam*.

24 See Moody, *Edwin Forrest*; and Moody, *Astor Place Riot*, 30, 122. Macready himself was sensitive to Forrest's popularity with the Bowery B'hoys as Trewin makes clear in *The Journal of William Charles Macready*, xxiii.

25 Moody, *Astor Place Riot*, 238–39. Moody also records a more enthusiastic account of Forrest by Whitman, where Whitman recalls the bawdy atmosphere and "full-blooded young and middle-aged men, the best average of American born mechanics" who surrounded Forrest's performances with their "electric force and muscle from perhaps two thousand full-sinew'd men" (29–30).

26 Elsewhere I have argued that notions of aesthetics and style are not so easily separated from what some call the "political." Many scholars curiously subscribe to the idea that, for example, photographic realism, because it is historically linked to progressivist and socialist activity, is ideologically more valuable and substantive. Trachtenberg, for example, dismisses Alfred Stieglitz's claims for photographic art as nothing more than a "history of

styles, of changing looks and aesthetic traditions" and, worse, it existed in "isolation of the aesthetic from social functions" (*Reading American Photographs*, 175; I will engage Stieglitz somewhat differently in chapter 4). Lewis Hine's philanthropic, creative, and "social" activity, on the other hand, "consists of social spaces, of active figures, the bodies of men and women and children bearing their identities in posture, clothing, physiognomy" (217). Hines is active, Stieglitz passive. Moreover, because Hines contributed to "social uplift" (201) in America and to the portraiture of "social labor," his work is viewed as more participatory and socially relevant. As I hope to demonstrate in this book, arguments such as Trachtenberg's seal the terms for democracy and equality by wrapping them in masculinist terms. Another example is given by Shi in *Facing Facts*, where he compares the painters William Merrit Chase and Robert Henri by posing Chase's creative sensibilities as artificial and Henri's as natural. Shi tells us that Chase's realism was "epidermal" and glossed with "dazzling surfaces and delicate details." Furthermore, Chase paraded around the streets of New York in "tailored morning coats and striking cravats . . . with his white wolfhound." Henri, on the other hand, was "more down-to-earth." He is characterized as "warm and unpretentious [and] promoted both the creation of a distinctive American 'style' of painting and the democratization of the art world" (257). For many scholars, American popular democratic art can only be envisaged as not effeminate, artificial, or decadent. Recent queer theorists have questioned such assumptions about aesthetics. See my essays "Queer Angels of History Take It and Leave It from Behind" and "Queer Modernism"; as well as Pollock's "Modernity and the Spaces of Femininity."

27　See, especially, Whitman's *Democratic Vistas*.

28　Staiger, in "The Eyes Are Really the Focus," shows that this nineteenth-century "realist" style was pivotal for cinematic performance some fifty years later. Although Staiger places the shift of acting styles—what she identifies as a move from a "presentational" to "representational" (15) mode or toward a performance of "naturalism"—between 1865 and 1890, Whitman's critique of those who could not equal Forrest's purported natural performance style suggests an earlier transition toward "conventionalized realism" (16).

29　Tocqueville, *Democracy in America*, 1: 275, 326.

30　Moody, *Edwin Forrest*, 31.

31　For discussions about Forrest's widely publicized involvement in politics, his divorce proceedings, his travels abroad, and his public commentary on popular culture and everyday affairs, see Moody, *Edwin Forrest*; and, especially, Moody, *Astor Place Riot*, 32, 43.

32　Alger, *Life of Edwin Forrest*, 239.

33　Moody, *Edwin Forrest*, 27.

34 Slotkin, *Regeneration through Violence*, 521.

35 Alger, *Life of Edwin Forrest*, 136. Moody also recounts this moment between Forrest and Push-ma-ta-ha: "Forrest shared the ancient Greek's delight in the beauty of the naked human form. Moreover, [Forrest] maintained that fashionable clothes degraded and obscured the beauty that God had created. One evening he asked the Chief to strip and walk back and forth before him between the moonlight and the firelight so that he might feast his eyes and soul on so complete a physical type of what man should be. The Chief obliged. Forrest said that it was as if a living statue of Apollo in glowing bronze had come to life" (47–48). Writing in the late 1950s Moody phrases the event somewhat differently. It is also worth noting Gilmore's contention that the secondhand versions of Forrest and Push-ma-ta-ha do not mitigate the import of the encounter since the tale is directly linked to the popular mythology of Forrest ("The Genuine Article," 42; I want to thank the author for sharing his rigorous and thoughtful work with me). Though Gilmore's later book, *The Genuine Article*, deals less directly with Forrest's encounter with Push-ma-ta-ha, he thoughtfully explores what he terms "literary manhood." Forrest, as Gilmore points out, was intimately linked to the development of this cultural by-product.

It is also quite possible that Forrest was echoing this tale from George Catlin's own observations of the American Indian. The painter/writer's work was exhibited extensively during 1841 in the Northeast. For examples of similar descriptions of Indians, see Catlin, *North American Indians*, 8, 10, 18, 27, 29, 48, 61.

36 See Butsch, *The Making of an American Audience*, 26; as well as Burrows and Wallace, *Gotham*, 453.

37 Gilmore, "The Genuine Article," 42. See also Alger's comments that "never did an actor more thoroughly identify and merge himself with his part than Forrest did in Metamora. He was completely transformed from what he appeared in other characters, and seemed Indian in every particular, all through and all over, from the crown of his scalp to the sole of his foot" (*Life of Edwin Forrest*, 239). See also Pearce, *Savagism and Civilization*, 176–78, for a thorough analysis of *Metamora*.

38 Deloria adds that twentieth-century "modernist Indians imitated and appropriated the Other viscerally through the medium of their bodies" (*Playing Indian*, 120). Forrest's experience with Push-ma-ta-ha suggests that such visceral appropriation of the Indian occurred well before the twentieth century. Gaul, in her essay " 'The Genuine Indian Who Was Brought upon the Stage,' " directly addresses Forrest's nonthreatening "imagined redness" in his role of Metamora that reaffirmed the privileged whiteness of the audience.

39 Gilmore, "The Genuine Article," 35.

40 For a historical overview of minstrelsy and American Indians, see Toll, "Social Commentary in Late Nineteenth-Century White Minstrelsy."

41 See Slotkin, *Gunfighter Nation*, 143–45; and Deloria, *Playing Indian*, 29, 68. The myth of the Indian functions through an endless, yet paradoxical, parade of useful narrative tropes at once good, evil, and savagely noble.

42 Deloria, *Playing Indian*, 37.

43 Quoted in Nelson, *National Manhood*, 89.

44 There has been much written on the white man's romanticization of the American Indian. See, for example, Fairchild, *The Noble Savage*; the excellent essay by Nash, "The American Cult of the Primitive"; Pearce, *Savagism and Civilization*; Berkhofer, *The White Man's Indian*; and Forster-Hahn, "Inventing the Myth of the American Frontier."

45 Bederman, *Manliness and Civilization*, 173.

46 Gilmore ("The Genuine Article," 41) quotes the 1829 definition from *Webster's American Dictionary*.

47 This is, of course, what Sedgwick in *Epistemology of the Closet* discusses as the late-nineteenth-century principle of the closet.

48 Nash, "The American Cult of the Primitive," 521.

49 See Berkhofer's discussion on nineteenth-century progressivist movements and the American Indian in *The White Man's Indian*, 166–75.

50 It would seem, in fact, that Alger's biography of Forrest serves as a treatise on the theatrical method wherein one might achieve a transcendent oneness with both oneself and the world. The "savage" is the starting point for man's creative and transcendent experience. See Alger's *Life of Edwin Forrest*, especially 82–95.

51 Slotkin's work in *Regeneration through Violence* (125), for example, demonstrates how the early Puritans (in order to overcome their fear of forced Indian marriages) wrote extensively (and perhaps with some pleasure) on incidents of cannibalism that occurred in captive narratives.

52 Slotkin, *Regeneration through Violence*, 125.

53 Alger, *Life of Edwin Forrest*, 136. Perhaps not surprisingly, Forrest "saw the stage Indian as an almost literal embodiment of the histrionic qualities he cherished: physical vigor and passionate expression. Nor was he unaware of the fact that the colorful, yet scanty, tribal regalia would permit a provocative display of his calves and biceps" (Alger, 89).

54 In the vein of nineteenth-century artistic notions, Forrest's directing of movement and light is suggestive of his contemporary Emerson's prerequisite for the condition to create beauty: "And as the eye is the best composer, so light is the first of painters. There is no object so foul that intense light will not make beautiful." (*The Essential Writings of Ralph Waldo Emerson*, 9).

55 I follow Belsey's definition of "common sense," especially as she posits it in relation to issues of realism. She writes: "Common sense proposes a *humanism* based on an *empiricist-idealist* interpretation of the world (*Critical Practice*, 7). In this way, the aesthetic of realism, as I discuss later, upholds humanist ideals through discursive and ideological principles where the "facts of nature are there for everyone to see and to be plainly expressed" (9). For an antidote to the androcentric conclusions about American experience, see Kolodny's *The Lay of the Land* and *The Land before Her*; see also Shohat, "Gender and Culture of Empire." It is worth noting that even Kolodny's reading of women's experience in America's new frontier remains tethered to the (masculine) binary that sees women as the civilized gardeners of the frontier while men chop and industrialize it.

56 Mitchell, *Westerns*, 30.

57 See Spiegel, *Fiction and the Camera Eye*; and Sypher, *Rococo to Cubism in Art and Literature*, especially 257–93.

58 Rovitt, "American Literature and 'The American Experience,'" 121. Rovitt goes on to say: "And the American experience possessed, at least as one of its major determining ingredients, an inevitable effect of thrusting man into temporal and spatial isolation without a framework of tradition or society which could give him the security of self-definition. The American has characteristically been alone — "the man against the sky" — fronting a wilderness with the force of his own personality, and even though the physical wilderness gradually succumbs to his efforts, the metaphysical wilderness remains" (116).

59 See Turner's essay "Contributions of the West to American Democracy," in his *The Frontier in American History*, 261.

60 Orvell, *The Real Thing*, 35.

61 Fried first discusses his concept of "absorption" in his book *Absorption and Theatricality* (43). He later develops the idea in an American context in his work on Thomas Eakins (*Realism, Writing, Disfiguration*). In cinema studies Gunning, in his essay "An Aesthetic of Astonishment" (827), begins an initial investigation into Fried's theory of "absorption." He does not, however, fully explore the dual and contradictory effects of contemplation and spectatorial "insertion" in the text. Singer, in *Melodrama and Modernity* (176–77) cavalierly announces a theory of "absorption" that is strikingly similar to Fried's argument for his study of the early cinema and realism. Singer does not, however, refer to Fried's work.

62 Fried, *Realism, Writing, Disfiguration*, 42.

63 This is, of course, the main thread of Fried's work in his *Absorption and Theatricality*. "The young man reading," writes Fried, "is plainly engrossed in his performance" (27).

64 Fried, *Absorption and Theatricality*, 108.

65 Fried, *Realism, Writing, Disfiguration*, 81.

66 Although not explicitly raised in the essay, Fried points to Eakin's own insertion into the work (from a cameo appearance to the pleasure of consistently using calligraphy graphics sketched on everything from sheets of music to sculls). Here I am simplifying a complex argument by Fried that takes up a rigorous Freudian analysis of Eakin's paintings in relationship to paternal hands (from his own father to Walt Whitman) whose presence seemingly grasps the painter and his paintings at every turn. Many critics, directly or indirectly, take up a Freudian treatment of artists and their engagement with realism as a way to reinvigorate their masculinity against the castration threat and the demonization of effeminacy as an artist. These analyses often occur around William Dean Howells and Henry James. See, for example, Habegger's rote *Gender, Fantasy, and Realism in American Literature* (62); and Shi, *Facing Facts*, 103–4, 124–25. Clark, in "Gross David with the Swoln Cheek," provides a more subtle reading of the philosophical concerns of the body and mind relationship in eighteenth-century France and the idea of self-portraiture.

67 To suggest that Forrest had been aware of such aesthetic and theoretical assessments by the likes of Diderot is not out of bounds. Given his social and creative circles, his voracious readings, and his travels to England and France, Forrest was assuredly put into direct contact with these critical concepts. The continental ideas and aesthetic concerns of Britain and France undoubtedly made their way into American discussions about modes of creative production. But in the hands of America's artists such theories were manipulated (or mutilated, to borrow Levine's term) to fit the colonies' own cultural forces and ideological spheres. For a consideration of American/European transAtlantic exchanges, see Franklin, *The Autobiography of Benjamin Franklin*; Tocqueville, *Democracy in America*; Alberts, *Benjamin West*; Douglas, *The Feminization of American Culture*, 170–71; Smith, *The Virgin Land*, 145; and Slotkin, *Regeneration through Violence*, 201, 204, 231, 314.

68 The title of this subsection is taken from Emerson's essay "The American Scholar," in his *The Essential Writings*, 49.

69 See Neil's discussion of this historical relationship in *Toward a National Taste*, 1–50.

70 "Art and Artists in America," *American Review*, 658.

71 On Arnold's reception in America, see Trachtenberg, *The Incorporation of America*, 155; and May, *The End of American Innocence*, 32–33.

72 Emerson, *The Essential Writings*, 11.

73 I am discussing a concept of nativist essentialism (the land, the American Indian) as a romantic ideal that identified a unique American sensi-

bility. Another form of nativism existed concurrently in the United States. In this instance, nativism referred to a biological connection with Anglo-Saxon bloodlines traceable to British heritage. This brand of nativism was a xenophobic response to the influx of immigrants and the simultaneous rise of Catholicism. See Burrows and Wallace, *Gotham*, 631; and Foner, *Free Soil, Free Labor, Free Men*, 196–260.

74 Fairchild, *The Noble Savage*, 498.

75 Quoted in Fairchild, *The Noble Savage*, 420–21. Fairchild mistakenly titles Emerson's poem, "Goodbye, Proud World." For Emerson's poem, see *The Essential Writings*, 685.

76 In his work "Frost and the American View of Nature," Griffith situates the poet (albeit transfigured in Frost's "modern" moment) with the romantics, "because of his preference for the situations, relationships and attitudes with the Nature of poetry of nineteenth-century romanticism" (21). This is to say that the poet is "fond of joining [man and nature] in a dramatic encounter" where man "discovers meaningful facts about himself and the world he dwells in" (21). Such "romantic" ideas cut across other media such as in the photography of Ansel Adams and the filmmaking of Stan Brakhage. And, again, although nature is perhaps somewhat more contaminated in these more "modern" works, the appeal to discover meaningful facts about the artist and his world continue to prevail.

77 For a discussion of Pearce's triadic model of "Idea, Symbol, Image" that sought to categorize America's cultural comprehension of the American Indian, see Arnold Krupat's foreword to Pearce's *Savagism and Civilization*.

78 The fraught cultural contest over the Indian body and the claims to an authentic Americanism were highly divisive. There was much debate from the moment the Puritans arrived in the seventeenth century, for example, about whether or not the "savage" was truly "noble." By the nineteenth century the sciences, arts, trading posts, and presses engaged at length with the "idea" of the Indian; it was a topic as popular as it was contested. What was certain, however, was that in all areas of the ideological debate, the white settler saw a democratic and Christian civilization as the ultimate goal. The ends for the American Indian were, of course, different in these arguments: the Indian hater wanted the "red man" dead, the so-called liberals hoped (and undoubtedly prayed) that the Indian would become a good agrarian and abide by good Christian practices. Whether through hatred or pity, the end result was the same: the Indian would perish. For a discussion of white America's historical idea of and relationship to the Indian, see Pearce, *Savagism and Civilization*; Berkhofer, *The White Man's Indian*, 33–111; Horsman, "Scientific Racism and the American Indian in the Mid-Nineteenth Century"; Bieder, "Anthropology and History of the Indian"; MacGregor,

"Tammany"; Saum, "The Fur Trader and the Noble Savage"; and Nelson, *National Manhood*, 61–67.

79 Thoreau, *Walden*, 58. On Thoreau and his embrace of the American Indian, see Gilmore, *The Genuine Article*, 67–97. Slotkin suggests that "Emerson echoes (knowingly or unknowingly) the thoughts of Leatherstocking in *The Pioneers* and *The Prairies* when he quotes Thoreau as saying, 'Thank God . . . they [Man] cannot cut down the clouds' " (*Regeneration through Violence*, 519).

80 Slotkin, *Regeneration through Violence*, 519.

81 Quoted in Sheehan, *Seeds of Extinction*, 96. The Indian, as Sheehan tells us, is no mere representation to be gazed upon: "More significant as part of the landscape of paradise, the noble savage reflected a unidimensional image. Rather than standing aside from his surroundings, as did civilized man, the noble savage blended into the surface of paradise. In effect, he could not be differentiated from a natural resource" (90).

82 Fried, *Absorption and Theatricality*, 132.

83 See Catlin, *North American Indians*; and Evans, "Cushing's Zuni Sketchbooks."

84 Smith, *The Virgin Land*, 83.

85 Nelson, *National Manhood*, 67.

86 Edelman, *Homographesis*, 50–51.

87 I discuss the ironies of over-determined masculine performance in my essay "Dancer from the Dance."

88 Gaines, *Fire and Desire*, 266.

89 Belsey points out that realism (what she calls "expressive-realism") raises more questions than it seemingly resolves: "What form does it take? . . . What do we mean by 'realism'? In what sense is fiction 'true,' and what constitutes evidence of that truth? What is the relationship between a text (a discursive construct) and the world? To what extent is it possible to perceive the world independently of the conventional ways in which it is represented? To what extent is experience contained by language, society, history?" (*Critical Practice*, 14). See also the feminist critiques of American realism in Miller, "The Feminization of American Realist Theory"; and Dougherty, "The Ideology of Gender in Howells' Early Novels."

90 See my "Unsinkable Masculinity: The Artist and the Work of Art in James Cameron's *Titanic*," where through the study of the contemporary film *Titanic* (1997) I trace the historical idea of American realism as an aesthetic anchor for masculine authorial privilege and preoccupation that upholds the male artist's heteronormative identity. In *Titanic*, James Cameron (not unlike Thomas Eakins) inserts his presence, his authorial signature, in the film as a gesture of authorial intent and authenticity. The trope of realism is play-

fully rendered in the film as director/artist (Cameron) symbiotically manages the narrative between himself and the diegetic artist (Leonardo DiCaprio). The realist aesthetic, I conclude, has been useful to the extent that its ideological underpinnings prescribe an erasure of "effeminacy," or cultural excess, of the film's female protagonist (Kate Winslet) and the director's role as artist.

91 See, for example, Richard Schickel's interviews with Hawks and Fuller in his films, originally shown on PBS, *The Men Who Made the Movies*.

92 Löwy and Sayre thoroughly argue that romantic thought has a complicated political history and served as a "reaction against the way of life in capitalist societies" (*Romanticism against the Tide of Modernity*, 17).

93 Douglas, *The Feminization of American Culture*, 255.

94 Bell, *The Problem of American Realism*, 37.

95 Matthiessen, *American Renaissance*.

96 Novak, *American Painting of the Nineteenth Century*, 61; Sundquist, introduction to *American Realism*, 3. Note also the use of the word "problem" in Bell's title *The Problem of American Realism*.

97 The anxieties over the burgeoning machine culture and the loss of nature will be explored more fully in my discussion in chapter 4 of America's avant-garde.

98 Foner, *Reconstruction*, 233, 278; McPherson, *Battle Cry of Freedom*.

99 Slotkin, *Gunfighter Nation*, 33.

100 Trachtenberg, *The Incorporation of America*, 184.

101 The work on the concept of American realism is vast, to say the least. In literary studies see, for example, Kaplan, *The Social Construction of American Realism*; Habbegger, *Gender, Fantasy, and Realism in American Literature* (for the heterocentric and complicitly masculinist version of American Realism); Sundquist's introduction to *American Realism*; Stovell, *American Idealism*; Matthieson, *American Renaissance*, 517–49; and, as mentioned, Bell, *The Problem with American Realism*. For a study of painting and American realism, see Lucie-Smith, *American Realism*; and, as cited, Novak's *American Painting of the Nineteenth Century*. Shi, in *Facing Facts*, provides a rigorous (if teleological) interdisciplinary overview of American realism with a stress on the masculinist premise of realism. See Corkin, *Realism and the Birth of the Modern United States*, for film and for what the author terms "interdisciplinary" approaches to realism (although his approach is certainly not as rigorous as that of Shi). Pollock's important feminist work across media (and especially film) in *Vision and Difference* is extremely productive and thoughtful on the topics of realism and ideology (note especially the chapter "Screening the Seventies: Sexuality and Representation in Feminist Practice—A Brechtian Perspective," 155–99). Further, see Klinger, "'Cinema/Ideology/Criticism' Revisited"; and Margulies's *Rites of Realism*.

For an overview of the debates on cinematic realism, see Williams's edited collection, *Realism and the Cinema*.

102 Fried, *Realism, Writing, Disfiguration*, 73.

103 Mumford, *The Brown Decades*, 218.

104 Sundquist, introduction to *American Realism*, 14.

105 Althusser, "Ideology and Ideological State Apparatuses"; Belsey, *Critical Practice*.

106 Thomas Paine, "Common Sense," 81. It is instructive to highlight Paine's use of language to describe Britain's relationship to America: "And as a man [America], who is attached to a prostitute [Britain], is unfitted to choose or judge of a wife, so any prepossession in favour of a rotten constitution of government will disable us from discerning a good one" (71).

107 James, "The Varieties of Religious Experience," 469. It is important to remember that James studied scientific analysis and had faith in it: he attended the Lawrence Scientific School at Harvard where he studied organic chemistry and comparative anatomy. See Dupree, *Henry James*, 50–51; as well as Menand, *The Metaphysical Club*, 73–95.

108 As Smith puts it, "practical" meant for James (and C. S. Peirce before him) "practice or action." Being practical was the surest way for meanings to be translated into actions (*The Spirit of American Philosophy*, 14).

109 Smith, *The Spirit of American Philosophy*, 68. James's philosophy of "pragmatism" illuminates an important caveat to the either/or regulatory confines of common sense as unilateral in its nature. As James writes in his lecture, "The Varieties of Religious Experience": "Nevertheless, in the interests of intellectual clearness, I feel bound to say that religious experience, as we have studied it, cannot be cited as unequivocally supporting of the infinitist belief. The only thing that it unequivocally testifies to is that we can experience union with something larger than ourselves and in that union find our greatest peace. Philosophy, with its passion for unity, and mysticism with its mono-deistic bent, both 'pass to the limit' and identify the something with a unique God who is the all-inclusive soul of the world. Popular opinion, respectful to their authority, follows the example which they set" (468). James, in a manner similar to, but more precisely than, Emerson, Thoreau, and Whitman, questioned dogmatic drills of common sense or mystical transcendence that "popular opinion" was likely to follow.

110 Blakemore, " 'Without a Cross,' " 33.

111 Quoted in Freeman, *The Feminine Sublime*, 72.

112 The canonical texts on the sublime include Kant's *Critique of Aesthetic Judgement*; and Burke's *A Philosophical Enquiry into the Origin of Our Ideas of the Sublime*.

113 Freeman, *The Feminine Sublime*, 11.

114 Jon Pareles, "His Kind of Heroes, His Kind of Songs," *New York Times*, July 14, 2002, section 2, p. 1.

115 For an excellent overview of the transition from American artist as "deviant" and un-American to legitimate cultural producer, see Bell's "Beginnings of Professionalism," 67–133.

116 Sundquist, introduction to *American Realism*, 11.

117 Wolf, "A Grammar of the Sublime," 322. Wolf treats Thomas Weiskel's theory of the sublime more thoroughly (although less satisfyingly) in his book *Romantic Re-Vision*. Wolf's reading of Thomas Cole's painting through Thomas Weiskel's theory of the sublime touches on the complex alterity of subject and object, yet never gets past the notion of the narcissistic sublime as Cole's "genius" of the "Romantic self as a signifying subject" (235).

118 Wolf, "A Grammar of the Sublime," 322. In his comparison between the British painter J. M. W. Turner and the American painter Frederic E. Church, Wolf argues that the way these two artists experience the sublime is (nationally) significant: "Unlike Turner's graffiti [signatorial practice] where verbal and graphic glosses qualify the meaning of the text by highlighting the impossibility of its sublime ambitions, Church's crosses [the artist's symbolic mark] tend to reinforce the substitution of self for world at the heart of the egotistical sublime. They place the painter at the center of his world, affirming emblematically what the painting has already achieved in more painterly fashion through color and tone" (334).

119 For a good overview of the competitive nature of the American arts, see Burns, *Inventing the Modern Artist*, especially 46–76.

120 Tuckerman quoted in Howat's *The Hudson River and Its Painters*, 44. Thomas Eakin's student, Thomas Anschutz, declared: "What I mean by truth in a painting is as follows: Get up an outfit for outdoor work, go out to some woe-begotten, turkey chawed, bottle-nosed, henpecked country and set myself down, get out my materials and make as accurate a painting of what I see in front of me as possible" (quoted in Shi, *Facing Facts*, 128). Novak confirms that "landscape painting, with true democratic spirit, required only the natural experience that was every man's rightful heritage" (*American Painting of the Nineteenth Century*, 62). The "rightful heritage" of the "natural experience" is nothing short of the work of common sense. In 1855 an article appeared in *The Crayon* appropriately titled "Common Sense in Art." In it the author states: "Let it be remembered that the subject of the picture, the material object of objects from which it is constructed, are the essential parts of it. If you have no love for them, you can have no genuine feeling for the picture which represents them . . . We love Nature and Beauty—we admire the artist who renders them in his works . . . The man to whom nature, in her inanimate forms, has been a delight all his early life,

will love a landscape and be better capable of feeling the merits of it than any city-bred artist, and so through the category of men and things. They are only capable of being just critics of art who have first learned to love the things that Art deals with" (quoted in Novak, *American Painting of the Nineteenth Century*, 62).

121 The version of the nineteenth-century nonartist set the stage for those who later refused the title of artist in the twentieth century (without refusing the cultural capital that went with it, of course). Frank Norris, for example, consistently denied the "literariness" of his writing. The painter Robert Henri similarly made claims for his masculine realist life when he played sports with his acolytes during their breaks from art class. For an account of Henri's gymnastics and (that which is apparently less than) art, see Perlman, *Painters of the Ashcan School*, 89; and Shi, *Facing Facts*, 254.

122 Bechte quoted in Lucie-Smith, *American Realism*, 197.

123 Noll, "Common Sense Traditions and American Evangelical Thought," 220.

124 As Max Weber's famous study argues, the "spirit of capitalism" is rooted (America especially) in Protestantism that not only eschews decadent excesses but insists that the "communion of God with the recipients of his grace can only take place and be consciously experienced by God *working* within them ('operatur') and by their becoming conscious of this—in other words, when their *actions* arise out of faith which comes from God's grace, and when the quality of those actions legitimates this faith as truly coming from God" (*The Protestant Ethic and the 'Spirit' of Capitalism and Other Writings*, 78; see also pp. 312 and 317 on relevant discussions of practicality and craftsmanship).

125 Nash, "The American Cult of the Primitive," 531.

126 Nash argues that the naturist John Muir delivered a message that "wilderness had religious significance" and "following the Transcendentalists, [Muir] argued that wild things provide the best 'conductor of divinity' because they are least affected by man's works" ("The American Cult of the Primitive," 530).

127 Weiskel, *The Romantic Sublime*, 28; see also Bloom's *The Anxiety of Influence*. It is interesting to note that Edmund Burke rebuked Thomas Paine's *Age of Reason* because it stripped away spiritual transcendence.

128 Shapiro, "From the Sublime to the Political," 233. Though I disagree with Angela Miller in her reading of a distinct effeminization of, and break from, the idea of a nineteenth-century masculinist sublime, her effort in *The Empire of the Eye* (243–65) to trace the shifts in how the sublime is rhetorically engaged in American painting is useful.

129 The Oedipal structure in this account has been crucial to scholars

such as Fried who unpack the superego anxiety at work in Eakin's artistic career and the artist's rendering of castration anxiety in such works as *The Gross Clinic*. Thus, the sublime moment facilitated by the overwrought and indeterminable real, the "beyond" real, of Eakin's *The Gross Clinic* speaks to what Shi identifies as a "splendid example of the epistemology of common-sense realism" (*Facing Facts*, 142).

130 Bloom, who adamantly refuses a feminist reading of such things, remarks that "all poetic ecstasy, all sense that the poet steps out from man into god, reduces to this sour myth, as does all poetic asceticism, which begins as the dark doctrine of metempsychosis and its attendant fears of devouring a former version of the self" (*Anxiety of Influence*, 117). For all Bloom's pleasure with Freudian interpretation, one may be assured that Weiskel's theory of the sublime as castration anxiety would leave the scholar speechless.

131 Nordau, *Degeneration*, 34, 42.

132 That is, to be American, one must break from the "dilettanti" cultures of Europe. As Whitman states: "In the prophetic literature of these States (. . . a new Literature, perhaps a new Metaphysics, certainly a new Poetry, are to be, in my opinion, the only sure and worthy supports and expressions of the American Democracy,) Nature, true Nature, and the true idea of Nature, long absent, must, above all become fully restored . . . I do not mean the smooth walks, trimm'd hedges, poseys and nightingales of the English poets" (*Democratic Vistas*, 249). See further Whitman's disgust with "abnormal libidinousness, unhealthy forms, male, female, painted, dyed, chignon'd, muddy complexions, bad blood, shallow notions of beauty" (212).

133 The political rights of the masses are founded in the "organization of republican National, State, and municipal governments" and "not for classes" (*Democratic Vistas*, 243).

134 "The idea of the women," writes Whitman, "(extricated from this daze, this fossil and unhealthy air which hangs about the word *lady*,) develop'd, raised to become the robust equals, workers, and, it may be, even practical and political deciders with the men" (*Democratic Vistas* 225–26).

135 Nordau, *Degeneration*, 15–18.

136 Shi, *Facing Facts*, 29.

137 Reynolds, *Walt Whitman's America*, 89.

138 For example, see Reynold's biography of Whitman, which thoroughly investigates a number of historical-biographical issues, including his sexuality, that inform the poet's aesthetic. See also Loving, *Walt Whitman*; and Aspiz, "The Body Politic in *Democratic Vistas*." Leverenz suggests that Whitman's work leaves the reader (because of the very position assumed by the author) in an androgynous position "[hovering] between yes and no" (*Manhood and the American Renaissance*, 32). However, in *Disseminating Whitman*

Moon's work on *Leaves of Grass* deconstructs Whitman's homosexuality as a queer sensual site that facilitates a commingling of the reader/author/text relationship. I will consider in chapters 3 and 5 Whitman's import to African American culture.

139 Shi, *Facing Facts*, 29.

140 The influence of Whitman on American visual artists is remarkably ubiquitous and, to use a Whitmanesque metaphor, potent. Robert Henri states that "*Leaves of Grass*, indeed (I cannot too often reiterate), has mainly been the outcropping of my own emotional and other personal nature—an attempt from first to last, to put a person, a human being (myself, in the latter half of the nineteenth century, in America) freely, fully, and truly on record in current literature that satisfied me" (quoted in Perlman, *Painters of the Ashcan School*, 46). Frank Lloyd Wright, eulogizing Louis Sullivan, tells us that "[Sullivan] adored Whitman, as I did" (*Collected Writings*, 172). Whitman was also "central" to the *Seven Arts* Round Table that was attended by Alfred Stieglitz, Van Wyck Brooks, Waldo Frank, Theodore Dreiser, H. L. Mencken, Sherwood Anderson, John Dos Passos, Paul Rosenfeld, and Lewis Mumford (Robinson, *Georgia O'Keeffe*, 227). Lowe further indicates Whitman's influence on Stieglitz in *Stieglitz: A Memoir/Biography*, 212. According to Trachtenberg, Paul Strand "grew up as a young photographer [trained by Lewis Hine at the Ethical Culture School] in the atmosphere of what historians call the 'Lyrical Left,' an openly romantic movement which declared Whitman to be its precursor and prophet" (Trachtenberg, "Introduction," 8). See also Garman, "'Heroic Spiritual Grandfather.'" In chapter 4 I will discuss in more detail the Stieglitz-circle aesthetics. As mentioned, in chapter 5 I will also show Whitman's significance for black artists, especially those aligned with the Harlem Renaissance.

2 *The Battle Cry of Peace* and Realism

1 See, for example, Staiger, "Dividing Labor for Production Control."

2 Burrows and Wallace, *Gotham*, 597.

3 Page, *The Creative Destruction of Manhattan*, 79.

4 See Singer's discussion of the tradition of "spectacular realism" and melodrama in *Melodrama and Modernity* (168–70). See also Vardac, *Stage to Screen* (144), for a discussion of "spectacular realism" in the cinema as a theatrical tradition. In addition, Vardac states that 1915 was the moment that film became a "full-fledged and autonomous art form [fusing] authentically spectacular production with . . . melodramatic structure" (225).

5 I'd like to thank Charles Silver of the Museum of Modern Art Film and

Media Studies Center for arranging a viewing of the few remaining pieces of film footage that are held at the George Eastman House in Rochester.

6 The complicated ideologies at work prior to World War I are usefully plotted in Cooper, *The Vanity of Power*. Cooper stresses that the significant isolationist position held at the time (or, in fact, the strong nationalist stance) was shaped through rural and agrarian "beliefs in the wickedness of Eastern big business" and metropolitan centers (197).

7 Many scholars discuss the highly charged angst about cultural effeminization during the end of the nineteenth century and into the early twentieth. See, for example, Chauncey, *Gay New York*; Gail Bederman, *Manliness and Civilization*; Kimmel, *Manhood in America*; and Douglas, *The Feminization of American Culture*.

8 See McCallum's biographical account in *Blood Brothers* of the Maxim brothers and their direct involvement with British and American industrial/military organizations.

9 Maxim quoted in McCallum, *Blood Brothers*, 159.

10 This was also the case with Henry Ford who took out a full-page advertisement claiming that *The Battle Cry of Peace* was nothing more than a campaign to sway the military to buy his product. Maxim countered that Ford and his other detractors were slanderous and treasonous. See McCallum, *Blood Brothers*, 201.

11 Fred, "The Battle Cry of Peace," *Variety*, August 13, 1915, n.p.

12 "Preparedness Plea as a Movie Theme: 'The Battle Cry of Peace' Pictures the Invasion of New York," *New York Times*, September 15, 1915, sec. 11, p. 1.

13 "New York Shelled on 'Movie' Screen: 'The Battle Cry of Peace' Meant to Show the Necessity of Preparedness," *New York Times*, August 7, 1915, p. 8.

14 "A Preparedness Play," *Independent*, October 11, 1915, p. 80; *New Republic*, October 9, 1915, p. 247.

15 In *The Vanity of Power* Cooper provides a good overview of the reasoning behind the reluctance of the United States to join the Great War in Europe.

16 Julian Johnson quoted in Slide, *The Big V*, 76.

17 Quoted in "Does Color Enhance Dramatic Realism?" *Moving Picture World*, July 1, 1916, p. 84.

18 See Singer's *Melodrama and Modernity* (172–77) for an overview of the particular relationship of realism to the cinema.

19 Blackton, "Silence Was Golden," J. Stuart Blackton Collection, Folder 33, p. 261, Academy of Motion Picture Arts and Sciences, Margaret Herrick Library, Department of Special Collections (hereafter cited as AMPAS). There is a second autobiography housed in the collection, " 'Hollywood with

Its Hair Down' or Hollywood Memories: Forty Years of Movies" (Folder 31). Although the Blackton manuscripts are not clearly dated, they appear to be written sometime in the late 1930s since the author discusses such films as Disney's *Snow White*, which was released in 1938 (Blackton was killed in an automobile accident in 1941). I'd like to thank Scott Curtis for his help in locating these works. According to Richard Schickel in *D. W. Griffith: An American Life* the wildly inflated costs of *Intolerance* were merely rumor (though the cost of the film may be why Albert Smith withdrew from Blackton's project). Schickel argues that Griffith's investment in the film was closer to $126,750 (326) while the total cost of *The Birth of a Nation* was $100,000 (244).

20 Blackton notes in his memoirs that he paid Maxim the $5,000 dollars up front without a clause for royalties because the author/inventor desperately needed the cash. This urgent need for an influx of cash gels with accounts of Maxim's history of uneasy finances.

21 Slide, *The Big V*, 73.

22 Brownlow, *The War, the West, and the Wilderness*, 30. Brownlow is somewhat inaccurate here regarding Roosevelt's public notoriety around the film. Roosevelt's involvement with the film was in fact quite public. In an article on August 7, 1915, the *New York Times* reports: "Furthermore, the Commodore [Blackton] claims for his film the endorsement and co-operation of many a notable from Theodore Roosevelt to Secretary Lansing" (8). The film reviews from the period indicate an active participation on his part in the promotion of the film (although, as we will see, there were some who claimed to be surprised by his work on the project).

23 See Cooper's thorough account in *The Warrior and the Priest* of the relationship between Roosevelt and Wilson.

24 Trimble, *J. Stuart Blackton*, 7.

25 For a thorough account of the emergence of American Vitagraph in relation to the Edison studios, see Musser, "American Vitagraph"; see also Musser, *The Emergence of Cinema*, 253–55. In addition, see Blackton's "'Hollywood with Its Hair Down,'" pp. 1–2, and "Silence was Golden," pp. 1–10, AMPAS.

26 Musser states that *The Spanish Flag Torn Down*, also known as *Tearing Down the Spanish Flag*, was released on February 4, 1899, with the subtitle of *Raising Old Glory over Morro Castle*. Musser conjectures that the "painted backdrop looks like it was drawn by Blackton" ("American Vitagraph," 26).

27 Blackton, "Hollywood with Its Hair Down," p. 52, AMPAS.

28 Trimble, *J. Stuart Blackton*, 22. Blackton himself opens his autobiography with a reprint of a contemporary "Who's Who" entry that reads in part: "For the past three years, Commodore Blackton has been engaged in

an intensive research in, and survey of, the non-theatrical and Educational field in Motion Pictures. The result of these investigations demonstrates that there is a very definite and increasing demand for clean, high moral films for education and entertainment in the hundreds of thousands of schools, colleges, churches, clubs and homes throughout the United States" ("Hollywood with Its Hair Down," p. 2, AMPAS). It should be said, however, that Commodore Blackton was not a real commodore in the military; rather, he was "elected Commodore of the Atlantic Yacht Club at Sea Gate in 1912" according to his daughter (Trimble, *J. Stuart Blackton*, 57). As Singer points out in his review of the Vitagraph serials circa 1915, the producers "aspired to some degree of high-brow appeal" and "humanist pretensions" (*Melodrama and Modernity*, 218).

29 "Hollywood with Its Hair Down," p. 3, AMPAS.

30 Katz, *The Film Encyclopedia*, 132.

31 Lucie-Smith writes, "Some fascinating notes describing a meeting with [Thomas Eakins] were made by Mariana Griswold Van Rennselaer, a sophisticated American with well-developed taste in the visual arts. One of the first writers on art to sense Eakins's potential importance, she went to interview him for a planned article in *The American Art Review* (which in the end was never published): 'He is most modest and unassuming [she wrote to the editor, Sylvester B. Koehler], like a big enthusiastic schoolboy about his work. I do not believe he knows how good it is or how peculiar . . . He seemed to me much more like an inventor working out curious and interesting problems for himself than an average artist . . . If you met him in the street you would say curious but most eccentric mechanic' " (*American Realism*, 39).

32 To my knowledge, this is the only place where Blackton describes his involvement with a major New York art club and with significant American artists outside the film industry.

33 Burns, *Inventing the Modern Artist*, 28, 252–53.

34 Blackton, "Silence Was Golden," p. 281, AMPAS.

35 By 1897 the French film company the Lumière Agency had closed shop in the United States. The Edison Manufacturing Company and Biograph were well on their way to dominating domestic film production for the next ten years or more (Musser, *The Emergence of Cinema*, 177). At the beginning of 1907, Vitagraph had established European branch offices to distribute their films overseas (473).

36 Blackton, "Hollywood with Its Hair Down," p. 39, AMPAS.

37 Trimble, *J. Stuart Blackton*, 50.

38 Anthony Slide's account of Blackton's first meeting with Roosevelt about *Battle Cry* indicates, at one level, the statesman's idea of moral art. Slide writes: "The producer [Blackton] claimed to have spent three days and

nights working on a scenario, which he then read to Roosevelt. 'As I finished,' wrote Blackton, 'he strode to his bookcase and took out a Bible. I can see him now, the book held close to his nearsighted eyes, rapidly turning over the pages. He literally pounced upon the desired passages. 'Here it is,' he cried in a vibrant tone, 'thirty-third chapter of Ezekiel, third verse. Whosoever heareth the sound of the trumpet, and heedeth it not, if the sword comes and takes him away, his blood shall be upon his own head. That's America today. Heedless! Put that in your picture, Blackton . . . Get every word of that in your picture . . . Drive it home to the peace-at-any-price creatures!' " (*The Big V*, 73). If Roosevelt allowed his name to be associated with any project of this sort, we can assume that not only must the content of the film meet his requirements, the aesthetic form of the film must have, unequivocally, met what he saw as the standards of American art.

39 On October 4, 1903, Roosevelt wrote the following to his son at college: "As I said, I am delighted to have you play football. I believe in rough, manly sports. But I do not believe in them if they degenerate into the sole end of anyone's existence. I don't want you to sacrifice standing well in your studies to any overathleticism" (*Selected Letters*, 330).

40 Letter to Cecil Spring Rice, August 13, 1897, *Selected Letters*, 146.

41 Theodore Roosevelt, "An Art Exhibit," in *Theodore Roosevelt . . . A Selection of His Writings*, 357.

42 Oliver, *Brander Matthews, Theodore Roosevelt, and the Politics of American Literature*.

43 See also Dyer's invaluable research in *Theodore Roosevelt and the Idea of Race* (especially 45–68) on Roosevelt's understanding of Teutonism and Anglo-Saxon heritage in the United States. Cooper points out as well that Roosevelt was among a group of intellectuals and politico progressives who "admired the Teutonic combination of national strength and social reform" (*The Vanity of Power*, 185).

44 In a letter to the writer Arlo Bates, Roosevelt states: "It did me good to see the straightforward fashion in which you dealt with Maeterlinck, Ibsen, Verlaine, Tolstoi [writers treated by Nordau in *Degeneration*] and the decadents generally. I wish Howells could be persuaded to read and profit by what you have written" (*Selected Letters*, 152–53).

45 Roosevelt, "An Art Exhibit," in *Theodore Roosevelt . . . A Selection of His Writings*, 358. European moderns were not alone in Roosevelt's diatribe against pretension. In a letter to Matthews, Roosevelt excoriates the aesthete's *Yellow Book* and remarks in the same breath: "What a miserable little snob Henry James is" (letter to James Brander Matthews, June 29, 1894, *Selected Letters*, 92). In chapter 5 I show how snobbery, sophistication, and pretension were the raison d'être of queer modernism.

46 Roosevelt quoted in Oliver, *Brander Matthews, Theodore Roosevelt, and the Politics of American Literature*, 113.

47 Roosevelt, "Dante and the Bowery," in *Theodore Roosevelt . . . A Selection of His Writings*, 351–52.

48 Ibid., 350.

49 Roosevelt and Burroughs spent a good deal of time corresponding and traveling in American's nature's preserves such as Yellowstone National Park, which was held so dear by both men.

50 Burroughs, *Whitman*, 11.

51 Letter to Anna Roosevelt, June 19, 1886 (*Selected Letters*, 47).

52 Letter to Brander Matthews, December 7, 1894 (*Selected Letters*, 98).

53 Orvell, *The Real Thing*, 3.

54 Roosevelt praises Hamlin Garland to Matthews: "I am glad that he should go back to writing good stories, and not try to evolve some little school of literary philosophy, where the propriety of his purpose is marred by the crudity of his half-baked ideas, and where he is not tempted to group himself and one or two of his friends under some such absurd heading as 'veritists'" (*Selected Letters*, December 7, 1894, 98–99). In *An Autobiography* Roosevelt suggests that, "with pen and pencil," Wister and Remington have made the men of the Spanish-America War "live as long as our literature lives" (122). Roosevelt's experiences with these men were captured by these realist artists: these men "might have walked out of Wister's stories and Remington's pictures" (122).

55 Roosevelt who, like Forrest, veiled his aristocratic wealth, posed as the champion of popular values, and was compared to such natural wonders as Niagara Falls. Henry James (of whom Roosevelt was not fond, as noted earlier) modernized the metaphor of Roosevelt's corporeal wonderment when he likened the statesman to a machine: "A wonderful little machine . . . destined to be overstrained perhaps, but not as yet, truly, betraying the least creak . . . it functions astonishingly, and is quite exciting to see" (quoted in Morris, *The Rise of Theodore Roosevelt*, 18. For the remarks comparing Roosevelt to Niagara Falls, see 20; for Roosevelt's negative comments about James, see 468).

56 The stories are legion about Roosevelt's flight to South Dakota to masculinize his perceived "Oscar Wilde" and dilettantish persona. Roosevelt's campaign of "violent exercise" soon became the standard by which Americans defined a vigorous and functional nation (Morris, *The Rise of Theodore Roosevelt*, 130 [also 184–225]; see also Brands, *TR*, 160–92). I'd like to thank Edmund Morris for his thoughtful correspondence during my writing of this chapter.

57 For the best accounts of Roosevelt's life, see Morris, *The Rise of Theo-*

dore Roosevelt; Morris, *Theodore Rex*; Brands, *TR*; and Roosevelt, *An Autobiography*. On Münsterberg, see Hale, *Human Science and Social Order*; Keller, *States of Belonging*; and M. Münsterberg, *Hugo Münsterberg*.

58 Hale, *Human Science and Social Order*, 66–67.

59 For the quote on James, see Morris, *The Rise of Theodore Roosevelt*, 92; for Roosevelt's experiences at Harvard, see 88–103.

60 Roosevelt's and Münsterberg's correspondence begins in 1901, and they remain in contact through letter writing and personal visits until Münsterberg's death in 1916. See *Theodore Roosevelt Papers*, Library of Congress, Manuscript Division. I read these papers at the City University of New York, Graduate Center Microfilm Collection of the Presidential Papers (hereafter cited as TRP). It is not entirely clear how Münsterberg's and Roosevelt's correspondence began, however from the letters in the TRP collection it seems that Roosevelt served on Münsterberg's LLD degree committee at Harvard, and a scandal occurred over the final decision and Roosevelt's involvement on the committee. The details of the affair remain vague, but it appears that their letter writing (occasionally emphasizing discretion over this issue) begins at this time (1901). See the letter dated June 3, 1901, TRP, Series 2, Volume 29; see also Hale, 102–3.

61 The quoted phrase here and in the sentence above are from Hale, *Human Science and Social Order*, 62, 68.

62 See further the letter of May 7, 1901, wherein Roosevelt praises Münsterberg's notion of "productive scholarship" (TRP, Series 2, Volume 28, pp. 813–15). Ironically, Roosevelt had earlier bestowed these terms on Woodrow Wilson, who later became his rival. For Roosevelt's remarks about Wilson's "productive scholarship," see Cooper, *The Warrior and the Priest*, 60.

63 Dyer, *Theodore Roosevelt and the Idea of Race*, 133. Ultimately, Münsterberg believed that Britain and, especially, America were "inferior to Germany" (Keller, *States of Belonging*, 68). Münsterberg's most pro-German stance and harshest criticism of Britain, in particular, are in his *The War and America*. This book suggests that England is envious of Germany's superior industrial position in Europe (which is just one among other arguments that insist that Germany was not to blame for the Great War). Münsterberg also refused to eliminate the hypen with his American identity. Unlike Roosevelt, Münsterberg believed he was truly American by keeping his identity as "German-American." See the Tocquevillian Hugo Münsterberg in *The Americans*; See also in TRP, Series 1, reel 200, the letter dated May 15, 1915, in which Münsterberg argues for the necessity of the hyphen. Roosevelt's clarification of the hyphen is further noted in a letter dated January 19, 1916.

64 Hale, *Human Science and Social Order*, 59.

65 Keller, *States of Belonging*, 48.

66 Münsterberg quoted in Hale, *Human Science and Social Order*, 128.

67 See Hale, *Human Science and Social Order*, 44, 149–63; and Keller, *States of Belonging*, 50.

68 Münsterberg, *Psychology and Industrial Efficiency*, 4.

69 In his lecture to Yale University (reprinted in *Science and Idealism*) Münsterberg states: "And certainly the work of art might entertain us and give us a pleasant feeling; but this enjoyment, again, does not make the value of beauty" (47). Thus, "And just as science and art cultivate systematically the naïve values of immediate appreciation, so civilization unfolds new values of purposive realization. Nature as a whole then becomes purposive to us, and we reach thus the values of technical civilization. Every mastery over stubborn nature becomes, then, of real absolute value. The material of our work fulfills by every technical advance in a higher degree its ultimate purpose, and every invention and discovery is thus an approach to a superpersonal ideal" (61).

70 Taylor, *The Principles of Scientific Management*, 5.

71 The TRP collection includes pages from Arthur MacDonald's article "A Place for the Study of Man," which argues for the precise import of attention and moral function: "As in machinery we must first repair the little wheels out of gear, so in society we must first study the criminal, crank, insane, inebriate or pauper who can seriously injure both individual and community" (Series 1, reel 15, collected by Roosevelt, circa May 10, 1901).

72 See Hale, *Human Science and Social Order*, 144–47; Keller, *States of Belonging*, 93–94; M. Münsterberg, *Hugo Münsterberg*; and Allan Langdale's essay "S(t)imulation of Mind: The Film Theory of Hugo Münsterberg," which serves as an introduction to Münsterberg's *The Photoplay*, 6–8.

73 See also Curtis, "Like a Hailstorm on the Nerves of Modern Man" (especially 61–80), for a rigorous consideration of Münsterberg's theoretical and aesthetic investigations.

74 Gillespie, "T. R. on Film," 39, 51.

75 Quote in Gillespie from "Theodore Roosevelt: The Picture Man," *Moving Picture World*, no. 7, October 22, 1910, p. 920.

76 I take this information about Roosevelt and the film from Brownlow's introduction to his book *The War, the West, and the Wilderness*.

77 One of the few comments made on the cinema is in a 1915 letter to Edward Grey where Roosevelt laments America's softening on the Allies' war position as well as on its own military preparedness. As Roosevelt writes: "I do not think that this was the case among the people who are best informed; but I do think it was the case among the mass of not very well-informed people who have little to go upon except what they read in the newspapers or

see at Cinematographe shows" (*Selected Letters*, 587–88). Considering Roosevelt's strong antitrust positions during his presidency, the motion picture industry's legal battles in 1908 over monopolization must have held great interest for him.

78 Brownlow states that Roosevelt provides the "sturdy link" that holds together his book *The War, the West, and the Wilderness* (xv). Although Brownlow is mainly interested in Roosevelt's relationship to what he calls the "factual film," he stresses that Roosevelt is "not a film-maker, not even a regular film-goer, but a man whose spirit and example imprinted themselves indelibly upon the minds of the prewar generation" (xv). But Roosevelt's impact most definitely resonates beyond the "prewar generation." As Slotkin argues in his discussion of the American myth of the frontier, "Roosevelt's version of the Myth is closer in style, emphasis, and content to the productions of industrial popular culture" (*Gunfighter Nation*, 26).

79 TRP, Series 1, reel 205, January 26, 1916, pp. 1–10, 10.

80 One can imagine Roosevelt infuriated by some of Münsterberg's suggestions that, for example, "your indignation against German warfare belongs therefore, in my mind, to the most superficial layer of your mental structure" (TRP, Series 1, reel 205, January 26, 1916), p. 4.

81 Langdale, "S(t)imulation of the Mind," 14.

82 In *The Transformation of Cinema* Bowser describes Paramount's public relations campaign in 1914 to move the movie-going experience into the realm of the better classes. Their greeting card to the trade that year read: "The Dawn of the New Era: Better Pictures, Finer Theatres, Higher Admission Prices" (135).

83 I am not suggesting that Münsterberg's only aim in his study of film was merely propagandistic. His analytical rigor, as with any project upon which he embarked, is undeniably present. But given the circumstances under which the study was completed, it is a mistake to completely separate his hope to win the hearts and minds of Americans from his scientific and philosophical studies. His article in *Cosmopolitan*, titled "Why We Go to the Movies," confirms his desire to express his views on the cinema's aesthetic properties and potentials to the largest possible audience (reprinted in *The Photoplay*, 171–82).

84 In a letter to Münsterberg, Roosevelt wrote that during the time of war "one must not look to the future with lofty philosophy" (TRP, Series 2, Volume 98, reel 257, October 3, 1914, p. 68).

85 TRP, Series 1, reel 202, October 29, 1915. It is worth noting that this letter was written during the period in which Münsterberg wrote *The Photoplay*.

86 TRP, Series 3A, volume 92–95, reel 385, November 6, 1915. Roosevelt

is not entirely honest here. His history of the frontier series, *The Winning of the West*, expresses considerable anger toward the British prior to and during the American Revolution. His diplomatic posture may have changed later during his political career, but it is arguable that Roosevelt fostered a long-standing resentment toward Britain.

87 Frederick Jackson Turner, "The Significance of the Frontier in American History," in *The Frontier in American History*, 1–38.

88 Slotkin, *Gunfighter Nation*, 30.

89 Morris, *The Rise of Theodore Roosevelt*, 465–66. Roosevelt and Turner knew one another and were familiar with one another's work. See Morris, *The Rise of Theodore Roosevelt* (1979), 410; Brands, *TR*, 263–64; and Dyer, *Theodore Roosevelt and the Idea of Race*, 54. Notably, Roosevelt writes Turner in 1894 declaring that Turner's "The Significance of the Frontier in American History" "comes at *the* right time for me, for I intend to make use of it in writing the third volume of my 'Winning of the West,' of course making full acknowledgement" (*Selected Letters*, 86–87).

3 African American Realism

1 See Roosevelt, "Race Decadence," in *Selected Writings*, 339–43. I would like to thank Paula Massood for her thoughtful and productive criticisms about this chapter.

2 Harlan, *Booker T. Washington* [1856–1901], 304–24; Harlan, *Booker T. Washington* [1901–1915], 3–5; Morris, *Theodore Rex*, 52–58.

3 Roosevelt, *The Rough Riders*, 88.

4 The identification of the Negro to the "criminal class" finds a direct link to the fear of black men raping white women. See Smith's important work on this issue in *Photography on the Color Line* (86–99). Interestingly, Smith demonstrates Du Bois's complicity in making similar connections between an African American criminal class and sexual prowess. Du Bois, however, reiterated the effects of African American social conditions over some sort of innate biological factor to create criminality.

5 Edmund Morris forthrightly suggests: "Even more distressing was the likelihood that redneck racists everywhere would applaud Roosevelt's willingness to act on what passed for evidence in lynch country: unsubstantiated charges of rape, instant identifications of black men last seen in darkness, the 'wooden, stolid look' of Negro terror, and a few dozen shell casings ejected from clean rifles" (*Theodore Rex*, 465). Brands goes so far as to argue that the Brownsville affair actually reversed Roosevelt's anti-lynching sentiment (*TR*, 589); see also Dyer, *Theodore Roosevelt and the Idea of Race*, 115–17.

6 Harlan, *Booker T. Washington* [1901–1915], 309.

7 See Roosevelt, "The Progressives and the Colored Man," in *The Works of Theodore Roosevelt*, 414.

8 For a thorough treatment of the "historical circumstances" in which Roosevelt moved, see Fredrickson's *The Black Image in the White Mind*.

9 Though Dyer argues that Roosevelt believed in "equipotentiality," which is to say that, whether black or white, men deserve their position based on merit (*Theodore Roosevelt and the Idea of Race*, 100), Gail Bederman links Roosevelt's imperialist projects and his anxiety of emasculation to his racism. According to Bederman, "Black Americans played no part in TR's frontier history, nor did he consider them part of the American race" (*Manliness and Civilization*, 179). Bederman's suggestion here, however, oversimplifes Roosevelt's relations with blacks. As noted earlier, the discursive shifts in Roosevelt's race ideology are indeed complex.

10 See, for example, Roosevelt's obituary in the *Cleveland Advocate* ("Colonel Theodore Roosevelt Passes Away; Last Word to His Faithful Colored Attendant," January 11, 1919, p. 1). See also the obituary in the *Union* whose editors stated that his "frankness, bravery and 'Color' blindness had again won for him the deep regard of our people" ("Sweetly Slumbering at Oyster Bay, Theodore Roosevelt Passed Away!" January 11, 1919, p. 1).

11 For discussions about Micheaux's enthusiasm for the frontier, see Moos, "Reclaiming the Frontier"; Butters, "Portrayals of Black Masculinity in Oscar Micheaux's *The Homesteader*"; VanEpps-Taylor, *Oscar Micheaux*; Johnson, " 'Stranger in a Strange Land' "; Herbert, "Oscar Micheaux"; Fontenot, "Oscar Micheaux"; and Brown, "Black Patriarch on the Prairie." The literature on Micheaux as the black man on the homestead often overshadows the role that African American women played in the same environment: see Riley, "American Daughters: Black Women in the West"; and Thompson's *American Daughter*.

12 In *The African Methodist Episcopal Church Review*, for example, John Burroughs is cited by the editors in a discussion about truth and religion (*AME Church Review*, July 1, 1893, p. 202); there are book reviews of Burroughs's "charming" books in the *AME* as well (October 1, 1892, p. 208). In his book *The Betrayal of the Negro* (162), Logan suggests that Walt Whitman was the only white American poet of the nineteenth century who did not subscribe to African American stereotypes as others had. James Weldon Johnson, a powerful voice in early-twentieth-century African American arts, writes, "But just at this time I came across Whitman's *Leaves of Grass*. I was engulfed and submerged by the book, and set floundering again. I felt nothing I had written, with the exception of the hymn for the Lincoln celebration, rose above puerility" (*Along This Way*, 158).

13 For an overview of the Washington/Du Bois debate, see Moore, *Booker T. Washington, W. E. B. Du Bois, and the Struggle for Racial Uplift.*

14 I do not mean to suggest that African American migration was strictly a "postslavery" phenomenon. As Gilroy has demonstrated in *The Black Atlantic,* black migration has a long, rich, and complex history.

15 Carby, *Race Men,* 69; Gaines, *Fire and Desire,* 205.

16 Gaines, in *Uplifting the Race,* points to the risks in making claims for social equality and black specificity when its terms are established by the white hegemonic rule already in place. Earlier, Frazier, in *Black Bourgeoisie,* infuriated the post–World War II black middle classes and their dull, apolitical sensibilities by suggesting they had subscribed to a sort of culture-industry effect on black society. But the uplift debate that occurred over platitudes of intellectualism versus common sense found fertile ground in which to unfold. On the one hand, critics such as Ishamel Reed, writing in his introduction to Washington's *Up From Slavery,* contend that Washington's brand of common-sense uplift was branded "accomodationist" by African American elitist and northern intellectuals [Du Bois, for example]. According to Reed, Washington's theories of practicality remain relevant today. Yet, as Moore writes, "the differences between [Du Bois and Washington] were not as great as they appeared" (*Booker T. Washington, W. E. B. Du Bois, and the Struggle for Racial Uplift,* 61). Levine recommends a more nuanced examination of the workings of black culture under the hegemony of white ideology where black culture is far from homogenized (*Black Culture and Black Consciousness,* 150–52). Bartling, in a manner similar to Frazier, sees Micheaux as one who, although attempting resistance, remains trapped within culture-industry ideology that proscribes the possibility of opposition ("Intentions as Mass Culture," 119–36).

17 Carby, *Race Men.* In the essay, "Frederick Douglass's Self-Refashioning" in *Manhood and the American Renaissance* (108–34), Levernz situates the exslave's later narrative style as well as his assimilationist lifestyle as an appropriation of genteel and androcentric culture. The urgency to reclaim a virile black manhood is an example of White's concept of ideological negation in times of "socio-cultural stress" (see chapter 1 in this volume). During the nineteenth century, the idea of mixed races and the black man as "effeminate" was strongly rooted in the scientific theories of the day. It was essential, therefore, to mark the body of the black male as manly; on this topic, see Menand, *The Metaphysical Club,* 115, 140.

18 See Johnson, " 'Stranger in a Strange Land,' " 232; Butters, "Portrayals of Black Masculinity in Oscar Micheaux's *The Homesteader,*" 55; Moos, "Reclaiming the Frontier," 367; Brown, "Black Patriarch on the Prairie," 132–35; VanEpps-Taylor, *Oscar Micheaux,* 13; and Bowser and Spence, *Writing Him-*

self into History, 20. Micheaux has been marshaled into the corner of white assimilation in Young's oversimplified book *Black Novelist as White Racist*. As Bogle states, "That [Micheaux's] films reflected the interests of and outlooks of the black bourgeoisie will no doubt always be held against him" (*Toms, Coons, Mulattoes, Mammies, and Bucks*, 115). Bone angrily denounces Micheaux's writing because he doesn't "face the hard facts." Instead his characters " 'play white' much the same sense as children 'play house' " (*The Negro Novel in America*, 49).

19 According to most scholars, when Micheaux discusses Du Bois it is either to reiterate his distance from the black leader's "abstract" ideology (Fontenot, "Oscar Micheaux," 118) or to aim "scathing remarks" at the northern leader (Brown, "Black Patriarch on the Prairie," 134). I argue that Micheaux engaged Du Bois more dynamically than most critics allow.

20 The word "organ" takes on a peculiar resonance in discussions of manhood. There is a rather ironic use of the term by Booker Washington where he describes Douglass's return from England and his interest in beginning his own journal for African Americans and his struggle to break from Garrison to begin the enterprise. Washington writes: "But [Douglass] wanted an 'organ' of his own. As time went on he believed that he perceived the need of it more and more" (*Frederick Douglass*, 120).

21 To the best of my knowledge, Du Bois does not refer to Micheaux's work. A letter exists, however, from Du Bois to Noble Johnson of Lincoln Motion Pictures requesting a photograph of the studio's president for an issue of *The Crisis* (February 7, 1918, UCLA Department of Special Collections, George P. Johnson Collection, General Files, Box 52, File 33). Since Du Bois was aware of Johnson's film productions (Du Bois was an avid filmgoer) he was most likely aware of Micheaux but refused to comment on his work. See Lewis, *W. E. B. Du Bois* [1919–1963], 153–82, for a thorough examination of Du Bois's patronizing and harsh critical position toward certain black artists during the period of the Harlem Renaissance (especially Alain Locke; and note in chapter 5 that Lewis does not treat Locke gently either). Du Bois, according to Lewis, had very clear (and conservative) ideas about art and its purposes. Du Bois worried both about the whitening of "New Negro" art milieus and practices as well as the effeminizing of the arts by the likes of Locke. Ironically, his favored son-in-law, the Harlem Renaissance poet Countee Cullen, turned out to be homosexual. For more on this topic, see Du Bois, "Criteria of Negro Art."

22 Information here is from a letter dated September 7, 1920, from Swan Micheaux (Oscar's brother) to George Johnson, General Booking Manager of Lincoln Motion Picture Company; an extract of a separate letter from Oscar to Swan is included. Oscar reports to Swan that he was preparing to

meet Johnson, Du Bois, and Chestnutt. (The letter is located in the UCLA Department of Special Collections, George P. Johnson Collection, Positive Reel 8 of 12).

23 Bogle, *Toms, Coons, Mulattoes, Mammies, and Bucks*, 110.

24 Carby, *Race Men*, 47.

25 Micheaux's textual doubleness is discussed by several critics including J. Ronald Green who argues that, in relationship to Griffith's "oneness," Micheaux espoused a "more dialectical approach to his art" that provided his work with a "more open-ended" political form (*Straight Lick*, 87; see also Green, "'Twoness' in the Style of Oscar Micheaux," 26–48). I would agree with Green that Micheaux's work is "more open-ended," but, as I will posit here, the textual range of his work far exceeds simple dialectical configurations and is, strangely enough, both similar and dissimilar to Griffith's work.

26 Creekmur, "Telling White Lies," 147–58, 48.

27 Derrida, "Signature, Event, Context," 318. I follow here Culler's suggestion regarding meaning and context insofar as "meaning is context bound but context is boundless" (*Theory and Criticism after Structuralism*, 128).

28 Johnson, "A Phenomenology of the Black Body," 123.

29 Warren, *Black and White Strangers*, 63.

30 Ibid., 68. On uplift, Dunbar, and Howells, see Gaines, *Uplifting the Race*, 182. According to Gaines, Dunbar regarded his popular dialect poetry as something not dissimilar to minstrelsy's racist predilections (see below for a discussion of minstrelsy). See also Gates, *The Signifying Monkey*, 177.

31 Martin suggests that a reason that Douglass could, at first, return Garrison's benevolent paternalistic favors with such ambivalence was because of his "nonrelationship with his white father" (*The Mind of Frederick Douglass*, 4). As Carby argues, however, there is a more powerful ideological current at work in Garrison. The abolitionist, for example, who often insisted on the slave women's spiritual inferiority, "could use the absence of the qualities of virtue and chastity in the lives of slave women as part of his campaign for the abolition of the slave system . . . Garrison's sexual metaphors for black women extended from passionate whore to hapless, cringing victim" (*Reconstructing Womanhood*, 34–35).

32 William Lloyd Garrison, preface to *Narrative of the Life of Frederick Douglass*, 5. Garrison further writes: "I am confident that [the narrative] is essentially true in all its statements; drawn from the imagination; that nothing has been set down in malice, nothing exaggerated, nothing drawn from imagination; that it comes short of the reality, rather than overstates a single fact in regard to SLAVERY AS IT IS" (6).

33 Gates writes, "Indeed, Douglass's major contribution to the slave narrative was to make chiasmus the central trope of slave narration, in which a

slave-object writes himself or herself into a human subject through the act of writing" (*The Signifying Monkey*, 172).

34 For an overview of white authentication of slave narratives, see John W. Blassingame's introduction to *Narrative of the Life of Frederick Douglass*, ix–xli, especially xvi–xxiii. Gates confirms the significance of locating the black voice in these narratives, since slave writings "retained their implicitly political import after the war and especially after the sudden death of Reconstruction, then it should not surprise us that the search for a voice in black letters became a matter of grave concern among black literati" (*The Signifying Monkey*, 171).

35 The three autobiographies are titled *Narrative of the Life of Frederick Douglass, An American Slave; My Bondage and My Freedom*; and *Life and Times of Frederick Douglass*. All three are collected in *Douglass: Autobiographies*.

36 Gilroy, *The Black Atlantic*, 69–70. Through a feminist lens, Gilmore makes the case for the significance of what she calls "autobiographics." Her Derridean reading of women's autobiography posits that her "work builds from that critique to analyze how women use self-representation and its constitutive possibilities for agency and subjectivity to become no longer primarily subject to exchange but subjects who exchange the position of object for the subjectivity of self-representational agency" (*Autobiographics*, 12). I subscribe to Gilmore's insistence on the radical struggle to forge autobiography as a tool of self-representational agency while I shift her feminist model toward the landscape of African American agency and the slave narrative.

37 The long-standing central place held for autobiography for African Americans is a cornerstone of black cultural politics. As we have seen, Douglass wrote three versions of his slave narrative. In addition, *The Life of Olaudah Equiano or Gustavas Vassa, The African* is most often considered the earliest of slave narrative texts. Following this work, exslaves such as Douglass, Washington, and Harriet Jacobs (aka Linda Brent) set pen to paper to politicize the slave experience (albeit certainly to different ideological ends). The tradition of autobiography as a political gesture and an announcement of black presence continued with Du Bois, James Weldon Johnson, Zora Neale Hurston, and, of course, Micheaux. Perhaps what is most striking about the authoring of these texts is the repetition; that is, Douglass, Washington, Du Bois, and Johnson all wrote more than one version of their autobiographical accounts of their life experience. Oscar Micheaux rewrote his autobiographical accounts many times over. Micheaux's novels that recount his life experience include *The Conquest: The Story of a Negro Pioneer* (1913), *The Forged Note: A Romance of the Darker Races* (1915), *The Homesteader* (1917), and *The Wind from Nowhere* (1944). His autobiographical films include *The*

Homesteader (1919) and, to varying degrees, *The Symbol of the Unconquered* (1920) and *Within Our Gates* (1920).

38 Wallace, *Constructing the Black Masculine*, 84.

39 As Walker writes, "For only after Douglass has been heard as a human individual will he begin to be understood as a black American whose presence in American history has loomed so large and has been so compelling that he has been drafted into service as a personified social program by such widely divergent ideologues as Booker T. Washington and Philip Foner" (*Moral Choices*, 213). Martin argues that Douglass "personalized and internalized the collective black struggle; he personified his people's cause" (*The Mind of Frederick Douglass*, 61).

40 For an excellent discussion of the complex usage of "positive" and "negative" black images in the media, see Wallace, "Oscar Micheaux's *Within Our Gates*," 53–66; see also Bogle, *Toms, Coons, Mulattoes, Mammies, and Bucks*. As VanEpps-Taylor remarks, Micheaux "scrutinized nearly everyone he encountered with the same jaundiced, irreverent, critical, and sometimes biased eye, caricaturing and commenting freely on personal qualities, foibles, follies, and prejudices" (*Oscar Micheaux*, 8).

On the historical relationship between race and genre, see William's *Playing the Race Card*, which draws the interconnectedness between cinematic realism and melodrama. For Williams, the divide between the two cinematic tropes is artificially constructed by film scholars. Rather than continue the scholarly distinction, Williams finds it more fruitful to consider the "combined function of realism, sentiment, spectacle, and action in effecting moral legibility" (19). As I have shown in chapter 1, realism can only be understood as an uneven, multilayered aesthetic and ideological prism through which the experience of masculinity is rendered.

41 Jean Baptiste is Micheaux's alter ego in *The Homesteader*. Jean Baptiste Point du Sable (1745–1818) was a Haitian who is considered to be Chicago's first settler. As Micheaux points out in several places, Chicago was his preferred city (as far as his preference for cities goes), and it is also the nearest major city of the state in which he was born. Micheaux assumes the role of Martin Eden in *The Wind from Nowhere*, which evokes Jack London's eponymous character who some read as a hero (although London intended a more ironic reading of Eden as something less than heroic). Micheaux's last novel, *Masquerade* (one of his many reworkings of Chestnutt's *The House Behind the Cedars*), stresses African American history as having a direct affect on the narrative (I will further explore this toward the end of this chapter). Like Douglass who, under different degrees of circumstance, changed his name as part of his shifting identities, Micheaux's pseudonyms evoked the complexity of the African American male self.

42 Du Bois, *The Souls of Black Folk*, 2.

43 "8000 Feet of Sensational Realism" was Micheaux's promotional tag for *Within Our Gates*, quoted in Bowser and Spence, *Writing Himself into History*, 135. Dyer argues that the "aesthetic technology of the photographic media, the apparatus and practice *par excellence* of a light culture, not only assumes and privileges whiteness but also constructs it" (*White*, 122). Yet Levine cautions, "It would be inaccurate to speak of a monolithic American ideology concerning color." Just as American society "insisted upon racial purity" in the twentieth century, it simultaneously "[indulged] in a fetish for dark skin" (*Black Culture and Black Consciousness*, 290).

44 Gaines, *Fire and Desire*, 202.

45 In reading Nella Larsen, Butler argues that "race" itself is "figured as a contagion transmissible through proximity" ("Passing, Queering: Nella Larsen's Psychoanalytic Challenge," in *Bodies That Matter*, 171). The very idea of race is, recalling Culler, context bound yet boundless. See further Ginsberg's excellent introduction to the collection *Passing and the Fictions of Identity*, 4.

46 Micheaux was quite angry with the way in which Hollywood capitalized on the "race film" for their own profit. Unfortunately, his anger often revealed an anti-Semitic strain (see *The Case of Mrs. Wingate*, 86–92). On Micheaux's anti-Semitism and other prejudices, see VanEpps-Taylor, *Oscar Micheaux*, 8.

47 Gates, *The Signifying Monkey*, 44–45. Gates's work traces the history of the "Signifyin(g) Monkey" and its import for the black trickster and African American "Signification" (3–43). Bowser and Spence point to Micheaux's "calculated" tricksterism in *Writing Himself into History*, 17. Levine gives an excellent overview of the African American trickster in *Black Culture and Black Consciousness* (see especially 121–33 and 370–86 where he discusses the "Signifying Monkey").

48 Wallace considers black male "identity as one articulated by the ways in which the mimetic architectures of black male inhabitation—closets and cabins, houses and homeplaces—project a material form of self" (*Constructing the Black Masculine*, 111).

49 Micheaux, *The Case of Mrs. Wingate*, 203.

50 Micheaux, *The Forged Note*, 178.

51 Micheaux, *The Homesteader*, 283.

52 Gaines points this out in *Fire and Desire*, 213.

53 See Gates, *The Signifying Monkey* (133) for a discussion of the mother's central place in the history of the slave narrative. King and Mitchell posit that "African American literature presents two extremes of black mother-to-son parenting: mothers who love their sons brutally 'for their own good'

and mothers who love their sons to destruction through self-sacrifice and overindulgence" (*Black Mothers to Sons*, 9). King and Mitchell, however, revise this dualistic principle directly toward what they see as an "Afrocentric" Black Aesthetic (63). Patton, in *Women in Chains*, makes the vital distinction between the sex and gender of the mother in her work on African American women. That is, sex indicates the birthing ability of the female whereas gender is the cultural dynamic of motherhood and its trappings. My argument looks to the repetition and revision of the mother-trope strategically utilized by black-male authors to produce a text of the free black man.

54 hooks, "Micheaux," 351.

55 If Micheaux followed the moral rightness espoused by Washington and Roosevelt, his films and novels evoked the difficulties of maintaining such moral high ground.

56 In *The Case of Mrs. Wingate*, Sydney Wyeth/Micheaux (a successful filmmaker and novelist) is the model of the good, industrious, and tolerant African American man. His breadth of intellectual knowledge and practical know-how affords him the capacity to understand and, therefore, properly guide his readers and audiences along the most ethical and suitable cultural paths. His ability to tolerate is inestimable. He not only "understood Negro philosophy and what pleased them," he also understood and sympathized with men who were not "normal" (50). In the novel the notion of not "normal" appears to cover a wide spectrum of perversion. On the one hand, Micheaux raises concerns that Kermit Early (Du Bois) was sometimes considered not normal (i.e., homosexual; charges that Micheaux relates to be untrue). Later, when Early becomes involved with the white Mrs. Wingate, she tells Early that she hasn't had sexual experiences with her husband because he is not a "normal man" (49). In this instance, her husband is likened to Leo Franks, the Jew who was accused of sexually abusing and killing a young girl. The racial implications in this case were severe since a black man's testimony indicted Franks; questions lingered regarding the African American's innocence (49–52).

57 As Martin argues, although Frederick Douglass supported universal suffrage, black-male suffrage superceded that of women's rights: "Douglass's acceptance of the black man's vote, without the vote of women, represented a compromise with, and tacit approval of, male supremacy" (*The Mind of Frederick Douglass*, 156).

58 Writers such as Morton in *Disfigured Images* and Doyle in *Bordering on the Body* demonstrate the problematics of black motherhood in the critical inquiry of African American politics.

59 On Douglass's relationship to the mother figure, see Martin, *The Mind of Frederick Douglass*, 3–6; and Walker, *Moral Choices*, 251–55. McFeely argues

that Douglass manufactured in "retrospect" the importance of his maternal relationship (*Frederick Douglass*, 6–7). On Du Bois and his mother, see Lewis, *W. E. B. Du Bois* [1868–1919], 23–30; Du Bois gives further praise to mothers in his "The Damnation of Women." On Washington, see Harlan, *Booker T. Washington* [1856–1901], 14, 32; on James Weldon Johnson, see his fictionalized, albeit significant, relationship to the mother in *The Autobiography of an Ex-Colored Man*. Johnson, in his autobiography *Along This Way*, privileges both parents yet expounds on his "poignantly tender" mother (11). Indeed, while his mother's love and extensive cultural teachings had great impact on Johnson's later creative experiences, his "father had underestimated my stage of development" as a young boy (13).

60 Doyle, *Bordering on the Body*, 4.

61 Quoted in Martin, *The Mind of Frederick Douglass*, 3.

62 Washington, *Up from Slavery*, 21.

63 Wallace, *Constructing the Black Masculine*, 123.

64 The organization of the African American family is complicated. Many books have tackled these family structures, including Du Bois's *The Philadelphia Negro*. More recently, Sudarkasa in "Interpreting the African Heritage in African America Family Organization" provides a concise overview of the historical organization associated with black families in America following the era of slavery and their relationship to such issues as urbanization and the African tradition.

65 The scandal that rocked Booker T. Washington late in his career is an ironic-tragic case in point. In 1911, Washington's accomodationist paternalism was brought into question when he was accused by a white man of drunkenness, voyeurism, and thievery. See Harlan's full accounting of the event in *Booker T. Washington* [1901–1915], 379–404.

66 Douglass's marriage to a white woman caused a furor even among his white supporters; Washington was never at home to supervise his children's upbringing because he was always fundraising for Tuskegee; Du Bois's marriage was cordial at best, given (similar to Washington and Douglass) his constant travels, adulterous affairs, emotional distance (due to separation), and unequal parenting. Undoubtedly, these are the travails of any heterosexual (or, indeed, homosexual) coupling. But because the politics of their manhood and the implications of their race were in the socio-cultural spotlight, the stakes to abide by white idealist principles or to radically resist them were all that much higher.

67 Martin, *The Mind of Frederick Douglass*, 5. See also Walker's discussion of Douglass's double imperatives of the autobiography: his mother's tradition of Africa and father's tradition of "Anglo-Saxonism" (254).

68 Quoted in Lewis, *W. E. B. Du Bois* [1868–1919], 419. On Du

Bois's feminism, see Morton, *Disfigured Images*, 55–65. "The Damnation of Women" is Du Bois's clearest tract on feminism.

69 Carby, *Race Men*, 21.

70 Micheaux quoted in VanEpps-Taylor, *Oscar Micheaux*, 15.

71 On Micheaux and his treatment of the clergy, see Bowser and Spence, *Writing Himself into History*, 185.

72 Unlike Chestnutt's original novel, Micheaux's Rena lives and finds succor in her new marriage and returns to her black family. Chestnutt's novel kills Rena off at the end, thereby underscoring, perhaps, the author's sympathies with Rena's brother who, like Chestnutt, was able to pass.

73 The quote here is from Child's "Introduction by the Editor" to Linda Brent's *Incidents in the Life of a Slave Girl*, 338.

74 Braxton, *Black Women Writing Biography*, 51.

75 Leverenz argues that Douglass held dear a white, masculine, genteel masculinity in his "self-refashioning" (*Manhood and the American Renaissance*, 121) of his former slave self. Douglass's genteel writing style is most apparent in his last two autobiographies and, according to Leverenz, indicates what amounts to Douglass's conservative Anglo-Saxon ideals. I concur to the extent that the repetition of style bears the marks of white bourgeois style in Douglass's texts, but it also bears the marks of rewriting the struggle with memory, space, and time in the slave narratives as well *as* Anglo-Saxon ideology.

76 Gaines, *Fire and Desire*, 7.

77 Wallace, "Oscar Micheaux's *Within Our Gates*," 66. My argument here is to complicate those who posit Micheaux's formal and narratological coherency as somehow aesthetically wanting or that his films appear less polished because of lack of funds and, therefore do not meet high-quality (white) illusionist standards. See, for example, Bordwell and Thompson, *Film History*, 181.

78 Elsaesser and Barker, "Introduction," 294.

79 Gunning, *D. W. Griffith and the Origins of American Narrative Film*, 77.

80 According to Elsaesser and Barker: "Parallel editing in the classical cinema (and to some extent this is true of *The Lonedale Operator*), increasingly came to connote temporal simultaneity/spatial" distance. Indeed, the "practice of analytical editing—i.e. classical cinema—generally came to mean articulating shots according to a form of alternation which privileged temporal successiveness (exemplified in shot-reverse shot) over spatial coherence, the former eventually absorbing the latter, and subsuming both under the new narrational logic" ("Introduction," 296–97).

81 For the aesthetic traditions through which Griffith aligned himself, see Gunning, *D. W. Griffith and the Origins of American Narrative Film*, 31–

56. One of the first to identify Griffith's bourgeois structure in filmmaking was Eisenstein in "Dickens, Griffith and the Film Today," 195–255. See also Schickel, *D. W. Griffith*, 44, 111, 113, 140–41.

82 "Although it is possible," writes Gunning, "that [in *A Corner in Wheat*] the dinner party, the actions at the bakery, and the farmers return from the market are simultaneous, these temporal relations are of less importance than their structural role as relations on the economic level. Such theoretically motivated editing makes the film less a conventional, character-based story than what the Spectator termed a film 'editorial,' channeling the power of filmic codes into the expression of ideas" (*D. W. Griffith and the Origins of American Narrative Film*, 247).

83 Although Micheaux emphasized that he couldn't hate anyone, his uneven approach to Jews in his work is discomfiting. VanEpps-Taylor is right when she states that Micheaux carried a "bitter anti-Semitism" particularly following the history of the moguls appropriating the race film (*Oscar Micheaux*, 116). Arguably, Micheaux's tolerance for the Other veils his resentment toward Jews. It is also possible that Micheaux takes his Kermit Early/Du Bois anti-Semitic narrative from actual events that raised the ire of American Jews against Du Bois. In 1937, Du Bois published "The German Case against the Jews" in which he presents a strange apologia for Germany's "fear of this foreign element [Jews]" entering the country after World War I, and in which he claims that the victimization of the Jews was legalistic while that of the Negro was constitutional. As Lewis asserts, "That he spoke of the German situation with an occasional inflection typical of the WASP of the day was because Du Bois was essentially a brown-skinned New England gentile and, less admirably, because he was willing to score points against his own country for the discrimination against Negroes by recourse to legalistic sophistries about the sufferings of another religious or racial group — sophistries of which he, of all observers, should have been ashamed" (*W. E. B. Du Bois* [1919–1963], 421). Although Micheaux posits Early's (Du Bois) anti-Semitism as dissimilar to his own in the novel, Micheaux's overdetermined emphasis on this difference-of-degree anti-Semitism between Wyeth/Micheaux and Early/Du Bois begs the question about what shape Micheaux's animosity toward the African American intellectual took. Since Micheaux saw himself, in part, as an intellectual, it seems likely here that there was more competitive jealousy than philosophical difference. For a thoughtful, historical overview of race relations toward Jews and African Americans and, in part, toward one another, see Fredrickson's *Racism*.

84 Frank, a Jew ("not a normal man" [*Case of Mrs. Wingate*, 50]), was convicted of murdering the thirteen-year-old Mary Phagan. A black ("simple, ignorant," 50) janitor, Jim Conley, testified against Frank claiming that the

accused made him carry Phagan's body away from the crime scene. Frank was convicted; his death sentence was commuted in 1915 and he was transferred to another prison where an inmate slashed his throat. While recovering, a group of men kidnapped him from the infirmary, brought him to Phagan's hometown of Marietta and lynched him. Questions remained about how significant a role Conley actually played in the murder and, in fact, if he was the murderer. In 1986 Frank was pardoned by the state of Georgia for its failure to protect the prisoner.

85 Micheaux, *The Masquerade*, 319.

86 In this way I part ways with Jane Gaines's assessment of Micheaux's use of the flashback. Gaines argues that Micheaux's flashback is a "distancing device" that safely 'cordons off' the film's present from a traumatic past. As I see it, Micheaux's flashback saturates the present ("Within Our Gates" 72–73).

87 I am paraphrasing Mary Ann Doane here when she refers to "the pen which writes the feminine body." In her argument Doane deftly demonstrates how, in her discussion of *Rebecca* and *Caught*, "female desire is linked to the fixation and stability of a spectacle refusing the temporal dimensions, while male desire is more fully implicated with the defining characteristic of the cinematic image—movement" (*The Desire to Desire*, 170–71). The ideological implications are significantly different between *Rebecca* and *Within Our Gates*. The use of the camera to project and inscribe masculine desire via female desire through a managed organization of cinematic time and space is worth noting, however, since Micheaux's "penning" of masculine desire shares in, as we have seen, the complex relationship of American feminism. It is precisely through this complexity that one might engage cinematic projection and inscription (issues at the very heart of Doane's work) as they open matters of race and gender.

88 Micheaux, *The Wind from Nowhere*, 47.

89 Perhaps what Micheaux found so prescient was, as Favor suggests about Johnson's work, "the possible implications of appropriation *within* racial borders but *across* an intraracial class divide" (*Authentic Blackness*, 43–44).

90 See Skerrett, "Irony and Symbolic Action in James Weldon Johnson's *The Autobiography of an Ex-Coloured Man*," 548.

91 DuCille, "Looking for Zora," 12.

92 Lhamon, *Raising Cain*, 91.

93 The recent scholarship on minstrelsy wrestles with the uneasy relationship between the overt racism yet resistant strategies attending minstrelsy. On this topic, see Gaines, "Assimilationist Minstrelsy as Racial Uplift Ideology"; Dormon, "Shaping the Popular Image of Post-Reconstruction Ameri-

can Blacks"; Lott, *Love and Theft*; Rogin, *Blackface, White Noise*; Williams, who works in dialogue with Rogin in her *Playing the Race Card*; and, as cited above, Lhamon, *Raising Cain*. See also Gilmore, *The Genuine Article*, 37–66; Curtis, *The First Black Actors on the Great White Way*, 41; and Douglas, *Terrible Honesty*, 328–30.

94 Kirby, *Parallel Tracks*, 80.

95 "On board a train," VanEpps-Taylor writes, "the porter was a servant as well as the host on his car" (*Oscar Micheaux*, 25).

4 *Manhatta*: A National Self-Portrait

1 May makes an important distinction between pragmatists and a resurgence of what he identifies as the "practicalists." "This group," he writes, "believed that what was measurable, immediate, and concrete was what was important. To distinguish these from the pragmatists, since they did not make their opinion into philosophical argument, we will call them 'practicalists'" (*The End of American Innocence*, 129).

2 Whitman quoted in Garman, "'Heroic Spiritual Grandfather,'" 91. See also Reynolds, *Walt Whitman's America*, 502–7. Both writers point to the contradictory positions that Whitman held about American business, socialism, and capitalism.

3 Wiebe, *The Search for Order*, 97.

4 Hartley, "Modern Art in America," in *Adventures in the Arts*, 61; Veblen, *The Theory of the Leisure Class*; Frank, *Our America*; Rosenfeld, "Alfred Stieglitz," in *Port of New York*, 245.

5 Brooks, *America's Coming-of-Age*, 59.

6 See Menand's *The Metaphysical Club* on the connections between American metaphysical spirituality and religion.

7 "They were quite literally soul-searching times," Wiebe succinctly remarks, "for throughout the nineteenth century a great many looked upon economic downturns as a moral judgment, precise punishment for the country's sins" (*The Search for Order*, 2).

8 Hofstadter, *The Age of Reform*, 16; Wiebe, *The Search for Order*, 12.

9 "Middle state," as Marx defines it, is the "reconciliation between the animal and rational, natural and civilized, conditions of man always . . . implied by the pastoral ideal" (*The Machine in the Garden*, 102).

10 On the hyperbolic "nature" of subjectivity, see Butler, *Bodies That Matter*, 10. See Chauncey, *Gay New York* (79–80), for a demonstration of nineteenth-century men masculinizing themselves with hyper-athletics at the gym; as well as Stansell's work on masculinity and modernism in *Ameri-*

can Moderns (203). See, further, Bederman, *Manliness and Civilization*, 12–20.

11 Abrahams points out in *The Lyrical Left and the Origins of Cultural Radicalism in America* (3) that in the same year, 1913, two significant events took place: the International Exhibition of Modern Painting (the Armory Show) and the Paterson Pageant at Madison Square Garden (the political event organized by the Industrial Workers of the World with the help of Mable Dodge-Luhan, who also had her hand in the Armory Show).

12 Brown's book, *The Story of the Armory Show* provides the most comprehensive history of the exhibition See also http://xroads.virginia.edu/~MUSEUM/Armory/armoryshow.html for an electronic tour of the show; and see Pach's "The Armory Show," in his *Queer Thing Painting* (192–203). The critics were many, with Theodore Roosevelt among them (as I have noted). Roosevelt's sarcastic essay infamously characterized the European artists at the exhibition as the "lunatic fringe," and he compared cubism to the "colored puzzle-pictures in the Sunday papers" ("An Art Exhibition," in *Selected Writings*, 356–59).

13 For discussions of the Strand and Sheeler film, see Horak, "Modernist Perspectives and Romantic Impulses"; and Suárez, "City Space, Technology, Popular Culture." Suárez seeks to expand the discussion of *Manhatta* by shifting the film from what he sees as Horak's "monolithic" modernism to a broader consideration of the film's relationship to a select few art journals (the *Soil* in particular). Unfortunately, Suárez's investigation remains too narrow to accomplish what he sets out to do. My aim in this chapter is to open the film within its larger discursive formations about modernism.

Strand and Sheeler shot *Manhatta* in 1920, and it was released as *New York the Magnificent* at the Rialto Theater in 1921. In 1922, the film was screened in Paris under the title *Fumée de New York* (*Smoke of New York*). The film's original title, *Manhatta*, was finally used at the 1927 screening at the London Film Society (see Horak, "Modernist Perspectives and Romantic Impulses," 9–10). In the text I will refer to the film's New York release date, 1921.

14 Frank et al., *America and Alfred Stieglitz*, 3.

15 Certainly several of the essays, such as Jean Toomer's (the only African American member of the circle) and Jennings Tofel's spill into romantic hagiography, but what is striking about the collection is how Stieglitz is often a tool with which the writers' explore the American cultural scene. For further discussion about Toomer's relationship to the Stieglitz circle, see Helbling, " 'Worlds of Shadow-Planes and Solids Silently Moving.' "

16 The exception to this is Brennan's excellent examination in *Painting Gender, Constructing Theory* of the Stieglitz circle and the theoretical discourses they espoused. Brennan considers what she calls "embodied formal-

ism" in her investigation of how Stieglitz and his contemporaries engaged a rhetoric that theorized the artist's body in direct, "embodied" relationship to the work of art. Her emphasis on "embodied formalism" identifies the key ways that Stieglitz, O'Keeffe, Marin, and Dove explored gender relations and corporeality as an intimate experience of art. Brennan's work differs from mine in that I seek to draw the connections not just between gender and the work of art. Rather, I analyze gender and art at the nexus at which the machine complicates, yet proves pivotal to, Stieglitz's concept of embodiment. On Stieglitz and his circle, see also Abrahams, *The Lyrical Left*, 93–203; Corn, *The Great American Thing*; Dijkstra, *Cubism, Stieglitz, and the Early Poetry of William Carlos Williams*; Norman, *Alfred Stieglitz: An American Seer*; Whelan, *Alfred Stieglitz: A Biography*; and Lowe, *Stieglitz: A Memoir Biography*. For discussions about the larger American avant-garde, particularly in New York, see Stansell, *American Moderns*; Watson, *Strange Bedfellows*; and Blake, *Beloved Community*.

17 I emphasize "tolerant" because, as Corn points out, Stieglitz tolerated homosexual artists to the extent that he marginalized artists such as Charles Demuth from the more hetero-virile artist works of, say, John Marin and, indeed, O'Keeffe. Stieglitz made room for homosexuality, it seems, when what he perceived as "vulgar" or "effeminate" was not an attribute of the artist's work of art—the artist's body included (*The Great American Thing*, 193–201). This might be why, following Weinberg's reading, Stieglitz entertained Marsden Hartley's work over that of Demuth's because Hartley disparaged both homosexuality and male effeminacy: his work was considered masculine, unlike Demuth's contributions. See Weinberg, *Speaking for Vice*, especially where the author quotes Pasolini: tolerance is nothing more than "a more refined form of condemnation" (210).

18 For a useful mapping (literally) of the entangled political-romantic relationships between New York's early moderns see Watson's *Strange Bedfellows*.

19 Frank, "The New World in Stieglitz," in *America and Alfred Stieglitz*, 213.

20 "Of course, we in America," the ever-verbose Stieglitz wrote in 1907, "fully acknowledge that in other countries there are enthusiastic workers who have done very much toward enhancing the dignity of pictorial photography, and even bodies of workers who have striven toward a goal; but it is borne in upon us that their spirit of loyalty and enthusiasm has been directed toward organizations, rather than toward broad and universal ideals. True to the American spirit, of which it has been said that even its transcendentalism and Puritanism have been tempered by practical considerations, there has been an incidental material side to all this, which the American worker

fully understands. Though the individual American photographer was sub-ordinated to the success of the cause, yet, in its success, the individual was enabled to achieve, and did achieve, a far greater distinction than could ever have been his portion if he had been compelled to rely upon his unaided effort . . . [photography is] one medium of individual expression" ("Pictorial Photography," 354–55).

21 "When it came to a showdown [with "The Eight," or Ashcan group], I could not see anything truly revolutionary or searching in their paintings. Their line, form, color seemed mediocre. Certainly they lacked freshness or a sense of touch. I could not feel committed to what was mere literature, just because it was labeled social realism" (quoted in Norman, *Alfred Stieg-litz*, 77). For an overview on the Ashcan School, see Perlman, *Painters of the Ashcan School*.

22 See Ohmann's *Selling Culture*; and Tashjian, *Skyscraper Primitives*, chapters 4 and 6.

23 Stieglitz-influenced journals included the *Seven Arts* (defunct by 1920), the *Dial, Manuscripts, 391, Broom*, and many others. See Dijkstra, *Cubism, Stieglitz, and the Early Poetry of William Carlos Williams*, 108–26.

24 MacMillan is more straightforward when she states that "proud, con-fident, rich Europe had torn itself to pieces" (*Paris 1919*, xxv).

25 McBride, "American Art Is 'Looking Up,'" in *The Flow of Art*, 165.

26 Brown, "The Three Roads," 22.

27 "The machine," Frank announces in *Our America*, "is simply an ap-pendage to the human body" (44). And for that reason it is necessary to harness modern energy because it is One: "it is neither material nor spiritual. It is both—or neither" (24).

28 Frank, *Our America*, 9.

29 Stieglitz quoted in Norman, *Alfred Stieglitz*, 31.

30 Stieglitz never took a commission from the art sold in his galleries. Money, for Stieglitz, was a necessity to the extent that it kept the artist alive. He considered lacking in integrity the many galleries in New York that blos-somed following his exhibition model—as he saw it (and rightly so), the gallery owners were in it for the money. Art was a means toward an end, whereas Stieglitz posited art as beyond such cash-driven occupations.

31 For an excellent overview of Stieglitz's aesthetic theories, see Dijkstra, *Cubism, Stieglitz, and the Early Poetry of William Carlos Williams*, 82–107.

32 Brooks makes a similar case in *America's Coming-of-Age*, 132–37.

33 As Corn demonstrates in *The Great American Thing*, the concept of "spirit" was central to the Stieglitz circle.

34 Although McBride would later be somewhat more generous in his con-sideration of the Hudson River School (by the 1950s he saw the group, if

not as artists per se, then as important pioneers for American art), during the 1920s and 1930s he stated that the movement "lacked style" (*The Flow of Art*, 196) and was "stodgy" (287).

35   Stieglitz quoted in Dijkstra, *Cubism, Stieglitz, and the Early Poetry of William Carlos Williams*, 94.

36   Stieglitz quoted in Whelan, *Alfred Stieglitz*, 54.

37   Ibid., 103. Ironically, Kodak became a major advertiser in *Camera Work*.

38   Whelan, *Alfred Stieglitz*, 54.

39   Stieglitz quoted in ibid.

40   Stieglitz consistently let the artist manqué know in no uncertain terms that their career was not merely short-lived but rather never existed.

41   Lowe, *Stieglitz*, 76. See also Whelan, *Alfred Stieglitz*, 120–21. Sherwood Anderson once wrote: "I have quite definitely come to the conclusion that there is in the world a thing one thinks of as maleness that is represented by such men as Alfred Stieglitz. It has something to do with the craftsman's love of his tools and materials" (quoted in Brennan, *Painting Gender, Constructing Theory*, 67).

42   Stansell, *American Moderns*, 34.

43   Henry Adams had similar, albeit more cynical, views on women's role in machine culture. In his well-rehearsed chapter "Vis Inertiae" in *The Education of Henry Adams*, he dolefully announces that because woman was "trying to find her way by imitating [man]" in American culture, she indeed succeeded, yet had "become sexless like the bees" (236). Adams envisioned machine culture as one of Stepford Wives–type sameness: "She must, like the man, marry machinery" (237). And as the "determined patriot," Henry McBride (a champion of Stieglitz) declared: "[The modern age] is an age in which all barriers are down; an age in which the women wish to be men" ("Brancusi," in *The Flow of Art*, 57).

44   Norman, *Alfred Stieglitz*, 204.

45   Wilson quoted in Whelan, *Alfred Stieglitz*, 372.

46   Norman, *Alfred Stieglitz*, 203.

47   Whelan, *Alfred Stieglitz*, 17. On the one hand, Stieglitz adored O'Keeffe's preponderance for black, simple, Puritan-like clothing. On the other hand, he was mesmerized by what he saw as O'Keeffe's purity to which he refers to as her "whiteness," her "metaphysical purity based on her clarity of vision and the lucid wholeness of her mind, which set[s] her apart from other women and, in fact, all other people" (Robinson, *Georgia O'Keeffe*, 195; on the simplicity of her dress and its sometimes-androgynous effect, see 60, 89, 174).

48   Unlike, say, Villier L'Isle Adam's *L'Eve Futur* or Henry Adams's ironic

squabbling over the place of woman as machine and, indeed, the troubling effect she had on machine efficiency, Stieglitz countenanced and embraced gender distinction—male and female—as cooperative material in the transcendent possibilities of the machine. See Adams's "Vis Inertiae" in *The Education of Henry Adams*, 225–39. See also Gerstner, "Unsinkable Masculinity."

49 Stieglitz quoted in Norman, *Alfred Stieglitz*, 161.

50 "My cloud photographs are *equivalents* of my most profound life experience, my basic philosophy of life" (quoted in Norman, *Alfred Stieglitz*, 144). Brennan takes up Stieglitz's "equivalents" in *Painting Gender, Constructing Theory*, 70.

51 Stieglitz quoted in Norman, *Alfred Stieglitz*, 136.

52 Ibid., 137.

53 Such logic befits Walt Whitman's exegesis on a "strong and sweet Female Race, a race of perfect Mothers" (*Democratic Vistas*, 328).

54 Hartley, *Adventures in the Arts*, 8 (note that the book is dedicated to Alfred Stieglitz).

55 Hartley was not alone among Stieglitz's entourage to elicit the spiritual necessity of the primitive in modern art. Abrahams (*The Lyrical Left*, 162–63) recounts de Zayas's insistence (possibly the strongest voice of such arguments that Stieglitz entertained) that the primitive object carried "physical" and "spiritual" presences essential to modernist practices. His abstract caricatures and his book *A Study of the Modern Evolution of Plastic Expression* were the artist/writer's evidence for his argument.

56 Robinson, *The Mind in the Making*, 80.

57 Rony, "Robert Flaherty's *Nanook of the North*," 310.

58 I borrow Gaines's use of the word "fascinated" from her discussion of the modernist film journal *Close-up* and, as she posits, "the Left's love affair with political modernism" but its "[flirtation] with the essentialism that should be starkly antithetical to it" (*Fire and Desire*, 4).

59 May provides a good overview of New York arts and intellectual culture during the particular period under discussion, 1910 to 1916 (*The End of American Innocence*, 279–301).

60 Rosenfeld, *Port of New York*, 288.

61 Freud's popularity as well as the much-touted fields of anthropology and ethnography at the time had much to do with the connections made between "childhood" and primitivism. See, for example, Freud's *New Introductory Lectures on Psychoanalysis*, 152. Douglas gives a good overview of Franz Boas and the rise of anthropology as a consecrated science and discipline in *Terrible Honesty*, 49–51.

62 See Scott and Rutkoff, *New York Modern*, 44–72.

63 Lucic, *Charles Sheeler and the Cult of the Machine*, 24.

64 Quoted in Tashjian, *Skyscraper Primitives*, 192–93. Stella's remarks are also partially quoted in Lucic, *Charles Sheeler and the Cult of the Machine*, 43. For a thorough discussion of Stella's place in American art and his relationship to New York City, see Corn, *The Great American Thing*, chapter 3.

65 Tomkins, *Duchamp*, 203.

66 Marx, *The Machine in the Garden*, 205.

67 Tomkins, "Profiles: Look to the Things around You," 56; Horak, "Modernist Perspectives and Romantic Impulses," 10.

68 Lindsay, *The Art of the Moving Picture*, 95. A year after Lindsay first published his book on film theory, Münsterberg published *The Photoplay*. Prior to both, the earliest critical study of cinema was found in Stieglitz's *Camera Work* by Sadakichi Hartmann. His essay, "The Esthetic Significance of the Motion Picture," was published in 1912. Moore, in *Savage Theory*, provides an insightful review of Lindsay, Hartmann, and other early discussions of film theory and modern primitivism. Other early film writings include Robert J. Coady, "Censoring the Motion Picture," *Soil* (December 1916); Kenneth Macgowan, "Beyond the Screen," *Seven Arts* (December 1916); and Robert Alden Sanborn, "Motion Picture Dynamics," *Broom* 5.2 (September 1923). Suárez discusses these works in "City Space, Technology, Popular Culture," 97–100.

69 Suggesting Griffith's work as democratically "Whitmanesque" is not as odd as it may seem given Lindsay's penchant for a peculiar mix of "masters," or as May identified them: "Jesus, Swedenborg, Tolstoy, St. Francis, Whitman, Emerson, and Shelley" (*The End of American Innocence*, 265). Lindsay's argument for "Whitmanesque scenarios" and poetic aesthetics in machine-based cinema also confirms Marx's idea that "it is fitting to consider Whitman here because he becomes closest to transmuting the rhetoric of the technological sublime into poetry" (*The Art of the Moving Picture*, 222). Randolphe Bourne ultimately distrusted the simplifications of popular cinema as democratic. He thought of it instead as "low-brow snobbery" (quoted in Rasmussen, "Mass Wasteland," 313).

70 "Man will not only see visions again, but machines themselves, in the hands of prophets, will see visions" (298). For Lindsay, the prophets were the American artist-poets who necessarily worked in unison with the "mechanical inventors" or "realists" (a list that includes Thomas Alva Edison and Hudson Maxim, author of *Defenseless America* and, as we saw earlier, inventor of the Maxim machine gun). As Moore argues: "America, with no significant artistic tradition of its own, according to Lindsay, effectively skips developing its own art history and turns directly to cinema, thus putting it ahead, for once, of the Old World" (*Savage Theory*, 54). As I have been arguing, however, Americans did not "effectively skip" a tradition of art.

They grappled with the terms of what "art history" meant through inherited traditions of painting and literature. The cinema was a new form grabbed for its fresh possibilities yet measured by conventional aesthetic standards.

71 It is noteworthy that Griffith shows up in the pages of his "Imagist film" discussion when Lindsay states, "Except for some of the old one-reel Biographs of Griffith's beginning, there is nothing of Doric restraint from the best to the worst" (*The Art of the Moving Picture*, 268). Lindsay emphasizes that his theory of hieroglyphics is not one that he insists the filmmaker follow. Rather, he wishes the filmmaker to "consent in his meditative hours to the point of view [hieroglyphics] implies" (209). As such, Griffith is the "king-figure" of long or short films.

72 For an excellent account of the role of the cinema in Sheeler's work, see Haas, "Charles Sheeler and Film."

73 Rourke's body of writing is precisely a project to identify the complexity of the American arts. See, for example, *The Roots of American Culture and Other Essays* and *American Humor: A Study of The National Character*.

74 Letter from Rourke to Sheeler, c. 1937, Archives of American Art, microfilm reel 1811, plate 178, p. 1.

75 Rourke, *Charles Sheeler*, 70.

76 Quoted in Rourke, *Charles Sheeler*, 143. As Fillin-Yeh writes in "Charles Sheeler's 1923 'Self-Portrait,'": "Although Sheeler's paintings took their structural underpinnings from the geometric and angular shapes of Cubist abstractions they still seemed true to life; thus they always remained popular works, never having to face the hostility of a public unsympathetic toward abstraction" (106–7). A great many scholars comment on Sheeler's realist-abstraction aesthetic: see, for example, Driscoll, "Charles Sheeler's Early Work," 128–29; William Carlos Williams's introduction to Sheeler, *Charles Sheeler: Paintings, Drawings, Photographs*, 8–9; and Lucic, *Charles Sheeler and the Cult of the Machine*, 13.

77 Oral history interview with Charles Sheeler, conducted by Martin Friedman, Archives of American Art, June 18, 1959. On-line transcript accessed June 21, 2003: http://www.archivesofamericanart.si.edu/oralhist/sheele59.htm.

78 See further Sheeler's discussions of "selective realism" in his unpublished autobiography (Archives of American Art, microfilm reel 1811, p. 8); and in Friedman's "The Art of Charles Sheeler," 47. When Sheeler was asked why his work *View of New York* did not represent a literal view of New York, he declared, "I wish I could give you an interesting story in connection with *View of New York*, but alas it would have to be drawn from imagination and I am a realist. It was painted in 1931 in a studio which I had at the time in

New York. So you see the title really is authentic" (quoted in Lucic, *Charles Sheeler and the Cult of the Machine*, 130).

79 Sheeler, unpublished autobiography, Archives of American Art, microfilm reel 1811, p. 7.

80 Ibid., 8; Rourke, *Charles Sheeler*, 133–36. For an excellent discussion of Sheeler's modernist folk art, see Corn, *The Great American Thing*, 293–337.

81 Friedman, "The Art of Charles Sheeler," 36; Rourke, *Charles Sheeler*, 27. Sheeler marks this date as well for the first time he witnessed these works (see Friedman, "Interview with Charles Sheeler," 2–3).

82 Much is written about the "perdurable" friendship between Sheeler and Schamberg, and how Sheeler was devastated by his friend's death in 1918 by the influenza epidemic. Their intimacy and love for one another are so well documented and inscribed as part of the Sheeler myth that it begs the obvious question that is never articulated. Rourke's sharp observations, however, may have slyly introduced the provocative possibilities of their relationship: "A still from an early motion picture of Sheeler's shows Schamberg partially reclining with a parraoquet on his·wrist, his narrow figure, the turned head and finely articulated hand against the dark. Here Sheeler did not scorn nature; the portraiture is explicit, indicating among other qualities the aloofness belonging at the time to both these young men, and their estheticism" (*Charles Sheeler*, 37). Haas also discusses Schamberg and Sheeler's experiments with motion pictures ("Charles Sheeler and Film," 122–23).

83 Lucic, *Charles Sheeler and the Cult of the Machine*, 39.

84 As is clear from Sheeler's works, the barn was central to his understanding of native and functional American architecture. In his 1959 interview with Friedman, Sheeler states: "Well, people—they built their own barns largely, that is, I mean the community built the barns for the individual, and they always had, first of all, its utility in mind; and that wasn't accidental because they knew how the barn had to function for their purpose. They weren't building a work of art. That is as a family objective. If it's beautiful to some of us afterwards, it's beautiful because it functioned. The functional intention was very beautifully realized" ("Interview with Charles Sheeler," n.p.).

85 Friedman, "The Art of Charles Sheeler," 36. For further discussion about Sheeler's lifestyle and art in Pennsylvania, see Corn, *The Great American Thing*, 298–302.

86 Marx, *The Machine in the Garden*, 356. Lucic, in *Charles Sheeler and the Cult of the Machine* (104–5), disagrees with Marx's assessment of Sheeler's work, stating that Marx underestimates Sheeler's "consciously or unconsciously" critical approach to the "worker's powerlessness" in *American Landscape*. I am not certain that Marx would disagree with Lucic that Sheeler's

work "unsettles" more than it "pacifies" a nervous machine-age spectator. Marx's entire book is precisely about the unsettling experience defining the tensions between pastoral/agrarian and industrial/machine cultures.

87 Rourke, *Charles Sheeler*, 87.

88 Lucic, *Charles Sheeler and the Cult of the Machine*, 132.

89 Fillin-Yeh, "Charles Sheeler's 1923 'Self-Portrait,'" 107; Troyen and Hirshler, *Charles Sheeler*, 96.

90 For further analysis of Sheeler's two works, see Lucic, *Charles Sheeler and the Cult of the Machine*, 95–97. Maroney, in his essay "Charles Sheeler Reveals the Machinery of His Soul," provides a thorough accounting of and challenge to analyses such as Lucic's that funnel Sheeler's work through a strictly machinist perspective. Maroney persuasively identifies Sheeler's quest for more personal and spiritual attainment. The illustrations discussed here were not available for publication as a pair, but they are reproduced in Lucic's book on pp. 96–97.

91 Sheeler quoted in Friedman, "Interview with Charles Sheeler, n.p."

92 Brennan discusses the centrality of the portrait in Stieglitz's work in relationship to his theories of embodiment with the photograph, especially through the fragmented "portraits" of O'Keeffe: "The symbolic fragments of her body could simultaneously function as a portrait of her and symbol of Stieglitz himself" (*Painting Gender, Constructing Theory*, 83).

93 Brown, "Three Roads," 30.

94 Alan Trachtenberg, "Introduction," 2. See also Weaver's "Dynamic Realist."

95 Strand, "Photography," 524. For an excellent overview of Strand's early writings and works, see Rosenblum, "The Early Years," 42.

96 Strand, "Photography," 524.

97 Yet, it is apparent from his photograph *Workman* (1916) that Strand (most likely because of his education at the Ethical Culture School) found himself attracted to the worker as humanist subject.

98 Greenough, *Paul Strand: An American Vision*, 32. Since there is no full biography written about Strand, the best sources for his background are Greenough's book, as well as Tomkins, "Profiles: Look to the Things Around You," and the individual essays in Maren, ed., *Paul Strand: Essays on His Life and Work*. On the Ethical Culture School, see Hutchinson's discussion in *The Harlem Renaissance in Black and White*, 39–42.

99 Trachtenberg's book *Reading American Photographs* rehearses the two versions of photography between which Strand found himself. See my note in chapter 1 that critiques Trachtenberg's masculinist account of American aesthetics, particularly in his dismissal of Stieglitz's aesthetics over Hine's (apparently) more relevant social art.

100 Rosenblum, "The Early Years," 31–51, 42.

101 Strand, "Photography and the New God," 258.

102 On this debate, see Bender, *The Unfinished City*, 34–37; and Scott and Rutkoff, *New York Modern*, 20–22.

103 When Daniel Liebskind, the architect charged with rebuilding the World Trade Center site in Manhattan after the September 11th terrorist attack, was asked in 2003 what inspired him to enter the competition, he responded: "I took out the Declaration of Independence and the Constitution and reread them so that I could get back to what America is about, and I read Walt Whitman, the poet of working-class New York, and I reread 'The Two Churches,' a short story by Melville" (quoted in Goldberger, "Urban Warriors," 74).

104 Douglas, *Terrible Honesty*, 119.

105 Strand, press release for *New York the Magnificent*, 1921, Museum of Modern Art Film Studies Center.

106 Horak, "Modernist Perspectives and Romantic Impulses," 14.

107 It is worth noting how Strand uses the word "register" twice in lieu of similar clichés in photography-speak such as "capture."

108 I discuss Trachtenberg's critique of Stieglitz in chapter 1. Bender champions John Sloan and The Eight's direct participation in city street culture over Stieglitz's less politically committed aesthetic vision of New York. For Bender, Stieglitz's photography is "not a place of working, living, and laughing; nor a place of homes, families, or neighborhoods" (*The Unfinished City*, 107–25). Corn argues something similar about Stieglitz, particularly during the era she identifies as the "second" Stieglitz circle that emerged following the war (*The Great American Thing*, 24–31). I would disagree with this assessment given what I see as the Stieglitz circle's embrace of the city precisely because of its potential as a place where, through art, one might bring equilibrium to disequilibrium. I also think that what these critics view as a sweeping dismissal of the "vulgar" city on the part of the Stieglitz coterie is nothing more than (albeit banal) New Yorker cynicism. Stieglitz, after all, continued to return to the city.

109 Horak, "Modernist Perspectives and Romantic Impulses," 13.

110 These are Horak's terms ("Modernist Perspectives and Romantic Impulses," 14). Suárez concurs with Horak that the human figures are "nearly turned into abstractions, reduced to pattern, movement, and type." Suárez goes so far as to suggest that the "reduction" of the human figure "is central to the film's modernism and seems to have been the primary purpose of *Manhatta*" (101). I find things to be somewhat more complicated, however. Hammen, in one of the first critical re-evaluations of the film, questions the critique that the film "does not move in the manner considered correct for

the true cinema" ("Sheeler and Strand's 'Manhatta,' " 6). Hammen states that Strand and Sheeler "examine" the "movements of man and machine from a distance" though he recognizes how the scale of the subjects may make especially the spectator experience a "suppressed anxiety" (6–7).

111 Bender, *The Unfinished City*, 107.

112 In this way the film sustains, as I have argued, Stieglitz's poetic "equivalents" over the narrative model that Horak suggests because each recorded moment in the film is presented as one that converges with the artist's lived experience and creative expression. Horak sees a teleological development from *Manhatta* through to Vertov's *Man with a Movie Camera* (1929) and Ruttman's *Berlin: Symphony of a City*. The film does not display, necessarily, the daily life of the city. In fact, the seasonal changes and the uncertain times of day (consider the film's shadows) in the film lead me to think otherwise. The film's concluding reference to drenching sunshine, moreover, leaves it far from certain that the film has followed a day-to-night scenario.

113 Moon, *Disseminating Whitman*, 69.

5   The Queer Frontier

1 Eleanor Lambert, uncatalogued press release, 1937, Shubert Archives.

2 Kirstein, *Dance*, 250–52. I want to thank Edward Miller for the engaging discussions we shared during the writing of this chapter.

3 Garafola, *Diaghilev's Ballets Russes*, 361.

4 "I was never told that creativity was unmanly," Minnelli declares. "Looking at Mr. Frazier's assistant [Frazier was Minnelli's boss at Marshall Field where he worked on window displays], a William Bendix type, and talking to the other display men who were all married and raising families, I saw by their example that one could happily function as the male animal and still give vent to his so-called feminine traits. As a result, I wasn't cowed at this impressionable age into more conventionally male avenues of expression. I'm thankful for that. I'd make a miserable football coach" (Minnelli, with Arce, *Vincente Minnelli*, 45).

5 I intend to use the word "queer" to cover the spectrum of people who broadly expressed, experienced, and performed sexuality in relationship to how they understood and embodied "American art."

6 Balanchine first saw Isadora Duncan late in her career when she visited Russia in 1922 (Taper, *Balanchine*, 58–59).

7 Although, as Banes argues in *Dancing Women* (80), Duncan's feminist

overtures through American dance were ultimately "conservative" because she linked "sexuality, nature, procreation, and motherhood as women's innate biological and social destiny," the dancer was an odd duck like her poetic mentor Whitman. Not surprisingly, Duncan's "conservative" notion of women was certainly close to Whitman's essentialist account of women.

8 Benton, *An Artist in America*, 262–67.

9 For a review of the filmmaker's interest in the arts, see Gerstner, "Queer Modernism"; and Naremore, *The Films of Vincente Minnelli*, 1–50. See also Harvey, *Directed by Vincente Minnelli* (11–35), for a complete biographical account of Minnelli and his modernist aesthetics.

10 See chapter 3 in this book for a discussion of Micheaux's relationship to urban and rural cultures. Allmendinger, in "The Plow and the Pen: The Pioneering Adventures of Oscar Micheaux" (559–60), indicates the way that Micheaux emphasizes in his novels the prairie as "chaste" while Chicago elicits "innuendo" and flirtation.

11 Lewis writes: "Altogether, the Harlem Renaissance evolved through three stages. The first, ending in 1923 with the publication of [Jean] Toomer's *Cane*, was deeply influenced by white artists and writers, all of them fascinated for a variety of reasons with the life of people of color. The second phase, from early 1924 to mid-1926, was presided over by the Civil Rights Establishment of the Urban League and the NAACP, a collaboration of 'Negrotarian' whites and the Talented Tenth. The last phase, from mid-1926 to the Harlem Riots of March 1935, was increasingly dominated by African-American artists and writers themselves" (*When Harlem Was in Vogue*, xxiv).

12 And, of course, the opposite was true. New York's Harlem Renaissance artists rarely if ever considered Micheaux a significant artist (see chapter 3). Lewis posits Micheaux as a producer of "curious folk novels" prior to the advent of the high modernist strains associated with the Harlem Renaissance (*When Harlem Was in Vogue*, 89). Micheaux wasn't considered to have what it took to be a member of this very urbane movement. Paradoxically (as we will see below), folk culture was instrumental to much of the theoretical thinking of black modernists at the time.

13 Lewis, *When Harlem Was in Vogue*, xxiv. For discussions about the continuing effects of the Harlem Renaissance, see, especially, Baker, *Modernism and the Harlem Renaissance*, 12, 91.

14 Lewis's *When Harlem Was in Vogue*; Douglas's *Terrible Honesty*; and Chauncey's *Gay New York* chronicle Manhattan's complicated spheres of social tolerance often framed by racism and homophobia.

15 Marquis's *Alfred H. Barr* gives a very good accounting of both Barr and MOMA's institutional development of art in the United States (142). As late

as 1940 Barr (unlike Henry McBride who, in 1922, claimed that Americans had finally broken from Parisian influence) claimed, "America is not yet, I'm afraid, the equal of France" (190).

16 Stieglitz quoted in Whelan, *Alfred Stieglitz*, 565. Stieglitz was most likely infuriated when MOMA refused his offer of Marsden Hartley works for an early exhibit (Marquis, *Alfred H. Barr*, 144). Later, Dorothy Norman, sensitive to Stieglitz's treatment by MOMA, contributed her collection of Stieglitz's photographs to the Philadelphia Museum.

17 Marquis, *Alfred H. Barr*, 236. On the history of American abstract painting, see Naifeh and Smith, *Jackson Pollock*; and Leja, *Reframing Abstract Expressionism*.

18 Guilbaut, *How New York Stole the Idea of Modern Art*, 23.

19 Indeed, Iris Barry, who Barr positioned as curator of the museum's film library, built the largest archive of Griffith films and papers anywhere in the world at the time. In addition, Lincoln Kirstein was Barr's friend and had some influence on the key decisions made regarding MOMA exhibitions. Marquis (*Alfred H. Barr*, 94) points out that in 1932 it was at Kirstein's insistence (as part of an advisory committee assembled by Abby Rockefeller) that an American muralist's show take place. More relevantly, Kirstein published one of Barr's articles, "Nationalism in German Cinema," in his Harvard-founded avant-garde journal *Hound and Horn*. Kirstein himself wrote several articles on, among other topics, Hollywood film, many of which are collected by Nicholas Jenkins in *By With To and From: A Lincoln Kirstein Reader*. See in the collection, for example, his 1932 essay, "James Cagney and the American Hero" (275–77) or his later essay "Marilyn Monroe: 1926–62" (301–8). Others directly or indirectly involved in Barr's circles who took pleasure in Hollywood film included Pavel Tchelitchev and Carl Van Vechten. I'd like to thank Kirstein's literary executor, Nicholas Jenkins, for pointing to Kirstein's remarks about Astaire and Rogers as prototypes for the "Balanchinian look" (correspondence with author, January 27, 2004; see also *By With To and From*, 196).

20 Chauncey, *Gay New York*, 303.

21 See Leddick's *Intimate Companions*, for a look at the queer sexual dynamic (especially within the vicinity of MOMA) that occurred at this time and the ways in which this sexuality permeated the artistic and critical practices of the period.

22 Marsden Hartley, who later befriended George Platt Lynes, spent time at his studio, and was photographed by him before he died in 1943, had his last show at Stieglitz's An American Place in 1937. In 1944, MOMA held a retrospective of Hartley's work. For the Hartley photograph, see Woody's *George Platt Lynes Photographs, 1931–1955*.

23 Lewis, *When Harlem Was in Vogue*, 28.

24 Douglas, *Terrible Honesty*, 76.

25 Hutchinson, *The Harlem Renaissance in Black and White*, 90. Hutchinson further asserts that the Harlem Renaissance of the 1930s should not be so quickly overlooked (22–3).

26 Litvak, *Strange Gourmets*, 3.

27 See Waters (with Charles Samuels), *His Eye Is on the Sparrow*. "Those bohemians [downtown]," writes Waters, "were like my own people, and I liked them. Your color or your bank account made no difference to them. They liked you for yourself. They were doing work they loved, kept what hours they pleased, and didn't care what Mr. and Mrs. Buttinsky down the hall thought of them and their odd ways. That all made sense to me" (193).

28 Minnelli continually let the press know about his painterly ambitions. "He limits his painting these days to designing stage sets and costumes for prima donnas," writes Birnie, "But he still nourishes a dream of turning out some serious canvases . . ." ("A Chorine Thought and Was Wrong," 3). In Shubert press releases he is identified as the "painter gone producer." Such publicity anecdotes were many. During the writing of my dissertation at UCLA I interviewed Lee Minnelli (Vincente's last wife) at their home in Beverly Hills in 1994. Prominently displayed in Minnelli's studio and overlooking the rose garden (filled with roses, gifts from Elizabeth Taylor) was his easel with an unfinished painting. Ms. Minnelli reasserted the centrality of painting to the director's work and life.

29 Minnelli, *Vincente Minnelli*, 51.

30 Minnelli cites Bakst in his memoirs especially in relationship to *Vanities* (58) and can't say enough about how he was "transfixed" early on by Jones's work in the theatre (46, 51, 57, 61). Jones also designed for *The Green Pastures* (1935) and served as managing director for Kirstein's Ballet Caravan's production of *Billy the Kid* (1939). Kirstein singled out Jones for his work as the only "American to collaborate with the Russians" (*Dance*, 295).

31 For an excellent discussion of Minnelli's work in New York see Harvey's "Vincente Minnelli and the Shuberts."

32 Minnelli, *Vincente Minnelli*, 54.

33 Regina Crewe, "Color Flair Wins Fame for Minnelli," *New York Journal-American*, October 24, 1937, np.

34 An 'aesthetic of excess' is, of course, what we might call "camp." There is much — perhaps, ironically, too much — written about it but for a thorough overview of its history and a solid collection of writings on this subject, see Cleto, *Camp: Queer Aesthetics and the Performing Subject*.

35 Quoted in Buckle, *George Balanchine*, 89. As Buckle points out, Kirstein was in search of "American themes, musicians and painters." In a letter

to Everett "Chick" Austin, director of the Wadsworth Atheneum in Hartford, Connecticut, who originally worked with Kirstein to bring Balanchine to America, Kirstein writes: "This will be the most important letter I will ever write to you . . . My pen burns my hand as I write . . . We have a real chance to have an American ballet within 3 years time . . ." (quote in Buckle, 69).

36 Franko, in *The Work of Dance* (122), derides Kirstein as an "[ideologue] of aesthetic modernism" in his Americanist sensibilities. Franko bases his argument on a handful of articles. As I show here, aesthetics and politics were grounded in something more complex and, indeed, queer. Kirstein, in fact, summoned "elegance" as a way to resist a "national manner [that] quickly grows defensively and complacently provincial." For Kirstein, dandyism and elegance "smack of revolt against the ordinary, the level, the average" (*By With To and From*, 179).

37 New York Public Library, Performing Arts Library at Lincoln Center, Lincoln Kirstein Collection, clippings file (folder "Before 1950").

38 Given Kirstein's central position and direct involvement with the Caravan, I presume the brochure to be in his words.

39 Writing in 1955, Duke recalls that as early as 1936 the word "gay," uttered by the "resplendent parade of homosexuals," was associated with the "boys" at the ballet (*Passport to Paris*, 328–29).

40 See, for example, the accounts of Kirstein's sexual affair with Carl Carlsen: "Carlsen, Crane," in *By With To and From*, (38–71); and "Crane and Carlsen, New York, 1931–1932," in *Mosaic* (187–210). Carlsen was apparently not the only "manly" boy who tickled Kirstein's fantasy. In a letter to Tchelitchev dated February 4, 1957, the impresario writes: "I have also a wonderful boy who is in the naval academy until June but he has a sympathetic commanding-officer who permits him to work at school. He is an Italian boy, rather small but extremely beautiful and manly" (Beinecke Rare Book and Manuscript Library, Yale University, Tchelitchev correspondence with Lincoln Kirstein, preliminary survey [not catalogued]).

41 See the New York City Performing Arts Library at Lincoln Center, Lincoln Kirstein Collection, "Before 1950" folder.

42 John Murray Anderson directed *Ziegfeld Follies*. Minnelli, at the same time he designed the *Follies*, directed Waters in *At Home Abroad* at the Majestic Theater. According to Harvey, Minnelli "found Baker a particularly inspiring mannequin for his fanciful chic. In a bow to her music-hall image as the pagan icon of exotica, he bared Baker in a bikini-dentata of white tusks for the Duke-Gershwin song, 'Island of the West Indies;' elsewhere he draped her in saris as a maharani at the race-track and in a gold-metallic gown in a sketch representing her weary-of-it-all existence in Paris" ("Vincente Minnelli and the Shuberts," 4). Their take on Baker is quite telling

of the two men. Minnelli thrilled at the opportunity to dress her in "gold mesh" while she performed in "a dusty pink room with African sculpture" (Minnelli, *Vincente Minnelli*, 78), while Balanchine, according to Taper, was assigned to "fashion some dances that would display to advantage her dusky elegance and her talented, world-famous *derrière* . . . but there was little original he could do for it" (*Balanchine*, 178). As Baker recalls: "Vincente Minnelli had provided gorgeous sets and costumes including an Asian version of my banana waistband, which substituted tusks for fruit." Though she admired Minnelli, she ultimately felt that for him she was "nothing but a body to be exhibited in various stages of undress" (Baker, *Josephine*, 101; this autobiography includes a photograph of Minnelli's "Asian version" costume for the *Follies*).

43 For good biographical information on Balanchine, see Buckle, with Taras, *George Balanchine*; Farrell, with Bentley, *Holding on to the Air*; Kristy, *George Balanchine*; McDonagh, *George Balanchine*; and Taper, *Balanchine*.

44 Although most biographies discuss Balanchine's work outside the ballet, McDonagh, in *George Balanchine*, provides the best coverage (see the chapter titled "Popular Entertainment" [79–95], which includes a discussion of his work with Minnelli [81]).

45 Quoted in Farrell, *Holding on to the Air*, 175.

46 Quoted in Taper, *Balanchine*, 181.

47 See Banes's informative essay "Balanchine and Black Dance." In 1926 Balanchine, for Diaghilev's Ballets Russes, performed in blackface as the character "Snowball" in *The Triumph of Neptune*, and he choreographed "The Black Dancer" in *Jack in the Box*. As Banes points out, Balanchine's admiration of black dance was part and parcel of his love for American culture (56), and because of this she does not read "Snowball" as racist minstrelsy. In addition Kirstein, perhaps because of his knowledge that Balanchine turned to African American culture for his choreography, told e. e. cummings that *Uncle Tom's Cabin* would be the first ballet performed upon Balanchine's arrival to the United States (from a letter quoted in Kisselgoff, "Retracing the Steps in Balanchine's Extraordinary Odyssey," E1, 8).

48 Buckle, *George Balanchine*, 13; McDonagh, *George Balanchine*, 3; Taper, *Balanchine*, 46.

49 Buckle, *George Balanchine*, 112.

50 The filmed version of "Slaughterhouse on 10th Avenue" in *On Your Toes* suggests the variations for camera that Balanchine sought in the relationship between dance and film. In one dramatic angle, the camera moves through the dancer's legs toward another set of action (there is a bit of Busby Berkeley here; a director that Balanchine admired). The rather funny story is told about Balanchine's first Hollywood work with Sam Goldwyn on *The*

Goldwyn Follies (1938) when he put the humorously inarticulate producer through a series of rigorously uncomfortable viewing positions to examine his multiple and complex camera setups. Goldwyn, although he admired Balanchine, told him to present the film's dance numbers in a traditional proscenium setup. For the best account of Goldwyn's response to Balanchine's cinematic choreography, see Taper, *Balanchine*, 187–90. See also Waleson, "When Balanchine Brought Ballet to Hollywood."

51 A full-scale ballet in homage to Gershwin's composition would not occur, of course, until 1951 when Minnelli directed *An American in Paris* for MGM, (although Balanchine choreographed Gershwin in *Who Cares?*). Minnelli's long takes, sweeping camera, and painterly mise-en-scène in *An American in Paris*, however, were far different from what Balanchine proposed for Gershwin's music. Indeed, the issue of mise-en-scène, dance, and the cinema was central to the different ways that Minnelli and Balanchine understood the relationship of the body to theatrical and cinematic art.

52 The quote by Kirstein is in *Mosaic*, 244.

53 Goffman, *The Presentation of Self in Everyday Life*.

54 Kirstein, *Mosaic*, 244; Duke, *Passport to Paris*, 178.

55 See Alice Hughes, "B'way Hails Minnelli as New Master," *New York American*, January 3, 1937, n.p. In addition, "That Felli Minnelli" (as S. J. Perelman called his friend) was described by Dorothy Tuttle Nitch, a contract dancer at MGM, as follows: "When Vincente [Minnelli] came to MGM he had the green eye shadow and the purple lipstick and a tam, etc. and we didn't quite think he would marry Judy [Garland] or anyone else" (interview in *Judy: Beyond the Rainbow*, A&E *Biography*, Peter Jones Productions, aired March 23, 1997. See also "That Felli Minnelli," *Stage*, May 1937, 66–68). Hugh Troy of *Esquire* describes Minnelli as "the incarnation of our preconceived notion of a 'Village type';—that black hat with a wide brim, loose collar and looser tie around his thin neck, a big portfolio of drawings under one arm and the cut of his long coat a triumphant marriage of *Harlem and The Left Bank*" ("Never Had a Lesson," 99).

56 Buckle, *George Balanchine*, 53.

57 Balanchine quoted in McDonagh, *George Balanchine*, 6.

58 Taper, *Balanchine*, 77. According to Taper, Balanchine found that "Diaghilev came to focus so much attention on décor and costumes; he was trying to distract the public from the inadequacies of the dancing" (78).

59 The interview with Balanchine on the DVD *Balanchine* covers many of the theoretical interests that the choreographer espoused (West Long Branch, N.J.: Kultur, 2004, produced by Thirteen/WNET New York with Societe Radio Canada and the BBC, directed by Merrill Brockway, produced by Judy Kinberg).

60 "Ballet is woman" is quoted in McDonagh, *George Balanchine* (15), and in Farrell, *Holding on to the Air* (201).

61 Balanchine quoted in McDonagh, *George Balanchine*, 15.

62 Balanchine quoted in Farrell, *Holding on to the Air*, 115.

63 As Edward Miller reminds us: "The pas de deux is a further extension of the idealized expressivity of the female form, not a romantic coupling or union . . . The male dancer is only the engine or enabler of this display of virtuosity." And, more significantly, the male dancer is the "surrogate" Balanchine (personal correspondence with author, March 9, 2004).

64 One might argue that his love of the Western film genre's open spaces had much to do with his adoration of his ballet's minimalist worlds (Isadora Duncan, who, as we have seen, was inspired by and inspired the ideals of the West, also stripped bare her stage).

65 Buckle, *George Balanchine*, 159.

66 Balanchine quoted in Taper, *Balanchine*, 214–15.

67 "In a way," Banes posits, "Balanchine's modernist ballet prefigures the sexual revolution of the 1960s" (*Dancing Women*, 213).

68 Even with their creative differences, "Tchelitchev," Kirstein posits, "allowed that Balanchine certainly had a gift for transforming movement and filling space with human bodies" (*Mosaic*, 235). On Tchelitchev's creative split with Balanchine, see Taper, *Balanchine*, 222; and Buckle, *George Balanchine*, 66.

69 As we will see, Kirstein devoted a great deal of energy and time to elevating Tchelitchev's position in the art world during the artist's lifetime and after his death in 1957. An early diary entry in 1933 by Kirstein is actually quite revealing. After seeing a rehearsal of *Errante* in Paris, Kirstein wrote, "Balanchine's choreography: activated Tchelitchev drawings; no dancing, but some startling effects *à la* Loie Fuller" (*By With To and From*, 133). And, as Taper further points out, Tchelitchev held a powerful grip on both Kirstein and Balanchine, "but on the whole Tchelitchev's influence on [Balanchine] was not so marked or lasting as it was on Kirstein" (*Balanchine*, 171). Kirstein's letters to Tchelitchev (1939–52) reveal the on-again off-again dynamic between Kirstein and Balanchine. By 1952, Kirstein admits that Balanchine had a "lack of visual imagination" (Beinecke Rare Book and Manuscript Library, Yale University, Tchelitchev correspondence with Lincoln Kirstein, preliminary survey [not catalogued]).

70 AMPAS, Margaret Herrick Library, George Cukor Collection, folder 835, letter dated November 10, 1945. The late George Custen kindly pointed out this material to me. The artist's name has been alternately spelled Tchelichieff, Tchelitchef, and Tchelitchew. I follow Kirstein's final spelling, Tchelitchev.

71 Tchelitchev's circles were led by his lover, the very attractive and mischievous Charles Henri Ford. Ford, with Parker Tyler, published their scandalous novel *The Young and the Evil* with the help of Gertrude Stein in 1933. The book, however, was banned in the United States and published in France. In any case, Ford's interest in magic realism and other decadent movements elicited scurrilous responses from cultural pundits—including some homosexuals such as Robert Duncan who wrote of Ford and his friends later in the 1940s. Appalled by the voodoo queers who refused to assimilate into mainstream culture, Duncan writes in the journal *Politics*, "Like early witches, the homosexual propagandists [read here Ford and his coterie] have rejected any struggle toward recognition in social equality and, far from seeking to undermine the popular superstition, have accepted the charge of Demonism. Sensing the fear in society that is generated in ignorance of their nature, they have sought not to bring about any understanding, to assert their equality and their common aims with mankind, but they have sought to profit by that fear and ignorance, to become witchdoctors in the modern chaos" ("The Homosexual in Society," 320).

As mentioned earlier, the new Americanist art movement was led by the art critic Clement Greenberg who placed Jackson Pollock front and center of his nationalist aesthetic goals. Much is written about the abstract expressionist movement, particularly about the androcentrism of the artists' circles. As some critics argue, surrealism (Greenberg's bête noir) was an instrumental aesthetic to Pollock's abstract works. Thus, no matter how hard Greenberg et al. hoped to jettison European tradition from American art, its trace always remained. See Cernuschi, *Jackson Pollock*, 163–66; and Chave, *Mark Rothko*, 64–77.

72 Jackson Pollock later declared, "I am Nature," to which Hans Hoffman quickly retorted, "Ah, but if you work from inside you will repeat yourself" (quoted in Naifeh and Smith, *Jackson Pollock*, 486). Hoffman, however, did not consider the way the "inside" might suggest something perverse.

73 Duke makes clear that "Dukelsky in no way resembles Duke." What he reiterates with great relish is that Dukelsky wrote the "serious or unrewarding" music while Duke wrote the "unserious but lucrative" sort of compositions (*Passport to Paris*, 4). Duke's biography is wonderful for its dilettant style and its many discussions of queer culture.

74 Duke comments on *The Show Is On* as an "almost girl-less musical"; and on the detail-oriented Minnelli, he states: "I don't think there has ever been a greater disciplinarian or a more exacting perfectionist in the musical theater than Vincente Minnelli . . . Where other directors wasted a lot of valuable time wrangling with costume designers, arguing with overpaid

stars or kidding around with chorus girls, with Vincente—once the rehearsals started it was all work and no play" (*Passport to Paris*, 337).

75 My biographical sources for Tchelitchev include Kirstein, *Tchelitchev*; Kirstein, "Biographical Notes"; and Tyler, *The Divine Comedy of Pavel Tchelitchew*. In addition, I consulted the Tchelitchev collections at the Harry Ransom Center at the University of Texas, Austin, and the Beinecke Rare Book and Manuscript Library at Yale University.

76 Kirstein, *Tchelitchev*, 20.

77 See the drafts for "Tchelitchew on His Art" and "Tchelitchew's Biographical Notes" for the author's version of how his life experience informed his art (Beinecke Rare Book and Manuscript Library, Yale University, uncatalogued box 1, ZA MS 243).

78 Windham, in his essay "The Stage and Ballet Designs of Pavel Tchelitchew," provides a very good description of Tchelitchev's theatrical work during this period and through 1944.

79 Tyler, *The Divine Comedy of Pavel Tchelitchew*, 63.

80 Breton's reliance on a bunch of queers to support surrealism in America was more than he could bear (American culture was already tipping his aesthetic scales). When, in 1940, Ford and Parker Tyler designed America's first surrealist/neoromantic/magic realist art journal, *View*, as a forum for Breton's entourage, Breton renamed the magazine "Pederasti Internationale." But *View*, much to Breton's chagrin, was the formidable surrealist forum for the emigrés just as it was the bulwark behind Ford's (failed) attempt to push neoromanticism, surrealism, magic realism, and the work of Tchelitchev into the clutches of the powerful reformation of the contemporary American art scene.

81 For an overview of Tchelitchev and Ford's creative circles, see Neiman's "*View* Magazine," xi–xvi.

82 Rosamond Frost writing in *Art News*, quoted in Kirstein, *Tchelitchev*, 64.

83 Kirstein, *Tchelitchev*, 48.

84 Tyler, *The Divine Comedy of Pavel Tchelitchew*, 336; Kirstein, *Tchelitchev*, 51.

85 The ballet gave Diaghilev much anxiety and he distanced himself from its production. Tchelitchev's schemes were even more extravagant than the impresario of extravagance.

86 Kirstein, *Tchelitchev*, 48. Both authors cite the libretto and claim that it is housed at the Museum of Modern Art. The museum cannot seem to locate a copy of it, however. Additional research for the material (at institutions such as the New York City Performing Arts Library at Lincoln Center

and at Yale's Beinecke Library) has also been unsuccessful. Unfortunately, the libretto appears to have been lost.

87 Garafola, "Dance, Film, and the Ballets Russes," 17. In the Tchelitchev collection (miscellaneous) are half-a-dozen circus programs, including those of the Medrano circus saved by the artist. In one of the programs a photograph of the performers (Véra, Skibine, Grekine) are seen in skin-tight, flesh-colored costumes acrobatically posed on a large ball covered in wire. The image recalls the production still of the *Ode* production (see Kirstein, *Tchelitchev*, 46). In the Tchelitchev collections at the Harry Ransom Center at the University of Texas, Austin, postcards from a trip to Florida in 1947, sent to Tchelitchev from Charles Henri Ford, excitedly tell the painter about Ford and his traveling companion's (Gertrude Stein) experiences with the circus.

88 Tyler, *The Divine Comedy of Pavel Tchelitchew*, 331.

89 The drawing that Tchelitchev completed for Balanchine's ballet, *Concerto*, indicates the painter's theatrical designs for fragmented and torn bodies (see the illustration in Ford, *View: Parade of the Avant-Garde*, 50).

90 Kirstein, *Tchelitchev*, 49; Tyler, *The Divine Comedy of Pavel Tchelitchew*, 334.

91 Tchelitchev writes: "For me color that expresses light has . . . autonomous and symbolic quality like that of (the divine) Arachne weaving with her threads of light the world of the five elements, the world of our illusion [in parenthesis above 'our illusion,' Tchelitchev inserts, 'of our conjuring?']" ("Tchelitchew on His Art," 6, Beinecke Rare Book and Manuscript Library, Yale University, uncatalogued box 1, ZA MS 243).

92 Quoted in Kirstein, *Tchelitchev*, 51.

93 Tyler, *The Divine Comedy of Pavel Tchelitchew*, 337. Tchelitchev's use of the cinema is an important counterpoint to arguments made by the likes of David Bordwell that all cinematic production (including cinemas of resistance) can only be realized in relationship to Hollywood. The cinema, as *Ode* demonstrates, was also conceived as a modern technology in relationship to the other arts.

94 Quoted in Tyler, *The Divine Comedy of Pavel Tchelitchew*, 328.

95 When the two worked together on the *Follies* the Minnellian-Balanchinian aesthetic was, as Harvey suggests, at its "most striking" and certainly its most revealing. The Balanchine number was presented in "abstract forms of green and black featuring Harriet Hoctor, the contortionist toe-dancer who had an inexplicable vogue in the mid-thirties" ("Vincente Minnelli and the Shuberts," 5).

96 The terms are those of Kirstein: "metamorphosis" ("Biographical Notes," 19), "simultaneity" (*Mosaic*, 38).

97 Kirstein, "Biographical Notes," 19, 38.

98 "Tchelitchew's Biographical notes," 1, Beinecke Rare Book and Manuscript Library, Yale University, uncatalogued box 1, ZA MS 243.

99 Kirstein, "The Position of Pavel Tchelitchew," 50. Given the intimate arrangement between the critics and the artists at *View* it is correct to surmise that Tchelitchev agreed with Kirstein's theoretical explanation of his work.

100 Kirstein, *Tchelitchev*, 38. Tchelitchev's paintings present the freak as an amorphous and violently ruptured body of "simultaneity," wherein disfigured multiple and mutated bodies merge and emerge from the central figure in the painting (*Clown* [1929]), or where disproportionately large cocks and buttocks encumber male figures (*Bullfight* [1934]; *Bathers*, [1936]), or where severed limbs dangle from whence a cohesive body once stood (*Spanish Dancer* [1930]; *Fallen Rider* [1930]).

101 As early as 1925 Tchelitchev's paintings were an explosion of corporeality and materialist affect, whether as seen in *Doubled Figure* (1925–26), which was constructed with oil paint and coffee grounds; or in the multifragmented bodily figures of *Clown* (1929) and *Spanish Dancer* (1930); or in the simultaneous circus portraits of *Madame Bonjean* (1931), *Lincoln Kirstein* (1937), and *Phenomena*.

102 Kirstein, *Tchelitchev*, 67. In his monograph, Kirstein identifies plate 60 as "Final Sketch for *Phenomena*" and attributes the illustration to the Hirshhorn Museum. I also include the illustration from the same source; however, the assigned title to the work by the Hirshhorn is "Final Sketch for *Phenomenon*." I confirmed this with the museum on March 21, 2005.

103 While in New York, Tchelitchew worked with Balanchine on *Magic* (1936, Hartford), *Orpheus and Eurydice* (1936), *Balustrade* (1941), and *Concerto* (1942).

104 Tyler, *The Divine Comedy of Pavel Tchelitchew*, 387.

105 Ibid., 90, 74.

106 Beaton, *Cecil Beaton's New York*, 235.

107 Naremore, *The Films of Vincente Minnelli*, 63.

108 Martin, "The Dance," 150.

109 On Martin's notorious claims about African Americans and ballet, see Aschenbrenner, *Katherine Dunham*, 27.

110 Aschenbrenner, *Katherine Dunham*, 47.

111 From my interview with Dunham on February 14, 2004. All subsequent quotes in the text attributed to Dunham are from this interview unless stated otherwise.

112 Given this view, Dunham's thoughts about Balanchine's 1926 blackface performance as "Snowball" in London are similar to Banes, who argues that Balanchine's performance was not racist minstrelsy but something more complicated in relationship to the choreographer's embrace of American

culture. On Balanchine's "Snowball," see Taper, *Balanchine*, 93; and Banes, "Balanchine and Black Dance."

113 Baldwin, *Beyond the Color Line and the Iron Curtain*, 52. The relationship between Russian and African American cultures is rich and varied across the arts and social exchanges. As Baldwin reiterates, the significance of communism cannot be underestimated for its appeal to disenfranchised African Americans. As Locke wrote in his essay "American Literary Tradition and the Negro": "But the work of Waldo Frank, Jean Toomer, Walter White, Rudolph Fisher, and Du Bose Heyward promises greatly; and if we call up the most analogous cases as a basis of forecast, — the tortuous way by which the peasant came in Russian literature and the brilliant sudden transformation his advent eventually effected, we may predict, for both subject and creative exponents, the Great Age of this particular section of American life and strand in the American experience" (*The Modern Quarterly*, 22).

114 Baldwin shows how Paul Robeson from the 1930s through the 1950s stressed the centrality of the folk and the inter-relationship between Russia and African Americans. Notably, this international connection was anchored, for Robeson, in sound: "Robeson strove to unite different peoples under a rubric of 'soul' that was inclusive, regardless of race, class, nationality, or gender. Advocating music was one of the 'quickest' ways to mutual understanding across national borders" (*Beyond the Color Line and the Iron Curtain*, 221).

115 Agee, "Psuedo-Folk," 316.

116 Agee unevenly championed Minnelli's work on several occasions (*The Clock* [1945] received high marks by the critic); but he did not comment on *Cabin in the Sky*. Although he appreciated the Halloween sequence in *Meet Me in St. Louis*, the film was "too sumptuously, calculatedly handsome to be quite mistakable for the truth" (Agee, *Agee on Film*, 356–59).

117 Lewis's distaste for the "effeminizing" effects of black culture derived not only from white culture. African American aesthetes, such as Locke, were also at the root of the "failed" project of the Harlem Renaissance (Lewis, *When Harlem Was in Vogue*; note especially the discussion about Locke's aestheticism, 149–55). In terms of Van Vechten's disappearance from the historical radar, queer studies has altered Lewis's perception of the impresario (although I'm not sure Lewis's view ever held much ground).

118 Favor, *Authentic Blackness*, 146. See also Helbling's introduction to *The Harlem Renaissance*.

119 http://members.aol.com/klove01/leroylck.htm, accessed April 5, 2004.

120 Lewis, *When Harlem was in Vogue*, 87, 93. Lewis's remarks are all the more unusual since he provides a correction in his preface to the 1996 edi-

tion of his book in light of Chauncey's *Gay New York*. Chauncey's recent scholarship, according to Lewis, "underscores the limitations of my rather too implicit discussion of gay and lesbian affections. If *Vogue* were being written today, both Zora Neale Hurston and Richard Bruce Nugent would be broken out of their caricatures and placed in a far fuller social 'context'" (xxii). Nowhere is there mention of a rethinking of either Locke's or, for that matter, Lewis's scholarly inspiration, Langston Hughes's sexuality.

121 Watson's *The Harlem Renaissance: Hub of African American Culture, 1920–1930* (54–61) stands out in this regard. Watson unapologetically discusses homosexuality and bisexuality among the artists, including Alain Locke, of the Harlem Renaissance.

122 See Washington, *A Journey into the Philosophy of Alain Locke* (131), for a discussion of this untitled work by Locke that he contingently titles "Insanity." As with others, Washington points to Locke's evaluation of homosexuality in his study but does not suggest how this essay bore on the philosopher's life, nor does he take up the issue in his biographical overview of Locke. Harris omits homosexuality from Locke's biography in his introduction to *The Philosophy of Alain Locke: Harlem Renaissance and Beyond*.

123 Cowley quoted in Lewis, *When Harlem Was in Vogue*, 91.

124 It is important to note here that most scholars indicate Locke's careful distinction between classical aesthetics and aesthetic decadence (although it seems to me that the line is not always so clear with the philosopher). Locke (like Du Bois) put a distance between himself and the more queer-radical African American element such as Richard Bruce Nugent and Wallace Thurman. On homosexuality and the Harlem Renaissance, see Douglas, *Terrible Honesty*, 97; Faderman, *Odd Girls and Twilight Lovers*, 67–88; Chauncey, *Gay New York*, especially 227–67; Cobb's excellent "Insolent Racing, Rough Narrative"; Mercer, "Dark and Lovely Too," 249; Kelley, "Blossoming in Strange New Forms"; and Watson, *The Harlem Renaissance*. Ethel Waters also tells the lovely tale about how she lent evening gowns to the "male queers" in Harlem (*His Eye Is on the Sparrow*, 149). See also the collection edited by Wirth, *Gay Rebel of the Harlem Renaissance*; and Schwarz, *Gay Voices of the Harlem Renaissance*. Schwarz is one of the few scholars to speak directly about Locke's homosexuality.

125 It is worth comparing Van Vechten's comments to the "pet hates" espoused by Harlem Renaissance queer writer Wallace Thurman: "All Negro uplift societies, Greta Garbo, Negro novelists including myself, Negro society, New York state divorce laws, morals, religions, politics, censors, policemen, sympathetic white folk" (quoted in Watson, *The Harlem Renaissance*, 88). Thurman's lover was the white, blond Harold ("Bunny") Stephanson.

126 Quoted in Pfeiffer's introduction to *Nigger Heaven*, xxi. It seems that

Van Vechten held fast to his friendships. For example, he maintained a long-standing friendship with Hughes that weathered a number of personal and cultural tensions over the years. They were photographed together by Richard Avedon in 1963 not long before Van Vechten's death (see Watson, *The Harlem Renaissance*, 177).

127 Waters, *His Eye Is on the Sparrow*, 195. Waters defended Van Vechten's *Nigger Heaven* and dined regularly at his home with other queer modernists such as Cole Porter, Noël Coward, and Somerset Maugham.

128 Faderman, *Odd Girls and Twilight Lovers*, 68.

129 Locke at one point had asked Van Vechten to write an essay about black American art, but Van Vechten was unable to do so (see Kellner's " 'Refined Racism,' " 95). In 1927, according to Coleman, Van Vechten was given a copy of *The New Negro* signed by James Weldon Johnson, Zora Neale Hurston, Du Bois, and Locke ("Carl Van Vechten Presents the New Negro," 125).

130 I do not refer to Derrida's signature term randomly. For a discussion of Locke and Derrida, see Mason's "Deconstruction in the Philosophy of Alain Locke."

131 Helbling, " 'Worlds of Shadow-Planes and Solids Silently Moving,' " 55. In this way, I part with Favor's assessment of Locke. Though he critiques Lewis's take on the philosopher, Favor points to Locke's "valorization of the folk" without indicating Locke's more ambiguous—indeed, sophisticated—challenge to the essentialist qualities of the folk tradition. See, for example, Locke's "Who and What Is 'Negro,' " (reprinted in Harris, *The Philosophy of Alain Locke*, 207–28).

132 Locke, "Values and Imperatives" (reprinted in Harris, *The Philosophy of Alain Locke*, 34–50).

133 Hutchinson, "The Whitman Legacy and the Harlem Renaissance," 207.

134 Lewis, *When Harlem Was in Vogue*, 95.

135 Locke and Brown, "Folk Values in a New Medium," 25–29; see also Everett's *Returning the Gaze*, 189–92. Later, in "Frontiers of Culture," Locke applauds Hollywood for *Intruder in the Dust*.

136 Locke and Brown, "Folk Values in a New Medium," 26.

137 Ibid., 27.

138 Baker, *Modernism and the Harlem Renaissance*, 71, 72.

139 Harris, *The Philosophy of Alain Locke*, 8.

140 Ibid., 9.

141 See Aschenbrenner, *Katherine Dunham*, 19–42.

142 Harvey, *Directed by Vincente Minnelli*, 37.

143 Horne and Schickel, "Lena," 140. From all accounts, Horne and Min-

nelli were quite close friends. Horne recounts sharing dinner at both his home and hers: "He [Minnelli] was living like a displaced New Yorker, just as I was, and we shared a dislike at that time for Hollywood life" (146). See also Minnelli, *Vincente Minnelli*, 115–16.

144 Minnelli, *Vincente Minnelli*, 103; in this memoir, Minnelli includes script selections from the *Serena Blandish* play (103–6).

145 Minnelli discusses his modernist-folk sets in *Serena Blandish* that "would take note of the black characters, but only in passing. The Countess's bedroom, for example, would be papered in newspapers, as was the humble shack where she'd been born, but all the furnishings and fittings would be luxurious and elegant" (*Vincente Minnelli*, 103).

146 Minnelli, *Vincente Minnelli*, 98. The opera *Four Saints in Three Acts* was first staged in 1934 (one year before *Porgy and Bess*) in Hartford, Connecticut. Its libretto was written by Gertrude Stein, the music was composed by Virgil Thompson, and the set and costume designs were by Florine Stettheimer.

147 Harvey, *Directed by Vincente Minnelli*, 41. Vernon Duke (who had been involved in many reincarnations of the *Serena* idea prior to Minnelli) entertained Marie-Blanche in Paris on a regular basis with his music from the production to be (at the same time, Duke had a parting of the ways with Tchelitchev over what Duke recalls as his "social triumphs" [*Passport to Paris*, 352]). Duke also recalls how he was surprised to learn how his name was at first aligned with the Minnelli production of *Serena Blandish*, and, then, removed from the production entirely (359). According to Minnelli, Cole Porter was thought to be a more saleable name by the backers and producers. Those are "the show business breaks" as Minnelli put it (*Vincente Minnelli*, 103).

148 The information on Dunham and MGM is from my interview with Dunham. Minnelli refers to Balanchine as his "old friend" while he remarks how little impressed he was by his filmed ballet for *The Goldwyn Follies*. "Much as I respect him," Minnelli goes on to say, the ballet sequence was "movie conventional" (*Vincente Minnelli*, 113). For Minnelli, Balanchine's expertise lay elsewhere.

149 Naremore, *The Films of Vincente Minnelli*, 53.

150 Guerrero, *Framing Blackness*, 51.

151 Harvey, *Directed by Vincente Minnelli*, 42.

152 Knee, "Doubling, Music, and Race in *Cabin in the Sky*," 197, 198.

153 Waters's ironic fluttering eyelashes during the more sentimental moments in the film as well as the tough and sly stand she takes with Little Joe's conartist buddies hardly point to a naive performance. Horne, likewise, plays Georgia Brown with a very knowing sensibility.

154 It is significant that the film differs from the stage version in that the latter does not incorporate a frame story that removes the narrative from a strictly fantasy-based scenario; indeed, Joe and Petunia live in a "real" world.

155 Kuntzel, "The Film-Work, 2," 7.

156 Harvey, Stephen. *Directed by Vincente Minnelli*, 44.

157 Petunia is, in many ways, similar to Waters: at once strongly religious and street tough.

158 I'd like to thank Joe McElhaney for his discussions about, and encyclopedic knowledge of, the performances in this sequence.

159 Kuntzel, "The Film-Work, 2," 13.

160 Bogle, *Toms, Coons, Mulattoes, Mammies, and Bucks*, 128.

161 Minnelli, *Vincente Minnelli*, 127.

162 Litvak, *Strange Gourmets*, 59.

163 Reynolds, "An Interview with Vincente Minnelli," 106.

164 For many African Americans, such as author Claude McKay (as Christa Schwarz shows), modernist-primitivism played a pivotal role in their aesthetic identity.

165 Litvak, *Strange Gourmets*, 73.

166 Tinckom, *Working Like a Homosexual*, 71.

Epilogue

1 Kleinhans and Lesage, "Listening to the Heartbeat," 120.

2 Recall in chapter 1 of this volume where I cite Richard Slotkin's work in neatly describing the early American fascination with this metaphor since the seventeenth century.

3 Initial work that has been undertaken in these areas includes Suárez, *Bike Boys, Drag Queens, and Superstars*; Doyle, Flatley, and Muñoz, *Pop Out*; Mercer, "Skin Head Sex Thing"; Wagner, "Warhol Paints History, or Race in America"; and Grundmann, *Andy Warhol's* Blow Job.

Bibliography

Abrahams, Edward. *The Lyrical Left and the Origins of Cultural Radicalism in America*. Charlottesville: University Press of Virginia, 1986.

Adams, Henry. *The Education of Henry Adams*. New York: Time Incorporated, 1964 [1918].

Agee, James. "Pseudo-Folk." In *Agee on Film*, vol. 1. New York: McDowell, Oblensky, 1958. 404–10.

Alberts, Robert C. *Benjamin West: A Biography*. Boston: Houghton Mifflin, 1978.

Alger, William Rounseville. *Life of Edwin Forrest: The American Tragedian*, vol. 1. Philadelphia: J. B. Lippincott, 1877.

Allmendinger, Blake. "The Plow and the Pen: The Pioneering Adventures of Oscar Micheaux." *American Literature* 75.3 (2003): 545–69.

Althusser, Louis. "Ideology and Ideological State Apparatuses (Notes towards an Investigation)." In *Lenin and Philosophy and Other Essays*. Translated by Ben Brewster. New York: Monthly Review Press, 1971. 127–86.

Altschuler, Glenn C., and Stuart M. Blumin. *Rude Republic: Americans and Their Politics in the Nineteenth Century*. Princeton: Princeton University Press, 2000.

American Citizen, An. *A Rejoinder to "The Replies from England, etc." to Certain Statements Circulated in this Country Respecting Mr. Macready. Together with an Impartial History and Review of the Lamentable Occurrences at the Astor Place Opera House, on the 10th of May, 1849*. New York: Stringer and Townsend, 1849.

"Art and Artists in America." *American Review: A Whig Journal of Politics, Literature, Art, and Science* 2 (December 1845): 658.

Aschenbrenner, Joyce. *Katherine Dunham: Dancing a Life*. Urbana: University of Illinois Press, 2002.

Aspiz, Harold. "The Body Politic in *Democratic Vistas*." In *Walt Whitman:*

The Centennial Years, edited by Ed Folsom. Iowa City: University of Iowa Press, 1994. 105–19.

Baker, Houston. *Modernism and the Harlem Renaissance*. Chicago: University of Chicago Press, 1985.

Baker, Josephine, and Jo Bouillon. *Josephine*. Translated by Mariana Fitzpatrick. New York: Harper and Row, 1976.

Baldwin, Kate. *Beyond the Color Line and the Iron Curtain*. Durham: Duke University Press, 2002.

Banes, Sally. "Balanchine and Black Dance." In *Writing Dancing in the Age of Postmodernism*. Hanover, N.H.: Wesleyan University Press, 1994. 53–69.

———. *Dancing Women: Female Bodies on Stage*. London: Routledge, 1998.

Bartling, Hugh. "Intentions and Mass Culture: Oscar Micheaux, Identity, and Authorship." In *Authorship and Film*, edited by David A. Gerstner and Janet Staiger. New York: Routledge, 2003.

Beaton, Cecil. *Cecil Beaton's New York*. New York: Lippincott, 1938.

Bederman, Gail. *Manliness and Civilization: A Cultural History of Gender and Race in the United States, 1880–1917*. Chicago: University of Chicago Press, 1995.

Bell, Michael Davitt. "Beginnings of Professionalism." In *Culture, Genre, and Literary Vocation: Selected Essays on American Literature*. Chicago: University of Chicago Press, 2001. 67–133.

———. *The Problem of American Realism: Studies in the Cultural History of a Literary Idea*. Chicago: University of Chicago Press, 1993.

Belsey, Catherine. *Critical Practice*. London: Routledge, 2001 [1980].

Bender, Thomas. *The Unfinished City: New York and the Metropolitan Idea*. New York: New Press, 2002.

Benton, Thomas Hart. *An Artist in America*. Columbia: University of Missouri Press, 1983 [1937].

Berkhofer, Robert F. *The White Man's Indian: Images of the American Indian from Columbus to the Present*. New York: Knopf, 1978.

Bieder, Robert E. "Anthropology and History of the Indian." *American Quarterly* 33.3 (1981): 309–26.

Birnie, William A. H. "A Chorine Thought and Was Wrong." *World Telegram* (November 14, 1936): 3.

Blake, Casey Nelson. *Beloved Community: The Cultural Criticism of Randolph Bourne, Van Wyck Brooks, Waldo Frank, and Lewis Mumford*. Chapel Hill: University of North Carolina Press, 1990.

Blakemore, Steven. " 'Without a Cross:' The Cultural Significance of the Sublime and Beautiful in Cooper's *The Last of the Mohicans*." *Nineteenth-Century Literature* 52.1 (1997): 27–57.

Blassingame, John W. "Introduction." In *Narrative of the Life of Frederick Douglass*. Toronto: Dover, 1995. xi–xli.

Bloom, Harold. *The Anxiety of Influence: A Theory of Poetry*. New York: Oxford University Press, 1997 [1973].

Bogle, Donald. *Toms, Coons, Mulattoes, Mammies, and Bucks: An Interpretive History of Blacks in American Film*. New York: Continuum, 1997 [1973].

Bone, Robert. *The Negro Novel in America*. New Haven: Yale University Press, 1958.

Bordwell, David, and Kristin Thompson. *Film History: An Introduction*. New York: McGraw-Hill, 1994.

Bowser, Eileen. *The Transformation of Cinema, 1907–1915*. Berkeley: University of California Press, 1990.

Bowser, Pearl, Jane Gaines, and Charles Musser, eds. *Oscar Micheaux and His Circle*. Bloomington: Indiana University Press, 2001.

Bowser, Pearl, and Louis Spence. *Writing Himself into History: Oscar Micheaux, His Silent Films, and His Audiences*. New Brunswick: Rutgers University Press, 2000.

Brands, H. W. *TR: The Last Romantic*. New York: Basic Books, 1997.

Braxton, Joanne M. *Black Women Writing Biography: A Tradition within a Tradition*. Philadelphia: Temple University Press, 1989.

Brennan, Marcia. *Painting Gender, Constructing Theory: The Alfred Stieglitz Circle and American Formalist Aesthetics*. Cambridge, Mass.: MIT Press, 2001.

Brent, Linda. *Incidents in the Life of a Slave Girl: Written by Herself, Linda Brent* [1861]. In *The Classic Slave Narratives*, edited by Henry Louis Gates Jr. New York: Penguin Books, 1987.

Brooks, Van Wyck. *America's Coming-of-Age*. Garden City, N.Y.: Doubleday, 1958 [1915].

Brown, Jayna. "Black Patriarch on the Prairie: National Identity and Black Manhood in the Early Novels of Oscar Micheaux." In *Oscar Micheaux and His Circle*, edited by Pearl Bowser, Jane Gaines, and Charles Musser. Bloomington: Indiana University Press, 2001. 132–46.

Brown, Milton W. "Cubist-Realism: An American Style." *Marsyas* 3, (1946): 139–60.

———. *The Story of the Armory Show*. New York: Abbeville Press, 1988.

———. "The Three Roads." In *Paul Strand: Essays on His Life and Work*, edited by Maren Stange. New York: Aperture Books, 1991. 18–30.

Brownlow, Kevin. *The War, the West, and the Wilderness*. New York: Knopf, 1978.

Buckle, Richard, with John Taras. *George Balanchine: Ballet Master*. New York: Random House, 1988.

Burke, Edmund. *A Philosophical Enquiry into the Origin of Our Ideas of the Sublime*. New York: Harper, 1846.

Burns, Sarah. *Inventing the Modern Artist: Art and Culture in the Gilded Age*. New Haven: Yale University Press, 1996.

Burroughs, John. *Whitman: A Study*. Amsterdam: Fredonia Books, 2001 [1895].

Burrows, Edwin G., and Mike Wallace. *Gotham: A History of New York City to 1898*. New York: Oxford, 1999.

Butler, Judith. *Bodies That Matter: On the Discursive Limits of "Sex."* New York: Routledge, 1993.

Butsch, Richard. *The Making of an American Audience: From Stage to Television, 1750–1990*. Cambridge: Cambridge University Press, 2000.

Butters, Gerald R. "Portrayals of Black Masculinity in Oscar Micheaux's *The Homesteader*." *Literature Film Quarterly* 28.1 (2000): 54–59.

Carby, Hazel V. *Race Men*. Cambridge, Mass.: Harvard University Press, 1998.

———. *Reconstructing Womanhood: The Emergence of the Afro-American Woman Novelist*. New York: Oxford University Press, 1987.

Catlin, George. *North American Indians*, edited by Peter Matthiesen. New York: Penguin Books, 1989.

Cernuschi, Claude. *Jackson Pollock: Meaning and Significance*. New York: Icon, 1992.

Charles Sheeler. Washington, D.C.: Smithsonian Institution Press, 1968.

Chauncey, George. *Gay New York: Gender, Urban Culture, and the Making of the Gay Male World*. New York: Basic Books, 1994.

Chave, Anna C. *Mark Rothko: Subjects in Abstraction*. New Haven: Yale University Press, 1989.

Clark, T. J. "Gross David with the Swoln Cheek: An Essay on Self-Portraiture." In *Rediscovering History: Culture, Politics, and the Psyche*, edited by Michael S. Roth. Stanford: Stanford University Press, 1994. 243–307.

Cleto, Fabio. *Camp: Queer Aesthetics and the Performing Subject: A Reader*. Ann Arbor: University of Michigan Press, 1999.

Cobb, Michael L. "Insolent Racing, Rough Narrative: The Harlem Renaissance's Impolite Queers." *Callaloo* 23.1 (2000): 328–51.

Cohen, Paula Marantz. *Silent Film and the Triumph of the American Myth*. New York: Oxford University Press, 2001.

Coleman, Leon. "Carl Van Vechten Presents the New Negro." In *The Harlem Renaissance Re-Examined*, edited by Victor A. Kramer. New York: AMS Press, 1987. 107–27.

Cooper, John Milton, Jr. *The Vanity of Power: American Isolationism and World War I, 1914–1917*. Westport, Conn.: Greenwood, 1969.

———. *The Warrior and the Priest: Woodrow Wilson and Theodore Roosevelt.* Cambridge, Mass.: Harvard University Press, 1983.

Corkin, Stanley. *Realism and the Birth of the Modern United States: Cinema, Literature, and Culture.* Athens: University of Georgia Press, 1996.

Corn, Wanda M. *The Great American Thing: Modern Art and National Identity, 1915–1935.* Berkeley: University of California Press, 1999.

Creekmur, Corey. "Telling White Lies: Oscar Micheaux and Charles W. Chestnutt." In *Oscar Micheaux and His Circle,* edited by Pearl Bowser, Jane Gaines, and Charles Musser. Bloomington: Indiana University Press, 2001. 147–58.

Culler, Jonathan. *Theory and Criticism after Structuralism.* Ithaca: Cornell University Press, 1982.

Curtis, Scott. " 'Like a Hailstorm on the Nerves of Modern Man': Cinema, Legibility, and the Body in Germany, 1895–1914." Ph.D. diss., University of Iowa, 1996.

Curtis, Susan. *The First Black Actors on the Great White Way.* Columbia: University of Missouri Press, 1998.

Deloria, Philip J. *Playing Indian.* New Haven: Yale University Press, 1998.

Derrida, Jacques. "Signature, Event, Context." In *Margins of Philosophy.* Chicago: University of Chicago Press, 1986 [1982].

Dijkstra, Bram. *Cubism, Stieglitz, and the Early Poetry of William Carlos Williams.* Princeton: Princeton University Press, 1969.

Doane, Mary Ann. *The Desire to Desire: The Woman's Film of the 1940s.* Bloomington: Indiana University Press, 1987.

Dormon, James H. "Shaping the Popular Image of Post-Reconstruction American Blacks: The 'Coon Song' Phenomenon of the Gilded Age." *American Quarterly* 40.4 (December 1988): 450–71.

Dougherty, Sarah B. "The Ideology of Gender in Howells' Early Novels." *American Literary Realism, 1870–1910* 25.1 (fall 1992): 2–19.

Douglas, Ann. *The Feminization of American Culture.* New York: Anchor, 1988 [1977].

———. *Terrible Honesty: Mongrel Manhattan in the 1920s.* New York: Farrar, Straus and Giroux, 1995.

Douglass, Frederick. *Douglass: Autobiographies.* New York: Literary Classics of the United States, 1994.

———. *Narrative of the Life of Frederick Douglass: An American Slave, Written by Himself.* Preface by William Lloyd Garrison. New Haven: Yale University Press, 2001 [1845].

Doyle, Jennifer, Jonathan Flatley, and José Esteban Muñoz, eds. *Pop Out: Queer Warhol.* Durham: Duke University Press, 1996.

Doyle, Laura. *Bordering on the Body: The Racial Matrix of Modern Fiction and Culture*. New York: Oxford University Press, 1994.

Driscoll, John. "Charles Sheeler's Early Work: Five Rediscovered Paintings." *Art Bulletin* 62.1 (March 1980): 124–33.

Du Bois, W. E. B. "The Criteria of Negro Art." In *The Crisis Reader: Stories, Poetry, and Essays from the N. A. A. C. P.'s Crisis Magazine*, edited by Sondra Kathryn Wilson. New York: Modern Library, 1999. 317–25.

———. "The Damnation of Women." In *Darkwater: Voices from Within the Veil*. New York: Schocken Books, 1969 [1920]. 163–86.

———. *The Philadelphia Negro: A Social Study*. Philadelphia: University of Pennsylvania Press, 1998 [1899].

———. *The Souls of Black Folk*. Toronto: Dover Publications, 1994 [1903].

DuCille, Ann. "Looking for Zora." *New York Times Book Review* (January 5, 2003): 12–13.

Duke, Vernon. *Passport to Paris*. Boston: Little, Brown, 1955.

Duncan, Robert. "The Homosexual in Society." *Politics* (August 1944): 319–22.

Dupree, F. W. *Henry James*. New York: William Sloane Associates, 1951.

Dyer, Richard. *White*. London: Routledge, 1997.

Dyer, Thomas G. *Theodore Roosevelt and the Idea of Race*. Baton Rouge: Louisiana State University Press, 1980.

Edelman, Lee. *Homographesis*. New York: Routledge, 1994.

Eisenstein, Sergei. "Dickens, Griffith and the Film Today." In *Film Form: Essays in Film Theory*, edited by Jay Leyda. New York: Harcourt Brace, 1977 [1949]. 195–255.

Ellis, Edward Robb. *The Epic of New York City: A Narrative History*. New York: Old Town Books, 1966.

Elsaesser, Thomas, and Adam Barker. "Introduction: The Continuity System: Griffith and Beyond." In *Early Cinema: Space, Frame, Narrative*, edited by Thomas Elsaesser and Adam Barker. London: British Film Institute, 1992 [1990].

Emerson, Ralph Waldo. *The Essential Writings of Ralph Waldo Emerson*. New York: Modern Library, 2000.

Evans, Brad. "Cushing's Zuni Sketchbooks: Literature, Anthropology, and American Notions of Culture." *American Quarterly* 49.4 (December 1997): 717–45.

Everett, Anna. *Returning the Gaze: A Genealogy of Black Film Criticism, 1909–1949*. Durham: Duke University Press, 2001.

Faderman, Lillian. *Odd Girls and Twilight Lovers: A History of Lesbian Life in Twentieth-Century America*. New York: Penguin Books, 1991.

Fairchild, Hoxie. *The Noble Savage: A Study in Romantic Naturalism*. New York: Columbia University Press, 1928.

Farrell, Suzanne, with Toni Bentley. *Holding on to the Air*. New York: Summit Books, 1990.

Favor, J. Martin. *Authentic Blackness: The Folk in the New Negro Renaissance*. Durham: Duke University Press, 1999.

Fillin-Yeh, Susan. "Charles Sheeler's 1923 'Self-Portrait.'" *Arts Magazine* 52.5 (January 1978): 106–9.

Foner, Eric. *Free Soil, Free Labor, Free Men: The Ideology of the Republican Party Before the Civil War*. New York: Oxford, 1995 [1970].

———. *Reconstruction: America's Unfinished Revolution, 1863–1877*. New York: Harper and Row, 1988.

Fontenot, Chester J. Jr. "Oscar Micheaux: Black Novelist and Film Maker." In *Vision and Refuge: Essays on the Literature of the Great Plains*, edited by Virginia Faulkner with Frederick C. Luebke. Lincoln: University of Nebraska Press, 1982. 109–25.

Forster-Hahn, Françoise. "Inventing the Myth of the American Frontier: Bingham's Images of Fur Traders and Flatboatmen as Symbols of the Expanding Nation." In *American Icons: Transatlantic Perspectives on Eighteenth- and Nineteenth-Century American Art*, edited by Thomas W. Gaehtgens and Heinz Ickstadt. Santa Monica, Calif.: Getty Center for the History of Arts and Humanities; Chicago: University of Chicago Press, 1992. 119–45.

Foucault, Michel. *The History of Sexuality. Volume 1: An Introduction*. New York: Vintage, 1990 [1978].

Frank, Waldo. *Our America*. New York: AMS Press, 1972 [1919].

Frank, Waldo, Lewis Mumford, Dorothy Norman, Paul Rosenfeld, and Harold Rugg, eds. *America and Alfred Stieglitz: A Collective Portrait*. New York: Doubleday, Doran, and Company, 1934.

Franklin, Benjamin. The *Autobiography of Benjamin Franklin*. New York: Modern Library, 1981.

Franko, Mark. *The Work of Dance: Labor, Movement, and Identity in the 1930s*. Middletown, Conn.: Wesleyan University Press, 2002.

Frazier, E. Franklin. *Black Bourgeoisie*. New York: Free Press, 1997 [1957].

Fredrickson, George M. *The Black Image in the White Mind: The Debate on Afro American Character and Destiny, 1817–1914*. Middletown, Conn.: Wesleyan University Press, 1987 [1971].

———. *Racism: A Short History*. Princeton: Princeton University Press, 2002.

Freeman, Barbara Claire. *The Feminine Sublime: Gender and Excess in Women's Fiction*. Berkeley: University of California Press, 1995.

Freud, Sigmund. *New Introductory Lectures on Psychoanalysis: The Standard Edition.* Translated and edited by James Strachey. New York: Norton, 1964 [1933].

Fried, Michael. *Absorption and Theatricality: Painting and Beholder in the Age of Diderot.* Berkeley: University of California Press, 1980.

———. *Realism, Writing, Disfiguration: On Thomas Eakins and Stephen Crane.* Chicago: University of Chicago Press. 1987.

Friedman, Martin. "The Art of Charles Sheeler: Americana in a Vacuum." In *Charles Sheeler: Essays by Martin Friedman, Bartlett Hayes, Charles Millard.* Washington, D.C.: Smithsonian Institution Press, 1968. 33–58.

———. "Interview with Charles Sheeler" (conducted June 18, 1959). http://www.archivesofamericanart.si.edu/oralhist/sheele59.htm.

Frohne, Ursula. "Strategies of Recognition: The Conditioning of the American Artist between Marginality and Fame." In *American Icons: Transatlantic Perspectives on Eighteenth- and Nineteenth-Century American Art,* edited by Thomas W. Gaehtgens and Heinz Ickstadt. Santa Monica, Calif.: Getty Center for the History of Arts and Humanities; Chicago: University of Chicago Press, 1992. 211–44.

Gaines, Jane. *Fire and Desire: Mixed-Race Movies in the Silent Era.* Chicago: University of Chicago Press, 2001.

———. "Within Our Gates: From Race Melodrama to Opportunity Narrative." In *Oscar Micheaux and His Circle,* edited by Pearl Bowser, Jane Gaines, and Charles Musser. Bloomington: Indiana University Press, 2001. 67–80.

Gaines, Kevin. "Assimilationist Minstrelsy as Racial Uplift Ideology: James D. Carrother's Literary Quest for Black Leadership." *American Quarterly* 45.3 (September 1993): 341–69.

———. *Uplifting the Race: Black Leadership, Politics, and Culture in the Twentieth Century.* Chapel Hill: University of North Carolina Press, 1996.

Garafola, Lynn. "Dance, Film, and the Ballets Russes." *Dance Research* 16.1 (summer 1998): 3–25.

———. *Diaghilev's Ballets Russes.* New York: Da Capo, 1998 [1989].

Garman, Bryan K. " 'Heroic Spiritual Grandfather': Whitman, Sexuality, and the American Left, 1890–1940." *American Quarterly* 52.1 (March 2000): 90–126.

Gates, Henry Louis Jr. *The Signifying Monkey: A Theory of African-American Literary Criticism.* New York: Oxford University Press, 1988.

Gaul, Theresa Strouth. " 'The Genuine Indian Who Was Brought Upon the Stage': Edwin Forrest's *Metamora* and White Audiences." *Arizona Quarterly* 56.1 (spring 2000): 1–27.

Gerstner, David A. "Dancer from the Dance: Gene Kelly, Television, and the Beauty of Movement." *Velvet Light Trap* 49 (spring 2002): 48–66.

———. "Queer Angels of History Take It and Leave It from Behind." *Stanford Humanities Review* 7.2 (winter 1999): 150–65.

———. "Queer Modernism: The Cinematic Aesthetics of Vincente Minnelli." In *Modernity*, edited by Stephen Eskilson. Eastern Illinois University 2 (2000): *http://www.eiu.edu/~modernity/modernity.html*.

———. "Unsinkable Masculinity: The Artist and the Work of Art in James Cameron's *Titanic*." *Cultural Critique* 50 (winter 2002): 1–21.

Gerstner, David A., and Janet Staiger, eds. *Authorship and Film*. New York: Routledge, 2003.

Gillespie, Veronica N. "T. R. on Film: The Theodore Roosevelt Association Collection at the Library of Congress." *Quarterly Journal of the Library of Congress* 34 (January 1977): 39–51.

Gilmore, Leigh. *Autobiographics: A Feminist Theory of Women's Self-Presentation*. Ithaca: Cornell University Press, 1994.

Gilmore, Paul. *The Genuine Article: Race, Mass Culture, and American Literary Manhood*. Durham: Duke University Press, 2001.

———. "'The Genuine Article': Race, Manhood, and Mass Culture in American Literature, 1826–1861." Ph.D. diss., University of Chicago, 1997.

Gilroy, Paul. *The Black Atlantic: Modernity and Double-Consciousness*. Cambridge, Mass.: Harvard University Press, 1993.

Ginsberg, Elaine K., ed. *Passing and the Fictions of Identity*. Durham: Duke University Press, 1996.

Goldberger, Paul. "Urban Warriors." *New Yorker* (September 15, 2003): 72–82.

Goffman, Erving. *The Presentation of Self in Everyday Life*. New York: Anchor Books, 1959.

Greeley, Andrew. *That Most Distressful Nation: The Taming of the Irish*. Chicago: Quadrangle Books, 1972.

Green, J. Ronald. *Straight Lick: The Cinema of Oscar Micheaux*. Bloomington: Indiana University Press, 2000.

———. "'Twoness' in the Style of Oscar Micheaux." In *Black American Cinema*, edited by Manthia Diawara. New York: Routledge, 1993.

Greenough, Sarah. "An American Vision." In *Paul Strand: An American Vision*. New York: Aperture, 1990.

Griffith, Clark. "Frost and the American View of Nature." *American Quarterly* 20.1 (spring 1968): 21–37.

Grundmann, Roy. *Andy Warhol's Blow Job*. Philadelphia: Temple University Press, 2003.

Guerrero, Ed. *Framing Blackness: The African American Image in Film*. Philadelphia: Temple University Press, 1993.

Guilbaut, Serge. *How New York Stole the Idea of Modern Art: Abstract Expressionism, Freedom, and the Cold War*. Translated by Arthur Goldhammer. Chicago: University of Chicago Press, 1983.

Gunning, Tom, "An Aesthetic of Astonishment: Early Film and the (In)Credulous Spectator." In *Film Theory and Criticism*, edited by Leo Braudy and Marshall Cohen. 5th ed. New York: Oxford University Press, 1999 [1974]. 818–32.

————. *D. W. Griffith and the Origins of American Narrative Film: The Early Years at Biograph*. Urbana: University of Illinois Press, 1991.

Haas, Karen E. "Charles Sheeler and Film." *The Magazine Antiques* 162.5 (November 2002): 122–29.

Habegger, Alfred. *Gender, Fantasy, and Realism in American Literature*. New York: Columbia University Press, 1982.

Hale, Matthew Jr. *Human Science and Social Order: Hugo Münsterberg and the Origins of Applied Psychology*. Philadelphia: Temple University Press, 1980.

Hammen, Scott. "Sheeler and Strand's 'Manhatta': A Neglected Masterpiece." *Afterimage* (January 1979): 6–7.

Harlan, Louis. *Booker T. Washington: The Making of a Black Leader, 1856–1901*. London: Oxford University Press, 1972.

————. *Booker T. Washington: The Wizard of Tuskegee, 1901–1915*. New York: Oxford University Press, 1983.

Harris, Leonard, ed. *The Philosophy of Alain Locke: Harlem Renaissance and Beyond*. Philadelphia: Temple University Press, 1989.

Hartley, Marsden. *Adventures in the Arts: Informal Chapters on Painters, Vaudeville, and Poets*. New York: Hacker Art Books, 1972 [1921].

Hartmann, Sadakichi. "The Esthetic Significance of the Motion Picture" [1912]. In *Alfred Stieglitz Camera Work: The Complete Illustrations, 1903–1917*. Cologne: Taschen, 1997. 626–29.

Harvey, Stephen. *Directed by Vincente Minnelli*. New York: Museum of Modern Art; Harper and Row, 1989.

————. "Vincente Minnelli and the Shuberts." *The Passing Show: Newsletter of the Shubert Archive* 13.1 (spring 1990): 2–7.

Helbling, Mark. "'Worlds of Shadow-Planes and Solids Silently Moving': Jean Toomer, Alfred Stieglitz, Georgia O'Keeffe, and Waldo Frank." In *The Harlem Renaissance: The One and the Many*. Westport, Conn.: Greenwood Press, 1999. 129–58.

Herbert, Janis. "Oscar Micheaux: A Black Pioneer." *South Dakota Review* 11.4 (1973–74): 66–69.

Hofstadter, Richard. *The Age of Reform: From Bryan to FDR*. New York: Vintage, 1955.

———. *Anti-Intellectualism in American Life*. London: Jonathan Cape. 1964.

hooks, bell. "Micheaux: Celebrating Blackness." *Black American Literature Forum* 25.2 (summer 1991): 351–60.

Horak, Jan-Christopher. "Modernist Perspectives and Romantic Impulses: *Manhatta*." *Afterimage* 14 (November 1987): 8–15.

Horne, Lena, and Richard Schickel. "Lena." In *Black Films and Film-Makers: A Comprehensive Anthology from Stereotype to Superhero*, edited by Lindsay Patterson. New York: Dodd, Mead and Company, 1975. 139–50.

Horsman, Reginald. "Scientific Racism and the American Indian in the Mid-Nineteenth Century." *American Quarterly* 27.2 (May 1975): 152–68.

Howat, John, ed. *The Hudson River and Its Painters*. New York: Viking Press, 1972.

Hutchinson, George. *The Harlem Renaissance in Black and White*. Cambridge, Mass.: The Belknap Press of Harvard University Press, 1995.

———. "The Whitman Legacy and the Harlem Renaissance." In *Walt Whitman: The Centennial Essays*, edited by Ed Folsom. Iowa City: University of Iowa Press, 1994. 201–16.

James, William. "The Varieties of Religious Experience: A Study in Human Nature." In *William James: Writings, 1902–1910*. New York: Library of America, 1987. 3–469.

Johnson, Charles. "A Phenomenology of the Black Body." In *The Male Body: Features, Destinies, Exposures*, edited by Laurence Goldstein. Ann Arbor: University of Michigan Press, 1994. 121–36.

Johnson, James Weldon. *Along This Way: The Autobiography of James Weldon Johnson*. New York: Da Capo Press, 2000 [1933].

———. *The Autobiography of an Ex-Colored Man*. New York: Dover Publications, 1995 [1912].

Johnson, M. K. " 'Stranger in a Strange Land': An African American Response to the Frontier Tradition in Oscar Micheaux's *The Conquest: The Story of a Negro Pioneer*." *Western American Literature* 33.3 (1998): 229–52.

Kant, Immanuel. *The Critique of Judgement*. Oxford: Clarendon Press, 1952.

Kaplan, Amy. *The Social Construction of American Realism*. Chicago: University of Chicago Press, 1988.

Katz, Ephraim. *The Film Encyclopedia*. New York: Harper Perennial, 1994.

Keller, Phyllis. *States of Belonging: German-American Intellectuals and the First World War*. Cambridge, Mass.: Harvard University Press, 1979.

Kelley, James. "Blossoming in Strange New Forms: Male Homosexuality and the Harlem Renaissance." *Soundings* 80.4 (winter 1997): 499–517.

Kellner, Bruce. " 'Refined Racism': White Patronage in the Harlem Renaissance." In *The Harlem Renaissance Re-Examined*, edited by Victor A. Kramer. New York: AMS Press, 1987. 92–106.

Kimmel, Michael. *Manhood in America*. New York: Free Press, 1995.

King, Joyce Elaine, and Carolyn Ann Mitchell, eds. *Black Mothers to Sons: Juxtaposing African American Literature with Social Practice*. New York: Peter Lang, 1995.

Kirby, Lynne. *Parallel Tracks: The Railroad and Silent Cinema*. Durham: Duke University Press, 1997.

Kirstein, Lincoln. "Biographical Notes." In *Tchelitchew: An Exhibition in the Gallery of Modern Art*. New York: Foundation for Modern Art, 1964.

———. *By With To and From: A Lincoln Kirstein Reader*, edited by Nicholas Jenkins. New York: Farrar, Straus and Giroux, 1991.

———. *Dance: A Short History of Classic Theatrical Dancing*. Princeton, N.J.: Princeton Book Company, 1987 [1935].

———. "The Position of Pavel Tchelitchew." In *View: Parade of the Avant-Garde*, edited by Charles Henri Ford. New York: Thunder's Mouth Press, 1991. 49–53.

———. *Mosaic: Memoirs*. New York: Farrar, Straus and Giroux, 1994.

———. *Tchelitchev*. Santa Fe: Twelvetrees Press, 1994.

Kisselgoff, Anna. "Retracing the Steps in Balanchine's Extraordinary Odyssey." *New York Times* (August 4, 2004): E1, 8.

Kleinhans, Chuck, and Julia Lesage. "Listening to the Heartbeat: Interview with Marlon Riggs." *Jump Cut: A Review of Contemporary Media* 36 (1991): 119–26.

Klinger, Barbara. " 'Cinema/Ideology/Criticism' Revisited: The Progressive Genre." In *Film Genre Reader 2*, edited by Barry Keith Grant. Austin: University of Texas Press, 1995. 74–90.

Knee, Adam. "Doubling, Music, and Race in *Cabin in the Sky*." In *Representing Jazz*, edited by Krin Gabbard. Durham: Duke University Press, 1995, 193–204.

Kolodny, Annette. *The Land before Her: Fantasy and Experience of the American Frontiers, 1630–1860*. Chapel Hill: University of North Carolina Press, 1984.

———. *The Lay of the Land: Metaphor as Experience and History in American Life and Letters*. Chapel Hill: University of North Carolina Press, 1975.

Kristy, Davida. *George Balanchine: American Ballet Master*. Minneapolis: Lerner Publications, 1996.

Kuntzel, Thierry. "The Film-Work, 2." Translated by Nancy Huston. *Camera Obscura* (spring 1980): 7–63.

Langdale, Allan. "S(t)imulation of Mind: The Film Theory of Hugo Münsterberg." In *Photoplay: A Psychological Study and Other Writings*, edited by Allan Langdale. New York: Routledge, 2002 [1916].

Leddick, David. *Intimate Companions: A Triography of George Platt Lynes, Paul Cadmus, Lincoln Kirstein, and Their Circle*. New York: St. Martin's Press, 2000.

Leja, Michael. *Reframing Abstract Expressionism: Subjectivity and Painting in the 1940s*. New Haven: Yale University Press, 1993.

Leverenz, David. *Manhood and the American Renaissance*. Ithaca: Cornell University Press, 1989.

Levine, Lawrence. *Black Culture and Black Consciousness: Afro-American Folk Thought from Slavery to Freedom*. New York: Oxford University Press, 1977.

———. *Highbrow, Low Brow: The Emergence of Cultural Hierarchy in America*. Cambridge, Mass.: Harvard University Press, 1998.

Lewis, David Levering. *W. E. B. Du Bois: Biography of a Race, 1868–1919*. New York: Henry Holt and Company, 1993.

———. *W. E. B. Du Bois: The Fight for Equality and the American Century, 1919–1963*. New York: Henry Holt and Company, 2000.

———. *When Harlem Was in Vogue*. New York: Penguin Books, 1997 [1979].

Lewis, R. W. B. *The American Adam: Innocence, Tragedy, and Tradition in the Nineteenth Century*. Chicago: University of Chicago Press. 1966 [1955].

Lhamon, W. T. Jr. *Raising Cain: Blackface Performance from Jim Crow to Hip Hop*. Cambridge, Mass.: Harvard University Press, 1998.

Lindsay, Vachel. *The Art of the Moving Picture*. New York: Liveright Publishing, 1970 [1915] .

Litvak, Joseph. *Strange Gourmets: Sophistication, Theory, and the Novel*. Durham: Duke University Press, 1997.

Locke, Alain. "American Literary Tradition and the Negro." *Modern Quarterly* 3 (1926): 215–22.

———. "Frontiers of Culture." *Crescent* 33 (spring 1950): 37–39.

Locke, Alain, and Sterling A. Brown. "Folk Values in a New Medium." In *Black Films and Film-Makers: A Comprehensive Anthology from Stereotype to Superhero*, edited by Lindsay Patterson. New York: Dodd, Mead and Company, 1975. 25–29.

Logan, Rayford W. *The Betrayal of the Negro: From Rutherford B. Hayes to Woodrow Wilson*. New York: Da Capo Press, 1997 [1954].

Lott, Eric. *Love and Theft: Blackface, Minstrelsy, and the American Working Class*. New York: Oxford University Press, 1993.

Loving, Jerome. *Walt Whitman: The Song of Myself*. Berkeley: University of California Press, 1999.

Lowe, Sue Davidson. *Stieglitz: A Memoir/Biography*. New York: Farrar, Straus and Giroux, 1983.

Löwy, Michael, and Robert Sayre. *Romanticism against the Tide of Modernity*. Translated by Catherine Porter. Durham: Duke University Press, 2001 [1992].

Lucic, Karen. *Charles Sheeler and the Cult of the Machine*. Cambridge, Mass.: Harvard University Press, 1991.

Lucie-Smith, Edward. *American Realism*. New York: Harry Abrams, 1994.

MacGregor, Alan Leaner. "Tammany: The Indian as Rhetorical Surrogate." *American Quarterly* 35.4 (fall 1983): 391–407.

MacMillan, Margaret. *Paris 1919: Six Months that Changed the World*. New York: Random House, 2001.

Macready, William Charles. *The Journal of William Charles Macready, 1832–1851, edited by* J. C. Trewin. London: Longman, Green and Co., 1967.

Maier, Pauline. *From Resistance to Revolution: Colonial Radicals and the Development of American Opposition to Britain, 1765–1776*. New York: Knopf, 1973.

Margulies, Ivone, ed. *Rites of Realism: Essays on Corporeal Cinema*. Durham: Duke University Press, 2003.

Maroney, James H. "Charles Sheeler Reveals the Machinery of His Soul." *American Art* 13.2 (summer 1999): 27–58.

Marquis, Alice Goldfarb. *Alfred H. Barr: Missionary for the Modern*. Chicago: Contemporary Books, 1989.

Martin, John. "The Dance: Elysian Jazz." *New York Times* (November 10 1940): 150.

Martin, Waldo E. *The Mind of Frederick Douglass*. Chapel Hill: University of North Carolina Press, 1984.

Marx, Leo. *The Machine in the Garden: Technology and the Pastoral Ideal in America*. New York: Oxford University Press, 1964.

Mason, Ernest. "Deconstruction in the Philosophy of Alain Locke." *Transactions of the Charles Peirce Society* 24 (winter 1988): 85–106.

Matthiessen, F. O. *American Renaissance*. London: Oxford University Press, 1941.

Maxim, Hudson. *Defenseless America*. New York: Hearst's International Library, 1915.

May, Henry F. *The End of American Innocence: The First Years of Our Own Time, 1912–1917*. New York: Oxford, 1979 [1959].

McBride, Henry. *The Flow of Art: Essays and Criticisms*, edited by Daniel Rich. New Haven: Yale University Press, 1997 [1975].

McCallum, Iain. *Blood Brothers: Hiram and Hudson Maxim, Pioneers of Modern Warfare*. London: Chatham Publishing, 1999.

McDonagh, Don. *George Balanchine*. Boston: Twayne Publishers, 1983.

McFeely, William S. *Frederick Douglass*. New York: Norton, 1991.

McPherson, James M. *Battle Cry of Freedom: The Civil War Era*. New York: Ballantine Books, 1988.

Menand, Louis. *The Metaphysical Club*. New York: Farrar, Straus and Giroux, 2001.

Mercer, Kobena. "Dark and Lovely Too: Black Gay Men in Independent Film." In *Queer Looks: Perspectives on Lesbian and Gay Film and Video*, edited by Martha Gever, John Greyson, and Pratibha Parmar. New York: Routledge, 1993. 238–56.

———. "Skin Head Sex Thing: Racial Difference and the Homoerotic Imaginary." In *How Do I Look*, edited by Bad Object Choices. Seattle: Bay Press, 1991. 169–212.

Micheaux, Oscar. *The Case of Mrs. Wingate*. New York: AMS Press, 1975 [1945].

———. *The Conquest*. Lincoln: University of Nebraska Press, 1994 [1913].

———. *The Forged Note: A Romance of the Darker Races*. Lincoln: Western Book Supply Company, 1915.

———. *The Homesteader*. Lincoln: University of Nebraska Press, 1994 [1917].

———. *The Masquerade: An Historical Novel*. New York: Book Supply Company, 1947.

———. *The Wind from Nowhere*. New York: Book Supply Company, 1944.

Miller, Angela. *The Empire of the Eye: Landscape Representations and American Cultural Politics, 1825–1875*. Ithaca: Cornell University Press, 1993.

Miller, Elise. "The Feminization of American Realist Theory." *American Literary Realism, 1870–1910* 23.1 (fall 1990): 20–41.

Minnelli, Vincente, with Hector Arce. *Vincente Minnelli: I Remember it Well*. Hollywood, Calif.: Samuel French Trade, 1990 [1974].

Mitchell, Lee Clark. *Westerns: Making the Man in Fiction and Film*. Chicago: University of Chicago Press. 1996.

Moody, Richard. *Astor Place Riot*. Bloomington: Indiana University Press, 1958.

———. *Edwin Forrest: First Star of the American Stage*. New York: Knopf, 1960.

Moon, Michael. *Disseminating Whitman: Revision and Corporeality in "Leaves of Grass."* Cambridge, Mass.: Harvard University Press, 1991.

Moore, Jacqueline M. *Booker T. Washington, W. E. B. Du Bois, and the Struggle for Racial Uplift*. Wilmington, Del.: Scholarly Resources, 2003.

Moore, Rachel. *Savage Theory: Cinema as Modern Magic*. Durham: Duke University Press, 2000.

Moos, Dan. "Reclaiming the Frontier: Oscar Micheaux as Black Turnerian." *African American Review* 36.3 (2002): 357–81.

Morris, Edmund. *The Rise of Theodore Roosevelt.* New York: Ballantine Books, 1979.

———. *Theodore Rex.* New York: Random House, 2001.

Morton, Patricia. *Disfigured Images: The Historical Assault on Afro-American Women.* Westport, Conn.: Praeger Publishers, 1991.

Mumford, Lewis. *The Brown Decades: A Study of the Arts in America, 1865–1895.* New York: Dover, 1955 [1931].

Münsterberg, Hugo. *The Americans.* New York: McClure, Phillips and Co., 1904.

———. *The Photoplay: A Psychological Study and Other Writings*, edited by Allan Langdale. New York: Routledge, 2002 [1916].

———. *Psychology and Industrial Efficiency.* Boston: Houghton Mifflin, 1913.

———. *Science and Idealism.* Boston: Houghton Mifflin, 1906.

———. *The War and America.* New York: D. Appleton, 1914.

Münsterberg, Margaret. *Hugo Münsterberg: His Life and Work.* New York: D. Appleton, 1972.

Musser, Charles. "American Vitagraph: 1897–1901." *Cinema Journal* 22.3 (spring 1983): 4–46.

———. *The Emergence of Cinema: The American Screen to 1907.* Berkeley: University of California Press, 1994.

Naifeh, Steven, and Gregory White Smith. *Jackson Pollock: An American Saga.* New York: Clarkson N. Potter, 1989.

Naremore, James. *The Films of Vincente Minnelli.* New York: Cambridge University Press, 1993.

Nash, Roderick. "The American Cult of the Primitive." *American Quarterly* 18.3 (fall 1966): 517–37.

Neil, J. Meredith. *Toward a National Taste: America's Quest for Aesthetic Independence.* Honolulu: University of Hawaii Press, 1975.

Neiman, Catrina. "*View* Magazine: Transatlantic Pact." In *View: Parade of the Avant Garde, 1940–1947*, edited by Charles Henri Ford. New York: Thunder's Mouth Press, 1991. xi–xvi.

Nelson, Dana T. *National Manhood: Capitalist Citizenship and the Imagined Fraternity of White Men.* Durham: Duke University Press, 1998.

Noll, Mark A. "Common Sense Traditions and American Evangelical Thought." *American Quarterly* 37.2 (summer 1985): 216–38.

Nordau, Max, *Degeneration.* Lincoln: University of Nebraska Press, 1993 [1895].

Norman, Dorothy. *Alfred Stieglitz: An American Seer.* New York: Aperture, 1973 [1960].

Novak, Barbara. *American Painting of the Nineteenth Century*. New York: Praeger Publishers, 1969.

Ohmann, Richard. *Selling Culture: Magazines, Markets, and Class at the Turn of the Century*. London: Verso, 1996.

Oliver, Lawrence J. *Brander Matthews, Theodore Roosevelt, and the Politics of American Literature, 1880–1920*. Knoxville: University of Tennessee Press, 1992.

Orvell, Miles. *The Real Thing: Imitation and Authenticity in American Culture, 1880–1940*. Chapel Hill: University of North Carolina Press, 1989.

Pach, Walter. *Queer Thing Painting*. New York: Harper Brothers, 1938.

Page, Max. *The Creative Destruction of Manhattan, 1900–1940*. Chicago: University of Chicago Press, 1999.

Paine, Thomas. "Common Sense." London: Penguin Books, 1986 [1776].

Patton, Venetria K. *Women in Chains: The Legacy of Slavery in Black Women's Fiction*. Albany: State University of New York Press, 2000.

Pearce, Roy Harvey. *Savagism and Civilization: A Study of the Indian and the American Mind*. Berkeley: University of California Press, 1988. [A revision of *The Savages of America*. Baltimore: Johns Hopkins University Press, 1953.]

Perelman, S. J. "That Felli Minnelli." *Stage* (May 1937): 66–68.

Perlman, Bennard B. *Painters of the Ashcan School: The Immortal Eight*. New York: Dover Publications, 1988. [Originally published as *The Immortal Eight: American Painting from Eakins to the Armory Show, 1870–1913*. Cincinnati: North Light Publishers, 1979.]

Pfeiffer, Kathleen. Introduction to *Nigger Heaven* by Carl Van Vechten. Urbana: University of Illinois Press, 2000 [1926].

Pollock, Griselda. "Modernity and the Spaces of Femininity." In *Vision and Difference: Femininity, Feminism, and Histories of Art*. London: Routledge, 1991 [1988]. 50–90.

Potter, David M. "The Quest for the National Character." In *The National Temper: Readings in American Culture and Society*, edited by Lawrence W. Levine and Robert Middlekauff. 2nd ed. New York: Harcourt Brace Jovanovich, 1972. 4–18.

Rasmussen, Chris. "Mass Wasteland: Michael Kammen's *American Culture, American Tastes: Social Change and the Twentieth Century*." *Reviews in American History* 28.2 (2000): 309–17.

Reynolds, Charles. "An Interview with Vincente Minnelli." *Popular Photography* (July 1962): 106–7, 116.

Reynolds, David. *Walt Whitman's America: A Cultural Biography*. New York: Vintage, 1995.

Riley, Glenda. "American Daughters: Black Women in the West." In *African*

Americans on the Western Frontier, edited by Monroe Lee Billington and Roger D. Hardaway. Niwot: University of Colorado Press, 1998. 160–80.

Robinson, James Harvey. *The Mind in the Making: The Relation of Intelligence to Social Reform*. New York: Harper and Brothers, 1939 [1921].

Robinson, Roxana. *Georgia O'Keeffe: A Life*. New York: Harper and Row, 1989.

Rogin, Michael. *Blackface, White Noise: Jewish Immigrants in the Hollywood Melting Pot*. Berkeley: University of California Press, 1996.

Rony, Fatimah Tobing. "Robert Flaherty's *Nanook of the North*: The Politics of Taxidermy and Romantic Ethnography." In *The Birth of Whiteness: Race and the Emergence of U.S. Cinema*, edited by Daniel Bernardi. New Brunswick: Rutgers University Press, 1996. 300–28.

Roosevelt, Theodore. *An Autobiography*. New York: Da Capo, 1985 [1913].

———. *The Rough Riders*. New York: Modern Library, 1999 [1899].

———. *The Selected Letters of Theodore Roosevelt*, edited by H. W. Brands. New York: Cooper Square Press, 2001.

———. *Theodore Roosevelt: An American Mind, A Selection of His Writings*, edited by Mario DiNunzio. New York: Penguin Books, 1995.

———. *The Works of Theodore Roosevelt: Memorial Edition*. 24 volumes. New York: Scribner's Sons, 1925.

Rosenblum, Naomi. "The Early Years." In *Paul Strand: Essays on His Work and Life*, edited by Maren Stange. New York: Aperture Books, 1991. 31–51.

Rosenfeld, Paul. *Port of New York: Essays on Fourteen American Moderns*. New York: Harcourt, Brace and Company, 1924.

Rourke, Constance. *American Humor: A Study of The National Character*. Tallahassee: University Presses of Florida, 1986 [1931].

———. *Charles Sheeler: Artist in the American Tradition*. New York: Harcourt, Brace and Company, 1938.

———. *The Roots of American Culture and Other Essays*. New York: Harcourt, Brace and Company, 1942.

Rovit, Earl H. "American Literature and 'The American Experience.'" *American Quarterly* 13.2 (summer 1961): 115–25.

Ruckstuhl, F. W. "Social Art: An Address Delivered to The Open Table of the National Arts Club, January 25, 1915." New York: National Arts Club Open Table Publications, 1915, n.p. [Archives of American Art, National Arts Club, roll 4262, frames 66–75.]

Saum, Lewis O. "The Fur Trader and the Noble Savage." *American Quarterly* 15.4 (winter 1963): 554–71.

Schickel, Richard. *D. W. Griffith: An American Life*. New York: Simon and Schuster, 1984.

Schwarz, A. B. Christa. *Gay Voices of the Harlem Renaissance*. Bloomington: Indiana University Press, 2003.

Scott, William B., and Peter Rutkoff. *New York Modern*. Baltimore: Johns Hopkins University Press, 1999.

Sedgwick, Eve Kosofsky. *Epistemology of the Closet*. Berkeley: University of California Press, 1990.

Shannon, William. *The American Irish: A Political and Social Portrait*. Amherst: University of Massachusetts Press, 1963.

Shapiro, Gary. "From the Sublime to the Political: Some Historical Notes." *New Literary History* 26.2 (winter 1985): 213–35.

Sheehan, Bernard W. *Seeds of Extinction: Jeffersonian Philanthropy and the American Indian*. Durham: University of North Carolina Press, 1973.

Sheeler, Charles. *Charles Sheeler: Paintings, Drawings, Photographs*. Introduction by William Carlos Williams. New York: Museum of Modern Art, 1939.

Shi, David E. *Facing Facts: Realism in American Thought and Culture, 1850–1920*. New York: Oxford University Press, 1995.

Shohat, Ella. "Gender and Culture of Empire: Toward a Feminist Ethnography of the Cinema." In *Visions of the East: Orientalism in Films*, edited by Matthew Bernstein and Gaylyn Studlar. New Brunswick: Rutgers University Press, 1997. 19–66.

Sinfield, Alan. *The Wilde Century: Effeminacy, Oscar Wilde, and the Queer Moment*. New York: Columbia University Press, 1994.

Singer, Ben. *Melodrama and Modernity: Early Sensational Cinema and Its Contexts*. New York: Columbia University Press, 2001.

Skerrett, Joseph T. Jr. "Irony and Symbolic Action in James Weldon Johnson's *The Autobiography of an Ex-Coloured Man*." *American Quarterly* 32.5 (winter 1980): 540–58.

Slide, Anthony. *The Big V: A History of the Vitagraph Company*. Methuchen, N.J.: Sacred Cow Press, 1987.

Slotkin, Richard. *Gunfighter Nation: The Myth of the Frontier in Twentieth-Century America*. Norman: University of Oklahoma Press, 1998 [1992].

———. *Regeneration through Violence: The Mythology of the American Frontier, 1600–1860*. New York: Harper Collins, 1996 [1973].

Smith, Henry Nash. *The Virgin Land: The American West as Symbol and Myth*. New York: Vintage, 1950.

Smith, John E. *The Spirit of American Philosophy: Peirce, James, Royce, Dewey, Whitehead*. London: Oxford University Press, 1974 [1963].

Smith, Shawn Michelle. *Photography on the Color Line: W. E. B. Du Bois, Race, and Visual Culture*. Durham: Duke University Press, 2004.

Spiegel, Alan. *Fiction and the Camera Eye: Visual Consciousness in Film and the Modern Novel*. Charlottesville: University Press of Virginia, 1976.

Staiger, Janet. "Dividing Labor for Production Control: Thomas Ince and the Rise of the Studio System." In *The American Movie Industry: The Business of Motion Pictures*, edited by Gorham Kindem. Carbondale: Southern Illinois University Press, 1982. 94–103.

———. "The Eyes Are Really the Focus: Photoplay Acting and Film Form." *Wide Angle* 6.4 (1985): 14–23.

Stange, Maren, ed. *Paul Strand: Essays on His Work and Life*. New York: Aperture Books, 1991.

Stansell, Christine. *American Moderns: Bohemian New York and the Creation of a New Century*. New York: Metropolitan Books, 2000.

Stieglitz, Alfred. "Pictorial Photography." *Camera Work* 18 (1907). [Reprinted in *Alfred Stieglitz Camera Work: The Complete Illustrations, 1903–1917*. Cologne: Taschen, 1997. 354–55].

Stovell, Floyd. *American Idealism*. Port Washington, N.Y.: Kennikat Press, 1943.

Strand, Paul. "Photography." *Seven Arts* 2 (August 1917): 524–26.

———. "Photography and the New God." *Broom* 3 (November 1922): 252–58.

Suárez, Juan A. *Bike Boys, Drag Queens, and Superstars: Avant-Garde, Mass Production, and Gay Identities in the 1960s Underground Cinema*. Bloomington: Indiana University Press, 1996.

———. "City Space, Technology, Popular Culture: The Modernism of Paul Strand and Charles Sheeler's *Manhatta*." *Journal of American Studies* 36.1 (April 2002): 85–106.

Sudarkasa, Niara. "Interpreting the African Heritage in African American Family Organization." In *The Strength of Our Mothers: African and African American Women and Families, Essays and Speeches*, edited by Niara Sudarkasa. Trenton, N.J.: Africa World Press, 1996. 123–41.

Sundquist, Eric. "Introduction: The Country of the Blue." In *American Realism: New Essays*, edited by Eric Sundquist. Baltimore: Johns Hopkins University Press, 1982. 3–24.

Sypher, Wylie. *Rococo to Cubism in Art and Literature: Transformations in Style in Art and Literature from the Eighteenth to the Twentieth Century*. New York: Vintage Books, 1960.

Taper, Bernard. *Balanchine: A Biography*. Berkeley: University of California Press, 1996 [1984].

Tashjian, Dickran. *Skyscraper Primitives: Dada and the American Avant-Garde, 1910–1925*. Middletown, Conn.: Wesleyan University Press, 1975.

Taylor, Frederick Winslow. *The Principles of Scientific Management*. New York: Norton, 1967 [1911].

Thompson, Era Bell. *American Daughter*. St. Paul: Minnesota Historical Society, 1986 [1946].

Thoreau, Henry David. *Walden, or, Life in the Woods, and On the Duty of Civil Disobedience* [1854]. New York: Harper and Row, 1965 [1854].

Tinckom, Matthew. *Working Like a Homosexual: Camp, Capital, Cinema*. Durham: Duke University Press, 2002.

Tocqueville, Alexis de. *Democracy in America*, vols. 1–2. Translated by Henry Reeve, edited by Phillips Bradley. New York: Vintage, 1945.

Toll, Robert. "Social Commentary in Late Nineteenth-Century White Minstrelsy." In *Inside the Minstrel Mask: Readings in Nineteenth-Century Blackface Minstrelsy*, edited by Annemarie Bean, James V. Hatch, and Brooks McNamara. Middletown, Conn.: Wesleyan University Press, 1996. 86–109.

Tomkins, Calvin. *Duchamp: A Biography*. New York: Henry Holt and Company, 1996.

———. "Profiles: Look to the Things Around You." *New Yorker* (September 16, 1974): 44–94.

Trachtenberg, Alan. *The Incorporation of America: Culture and Society in the Gilded Age*. New York: Hill and Wang, 1982.

———. "Introduction." In *Paul Strand: Essays on His Work and Life*, edited by Maren Stange. New York: Aperture Books, 1991.

———. *Reading American Photographs: Images as History, Mathew Brady to Walker Evans*. New York: Noonday Press, 1989.

Trimble, Marion Blackton. *J. Stuart Blackton: A Personal Biography by His Daughter*. Metuchen, N.J.: Scarecrow Press, 1985.

Troy, Hugh. "Never Had a Lesson." *Esquire* (June 1937): 99, 138, 141.

Troyen, Carol, and Erica Hirshler. *Charles Sheeler: Paintings and Drawings*. Boston: Museum of Fine Arts, 1987.

Turner, Frederick Jackson. *The Frontier in American History*. New York: Dover Publications, 1996 [1920].

Tyler, Parker. *The Divine Comedy of Pavel Tchelitchew*. New York: Fleet Publishing, 1967.

VanEpps-Taylor, Betti Carol. *Oscar Micheaux . . . Dakota Homesteader, Author, Pioneer Film Maker*. Rapid City, S.D.: Dakota West Books, 1999.

Vardac, A. Nicholas. *Stage to Screen: Theatrical Origins of Early Film: David Garrick to D. W. Griffith*. New York: Da Capo Press, 1987 [1949].

Veblen, Thorstein. *The Theory of the Leisure Class*. New York: Penguin Books, 1994 [1899].

Wagner, Anne M. "Warhol Paints History, or Race in America." *Representa-tions* 55 (summer 1996): 98–119.

Wakin, Edward. *Enter the Irish American*. New York: Thomas Y. Cromwell Company, 1976.

Waleson, Heidi. "When Balanchine Brought Ballet to Hollywood." *New York Times* (March 13, 1988): 24.

Walker, Peter F. *Moral Choices: Memory, Desire, and Imagination in Nine-teenth Century American Abolition*. Baton Rouge: Louisiana State University, 1978.

Wallace, Maurice O. *Constructing the Black Masculine: Identity and Ideality in African American Men's Literature and Culture, 1775–1995*. Durham: Duke University Press, 2002.

Wallace, Michelle. "Oscar Micheaux's *Within Our Gates*: The Possibilities of Alternative Visions." In *Oscar Micheaux and His Circle*, edited by Pearl Bowser, Jane Gaines, and Charles Musser. Bloomington: Indiana University Press, 2001. 53–66.

Warren, Kenneth. *Black and White Strangers: Race and American Literary Realism*. Chicago: University of Chicago Press, 1993.

Washington, Booker T. *Frederick Douglass*. London: Hodder and Stroughton Publishers, 1906.

———. *Up from Slavery*. New York: Penguin Books, 2000 [1901].

Washington, Johnny. *A Journey into the Philosophy of Alain Locke*. Westport, Conn.: Greenwood Press, 1994.

Waters, Ethel, with Charles Samuels. *His Eye Is on the Sparrow: An Autobi-ography by Ethel Waters*. Garden City, N.Y.: Doubleday, 1950.

Watson, Steven. *The Harlem Renaissance: Hub of African American Culture, 1920–1930*. New York: Pantheon Books, 1995.

———. *Strange Bedfellows: The First American Avant-Garde*. New York: Abbeville Press, 1991.

Weaver, Mike. "Dynamic Realist." In *Paul Strand: Essays on His Work and Life*, edited by Maren Stange. New York: Aperture Books, 1991. 197–207.

Weber, Max. *The Protestant Ethic and the "Spirit" of Capitalism and Other Writings*. Translated by Peter Baehr and Gordon C. Wells. New York: Penguin Books, 2002 [1905].

Weinberg, Jonathan. *Speaking for Vice: Homosexuality in the Art of Charles Demuth, Marsden Hartley, and the First American Avant-Garde*. New Haven: Yale University Press, 1993.

Weiskel, Thomas. *The Romantic Sublime: Studies in the Structure and Psychol-ogy of Transcendence*. Baltimore: Johns Hopkins University Press, 1976.

Whelan, Richard. *Alfred Stieglitz: A Biography*. New York: Little, Brown, 1995.

White, Hayden. *Tropics of Discourse: Essays in Cultural Criticism.* Baltimore: Johns Hopkins University Press, 1985.

Whitman, Walt. *Democratic Vistas: Complete Prose Works.* Philadelphia: David McKay, 1897.

Wiebe, Robert H. *The Search for Order, 1877–1920.* New York: Hill and Wang, 2001 [1967].

Wilentz, Sean. *Chants Democratic: New York City and the Rise of the American Working Class, 1788–1850.* New York: Oxford University Press, 1986.

Williams, Christopher, ed. *Realism and the Cinema: A Reader.* London: Routledge and Kegan Paul, 1980.

Williams, Linda. *Playing the Race Card: Melodramas of Black and White From Uncle Tom to O. J. Simpson.* Princeton: Princeton University Press, 2001.

Wilson, Sondra Kathryn, ed. *The Crisis Reader: Stories, Poetry, and Essays from the N.A.A.C.P.'s "Crisis Magazine."* New York: Modern Library, 1999.

Windham, Donald. "The Stage and Ballet Designs of Pavel Tchelitchew." *Dance Index* 3.1–2 (January-February 1944): 4–32.

Wirth, Thomas H., ed. *Gay Rebel of the Harlem Renaissance: Selections from the Work of Richard Bruce Nugent.* Durham: Duke University Press, 2002.

Wittke, Carl. *The Irish in America.* Baton Rouge: Louisiana State University Press, 1956.

Wolf, Bryan J. "A Grammar of the Sublime, or Intertextuality Triumphant in Church, Turner, and Cole." *New Literary Review: A Journal of Theory and Interpretation* 2.16 (winter 1985): 321–41.

———. *Romantic Re-Vision: Culture and Consciousness in Nineteenth-Century American Painting and Literature.* Chicago: University of Chicago Press, 1986.

Woody, Jack. *George Platt Lynes Photographs, 1931–1955.* Los Angeles: Twelvetrees Press, 1980.

Wright, Frank Lloyd. *Collected Writings: Volume Two, 1930–1932,* edited by Bruce Brooks Pfeiffer. New York: Rizzoli, 1992.

Young, Joseph A. *Black Novelist as White Racist: The Myth of Black Inferiority in the Novels of Oscar Micheaux.* New York: Greenwood Press, 1989.

Index

Abrahams, Edward, 122
Adams, Brooks, 65
Adams, Henry, 65, 257 n.43
Adventures in the Arts, 134
Aesop, 187
African Americans: influence of,
on American Modernism, 167–
170, 173–174, 191–196, 199–200;
black bodies, 90, 92, 96, 98–103,
105, 108–110; black desire, 94,
97–104, 252 n.87; black masculinity, xi, 87–90, 92, 94, 96–98,
100–102, 116–118, 169; and cultural uplift, x, 83–85, 87–89,
99, 169–170; folk culture of,
90–91, 181, 191–195, 198–200,
203–204, 276 n.114; and trope
of the mother, 97–104, 247 n.53,
248 n.59; and queer culture, xi,
167, 170, 173, 178, 181, 182, 196–
198, 200–205, 208, 210–211, 213;
and race relations, 16, 30, 84–
88, 103, 108, 118, 170, 193, 196,
213, 247 n.46; racial realism in
cinema, 87, 92–94; and white
paternalism, 83, 86, 91, 100. *See
also* Harlem Renaissance
Agee, James, 194–196, 204,
267 n.116
*Age of Reform: From Bryan to FDR,
The*, 119

Alger, William Rounseville, 14–16,
18, 22
Althusser, Louis, 35
America and Alfred Stieglitz, 123
American art: and artist's bodies,
xii, 1–5, 10–11, 13–16, 18–22, 27–
28, 33, 42, 44, 48, 50, 127, 131,
133–136, 139, 143, 150, 167–169,
174–175, 179, 181–184, 186–189,
194, 255 n.16; and democracy,
ix, 1, 4, 7–8, 10–11, 20, 27, 34,
37, 39–41, 47–48, 51, 58, 68, 81,
86, 121, 141; as masculine, ix, xii,
1–5, 8–13, 20, 22, 26–27, 29–
30, 36, 38, 41–42, 47–51, 68,
119, 127, 132–133, 164, 167, 180–
181, 184, 210, 213–214; and Old
World/New World dialectic, ix,
8, 47–48, 51, 66–67, 119, 121–126,
140, 164, 168, 176
American Citizen, 7–9, 19, 38, 47,
217 n.18
American frontier, 15, 25, 33, 42,
80–81, 83, 86, 96, 122, 211,
239 n.78
American immigrants, 3–5, 10–11,
66, 71
American Indians. *See* Native
Americans
American Historical Society, 66
American in Paris, An, 178, 270 n.51

American Landscape, 146, 147
American Legion, 57
American Place, An, 172, 266 n.22
American Review, 25
American Vitagraph, 51, 53, 56, 60–61, 63, 64, 74, 78
Anderson, Eddie "Rochester," 201, 208, 209
Anderson, Sherwood, 123, 175
Apollo, 179–180, 186
Apollon Musagète. See Apollo
Arabian Nights, 187
Arensberg, Walter, 125, 145
Armory Show, 65, 123, 141, 146, 154, 254 n.12
Armstrong, Louis, 203
Arnold, Matthew, 25
art. *See* American art
Art of the Moving Picture, The, 140–141
Ash Can School, 49, 125, 128, 160, 256 n.21
Astaire, Fred, 181, 266 n.19
Astor Place Opera House, 1, 216 n.3
Astor Place Riot, xii, 1, 3, 6–8, 215 n.1, 216 n.3, 218 n.25
Autobiography of an Ex-Colored Man, The, 115
Avedon, Richard, 278 n.126

Bailey, Bill, 205, 208, 209
Baker, Houston, 195, 199
Baker, Josephine, 98–99, 177, 198, 268 n.42
Bakst, Léon, 175, 185
Balanchine, George, 168, 172, 174, 189, 201, 208; and bodies, 179–183, 186; as collaborator, 176–178, 184–185; *Cabin in the Sky*, 191–195, 199–200
Balanchivadze, Georgi Melitonovich. *See* Balanchine, George
Baldwin, Kate, 193, 276 n.114

Ballet Caravan, 176
Ballets Russes, 165, 175, 176, 185, 269 n.47
Baptiste, Jean, 92, 94, 96
Barker, Adam, 105–106, 110
Barr, Alfred H., 170–172, 265 n.15, 266 n.19
Barry, Iris, 266 n.19
Barton, Ralph, 204
Battle Cry of Peace, x, 51, 53, 55, 56, 69, 83, 140, 156, 232 n.10, 233 n.22; as moral art, 59–60, 73–75, 81; as "living Corot," 62–64; as propaganda, 57–58, 78–80
Battle of Manila Bay, 60–61
Baudelaire, Charles Pierre, 45, 47
Beardsley, Aubrey, 142, 175
Beaton, Cecil, 189, 197
Bechte, Robert, 40, 58
Bederman, Gail, 17, 86, 241 n.9
Bell, Michael Davitt, 31
Belsey, Catherine, 35, 225 n.89
Bender, Thomas, 159, 160
Bendix, William, 264 n.4
Benjamin, Walter, 164
Benny, Jack, 209
Benon, Herbert, 73
Benton, Thomas Hart, 169
Bérard, Christian, 180
Berkeley, Busby, 205
Berst, J. A., 58
Bible, The, 54
Bierstadt, Albert, 48
Birth of a Nation, The, xi, 56, 60, 83, 105, 140, 233 n.19
Black Americans. *See* African Americans
Black Bohemia, 173
blackface. *See* minstrelsy
Blackton, J. Stuart, x, 78, 83, 156, 169, 233 n.22; and cultural uplift, 77, 80, 82, 172; and Isadora Duncan, 167–168; and moral art, 53, 55, 58–61, 74–76, 233 n.28,

234 n.38; on painting, 62–64; as propagandist, 56–57

Blackwood's Magazine, 17

Blakemore, Steven, 36

Body and Soul, 89, 94, 108

Bogle, Donald, 89

Bolger, Ray, 178

Bordwell, David, 274 n.93

Bourdieu, Pierre, 213

Bourne, Randolph, 125, 154

Bowery B'hoys, 11

Brakhage, Stan, 213, 224 n.76

Brancusi, Constantin, 124

Braxton, Joanne, 104

Brennan, Marcia, 262 n.92

Brent, Linda, 104

Breton, André, 185, 273 n.80

Bridge, The, 139

Brooklyn Bridge, 139

Brooklyn Eagle, 12

Brooks, Van Wyck, 120, 146, 159

Brothers Grimm, 187

Brown, Milton, 126, 142, 152

Brown, Sterling A., 198–199

Browning, Todd, 183, 188

Brownlow, Kevin, 59, 233 n.22, 239 n.78

Brownsville Riot (Texas), 86, 240 n.5

Bryner, Edna, 123

Buckle, Richard, 179

Burke, Edmund, 25, 36, 42, 43

Burns, Sarah, 62

Burroughs, John, 59, 65, 67–69, 87

Cabin in the Sky (film), xi, 165, 177, 206–207, 209; and African American folk culture, 191–195, 199–200, 203–204; sophisticated mise-èn-scene in, 200–201, 205, 208; as urban modernism, 167, 173–174, 202

Cabin in the Sky (play), 178, 191, 193–195, 200

Camera Work, 124–126, 153

Cameron, James, 214, 225–226 n.90

Carby, Hazel, 87, 88, 89, 92, 94, 97, 99, 102

Carlsen, Carl, 177, 268 n.39

Carter, Nick, 177

Case of Mrs. Wingate, The, 97, 98, 108, 248 n.56

Catlin, George, 28, 220 n.35

Cézanne, Paul, 124, 126, 145, 146

Charles Sheeler, 143

Chartres Cathedral, 150

Chauncey, George, 172

Chenault, Lawrence, 95

Chestnutt, Charles, 89, 102–103, 109

Chicago Art Institute, 174

Child, Lydia Maria, 104

Christian progressivism. *See* progressivism

Church, Frederic, 39–40, 48

cinema: as American art, ix, 51, 64, 81, 83, 129, 140, 142, 155, 164; classical Hollywood style, x, 51, 105–107, 172; use of flashback in, 109, 111, 114–115; and morality, 53, 55, 58–61, 64, 68, 73–76; and national identity, ix, xiii, 30, 49–51, 53, 60, 64–65, 76–78, 82; use of parallel editing in, 106, 108–110, 112–115, 250 n.80; as popular entertainment, 51, 53, 59, 63–64, 74, 76, 81; and propaganda, x, 51, 57–60, 73, 75, 78, 80

Circus Polka, 178

Clarke, Shirley, 213

Clock, The, 276 n.116

Cochran's 1930 Revue (musical revue), 178

Cole, Tom, 48

Conquest, The, 115–117

Cooper, James Fenimore, 14, 20, 27

Corn, Wanda, 159, 255 n.17

Corner in Wheat, A, 106, 108, 251 n.82
Corot, Jean Baptiste Camille, 62–64, 167
Corarrabius, Miguel, 204
Cosmopolitan, 73
Covered Wagon, The, 74
Coward, Noël, 278 n.127
Cowley, Malcolm, 196
Crane, Stephen, 65
Creekmur, Corey, 89
Criss-Cross Conveyors, 150
cubism, x, 45, 122, 126, 170
cubist realism, 126, 142, 146, 163
Cukor, George, 184
Cullen, Countee, 197
cultural assimilation, 71
cultural uplift. *See* African Americans: and cultural uplift
Cunard, Nancy, 197
Cushing, Frank Hamilton, 28

Dada, 125, 138, 155, 170
Dance: A Short History of Classical Theatrical Dancing (Kirstein), 168
D'Annunzio, Gabrielino, 141
Dante, 67, 136
Darwin, Charles, 47, 66, 128, 135–136
Davies, Arthur, 146
Day, F. Holland, 124
Debord, Guy, 16
Defenseless America, 53–55, 64
Degeneration, 47, 54, 168
Deloria, Philip, 17
Democratic Vistas, 47
Demuth, Charles, 123, 124, 145, 255 n.17
Derain, Alain, 180
Derrida, Jacques, 90, 245 n.36, 278 n.130
Destruction of Gotham, 53
Devereaux, Oscar, 92, 94, 96

Dewey, Admiral George, 59, 173
Diaghilev, Serge, 165, 176, 177, 179, 180, 182, 185, 186, 200, 270 n.58, 273 n.85
Diderot, Denis, 23, 24, 28
différance, 198
Doane, Mary Ann, 252 n.87
Dokstader, Lew, 117
Douglas, Ann, 31, 157, 173
Douglas, Steven, 109
Douglass, Frederick, 91–92, 94, 99–102, 104, 116, 244 nn.31, 33, 248 nn.57, 59, 249 n.66, 250 n.75
Dove, Arthur, 124, 171
Dovzhenko, Alexander, 194
Doyle, Laura, 100
Dred-Scott decision, 109
Dreiser, Theodore, 48, 125, 175
Du Barry, 175
Du Bois, W. E. B., 87–88, 93, 99–102, 116, 125, 198, 240 n.4, 243 nn.19, 21, 249 nn.59, 66, 251 n.83, 277 n.124
Duchamp, Marcel, 125, 140, 145, 175, 185
DuCille, Ann, 116
Duke, Vernon, 177, 179, 183, 185, 201, 205, 268 n.39, 272 nn.73, 74, 279 n.147
Dukelsky, Vladimir. *See* Duke, Vernon
Dunbar, Paul, 91
Duncan, Isadora, 63, 167, 168, 264 n.7, 271 n.64
Dunham, Alfred, 199
Dunham, Katherine, 178, 192–195, 199–201, 210, 275 n.112
Dyer, Richard, 93, 191
Dyer, Thomas, 71, 86

Eakins, Thomas, 24, 34, 144, 223 n.66, 230 n.129, 234 n.131
Edelman, Lee, 29
Eden, Martin, 92, 94

Edison, Thomas Alva, 60, 61, 64, 259 n.70
Eight, The. *See* Ash Can School
Eisenstein, Sergei, 175
Eliot, Charles, 70
Ellington, Duke, 203
Elsaesser, Thomas, 105–107, 110
Emancipation Proclamation, 109
Emanon, 55, 56
Emerson, Ralph Waldo, 14, 22, 25–28, 31, 35–36, 54, 66, 221 n.54, 225 n.79
Ernst, Max, 180, 185
Errante, 186
Ethical Culture School, 153, 262 nn.97, 98
Evans, Walker, 204

Faderman, Lillian, 197
Fairchild, Hoxie, 26
Fashion Group, the, 165, 169, 175, 177
fauvism, 45, 146
Favor, J. Martin, 195, 278 n.131
Feyder, Jacques, 175
Fillin-Yeh, Susan, 148, 150
film. *See* cinema
Firbank, Ronald, 175
Flaherty, Robert, 137
Flatiron Building, 139
Flemish masters, 175
Fokine, Michel, 168
"Folk Values in a New Medium," 198
Ford, Charles Henri, 185, 186, 189, 272 n.71, 273 n.80
Ford, John, 31, 45
Ford, Henry, 232 n.10
Forged Note, The, 89, 116
Forrest, Edwin, 38, 93, 165, 173, 189; and Astor Place Riot, xii, 1, 3–4, 6–8; rivalry with William Macready, 1, 3–9, 11; masculine body of, xii, 3–4, 6, 8–11, 13–15,
19, 40, 42, 49–50, 96; as Metamora, 2, 16, 19; and national identity, 1, 3–13, 19–22, 68, 152, 212–213; and Push-ma-ta-ha, 14–16, 18, 20, 23–24, 26–28, 36, 44–45, 133, 135, 181, 210, 212, 220 n.35
Foucault, Michel, 34
Four Saints in Three Acts, 201, 279 n.146
Frank, Leo, 108
Frank, Waldo, 120, 123, 125, 127
Freaks, 184, 188
Freed, Arthur, 208
Freeman, Barbara Claire, 36, 44
French impressionists. *See* impressionism
Freud, Sigmund, 43, 72, 258 n.61
Fried, Michael, 22–24, 28, 34, 37, 150, 222 n.61, 223 n.66
Friedman, Martin, 143–146
Frohne, Ursula, 6
frontier myth. *See* American frontier
Fuller, Loie, 187
Fuller, Sam, 31

Gaines, Jane, 30, 87, 93, 94, 104–105, 107, 108, 252 n.86, 258 n.58
Gaines, Kevin, 88, 117
Garafola, Lynn, 165, 187
Garbo, Greta, 277 n.125
Garland, Hamlin, 65
Garland, Judy, 204
Garreto, Paolo, 204
Garrison, William Lloyd, 91, 94
Gates, Henry Louis, 95, 105, 107, 244 n.33, 245 n.34
Gershwin, George, 177, 178
Gershwin, Ira, 177
gesamtkunstwerk, 22, 157
Gibson, Mel, 214
Gilliespie, Veronica, 74
Gilmore, Leigh, 92, 245 n.36

Gilmore, Paul, 15–16, 18
Gilrory, Paul, 91
Gish, Lillian, 93
God, 15, 128, 137, 155, 156, 227 n.109, 229 n.124
God (sculpture), 155
Goffman, Irving, 179
Goldwyn, Samuel, 178, 269 n.50
Goldwyn Follies, The, 178, 270 n.50, 279 n.148
Goodbye, 26
Greco, El, 145
Greenberg, Clement, 171, 184, 213, 272 n.71
Griffith, D. W., 62, 104–107, 108, 110, 118, 141, 159, 233 n.19, 250 n.81, 251 n.82, 260 n.71, 266 n.19
Gross Clinic, The, 34
Guerrero, Ed, 202
Guilbaut, Serge, 171
Gunning, Tom, 106–107, 108, 110

Hale, Matthew, 70, 71
Hall, Iris, 95
Hallelujah, 94, 199
Hals, Frans, 145
Harlan, Louis, 86
Harlem Renaissance, 170, 195–196, 198, 213, 265 n.11, 267 n.25, 276 n.117, 277 nn.121, 124
Hartley, Marsden, 120, 124, 134–135, 137, 173, 255 n.17, 266 nn.16, 22
Harvard University, 69, 70, 71, 198, 266 n.19
Harvey, Stephen, 201, 203, 204
Hawks, Howard, 31
Hawthorne, Nathaniel, 48
Haynes, Todd, 214
Hearst International, 54
Hearts in Dixie, 199
Hegel, Georg Wilhelm Friedrich, 35

Helbling, Mark, 198
Hemphill, Essex, 212
Henri, Robert, 45, 66, 125, 229 n.121
Hine, Lewis, 153, 160
Hirshler, Erica, 148
Hoctor, Harriet, 274 n.95
Hofstadter, Richard, 119
Holmes, Sherlock, 177
Hollywood style. *See* cinema: classical Hollywood style
Homesteader, The, 96, 102, 115
hooks, bell, 98–99
Horak, Jan-Christopher, 154, 157, 264 n.112
Horne, Lena, 174, 200–201, 203–205, 278 n.143, 279 n.153
House Behind the Cedars (Chestnutt), 102–103, 109
House Behind the Cedars (film), 104
Howells, William Dean, 48, 68, 91, 141
Hudson River School, 39, 49, 256 n.34
Hughes, Langston, 198, 277 n.120
Hurston, Zora Neale, 116
Huysmans, Joris-Karl, 47

Ibsen, Henrik, 47
imagism, 141–142, 160
immigration. *See* American immigrants
Imperative Duty, An, 91
Imperial School of Ballet, 178
impressionism, 45, 128, 175
Ingram, Rex, 202
Inness, George, 62
Intolerance, 56, 108, 233 n.19
Irving, Washington, 14, 27, 28

James, Henry, 47, 48
James, William, 35–36, 40, 54, 70–71, 157, 198, 227 n.109
Jimmie Marshall's Hotel, 173

Johnson, Charles, 90
Johnson, James, Weldon, 88, 89,
    101, 115, 116, 173, 249 n.59
Jones, Robert Edmond, 175

Kant, Immanuel, 25, 35–36, 42, 69,
    71, 76, 77
Karinska, Barbara, 177
Käsebier, Gertrude, 124
Keller, Phyllis, 72
Kemble, Fanny, 14, 96
Kinkade, Thomas, 214
Kipling, Rudyard, 65
Kirby, Lynn, 117–118
Kirstein, Lincoln, 165, 168, 172,
    176–177, 179, 182, 186–188,
    266 n.19, 267 n.35, 268 n.36, 271
    nn.68, 69
Knee, Adam, 203
Kochno, Boris, 187
Kodak, 129
kultur, 80
Kuntzel, Thierry, 203–204

Lambert, Eleanor, 177
Langdale, Allan, 75
Lathe, 153, 154
Leatherstocking Tales, 20
Leaves of Grass, 12, 68
Leroy, Mervin, 209
Let Us Now Praise Famous Men, 194
Leverenz, David, 250 n.75
Lewis, David Levering, 170, 195–
    198, 265 n.12, 276 n.120, 278
    n.131
Lewis, R. W. B., 11
Lhamon, W. T., Jr., 117
Liebskind, Daniel, 263 n.103
Lifar, Serge, 187
Lillie, Beatrice, 177
Lincoln, Abraham, 109
Lindsay, Vachel, 140–142, 152, 159,
    160, 259 n.70, 260 n.71

Little Galleries of the Photo-
    Secession, 124
Litvak, Joseph, 174, 208, 210
Locke, Alain, 196–199, 276 n.113,
    277 nn.121, 122, 124, 278 nn.129,
    131
Lomonosov, Mikhail V., 187
Lonedale Operator, The, 106
Lonely Villa, The, 106
Louvre, 138
Love Me Tonight, 175
Lucas, Charles, D., 84, 96
Lucic, Karen, 139, 150, 261 n.86
Luhan, Mabel Dodge, 125
Lusitania, 54, 73
Lynes, George Platt, 172, 173

Macready, William, 1, 93, 165; body
    as British spectacle, 3–9, 11
Mamoulian, Rouben, 175
Manet, Edouard, 22
Manhatta, x, 119, 122–123, 129, 140,
    142, 148, 152, 162, 263 n.110; as
    national art, 156–159; and Walt
    Whitman, 161, 163–164
Mapplethorpe, Robert, 213
Marie-Blanche, 279 n.147
Marin, John, 124, 138, 171, 255 n.17
Marinoff, Carl, 197
Marinoff, Fania, 197
Markham, Edwin, 63, 64
Maroney, James, 150, 262 n.90
Marquis, Alice Goldfarb, 171
Marshall Fields Department Store,
    174, 264 n.4
Martin, John, 191, 192, 196, 200,
    202
Martin, Waldo, 100, 101, 248 n.57
Marx, Leo, 121–122, 140, 146,
    261 n.86
masculinity: and creativity, 13, 17–
    22, 28–29, 49–50, 51, 133; and
    democracy, 1, 4, 7–13, 19, 27, 30–

masculinity (*continued*)
37; and masculine bodies, xii, 1–
6, 10–15, 21, 48, 50, 65, 72, 131;
and narcissism, 24, 29–31, 38–
39, 96–98, 150, 157; and national
identity, ix, xiii, 3–7, 10–12, 18–
19, 21–22, 28–29, 44, 49–51, 60,
64–65, 67–68, 213, 214; and the
sublime, 20, 25–29, 35–37, 39–45,
58, 82
Masquerade: An Historical Novel,
The, 103, 108, 109
Massine, Léonide, 187
Matisse, Henri, 66, 124, 180
Matthews, Brander, 65–67, 71, 116
Matthiessen, F. O., 32, 35
Maugham, Somerset, 184, 278 n.127
Maxim, Hudson, 53–55, 58–59, 64,
232 n.10, 259 n.70
Maximite explosives, 54
May, Henry, 119–120, 253 n.1
Mayer, Louis B., 200
McBride, Henry, 126, 266 n.15
McDonagh, Don, 180
Medrano Circus, 187
Meet Me in St. Louis, 204, 276 n.116
Melville, Herman, 48, 263 n.103
Mencken, H. L., 197
Men's Open Table. *See* National
Arts Club
Metamora, 2, 16, 19
metamorphosis, 188
Micheaux, Oscar, 84, use of African
American forms, xi, 84, 90–93,
97–104; and black desire, 94–
97, 99, 105, 107–111; and bodies,
90, 92, 96, 98–103, 105, 108, 110;
and cultural uplift, x, 83–85, 87–
89, 99, 169–170; use of flashback,
109, 111, 114–115; and masculinity,
87–90, 92, 96, 98–99, 105, 107–
110, 114–118; trope of the mother,
97–104; use of parallel editing, 108–110; and queer culture,

166–167; and racial realism, 87,
92–94; and Theodore Roosevelt,
83–87
Miller, Joaquin, 53
Mind in the Making, The (Robinson), 135
Minnelli, Lee, 267 n.28
Minnelli, Vincente, x–xiii, 165; and
African American aesthetics, 167,
170, 173, 196–198, 200–203, 213;
bodies as mise-èn-scene, 167–
169, 178–179, 187–189; *Cabin in*
the Sky, 191, 200–205; and the
Other, xiii, 170, 173, 182–183,
189; and queer modernism, 166,
172–175, 177, 183–185, 187, 208,
213
Minnellium, The, 174, 183, 184, 188
minstrelsy, 16, 117, 166, 244 n.30,
252 n.93, 269 n.47, 275 n.112
Miró, Joan, 180
Mitchell, Lee Clark, 20–21
Mitchell, W. J. T., 36
Mitchell's Christian Singers, 194
MOMA. *See* Museum of Modern Art
Moody, Richard, 12–14, 18, 22,
218 n.25, 220 n.35
Moon, Michael, 163
Morris, Edmund, 81
Muir, John, 229 n.126
Mumford, Lewis, 34, 123
Münsterberg, Hugo, 198; and
cinema, 72–78; and Theodore
Roosevelt, 53, 59–60, 69–71,
79–80
Museum of Modern Art, 170–172,
184, 265 n.15, 266 nn.16, 19
Musser, Charles, 60

NAACP, 265 n.11
Nabokov, Nicholas, 181, 187
Nanook of the North, 137
Naremore, James, 191, 202
Nash, Roderick, 42, 229 n.126

National Arts Club, 45, 66, 80
National Association for the Advancement of Colored People, 265 n.11
National Guard, 57
National Security League, 57
Native Americans: masculine bodies of, 14–16, 18–22, 27–28, 134–135, 224 n.78; as noble savages, 17–19, 25–26, 29, 33–34, 135, 212, 224 n.78; as Other, 15–19, 24, 29–30, 36, 44, 50, 93, 133, 173. *See also* Push-ma-ta-ha; Tallchief, Maria
Navy League, 57
Neal, John, 17
Nelson, Dana, 29
Neptune's Daughter, 73
New Negro Movement, 196
New School for Social Research, 135
New York City Ballet, 177
New York Journal-American, 175
New York the Magnificent, 140, 157, 158. See also *Manhatta*
Nibelungenlied, 70
Nicholas II, Czar, 178
Nietzsche, Friedrich Wilhelm, 45, 47, 168
Nigger Heaven, 197, 278 n.127
Nijinsky, Waslaw, 165
Noll, Mark, 41
Nordau, Max, 47, 48, 54, 67, 168
Norman, Dorothy, 123, 124, 127, 131, 266 n.16
Norris, Frank, 33, 34, 48, 49, 229 n.121
Novak, Barbara, 32
Nugent, Richard Bruce, 197

O'Brien, Neil, 117
Ode, 186–188, 274 n.93
Ode to the Grandeur of Nature and to the Aurora Borealis, 187

O'Keeffe, Georgia, 124, 131, 171, 255 n.17, 257 n.47, 262 n.92
Oliver, Lawrence, 66
On Your Toes (film), 178, 269 n.50
On Your Toes (musical), 178
Ophüls, Max, 175
Orvell, Miles, 22

Pach, Walter, 145
Page, Max, 53
Paine, Thomas, 35, 227 n.106
Palmer, George Herbert, 70
Paradise Night, 166, 204
Paramount Pictograph, 73, 76, 77
Paramount Studios, 74, 76, 239 n.82
Parkman, Francis, 65
Partisan Review, 171, 194
Pathé, 58
Pearce, Roy Harvey, 27
Phenomena, 188–189, 190
Photoplay, The, 75, 77, 239 n.85
Picabia, Francis, 125, 145
Picabia, Gabrielle-Buffel, 125
Picasso, Pablo, 124, 125
Pinkerton crime novels, 177
Pip and Flip, 188
Pollock, Jackson, 171, 272 nn.71, 72
Porgy and Bess, 279 n.146
Porter, Cole, 278 n.127, 279 n.147
Portrait of Jason, 213
Potter, David, 10–11, 33
Pound, Ezra, 141
precisionism, 126, 151
primitivism, xii, 14, 16–19, 24, 44, 129, 134–140, 142, 146, 148, 152, 158, 173, 181
Preer, Evelyn, 84
progressivism, 25, 86, 91, 119, 121
Progressivist Party, 86
Psychology and Industrial Efficiency, 72
"Pseudo-Folk," 194–195
Puritans, 19, 202, 257 n.47

Push-ma-ta-ha, 14–16, 18, 23–24, 27–28, 30, 36, 45, 133, 135, 137, 181, 200, 210, 212, 220 n.35

Radio City Music Hall, 176
Ragtime, 181
realism: and absorption theories, 22–25, 37, 150, 222 n.61; and common sense, 20, 34–37, 40–42, 51, 58, 61, 64, 81, 127, 184; and idealism, 11, 13–14, 20–22, 32, 37–38, 44, 51, 120, 127, 129; as national aesthetic, 125–127, 129, 164; and naturalism, 13, 30, 45, 49; as spectacle, 51, 53–55, 57–60, 78, 231 n.4; and the sublime, 20, 24–26, 35, 37, 127
Rebecca, 252 n.87
Remington, Frederic, 45, 65, 66
Rialto Theatre (New York), 157
Rice, Cecil Spring, 65
Riggs, Marlon, 212, 214
Riis, Jacob, 65, 67
Robeson, Paul, 89, 198, 276 n.114
Robinson, James Harvey, 135–136
Rodin, Auguste, 124
Roditi, Edouard, 185
Rony, Fatimah Tobing, 137
Roosevelt, Franklin Delano, 59
Roosevelt, Theodore, x, 45, 49, 52, 68, 81, 102, 116, 118, 120, 122, 139; on art, 66–67, 83, 160; *Battle Cry of Peace*, 56, 59–60, 64, 73–80, 82, 156, 233 n.22, 234 n.38; and masculinity, xii, 51, 54, 60, 65, 169; and Oscar Micheaux, 84–87, and Hugo Münsterberg, 53, 59–60, 69–71
Root, Elihu, 59
Rosenblum, Naomi, 154
Rosenfeld, Paul, 120, 123, 138, 157, 163
Rouault, Georges, 180
Rough Riders, 60, 71, 85

Rough Riders, 74
Rourke, Constance, 143–145, 146, 150, 261 n.82
Rousseau, Jean Jacques, 25, 168
Rovit, Earl, 21
Royce, Josiah, 70
Rubenstein, Helena, 185
Ruckstuhl, F. W., 45, 47, 48, 80
Rugg, Harold, 123

Salamagundi Club, 62, 63, 172, 188
Schamberg, Morton, 145, 146, 155
School of American Ballet, 176
Scott, Raymona, 194
Search for Order, The, 119
Self-Portrait, 148, 149, 150–152
Serena Blandish, 200–201, 203, 279 nn.144, 145, 147
Shakers, 144, 145, 151
Shapiro, Gary, 42
Sharaff, Irene, 177
Sheeler, Charles, 125, 134, 138, 149, 154, 169, 171, 175, 189, 261 nn.82, 84; and machine art, x, 123, 150–152, 155, 157–158, 163, 186, 261 n.86, 262 n.90; *Manhatta*, x, 122, 129, 140, 142, 157–159, 161, 162, 163; and realism, 143–148
Shi, David, 48, 49
Show Is On, The, 166
Shuffle Along, 198
Side of White Barn, 148
Slide, Anthony, 59, 234 n.38
Slotkin, Richard, 14, 19, 28, 33, 81
Smith, Albert E., 58, 60
Smith, Henry Nash, 29
Song of the Sky, 132
Spanish Flag Torn Down, The, 61, 233 n.26
Spencer, Herbert, 54, 128
Spencer, Kenneth, 202
Spring, 63, 167
Springsteen, Bruce, 37, 38
Square Dance, 181

Stansell, Christine, 131
Stars and Stripes, 181
Star-Spangled Rhythm, 178
Steichen, Eduard, 124
Stein, Gertrude, 125, 186, 187, 189, 272 n.71, 279 n.146
Stein, Leo, 125
Stella, Joseph, 138–139, 169
Stettheimer, Florine, 185, 279 n.146
Stieglitz, Alfred, 169, 171, 172, 175, 218 n.26, 255 n.17, 256 n.30, 257 n.47, 266 n.16; and bodies, 131–133, 139, 163–164, 254 n.16, 255 n.20, 262 n.92; influence of, on American art, 123–125, 127–131, 145–146, 157–58, 263 n.108; as nonartist, 131; and primitivism, 133–137, 139–140, 151–152; and Paul Strand, 152–156
Stowe, Harriet Beecher, 91
Strand, Paul, 124, 128, 145, 169, 175, 186, 189, 262 n.97; *Manhatta*, x, 122–123, 129, 140, 142, 156–163; and photography, 152–156; and primitivism, 134, 139, 148
Stravinsky, Igor, 178
Sublett, John William, 202, 205
Sundquist, Eric, 32,33,38
Swift, Kay, 174
Symbol of the Unconquered, 95, 96, 102, 108

"Tableau," 197
"Takin' a Chance on Love," 205, 208, 209
Tallchief, Maria, 181
Tanguy, Yves, 185
Tanner, Allen, 185
Tatum, E. G., 95
Taylor, Elizabeth, 267 n.28
Taylor, Frederick Winslow, 72–73
Taylorism, 72–73
Tchelitchev, Pavel, 172, 174, 177, 180, 190, 191, 200; and bodies, 187–189, 204; as queer modernist, 182–186, 208
Ten Minutes to Live, 98
Terrible Teddy: The Grizzly King, 74
Thompson, Virgin, 279 n.146
Thompson, Walker, 95
Thoreau, Henry David, 14, 27, 28, 31, 32, 35
Three Plays for a Negro Theatre, 175
Tiffany family, 64
Tinkcom, Matthew, 210
Titanic, 225 n.90
Tocqueville, Alexis de, 13
Toklas, Alice B., 189
Tolstoy, Leo, 68
Toomer, Jean, 254 n.15
Tongues Untied, 212
Trachtenberg, Alan, 34, 159, 262 n.99
Troyen, Carol, 148
Tuckerman, Henry, 39
Turner, Frederick Jackson, 21, 33, 80–81, 87, 240 n.89
Twain, Mark, 48, 141, 187
291 (gallery), 124–125, 129, 145, 153, 154
Tyler, Parker, 187, 188, 204, 272 n.71, 273 n.80

Uncle Tom's Cabin (ballet), 166, 269 n.47
University of Chicago, 200
Upper Deck, 148
Urban League, 265 n.11
Utrillo, Maurice, 180

VanEpps-Taylor, Betti Carol, 102
Vanities, 175
Vanity Fair (magazine), 175, 204
Van Vechten, Carl, 172, 174, 185, 195, 197–198, 276 n.117, 277 n.125, 278 nn.126, 127, 129
Veblen, Thorstein, 120
Veiled Aristocrats, 103

Velásquez, Diego Rodríguez de Silva, 145, 175
Verne, Jules, 177
Vidor, King, 94, 199
View from New York, 148
Vitagraph. *See* American Vitagraph
Vitascope Company, 60

Wagner, Richard, 47
Wallace, Maurice, 92, 97, 101
Wallace, Michelle, 105
Warhol, Andy, 213
Warren, Kenneth, 90–91
Washington, Booker T., 85–89, 92, 96, 99, 100–102, 116, 118, 249 nn.65, 66
Waters, Ethel, 174, 177, 192, 197, 200–201, 203–205, 208, 209, 267 n.27, 278 n.127, 279 n.153, 280 n.157
Wayne, John, 45
Weiskel, Thomas, 42–44
Western Symphony, 181
Wheeler, Monroe, 172, 184
Whelan, Richard, 130
Whistler, James Abbott McNeill, 175
White, Hayden, 4
Whitman, Walt, 46, 50, 120–121, 126, 127, 132, 141–142, 146, 163, 168, 198, 212, 230 nn.132, 134, 138, 231 n.140, 241 n.12, 263 n.103; and democratic art, 11–13, 33–35, 45, 47–49; *Manhatta*, 156–161; and Theodore Roosevelt, 67–69, 87
Wiebe, Robert, 119
Wilde, Oscar, 236 n.56
Williams, Bert, 173
Williams, William Carlos, 125
Wilson, Edmund, 131
Wilson, Woodrow, 57, 59, 75, 237 n.62
Wind from Nowhere, The, 115
Wings of Eagles, The, 45
Winning of the West, The, 81
Wister, Owen, 65
Within Our Gates, xi, 84, 105, 108, 110, 112–113, 252 n.87
Wizard of Oz, The, 202
Wolf, Bryan, 39
Women's Peace Party, 54
World (newspaper), 175
World of Art, 185
Wyeth, Sydney, 92, 94, 97, 108

Zayas, Marius de, 125, 258 n.55
Ziegfeld Follies of 1936, 177, 178, 188, 268 n.42

DAVID A. GERSTNER

is an associate professor of cinema

studies at the City University of

New York, College of Staten Island.

Library of Congress Cataloging-in-
Publication Data

Gerstner, David A.

Manly arts : masculinity and nation in early

American cinema / David A. Gerstner.

p. cm.

Includes bibliographical references and index.

ISBN 0-8223-3775-4 (cloth : alk. paper)

ISBN 0-8223-3763-0 (pbk. : alk. paper)

1. Men in motion pictures. 2. Masculinity

in motion pictures. 3. Homosexuality and

motion pictures. 4. Motion pictures—

United States. I. Title.

PN1995.9.M46G47 2006

791.43′653—dc22

2005028221